GLOBALIZATION

The **Institute of Southeast Asian Studies (ISEAS)** was established as an autonomous organization in 1968. It is a regional centre dedicated to the study of socio-political, security and economic trends and developments in Southeast Asia and its wider geostrategic and economic environment. The Institute's research programmes are the Regional Economic Studies (RES, including ASEAN and APEC), Regional Strategic and Political Studies (RSPS), and Regional Social and Cultural Studies (RSCS).

ISEAS Publishing, an established academic press, has issued more than 2,000 books and journals. It is the largest scholarly publisher of research about Southeast Asia from within the region. ISEAS Publishing works with many other academic and trade publishers and distributors to disseminate important research and analyses from and about Southeast Asia to the rest of the world.

GLOBALIZATION
Power, Authority, and Legitimacy in Late Modernity
Second and Enlarged Edition

Antonio L. Rappa

INSTITUTE OF SOUTHEAST ASIAN STUDIES
Singapore

This second edition first published in Singapore in 2011 by
Institute of Southeast Asian Studies
30 Heng Mui Keng Terrace
Pasir Panjang
Singapore 119614

E-mail: publish@iseas.edu.sg
Website: <http://bookshop.iseas.edu.sg>

All rights reserved. No part of this publication may be reproduced, stored in a retrieval system, or transmitted in any form or by any means, electronic, mechanical, photocopying, recording or otherwise, without the prior permission of the Institute of Southeast Asian Studies.

© 2011 Institute of Southeast Asian Studies, Singapore

The responsibility for facts and opinions in this publication rests exclusively with the author and his interpretations do not necessarily reflect the views or the policy of the publisher or its supporters.

ISEAS Library Cataloguing-in-Publication Data

Rappa, Antonio L.
    Globalization : power, authority, and legitimacy in late modernity. 2nd & enl. ed.
    1. Globalization.
    2. Civilization, Modern—21st century.
    3. United States—Politics and government—21st century.
    4. United States—Foreign relations—21st century.
    5. United States—Foreign economic relations—Asia.
    6. Asia—Foreign economic relations—United States.
    7. Global Financial Crisis, 2008–2009.
    I. Title.
    II. Title: Globalization : an Asian perspective on modernity and politics in America
JZ1318 R21 2010   2010

ISBN 978-981-4279-99-4 (soft cover)
ISBN 978-981-4311-02-1 (E-Book PDF)

Typeset by Superskill Graphics Pte Ltd
Printed in Singapore by

For George and Quentin

CONTENTS

Preface to the 2nd and Enlarged Edition		ix
Preface		xii
Acknowledgements		xxi
1	Introduction	1
2	Cultural America and the Globalization of (Im)perfection	35
3	Asia	61
4	Money	133
5	Terrorism	168
6	Culture	187
7	Norms and Values	218
8	Technology and Population	239
9	War	261
10	End Thoughts	286
References		311
Index		323

PREFACE TO THE 2ND AND ENLARGED EDITION

What does it mean to be alive in late modernity today? The second edition, *Globalization: Power, Authority and Legitimacy in Late Modernity*, analyses the competition for global control over scarce resources. Despite the failure of economic instruments and the loss of economic confidence across the world (2007–10), the United States (U.S.) remains a superpower *primus inter pares*. U.S. power is embedded within a domestic military-industrial complex that is legitimized by civil society under the authority of a democratic ethos that is presumed to be universal. The United States is the only country that has been continuously at war for over a century with a global impact. Indeed, the Cold War (1955–89) galvanized the United States and the rest of the "Free World" under the ideological umbrella of neoliberal capitalism. Not surprisingly, most nations today are tied directly or indirectly to the U.S. economy. This means that if the U.S. sinks, the weight of its debt will have a significant impact on the balance of trade with the rest of the world. Francis Fukuyama proclaimed Western liberal democracy, in *The End of History and the Last Man* (1992), as the conclusive form of government. Current cultural history keeps proving Fukuyama wrong. If it took Americans 233 years to inaugurate the first male African American as president, what more can be expected of nation states that are much younger along the transition to democracy? What is the point of *democracy* if half of the world's population owns less than 10 per cent of the world's resources? What does it say about democracy if there has never been a woman president for over 200 years although women make up at least half the U.S. population? Does the United

States represent the end-state in which fledgling democracies in Southeast Asia, Africa, Latin America, and the Pacific can look forward to? Despite its long years at empire-building and shoring up the democratic ideological belief system, the United States continues to face many domestic challenges along the lines of class, ethnicity and gender. President Obama's domestic policies are tied to foreign policy. The one impacts the other. The globalized world in the post-Iraq, post-Afghanistan, and post-terrorist world will be surfeit with a new protectionism. This new protectionism is already on the rise.

Under the neoliberal capitalist world order, the United States, Western Europe, and the OECD (Organisation for Economic Cooperation and Development) countries have developed authoritative local, regional, and international structures that have paved the way for a more unified and dependent world. Everything done in any place is eventually reported as news. The global funk today was created by greedy financial "terrorists" and avaricious investors. People cannot seem to get enough money. As a result the negative sentiments and economic impotence that were catalysed by the sub-prime crises in the United States and the United Kingdom have made investors very cautious about securities, equities, hedge funds, unit trusts, derivatives, futures and commodities, currencies, and virtually all structured products. The stock market bubble burst after Lehman Brothers and many smaller banks (like Washington Mutual) collapsed. The U.S. government had to bail out AIG, and the Bank of America acquired Merrill Lynch. Others, like Fortis and the Royal Bank of Scotland, were all nationalized by their respective Dutch and British Governments. Fannie Mae and Freddie Mac received lifelines from the state. By the end of December 2008, over 500,000 Americans lost their jobs. "Black October" de-legitimized the rhetoric of financial liberalism that the United States has been promulgating for decades. Democratic administrations in the United States have tended to focus on domestic issues rather than long, protracted wars. The United States is becoming increasingly inward-looking. Its foreign policy is also shifting away from hawkish global behaviour. Obama's first official act as President was to sign off on the Lilly Ledbetter Fair Pay Act (2009). The act serves to promote precisely what its title says. However, it only protects Americans, not foreigners, working in American companies overseas. America is turning inwards. President Obama has the onerous task of having to unravel the problems created by his predecessor. Overseas, Australia, Germany, and Singapore have had to guarantee deposits in banks to normalize the situation. Sixteen trillion U.S. dollars in stock value were lost in a period of thirty days. Some financial analysts argue that this was the lowest low score in over seven decades. When Congress first rejected a state bailout to rescue U.S. financial markets, the Dow lost 778 points. Congress authorized the use of US$700 billion to buy out toxic assets and devalued securities. Desperate times call for desperate measures. America, once the bastion of hope, optimism, and progress, is now showing more signs of a superpower in decline. The first sign of the American decline since 1941 in Pearl Harbour was the destruction of the World Trade Center in New York City on 11 September 2001. The other signs are the Vietnamization of Iraq, a nuclear stand-off with North Korea, increasing trade imbalances with China and India, a stalemate with terrorists in Afghanistan, the challenge of European protectionism, a belligerent politics in the Middle East, overt American dependence on oil and fossil fuels, and the mushrooming of various sub-prime crises into an escalating global recession. This second edition of the earlier book incorporates the latest developments in terms of culture, wealth, and terrorism around the world.

The central argument in this book is that competition over the political goods of "power", "authority", and "legitimacy" are ironically the source of the problem as well as part of the solution in late modernity. Globalization runs on the sentiments of the acquisition of power, the maintenance of authority, and the establishment of legitimacy. If we allow our sentiments of hope, optimism, and progress to fail, then we are doomed to board that final Foucauldian *Ship of Fools*. The *Ship of Fools* metaphor that Foucault used was important because it contains all the trials and tribulations of power structures, authority figures, and legitimate "rights". In late modernity, the highest value that is celebrated is what Vattimo calls the feeling of being modern; to celebrate the idea of being modern as the highest among modern values. But given the nature of power distribution, authority structures, and the de-legitimization of states, societies, and businesses, it is better not to lose one's nerve over the challenges that globalization presents. Being alive in late modernity today means surviving alongside the problems caused by the globalization of terrorism, technology, and money. So while globalization simply refers to taking something that is produced locally and then making it available in as many places as possible, it does not mean that local products and practices will be readily accepted in the global markets.

PREFACE

Modernity has proven itself to be the accumulative basis of civilization since the Industrial Revolution in the West. The emergent European states, Great Britain in particular, began using new and complicated economic tools during the Renaissance between the fourteenth to sixteenth centuries. Italy was the centre of the Renaissance but this shifted to the rest of Western Europe. Eastern Europe was not yet ready for the intellectual and cultural changes that were associated with the Roman rebirth. The decline in Italian fortunes, the continuation of Dutch mercantilism, rising French imperialism, and the British control of international waters concentrated the loci of global power into the hands of these rapidly modernizing European states. We are told that a political explosion of European principalities concluded with the Treaty of Westphalia in 1648 which led to the mapping of universal political principles and laid the basis for modern forms of governance. A modern politics was born and exported as rudimentary experimental versions across the far-flung European colonies. The end of the seventeenth century and the beginning of the eighteenth century witnessed economic and technological developments that would reach a critical turning point, called the Industrial Revolution (IR). The IR is important to this narrative of globalization because it gives modern people a point of reference. The IR coincided and was coterminous with the political and military changes that were sweeping the world and laying the basis for internationalization and, subsequently, globalization. By the nineteenth century and right up till the early twentieth century, European historians would have us believe that only a few great powers existed. Yet, Europe was itself in the throes of turmoil and upheaval. The *fin-de-siècle* witnessed the end of Czarist Russia, the destruction of the short-lived Austro-

Hungarian Empire, and the end of the Ottoman Empire (dating back to the thirteenth century) in World War I that ended in 1918. An immense and irreparable political culvert began undermining the old European monarchies, their power bases, and networks.

In Asia, the old absolutist monarchies were also under siege. In China, the last Chinese dynasty was fighting a powerful and hidden ideological force. The May Fourth intellectual movement and Karl Marx's influence on the fledgling communists were markers for the end of a 5,000-year-old way of life. Indeed, some still believe that Marx's *Communist Manifesto* was translated into Chinese one hundred years before it was translated into English. The other great Asian power, India, was not one. It was still under British control as was coastal Africa, Australia, New Zealand, the Pacific, and the rest of Southeast Asia, with the exception of Thailand. The Japanese naval victory in 1915 over the Russian fleet in Asian waters rejuvenated the militarization of Japan and that famous putsch against the Japanese emperor. Korea and Formosa (Taiwan) would soon come under Japanese control. Japanese intelligence officers had already begun scouring various Southeast Asian cities such as Vientiane, Saigon, Rangoon, Bangkok, Kuala Terengganu, Kuantan, Kuala Lumpur, Singapore, Djakarta, Port Moresby, and Manila. World War I significantly depleted the colonial economies and contributed to the first truly worldwide economic downward economic spiral known as the Great Depression. The loss of economic confidence became the backdrop for what the communists believed would lead to another powerful class revolution. But there was not enough time for the workers to unite and organize because they had no jobs in the first place. The oppression was primarily political. Economic oppression merely served political interests of the now weakening great powers. The Great Depression was the window into a new kind of economic hell, because in less than half a decade thereafter, the world would again be on the brink of disaster and turmoil. Even those idyllic, self-sufficient, and independent Asian communities far away from international trade and economics would eventually become embroiled in the problems of the West. World War II led to the fracturing and breakdown of the "Great Empires" of Britain, France, and to a lesser extent, Spain, Portugal, and Soviet Russia. The Japanese attack on Pearl Harbor in Honolulu, Hawaii, indelibly radicalized American political, diplomatic, economic, and military strategies. An immense wave of nationalist movements led to new nation states at the end of World War II. It was only after World War II that one could call the world as "internationalizing".

Over the course of a 500-year sketch of modernity, we saw power shift away from Rome, to Paris, the Netherlands, and London to Moscow and Washington DC. Pax Britannica would make way to the emergence of superpower rivalry between the Soviet Union of Socialist Republics and the United States of America. Competition over territory between the two superpowers through the influence of ideological proxies would compress ethnic and religious conflicts across the world. There were problems of decolonization in the 1950s and 1960s, which along with the Korean War, the Vietnam War, the abortive Soviet occupation of Afghanistan, and the Cold War between 1955 and 1989 made for life in interesting times. The global economic recessions in 1973 and 1985 marked a new kind of global political economics based on neoliberal assumptions and the rapid rise of the multinational corporations (MNCs). Beginning as transnational corporations (TNCs) in the early 1970s, the new MNCs would become the main vehicle for globalization's activities. Reagan's Star Wars programme helped hammer the final nail into the Soviet coffin. The fall of the Berlin Wall and the end of the Warsaw Pact ushered in the new era called Pax Americana. America remains dominant in this world of culture, money, and terror. American culture has had an impact on virtually every person on this planet. American money has been the safe haven for many an entrepreneur and investor. American technology is *primus inter pares*. America and Americans are also the targets of the worst forms of terrorism. 9/11 was a horrific experience and a terrible symbolic blow to capitalism. But the economic recession and the loss of over US$16 trillion by January 2009 is another kind of terror — financial terrorism. These events and accidents of time are part of the reason why many are unable to distinguish between Americanization and globalization. Nevertheless, globalization and its processes of power, authority, and legitimacy, are singularly contingent on modernity. This is true inasmuch as people eventually need to refer to some kind of urban dictionary to keep moving forward. Power creates windows to make money to "survive", discover medical facts, engage new cultural structures, de-authorize terrorists, or to predict the future. There are many dilemmas in modernity and globalization is indeed one of them. Globalization is a dilemma because it is the source of problems and solutions.

So what exactly is globalization?

Think about a world without email. No Internet access. No handphones, cable television, or Music Television (MTV) Music Awards; a utopian world where people actually look up at the sky. A world without weather channels, sports channels, digital calendars, PCs, Macs, palmtops, personal digital assistants (PDAs), or game consoles. A world without having to decide between PS3, Xbox360, and Nintendo Wii (popular computer games) for your grandchild's Christmas gift in 2009. A world where you do not have to care about whether old generation technology is being used as the basis for new generation electronics. Think about a world where air travel is still too expensive. Where you actually remember the last city you visited, and where all your relatives and the people in the town showed up to watch the train run into the station. A fantastic world where the pace of life is so slow that everyone watches the sun set, and then spends the next two hours looking up at the night sky. A world where there is no constant electricity supply, no threat from the ozone layer, environmental damage, or Al Gore to make you feel guilty. One where there are no watches with global positioning systems (GPS), 25-megapixel cameras, no flash memory sticks. No fast food. No second car. No Sport Utility Vehicle (SUV). No Adobe, Apple, Barney, Casio, Clementine, Dell, Facebook, Geico, Hitachi, i-phone, J-Lo, K-Mart, Lexus, Microsoft, Nokia, Oakley, Prada, Quattroporte, Reebok, statistical analysis system (SAS), statistical package for the social sciences (SPSS), Sponge Bob Square Pants, Tony Roma's, Universal Pictures, Versace, World Wide Web, X-Men, Yahoo! or Zip files to extract. These are only some of the ABCs of culture, money, and terror. Our dystopia in late modernity is a world without globalization. Brands are part of our late modern culture. We only need money to buy culture. But then we are eventually terrorized by culture itself. We note that there is a gulf of difference between buying culture and being cultured. They are not one and the same. This is because one does not have to be rich to be cultured, and contrary to popular belief, one does not have to possess money to have class.

Despite the challenges of culture, money, and terror, globalization continues to be driven by sentiments of hope, optimism, and progress. The new rhetoric involves a kind of politics of forgetting; it involves phrases like "letting go", "moving forward", and "moving on".

I began writing this book because of the questions that arose out of several undergraduate and master's courses that I taught in globalization, politics, and modernity at the National University of Singapore. I kept getting the same interrogatives such as: What is the difference between globalization and Americanization? Are we really global simply because we consume goods and services produced by different countries under different systems and cultures within a short span of time by people we are likely never to meet in our life? What is "political" about globalization? How can anyone survive the financial terrorism of 2008? What will Obama's America be able to do that McCain's America won't destroy? Looking at the various texts that are available, one finds that most of them raise important and similar ideas about globalization. Most of these books include economic and political dimensions and tend to separate their conceptual frameworks from their practical illustrations. We discovered that there were too many issues to be explained by current works on globalization. Some works appeared very concerned about specific items in globalization such as fast food, environmental damage and green politics, or business development and human management strategies. Many of these works asked more questions than provided answers. At other times, some books suggested solutions that complicated and clouded global issues rather than make them more lucid. A participant at a political theory conference in Illinois many years ago asked me what I thought about the nature of globalization. I replied, "there was none". That is the beauty and perhaps the horror of it all. You cannot really second guess meaning and content in globalization. What we can do is try to analyse the patterns that emerge from different ways in which individuals, communities, and states respond to the forces of global culture (American culture for many), money politics, and financial terrorism. We are interested here in how the world has risen and fallen and risen again in this global sea, and how globalization tends to be about struggles with the self. Not a religious struggle nor a Marxist revolutionary struggle, but a struggle to make the world more complete, more predictable, more manageable, and more meaningful. Answering questions on globalization often entails the expectation of more questions. Interrogatives are indeed part of the meaning of globalization. However, we might be able to say with some degree of confidence that globalization is a series of experiences that has not been felt in previous centuries to the same depth and extent that it is today.

I wrote this book because I was also unhappy with the different approaches and themes that various books, articles, reviews, and commentaries on globalization have provided so far. Many texts are either too full of academic jargon or too full of accusations of corruption and nepotism. Globalization tends to be confusing, not only for students in the humanities and social sciences but also for scholars and the general reading public. The confusion is demonstrated in the lack of agreement among scholars about the definition of globalization. But while globalization and its processes may be complex, it would be naïve to think that the best answer or solution is the simplest one. It is not.

"Man is by nature political", as Aristotle's supporters believe, is a misleading and essentialist (that is to say, wrong) statement. His axiom should be treated as a wrong idea because man is not only a natural being but both an unnatural and a supernatural one (Nietzsche). Aristotle's problematic phrase caused confusion because it took the "spirit" out of being human. This seemed to influence many generations of philosophers and thinkers who set the scene for the creation of modern indignities. And Aristotle was only one of the many problematic philosophers. Had Aristotle been the great philosopher of his time, he would have not been thus misrepresented by the generations of scholars, now long dead, some dying, who so faithfully clung to his wisdom. But I think Aristotle did not mean to use it for all time because he did not expect someone to come along much later to overturn the entire corpus of his epistemology. I am referring to Nietzsche, of course. Had those great thinkers who came after Aristotle mapped out more carefully those ancient Greek urns of wisdom that Aristotle bequeathed to the West, we would certainly have a much better world today than globalization could ever provide.

Nevertheless, if we understand man as being temporarily grounded by his biological self, and by his desire and greed for power, and taint this with the brilliance of speaking truth to power as Foucault suggested, then we might be able to undo some of the damage already done. This would be my compromise. And in order to survive in this globalized world of technological dependence and control, one has to play by formal rules and informal norms — or forever remain quiet about never "making it big". There appears to be a set of very fine lines that continue to criss-cross that abstract divide between permitted behaviour and rule-bending and impermissible behaviour and rule-breaking.

In late modernity, higher institutions of education are emphasizing life sciences, earth sciences, alternative food sources, water research, stem cell research, and the use of nano-technology and nano-bacteria against viral complexes in medical terrorism. All of these depend on power structures, authority figures, and legitimate scientific systems. Bioterrorism is another watchword on Interpol. But the more things change, the more they appear to remain the same. We are bound and tied to the technologies we create. Technology is defined as man's attempt to control his environment. And globalization by extension is the use of technology to enhance human life. This means that globalization often demands all its participants — citizens, individuals, communities and organizations of democracies, and authoritarian states — to partake in corrupt behaviour for the larger good. It may require honest citizens to close an eye to corporate greed and malfeasance if only to take home a small piece of the pie, to keep that paycheck coming or to keep that cushy job. Globalization may cause state bureaucrats to sell off trade secrets, employ creative and crafty accounting strategies to waylay the unsuspecting tax official, or bribe foreign government officials to get the job done. And now look at what happened to those wonderful new financial products that preyed on people who could not afford another mortgage. The sub-prime terror was ill-contained and mushroomed into a global financial problem. Heidegger's notion of technology is valuable if not instructive. He warned of the technological dehumanization that would plunge the world into darkness. But Heidegger could not and did not anticipate the depth of the commodification of culture, the extent of the human propensity for greed, and the willingness to tolerate financial, cultural, and political terrorists to take over our lives.

Using 1776 as a base year, Americans have almost continuously voted for their governments for 233 years. Despite that great democratic achievement, there is still much unhappiness with the domestic and foreign policies of American government. It appears that America while suffering from the horrendous attacks on 9/11, turned conservative overnight and voted in a highly conservative government that resulted in the deaths of even more American soldiers in Iraq and Afghanistan than all of the victims of 9/11. The system invented weapons of mass destruction (WMD) when the real WMD was churning in the cesspool of sub-prime financial terrorism. The disproportionate level of passion and outpouring of anger and fear in the aftermath of 9/11 does not seem to be easily reconciled with the many more military and civilian deaths in Iraq and Afghanistan. Clearly, this is a case of reactions to political symbols rather than just cause. An attack on the American homeland was something that seemed unthinkable because the last attack on American soil was when the Japanese attacked Pearl Harbor. Government has a large and important role to play. The paradox of Americanization is writ large in the fact that the distance between what is said and what is done seems to be increasingly widening. The paradox is critical because America continues to be highly influential and oftentimes the most and only outspoken member of the West. Asia viewed the West with fear in the past because Asia was outdated and colonized. Globalization helped propel Asia's view of the West to one of learning, adaptation, and innovation. Asia continues to view the West because it continues to learn from Western mistakes while trying to avoid them.

When we use the word Asia, we have to use it with some degree of accuracy. It is too large of course, to place the whole of Asia and its billions of people and thousands of cultures into a single category, inasmuch as it is too easy to place all advanced, post-industrial societies into a single bag called the West. But there are differences, and the differences that separate Asia from the West are far greater than the similarities that combine them.

Since the PC and IT revolutions of the 1970s and 1980s, there has been a tremendous widening and deepening of the chances and opportunities for making those political promises come true. The bid by a powerful conglomerate of Middle Eastern MNCs to run American seaports ended in failure because it was too soon for American culture to absorb. American theological-conservatives (theocons) and neo-conservatives (neocons) would not be able to accept such a cultural shock so soon after 9/11. The wounds had not yet healed. The facilitation of mass media and global communications has resulted, for example, in the clearance of *Al Jazeera English* for broadcasting in Asia. In the first few years after 9/11, the establishment of the Qatari news agency would have not been appropriate. Or even possible.

The U.S. Government is at the heart of the central nervous system of the most powerful business, political, and military nation the world has seen since 1989. This is why any view of the West cannot ignore America. Any view from Asia of the West cannot ignore American government and politics. If America gets its government wrong, the rest of the world is affected at some level.

The framework for this book is designed around the historical, social, cultural, and normative perceptions of late modernity in ten different chapters that explore the central metaphor and the themes of hope, optimism, and progress in modernity. The book was written to explore the meaning of globalization using America as the primary case and Asia as its sounding board.

ACKNOWLEDGEMENTS

I am deeply thankful to Joel B. Grossman, Benjamin Hermalin, John Quelch and Emeritus Professor Deane E. Neubauer for their intellectual thought, earnest criticism, and sincere advice. I also thank the two anonymous readers for their comments on the manuscript for the first edition. Some of the readers of this manuscript had serious reservations about the controversial political and business issues that were raised in the book while others preferred deeper readjustments to be made away from the postmodern method of overlapping arguments that requires a kind of pendulous return to previous ground.

I have resisted the temptation to write in a linear chronology that forces a conclusion at the end, so I hope the readers will forgive me for the blizzard of analysis that is globalization.

I would like to thank Aryeh Botwinick, Joshua Cohen, J. Peter Euben, Amy Gutmann, Joseph LaPalombara, Anne Norton, and Marshall Sahlins for their words of encouragement and more importantly, for their profound sense of theory. I also thank Michael Perelman for his unsolicited review of the first edition in 2005. I still have not had the pleasure of meeting him in person or over the Internet but I have tried to incorporate his criticisms into this edition. I remember and cherish the important role that approximately 186 undergraduate and graduate students played at the place where I used to teach "Contemporary Issues in Political Theory", "Globalization's Impact on Society and Culture", and "The Politics of Globalization" from the academic years 2000/2001 to 2005/2006. I am delighted to be associated with my distinguished colleagues at the Institute of Southeast Asian Studies (ISEAS), SIM University, my graduate students at the S. Rajaratnam School of International Studies (RSIS), Nanyang Technological University, and my undergraduate students at the SIM University Business School. In particular, I am very thankful to Barry Desker, Tsui Kai Chong, and Koh Hian Chye for their scholarly advice and philosophical discussions about power, authority and legitimacy.

I would like to thank the ISEAS Manuscript Review Committee; the two anonymous reviewers for their comments; and especially the Managing Editor of ISEAS Publishing, Triena Ong, and her wonderful staff at the Institute of Southeast Asian Studies, Singapore.

Finally, I thank my two sons, George and Quentin for being my inspiration.

1

INTRODUCTION

Culture, believed the Greek writer Herodotus, was a means of understanding the world.¹ His globe held the tragic prospect of unknowable and inestimable space. The modern political theorist, J. Peter Euben, argued that Greek tragedy represented a powerful cultural context for classical thought as it anticipates modern struggles with power, authority, legitimacy, freedom, justice, and tolerance.² The world that Euben describes seems far less spacious and more catastrophic than the one described by Herodotus. Euben's globe is a "culture" of money and terror. But whether or not it anticipates modern struggles from the basis of the classical lifestyle of the Greeks is in doubt. This is because the catastrophic nature of the world in late modernity is markedly different. There is a greater sense of disaffection, alienation, and anomie in the Age of Globalization than in the Age of Antiquity. The twentieth and twenty-first centuries in particular, have been about the mismanagement of war and global terror. If the twentieth century was characterized by a clash of political ideologies, then the twenty-first century manifests itself in neoliberal capitalism and the challenges of globalization. It is also the age of terror where the adage "one man's terrorist is another man's freedom fighter" bears itself onto the template of a commoditized world complicated by competition, technological convergence, uneven development, greed, poverty, culture, money and terror.

The seeds of such disaffection lie in the period of decolonization and rising nationalism of the past twentieth century. American Republicans tend to miss the point that the terrorists are made when innocent families are bombed. But the bombing of other cultures did not begin with Iraq. In our late modern era, the American bombing of Hiroshima City and Nagasaki

City were the first illustrations of the efficacy of weapons of mass destruction (WMD). That was the only way, they said, to stop the Japanese war from advancing. Innocent blood had to be spilled. The Japanese Imperial Army and the Japanese Kempetai committed many atrocities all over the Pacific, in Southeast Asia, and China. Iris Chang describes the six weeks of horror in the *Rape of Nanking* (1997) as the soldiers raped and murdered close to 300,000 Chinese women, men and children — mostly civilians — in 1937. When America dropped the atomic bomb on Japan, close to 140,000 people were killed instantaneously or died from the side effects of the bomb eventually.

George W. Bush searched all over Iraq for WMD and ended his presidency without finding them or Osama bin Laden. President Barack Hussein Obama will acknowledge that there are no WMD. The world has spent over fifteen years searching for a single terrorist to no avail. Unless he is caught, Osama will eventually become a mythical anti-hero, an icon for extremist Islamicist terrorists. Terror dehumanizes civilization whether they claim to be Communist or Fascist. Left or Right, both ideological hands are tainted with the blood of the innocent.

After World War II, the age of terror manifested itself in many small spaces: left-wing African nationalist forces; left-wing Cuban movements; left-wing neo-Marxists in Europe; and left-wing Maoists in Southeast Asia. For example, elements of the Malayan People's Anti-Japanese Army formed the nucleus of the Malayan Communist Party. Six hours away by plane, in the Philippines, the People's Anti-Japanese Army evolved into the Maoist-inspired People's Liberation Army (Hukbong Mapagpalaya ng Bayan). Re-tuning to more disasters: Over 58,000 Americans were killed in the Vietnam War; six million Jews were massacred by Nazis in concentration camps in World War II; and more than one million Cambodians were killed by the Khmer Rouge between 1975 and 1979 based on immoral authority and illegitimate government. These were all innocent people who were killed for no justifiable cause. When China attacked Vietnam in 1979 how many Chinese soldiers' lives were sacrificed in order for China to teach Vietnam "a lesson"? How many Iranians were killed by Iraqi forces? How many Kuwaitis were killed by the invading Iraqi Republican Guard in 1991? How many Jews and Palestinians have killed one another?

Ten hours away by plane, in the Middle East, the two fights for political autonomy continue, one Palestinian and the other Israeli. Over and above these are Arab states who continue to exist uncomfortably with the changing borders and the interference of Western powers. Border conflicts between Saddam Hussein's Iraqi dictatorship and the Ayatollah Khomeini's Iranian theocracy eventually erupted into the Iraq-Iran war between 1980 and 1988 and ended in a pyrrhic victory. Over a million Iraqis and Iranians were killed in those eight years. Saddam invaded Kuwait on 2 August 1990, ostensibly to gain access to a southern port for Iraqi oil. Border disputes and other local incidents are often primers for large-scale violence as shown in the Russo-Japanese War, the Sino-Vietnamese War, and the ongoing African wars that are often mistaken for tribal conflicts or do not have sufficient newsworthiness to be covered by the international media.

What then is the difference between a terrorist and a freedom fighter in late modernity? The difference is in the abuse of power and the willingness to thwart moral values, de-authorize legitimate structures, and kill innocent people. The Huk Rebellion from central Luzon is a clear example that ended in 1954 with U.S. military support.[3] The Moro Islamic Liberation Front (MILF), a powerful splinter group formed in 1981 from elements of the Moro National Liberation Front (MNLF), was responsible for the beheading of ten Philippine marines in Basilan on 17 July 2007. Are these terrorists bringing death and destruction or freedom fighters like American minutemen who sniped and killed British "Red Coat" Regulars in the American War of Independence (or was it the American Rebellion)? In the globalized world, it is critical that the point-of-view approach be carefully understood, because it reveals an entirely different understanding of any conflict. The Islamic Revolution led by Ayatollah Khomeini was described by the Shah of Iran's media as an illicit, illegitimate, and ill-organized attempt by insurgents to overthrow the rightful and sovereign emperor. When the Shah fell, the militant Iranian ayatollahs turned their theocratic values inwards as power struggle after power struggle ensued. They attempted to undermine (with the aim of overthrowing) the absolutist dictatorship of Saddam Hussein for two reasons. Iraq in those days was getting diplomatically closer to the United States and the brand of Islam practised by Saddam was perceived to be unIslamic by the Iranian theocracy. Saddam on the other hand wanted to liberate his Muslim brothers under the rule of the Iranian ayatollahs.

In Southeast Asia, like other parts of the globe, news consumers receive daily reports of terror instantaneously. For example, the demonstrations in July 2007 by anti-junta organizations in Bangkok have drawn the wrath of a nine-month-old military regime. This comes amidst a deepening three-sided crisis in the southern provinces of Pattani, Narathiwat, and Yala among elements of the 4th Army, special anti-terrorist police units, local Thai Buddhists and Buddhist monks, and local Thai Muslims agitating for a separate Islamic state. This is complicated by a decades-old political situation with the Muslim-dominant Malaysian states of Perlis, Kedah, Perak, and Kelantan. Political analysts believe that Malaysian Islamic radicals based in the jungle areas of these states are fuelling the demands for greater Islamic autonomy in southern Thailand. There are specific organizations located in Malaysia, Indonesia, and Thailand which make the insurgency difficult to control.[4] Despite these differences, Malaysia's Deputy Prime Minister Najib Tun Razak has (since 2006) openly spoken of cooperation with the current military junta in Bangkok to resolve the violence which has left over 2,300 people dead. On 28 January 2007, a suicide bomber injured thirty-one people and killed fifteen in Pakistan's northern city of Peshawar. This came after an earlier hotel bombing that killed a local police commander. Indeed, a day without any suicide bombing, death threat, revenge killing, religious-motivated murder, act of piracy, or the detonation of weapons of mass destruction in a public arena has become a rare commodity. The globalized world is one marked by global terror from invidious individuals and secret communities leading double lives and willingly using biological and computer viruses that add to the threat, panic, and mayhem of natural and artificial disasters in late modernity. This is what Kupperman, Opstal, and Williamson, Jr., described in 1982 as the strategic tool of terror.[5]

This book explains the power, authority, and legitimacy of globalization in late modernity. One of the most powerful metaphors that has become commonplace since the end of the Cold War in 1989 is U.S. neo-imperialism. The United States has wrought international political, economic, security, cultural, social, and religious connections that have affected the lives of people in most countries. However, the impact of the United States is neither seamless nor watertight as seen in the first and second Gulf Wars, the inability to deal with natural disasters such as Hurricane Katrina on continental United States, and the earthquakes in Pakistan, one of the United States' apparently strongest allies in the fight against global terrorist organizations. This book neither claims an epistemology of global proportions nor does it entirely agree with the argument that American hegemony equals neo-imperialism. Rather, this book unravels several ideas that impinge on the complexities of American globalization and the surfeit of problems that occur at all levels of international political, economic, cultural, social, and religious activity.

What are the considerations that support the power and legitimacy of American culture and American money alongside the critical pauses embedded within the epistemological reasons for these capitalist achievements? One thing seems clear from the problematic of neo-imperialism: there can be no wealth without poverty, no freedom without transparency, no rights without struggle, and no values without norms. The idea of the norm itself has taken on a different meaning from what it was half a century ago. Because of international broadcast media in the age of information and the age of the Internet, we now experience a more rapid process of normalization through the global dissemination of blips of information. This is known in contemporary political theory as the age of cybernetic capitalism that investigates the interface between the physical world and the biological one.[6]

There is a "politics of globalization" because of the unequal distribution of power. Human beings seem to be both attracted to and repulsed by power. It is clear that human beings possess the quality and proclivity for politicizing issues. As long as there is power to be gained or deployed, dispensed or resisted, there will be politics. There is a "politics of American globalization" because American financial cities are very much a subset of global movements in information, technology, commerce, investment capital, trade, finance, banking, and services. America is wired into a network of seemingly sleepless financial markets from New York and Philadelphia in the east to Los Angeles, San Francisco and Seattle in the west. The international chain of events are marked by stock exchanges in Frankfurt, London, Zurich, New Delhi, Bangkok, Kuala Lumpur, Singapore, Jakarta, Sydney, Hong Kong, Seoul, Taipei, and Beijing. The unequal power of these stock exchanges has long started buying into each other in a manner that thickens the bonds of interest across the world. The global financial interdependence and reliance on global currencies like the U.S. dollar have made America even more powerful than it has ever been in its previous incarnations. America is vocal, loud, and internationally "present".

The word "globalization" can also be potentially differentiated for every country in the world. The use of the word "American" is a point of reference that informs the title of this book, and not a suggestion that American globalization is globalization. Neither is the use of the word "America" to mean the United States of America in any way meant to marginalize Canada, Mexico, and the other countries in North America and Latin America. The politics of American globalization has never been written. This book might be seen as an original survey of the material things that encapsulate American modernity. This area of research is also important because America has severely (and severally) impacted the modern world in so many ways as to make it both fascinating and horrifying as more data is revealed through the global and international media. On the other hand, legislation such as the Freedom of Information Act that came into effect on 4 July 1967 in the United States that must be honoured by the bureaucracy, is not self-enforcing. The bureaucratic lag, malaise, or foot-dragging that confronts seekers of public information is not surprising since the act itself is a tool of investigation and transparency that may be used against the bureaucracy itself.[8]

We live in an age the self-contradictions of a soft determinist paradox[9] in which the rational utilitarianism of Friquegnon is oriented towards hedonistic culture. However, what appeared only in the rarified atmosphere of phenomenological research in the early 1970s has become a reality today. The age of globalization is about the satisfaction of the self above all selves. The age of globalization is a combination of hegemonic powers such as the United States, with its preponderance for neoliberal capitalism (read: MNCs freely flowing across the globe), global media corporations, Microsoft and Apple, cybernetic capitalism, and freedom of information and disinformation from competing pharmaceutical companies competing for market shares that are embroiled in a slow but rapid torque of infinite, artificial but very real possibilities. The age of globalization is about paradoxes. These include technological, cultural, social, economic, and political varieties. This book investigates one such paradox and its attendant vicissitudes.[10]

There is a central paradox in politics. This puzzle has something to do with neoliberalism, domestic politics, war motifs, popular culture, and the institutional problems of government. The paradox involves the relationship between the citizen's obligation to the state on one hand and the state's responsibility to its citizens on the other. It is a social contract that appears to be too readily ignored by many till it becomes too late for the few. The state has failed in several areas in terms of responsibly dealing with the trust it has received from Americans. The reason, if there can be such a thing in politics, is to be discovered in the political institutions that make up the system and the system that generates the culture. It is a paradox that Americans have known for years. America is like a barometer for the rest of the world.

OVERVIEW

Chapter One introduces the basic themes of the book alongside power structures, official authority, and legitimate government. It looks at the main assumptions involved in the major debates in globalization. The chapter also surveys the literature on globalization and politics, and suggests two examples of what might be considered as representing the positive stream of globalization books, and another that represents the negative stream of globalization. It also examines the ideas behind American domestic politics, globalization and Americanization, globalization and religion, and an analysis about the globe.

Chapter Two is about the cultural America and the globalization of perfection and imperfection. This chapter analyses the contradictions and complementarities that make American globalization worth researching. This chapter explains why America is so important to the rest of the world and how its importance might be tempered for the international public good. The chapter illustrates the integral complements within the American neoliberal system and highlights some contradictions within the American polity that do not seem to be synchronous with the most powerful nation on earth at the turn of the twenty-first century.

Chapter Three is about Asia and what works and does not work in this part of the world in terms of government policies, businesses, and the military. This chapter also examines the problems that globalization has foisted on its 500 million people who live across a vast territory that encompasses the Eurasian Steppes, the Himalayas, the tropical jungles of Malaysia, the forests of Thailand, and the volcanoes of Indonesia. This chapter highlights Singapore Airlines as a highly successful example of an indigenous Asian MNC. The chapter also criticizes the nature of globalization and military special forces in Southeast Asia.

Chapter Four is about money. This chapter details the economic aspects of globalization and the impact of its economic activities on the rest of the world. A special point of emphasis here is the work on MNCs and their management. This chapter deals with the business of American business and uses the story of the Panama Canal and the meaning of "outsourcing" to distinguish the interlocking of politics, business, and labour in achieving MNC status. The chapter uses successful economic narratives of several American chief executive officers (CEOs) as a segue into understanding the modernity of American businesses and its relationship to globalization.

Chapter Five considers terrorism. It invites the reader to consider the primordial desire to destroy and to violate. This curse dogs the human being and prevents him or her from ever fully achieving peace. And human technologies are designed to be inherently useful tools for terror. The Egyptians built the pyramids ostensibly as monuments to their dead pharaohs but they were substantially monuments about war. And the imposition of war on all others through supernatural forces. The technology used to build the pyramids continues to amaze us. Americans have the supreme technology like the Egyptians did in their time. *Pax Americana* was built on America's ability to defend and protect its interests locally and overseas and those of its allies. The foreign and domestic policies of several administrations are used as a clue to American military might. The position that America has achieved in late modernity is not only due to technological supremacy or brute force. If it were merely technological supremacy of arms, then there are many other advanced nations that could lay claim to being a superpower. Neither is America's position a result of brute force. Rather, it is the consistency of the neoliberal rhetoric contained within foreign and domestic policies coupled with the military industrial complex that have made *Pax Americana* what it is today. Military power is the foundation of America as a superpower. American military hegemony is a serious responsibility that when taken lightly bestows untold death and destruction. This chapter highlights the main problems hidden within the recesses of American military power and reveals the single most predatory problem that faces America today as a global power.

Chapter Six illustrates how important culture is to our understanding of the politics of American globalization in terms of the sociology of leisure and the psychology of escapism. The chapter shows why American popular culture in particular, including its idioms, images, and idols continue to impact the world. This is the politics of mimicry par excellence. Part of the power of American globalization's politics is the highly successful cultural idioms that have evolved, at least since 1776. This chapter also shows how these genuine American inventions are themselves important cultural stake-points for all Americans in modernity.

Chapter Seven is about the norms and values that dominate a vital aspect of globalization. In describing and explaining the meaning of norms and values, the chapter also serves a complementary function to the major themes of the book. These norms and values are built on a civil-society ideal in democratic countries but are not limited to such motifs.

Chapter Eight is about technology and population. It shows how both concepts are integrated within the larger neoliberal economic world order within the themes of hope, optimism, and progress in late modernity. It endeavours to reconcile the problems of the lack of neutrality in human technologies where it can be used for both good and evil.

Chapter Nine is about war that occurs conceptually along political, social, cultural, and economic lines. It specifically examines the complex connections between globalization, war, and peace. It shows how the locus of the firm is not always congruent with the location of the global industry. The chapter illustrates why neoliberal capitalist states sometimes go to war even in times of a general peace. It tries to show what exactly matters during the peaceful periods of globalization when the levels of local and global creativity are high. The chapter also examines the global interests in Asia and explains the advantages of investing in Asia, Africa, Latin America, the Pacific, the Middle East, and America with a special focus on countries that have specific value and meaning for America and Americans. This chapter considers the use of WMD and other aspects of culture, money, and terror in Asia including the fallout from the Crusades and the consequences of cultural wars cloaked or disguised as religious ones while rejecting notions of moral perfectionism and ethical idealism in late modernity. This chapter reviews the American case as a barometer of change and non-change in Asia. It highlights several small instances that are problematic when one considers Asia as a whole.

Chapter Ten proffers some end thoughts with the general argument that no single definition of American globalization will suffice, nor any particular theory or school of thought, in comprehensively showing the "what", "how", and "why" of globalization, politics, and modernity in America. The conclusion also reveals that the current strength of America's politics of globalization will gradually erode to be replaced by a new startling paradigm that does not involve American dominance but the dominance of an "other".

MODERNITY AND LATE MODERNITY

Modernity and late modernity can assume several hermeneutical forms. These centre on the work of critics like Schlomo Avineri, Zygmunt Bauman, Ulrich Beck, Hans Blumenberg, Aryeh Botwinick, Noam Chomsky, William E. Connolly, J. Peter Euben, Alvin Gouldner, Jürgen Habermas, Martin Heidegger, David Harvey, Fredric Jameson, Peter J. Katzenstein, Charles Larmore, Scott Lash, Jean Francois Lyotard, Herbert Marcuse, Deane E. Neubauer, Mario Puzo, Roy A. Rappaport, Richard Rorty, Marshall D. Sahlins, Charles Tilly, Gianni Vattimo, and Zhang Yimou. There are very many more scholars of equal intellectual girth whom I have not read sufficiently to address here and will leave it to the reader to expand the list. There appear to be three main forms of defining modernity. One way is through a genealogical looking-glass from a contemporary perspective. This would mean that everything in the past that can be recalled or reconstructed might be compared either erroneously or deliberately with contemporary life. The second common form for defining modernity is through the use of relative platforms: That every age has its own modern and traditional periods and ought to be understood as such. Hence we have knowledge that could potentially be based on a series of overlapping modernities. A third form for defining modernity is chronological. This means that it tends to use dates and years as a marker of beginnings and endings. I like to use this form to explain to new students of modernity. If this form is used, then we might argue that modernity's characteristics became particularly apparent and prominent in the Industrial Revolution of the West. Late modernity is marked at around the time of the personal computer (PC) and information and communications revolutions in the late 1970s and early 1980s. Readers are requested to think about the possibilities associated with all three forms of modernity that they encounter in this book.

DOMESTIC POLITICS

American domestic politics impacts globalization. The world watches whenever there is a presidential election, or when there is a change of party control over the House of Representatives and the Senate. The world's economists always keep an eye on who runs the Federal Reserve or Fed, the International Monetary Fund (IMF), and the World Bank. Financiers are concerned with the nature of local politics in America and many know more about America than they know about their own countries.[11] American politics impacts the world economy but is achieved with different levels of intensity and only in many parts of the globe, and not most of its parts. It is not unthinkable, however, for a national plan, economic strategy, and global philosophy that is crafted by a U.S. senator or U.S. president to have immediate, pervasive, and wide influence on states and societies they have never seen or will ever visit. But that does not mean America shapes the world perfectly. This is because history is a poor and inaccurate predictor of political modalities. And American "history" has shown itself to be more than a complex mixture of ideological norms and propagandistic values that have gained increasing predominance since the end of the nineteenth century on the world political stage. Modern America's search for global control since World War I has demonstrated the extent of its global reach. Yet, despite the international prominence of America, the greatest impact that America has had for the past 200 years is on its own domestic politics. While the trend is for America to think of itself more often than it thinks of the rest of the world, it is also true that America thinks of itself by "out-thinking" the rest of the world. For this we need to understand its domestic politics because American domestic policies influence the nature of America's response to globalization and the world.

American globalization is defined as all those activities involving multinational business corporations headquartered in one of the fifty U.S. states that provide goods and services for America and the rest of the world. American MNCs may principally serve a domestic market, but make its products in several countries overseas. This also counts towards globalization activity. If an American company is based in Arlington, Texas or Casper, Wyoming, but outsources its backroom operations to New Delhi in India or to Bangkok in Thailand, it is considered part of American globalization. If a company overseas purchases an American franchise and has an American customer base, it is American globalization. If a company uses American technology, information, and communications in its daily business activities, it is considered part of American globalization. American globalization is informed and moderated by the U.S. government and to a lesser extent by the governments of host countries where the MNCs are landholders and labour employers. An act of the European Parliament may have an effect on American globalization, especially now after the 1 May 2004 celebrations of European unity in Dublin. Police action against local saboteurs on Bintan Island, Indonesia, may affect an American subsidiary located there. This is also part of American globalization. Acts of Congress, executive pronouncements, and congressional committees may have an effect on American global companies.

Decisions made within the federal and state systems of courts, the political views of U.S. judges, and the costs of legal action in the U.S. system of civil law also have an impact on the conduct of American globalization. For example, George W. Bush might not have become president if not for a bureaucratic deadline involving Florida state law.[12]

But what does this mean for globalization? In the short run it appears to have created a better situation with regard to U.S. corporate taxes, but in the long run, it has placed someone in a position of extreme power who has appointed people who have cost American lives in Iraq. American global business practices are also subject to the former Immigration and Naturalization Service (INS), now known as the U.S. Bureau of Citizenship and Immigration Services (USCIS), the Drug Enforcement Administration (DEA), the Internal Revenue Service (IRS), the Department of Defence (DOD), and a whole host of other bureaus and departments that make the United States of America one of the most densely bureaucratized places in the world.

There is therefore only a superficial sense of difference between the Democratic Party and the Republican one. This has become common knowledge in first-year courses in political science and government at colleges and university campuses across the United States since the mid to late 1980s. Over the past fifty years, the primary distinctions between the two parties have all but completely evaporated. It is better to think of the Democrats and the Republicans in terms of their "position" on the political spectrum. In other words, it is better to think of the senators, representatives, and elected judges as either conservative or liberal in political outlook.

Conservatives prefer big business, free trade, less government intervention in the private lives of Americans but more intervention in the private lives of foreign nationals that are domiciled locally or abroad, tend to be pro-life proponents, and prefer incremental policy changes. Liberals on the other hand are usually pro-choice, and emphasize minority rights over business rights, prefer more government intervention and larger kinds of community differences acting within a non-violent arena. These are gross representations of what conservatives and liberals are in daily political life. For example, there are situations where you can mix up all of the above characteristics and end up with either a Republican or a Democratic political view. There are also many shades of differences within the parties themselves. If acting in concert, the party may give an impression of overall unity although this is not quite the same unity as that found in parliamentary-type governments modelled on the Westminster system in Europe, Asia, Africa, and the Pacific since 1945. However, the divergences between the so-called conservatives and so-called liberals are more often than not cosmetic. The impact of terrorism's global agents has narrowed the field of difference between conservatives and liberals to the extent that they have become encrusted within the shells of their former selves.

Nevertheless, shades of difference tend to colour the political map especially around the time of major elections. The shades of difference within party caucuses as politicians behave differently as individual representatives of the people and as collective representatives of the nation. This was seen clearly when the congressional Black Caucus spoke vehemently against the administrative lethargy of the Bush government to effectively tackle the hazards of Hurricane Katrina. The problem of political correctness in the United States and the complexity of its bureaucratic regulations have severely handicapped its policy delivery and regulatory systems. It has weakened the U.S. public's ability to deal with natural and artificial disasters in the same emotionally detached and rational manner it has dealt with the illegal invasion of Iraq and the continuing ruse about hidden caches of WMD. Recall that it was only in late December 2007 that the Senate began investigating a CIA torture technique called "waterboarding" which has the effect of making one think that one is drowning. This is only the tip of a deeply sunken iceberg. It is part of modern torture as Darius Rejali argues in his award-winning and valuable work.[13]

As an individual representative, a politician may emphasize a greater willingness to change over a given policy or to provide leadership on another issue. As a collective representative, s/he may or may not (legislatively) act in the same manner. There are also differences within the parties themselves in terms of seniority and rank. This cuts across conservative, radical, and right-wing members of the same party. This is why it is better to think of the two parties as generally possessing the same characteristics and the capacity and resources to reinvent themselves to adapt and take a stand on virtually any political and non-political issue, to politicize or depoliticize any political or non-political issue, and to issue warrants of political rhetoric at appropriate times. Many have refused to go to the polls. Others have voted with their feet. For example, there are currently over 3.5 million Americans living overseas, mostly in Canada and Mexico. Why? The whole problem began with the 16th Amendment to the U.S. Constitution that provides for the federal government to collect income tax. This has resulted in the evolution of the IRS into one of the most tax-efficient authorities in the globalized world. But this has also worked in a positive sense for America because the power that lies in the large number of Americans overseas means that these citizens will not bring their political disaffection to Congress because they are simply too geographically displaced. But their presence overseas is not only cultural and, or, political. Many are overseas because of the money.

American global businesses come under the protection and control of U.S. laws including ones involving anti-trust legislation. This means that "wise" American investors and corporate managers summarily create different pockets overseas in tax shelters such as the Bahamas. With the exception of insurance, reinsurance, banks, or trust companies, the Bahamas is where international business companies (IBC) can be formed to provide a tax shelter for profit. So what do you do when you have insurance, re-insurance, banks, or trust companies and want to open an IBC in the Bahamas? Just do not use the forbidden names. This only requires a minimum authorized capital of US$5,000 upon approval for incorporation of foreign companies. While offshore bank accounts are useful, they cannot really compete with the proximity and tropical attraction of the Bahamas and its fabled beaches of pink sand. The biggest selling point is the absence of a U.S.-Bahamas double taxation agreement.

Many Americans work overseas under the U.S. Department of State, the departments of the Army, Navy, and Air Force. However, a significant number of ordinary, non-military and non-state employed Americans (about 1.05 per cent of all Americans) live on expatriate terms outside the United States. Why? Because money accrued to individual work and profits in the United States can be comfortably and legally "sheltered" in the Bahamas, Barbados, Berlitz, the Cayman Islands, Gibraltar, Singapore, and Switzerland. These Americans live overseas in order to fully realize their version of the American Dream. This serves to lower the incidence of tax from x per cent to (close to, or exactly at) zero. And if you use your credit cards, corporate, personal or otherwise, the credit card's bank does not really care where the money comes from as long as you remain a customer in good standing. The Bahamas and other tax shelters have been used for decades by American companies seeking greater global opportunities to expand by taking advantage of IBC status that offers its shareholders exemption from all income taxes, capital gains tax and corporate taxes, inheritance, succession and gift taxes, stamp duties, and foreign exchange control regulations. Some Americans have even given up American citizenship in order to enjoy a slower pace of life with the profits realized from sheltered investments gleaned over a decade to thirty years.

Neoliberal capitalist profits are supposedly derived from honest, hardworking, and efficient Americans in the United States. Consider the Articles of Confederation. These were constructed to protect, in a large part, the present and future of American businesses and property rights of the early seaboard states from the aggressive colonial control of Great Britain. But as a result of breaking away, the new states had to pay for everything themselves. About 230 years later, the cost of the U.S. Government has become the highest in the world. According to the U.S. Bureau of Public Debt, the total U.S. deficit runs over US$7 trillion, rising at an increasing rate currently standing at over US$1.58 billion per annum before adding the future costs of the current Second Gulf War. The average debt owed by each American on paper is US$24,248. There is certainly a politics of American globalization because a large part of the deficit is due to American provisions of free international public good (such as "peace" and "stability") and the total cost of the Cold War programme (1955–89).

While the rest of the book and the chapter on war analyse the numbers that construct the politics of American globalization, it is also important to note another evolution. The founding fathers' fear of the absolutism of King George led them to construct the two basic principles of American governance, that is, a system of shared powers, and a system of checks and balances. In terms of political theory, many of the problems that American businesses face today are directly traceable to these two political fundamentals. The first reason is that the principle of shared power is not about equally shared power between the three arms of government. This is because the U.S. executive branch really has only one person-in-charge: the President. While the House of Representatives has 435 seats, the U.S. Senate has 100. This makes a total of 535 (different) individuals who have different terms of elected office and much lower access to the national media than the chief executive. That makes 535 individuals who have to share power. The U.S. Supreme Court has nine judges appointed by the President.

The second governance principle — a system of checks and balances — has shown a tendency to emphasize the "checks" and not the "balances". This leads to a potentially disastrous situation where an entire coterie of complex rules and regulations confounds the process rather than simplifying it. It is better to understand American politics in terms of political personalities, political issues, recent legal tradition, and the norms and values that determine the place on the political spectrum from conservative to liberal, and from the "left" to the "right" rather than simply ingest Senator's or Congressperson's political rhetoric, logical arguments, and "charts and graphs" debates on C-SPAN. For over 30 years, C-SPAN has been funded by a consortium of cable networks and provides news and information free of advertising and commercials.

Globalization is not beyond the reach of every one, but neither is globalization's reach able to touch everyone and everything. Perhaps one way of understanding globalization is to see it as a process rather than a goal. Once one is convinced of this starting point, accepting the idea of globalization as belonging to everyone and simultaneously belonging to no one is more easily attained. There are rational reasons for this paradox as seen in the competing array of challenges that the globe throws up every day: the variegated responses that are designed to match these challenges. There is a politics of globalization because it is a process that involves the complex borrowing, sharing, stealing, and copying of ideas, visions, concepts, and norms of technology's uses. Globalization is more than the human control of the external environment as Martin Heidegger suggested in the early twentieth century, perhaps to the chagrin of Hannah Arendt. Neither is globalization the Panopticonian vehicle that acts to chauffeur the current worldwide democratic transformation in a forward and linear motion, as Fukuyama and his supporters would be apt to believe.

Globalization involves all these different ideas and more. It is not moving only forward and back but also sideways and upwards. And globalization is reversible. Globalization is

> not an irreversible process, as some liberal economists insist, that is sweeping away the residues of resistance, be they national or regional. And with the end of the Cold War the world is not breaking up into rival economic blocs as some neo-mercantilists have argued. Instead globalization and regionalism are complementary processes. They occur simultaneously and feed on each other, thus leading to growing tensions between economic regionalism and economic multilateralism.[14]

But politics as we know it through the millennia is much more than the question of irreversibility. Alas, we are unable to completely learn from the past or else we could, inter alia, summon the greatest philosophers of each age to envision their map of their world. What would be the result? We would see that globalization has in effect taken on an enlarging series of cartographic experiences overlapping, questioning, interrogating, rejecting, and informing the preceding periods. The earliest Chinese philosophers saw the world as being inscrutably centred on China. The ancient Hindu philosopher kings thought that the world was best understood as unchallengeable but profound karmic interventions. The great Greek heroes of our own philosophical age saw the world as being divided between barbarians and civilized men. Later, some medieval Christian philosophers viewed the world as being symbolically four-cornered and flat. At every age there was talk and discussion about the world. As students of philosophy today, we need to take cognizance of the fact that we are dispossessed of sufficient life to seek out the ends of globalization, and must quickly retreat to the places that support discernible patterns of what can be observed about our past and present futures lest we forget. For the first quarter of the twenty-first century, there is significant data to support an assurance that there is likely to be an increase in total world output in trade. Additionally, sub-epistemological increases in human knowledge of food production vis-à-vis population growth[15] are also likely in terms of the volume of trade, commercial activities, and the value of global stock markets as Philippe Jorion and William N. Goetzmann have previously discovered. But this scenario is only likely if and when centres of economic production (that range from small farms and family holdings to multinational outsourcing powerhouses that pressure other conglomerates to perform and compete) perceive each other as complements.

ON ASSUMPTION

There can be no single school of thought that explains globalization. I do not support any single anarchic, realist, structural, Marxist, neo-Marxist, or liberal interpretation of the word and invite readers to create alternative critical modes of reading globalization.

Robert Gilpin's work on international political economy is a useful precursor to this book. But Peter J. Katzenstein's work is the one with the greatest influence over the form that this book has taken in the area of global political economy. While there are some obvious theoretical problems with areas of Gilpin's theoretical constructions, he provides an intellectual survey of the kind of introductory landscape that we are still trying to navigate.

Part of this book's intention is to generate sufficient evidence and intellectual provocations to challenge the theories that continue to dominate the intellectual scene. However, if you are a general reader and have already been thrown off course, suffice to know that there are two main debates that need to be understood to make more sense of the following chapters.

The first one is known as realism. While realism has a long tradition across the European philosophical landscape, and has been deployed in many different ways, it also has a central binding argument. The argument begins with assumptions of a certain kind of human nature and an anarchic world order where all nations are in competition for limited resources and for political, economic, and cultural survival. Realism involves the use of military force, combat power, and other coercive elements of the state to support what used to be called the national interest and national interest objectives. Thucydides, Hobbes, Machiavelli, Clausewitz, Niebuhr, Morgenthau, Kennan (the "king of containment"), and their disciples would tend to support an argument that celebrates the centrality of the state as an actor that is sovereign above all other entities. Realism and its derivatives (such as neorealism and structural realism) are mainly concerned with the state as the basic unit of analysis, state actions, and relationships between nations such as foreign policy, and diplomacy. The egotism of realism and its central invocation of the word "power" in its classical and modern forms tend to obscure the finer details of life within the state itself and the prospects for safeguarding a stable future. As a result, neo-liberalism was created. Neoliberalism shares many of the basic statist views of modern realism but defines the use of power as a means of achieving relative gains rather than realists' and realism's absolute ones. Neorealism in political science has to do with analysing the broad spectrum of international strategic studies. Neorealist experts also seem to be their harshest critics and include Kenneth Waltz, John Mearsheimer, Robert Gilpin, and Joanne Gowa. There is another residual consequence of realism called structural realism that focuses on civil society, deep structure, and variations on a theme of what Joseph Nye has now reclaimed as "soft power". The great contributions of realism include classical balance of power theory, hegemonic stability theory, security dilemma, and game theory.

The second debate involves the neoliberalism position. This is different from the kind of liberalism used in U.S. domestic politics by scholars who wish to emphasize the importance of individual rights, constitutionalism, and more or less government intervention in private life. Neoliberal discourse stresses the importance of MNCs and international organizations that support capitalism, non-protectionism, and "free trade". Proponents of neoliberalism tend to support the opening up of markets that are protected from or closed to capitalist intervention. Neoliberals also tend to support the WTO, IBRC, and the IMF. Neoliberals tend to marginalize the work of the United Nations (UN) although some weaker ones tend to accept it grudgingly. Neoliberal theory is idealistic in nature and purpose because it thinks that the world can be made a better place through openness and trade. At its best, neoliberalism is concerned with using capitalist machines to achieve worldwide freedoms for everyone. But as we will see, this is a political conceit. The neoliberals know that capitalism through MNCs and other business units have created widening and deepening divisions between the rich and the poor. Neoliberals are everywhere. Many of us often expose our neoliberal sides when making big purchases of consumer products, but are classical liberals when showing our desire for more wealth. The primary academic philosophy of neoliberalism can be traced directly to the work of Adam Smith, John Maynard Keynes, and the structure of the Bretton Woods' system.

For many of the poor and the marginalized, neoliberalism is not the "giver-of-gifts" but the "extractor-of-surplus value" we now call "productivity". My work remains generally critical of both realist and neoliberal schools but I do concede that there are certain advantages and prospects in both schools. These two debates were very briefly introduced because I intend to use them as lenses to explain the politics of American globalization.

Therefore when we use the word "realist" we are referring to the assumptions made above and are concerned with the hawkish or dove-like actions of states as unitary actors in their bid for survival and their strategies for surviving modernity. When we use the word neoliberal, we are referring to the working of MNCs and other driving forces of globalization that want to open up and deepen the world. When I use the word "conservative", it usually refers to something that is not positive; as for the word "socialist", it is too far to the left for it to be practical.

THE LITERATURE

There are more than 17,000 books on globalization and global-related industries. Most refer to politics and/or political economy in some form or manner. Much of the literature on globalization involves money, finance, or economics. Out of the hundreds of excellent books on the subject, there are two that are fairly representative of the main stream of arguments made in the literature.

One of these is Philippe Aghion and Jeffrey G. Williamson's *Growth, Inequality, and Globalization: Theory, History, and Policy* (Cambridge University Press, 1999). This book has been expertly written and leaves the reader with the impression of authors who are widely read and firmly acquainted with the economic literature on the subject. The reader quickly digests their arguments which are clear and lucid but may raise questions about globalization that occur in daily life, but are not present in their work. For example, how is it possible for Aghion and Williamson to consider inequality measures that converge on economic issues of the past without considering the political modalities that inform inequality of resource distribution on one hand with the inequality of political rights on the other? While their economic theory is certainly superior for its clarity and carefully worded sentences, they appear to have marginalized the most important cause of unequal human behaviour in three distinct areas: Political ideology, political structures, and advances made in international political economy (IPE). If, indeed, Aghion and Williamson's analysis seems a little "out-of-touch" with political life, then it leaves me as one of their readers purely convinced along the lines of an excellent academic argument.

James H. Mittelman's *The Globalization Syndrome: Transformation and Resistance* (Princeton University Press, 2000) is conceived along more didactic and moralizing lines. Mittelman is conservative and remains satisfied with describing globalization's assets and liabilities. For example, he discusses the matter of time management as being central to "the structural changes in management" but fails to pursue the matter of the speeding up of time within space as seen in the work of William E. Connolly, Lash and Urry, Geiger and others. Does he not feel that there are important measures to be considered when his own notion of global dynamics is subjected to the compression of space precisely because of the speeding up of time, and the compression of time because of the collapse of space? The book also tries to promote a causality of coherence that simply does not exist within its covers. Mittelman falls into the trap of trying to place an original starting point of globalization, which of course leads to needless arguments about which civilization was the first to globalize. The book does not raise the greater question of understanding the implications of knowing more about the kinds of contributions that were made in anticipation of what we have received today by default or design. The book's co-authored chapters cannot lay claim to the larger voices they seem to want to represent and therefore sit uncomfortably with the single-authored chapters. This gives the book an uneven style and "feel". But the most disconcerting point about the book is the misleading title: there is no clear, coherent, or sustained argument about globalization's syndrome. However, I am sure that there are clear reasons for all these sins that I myself am about to commit in this book, but hopefully with a little more pizzazz, and wit. Let us now begin with three themes of hope, progress, and optimism.

HOPE, PROGRESS, AND OPTIMISM

While it remains one thing to say that the world will never come to an end, simplistically or otherwise, it seems equally probable that all human concepts of "hope", "progress", and "optimism" are deeply embedded within the psychological paradigm of social scientific analyses. Hidden within the artificial concepts of social science are probably linguistic-based explanations that constitute human fantasies of hope, optimism, and progress. The macro-world is simultaneously a large container of billions of microcosmic individuals, of which a tiny percentage are interested in the philosophy of body and mind vis-à-vis the rest of the world. Today's globe is both reflector and reflection. The globe reflects human values and norms that bring celebration and tragedy. The globe is also a reflection of human minds in their quest towards developing the outermost fringes (or the innermost core) of human hope, optimism, and progress.

Globalization has generated its own global publishing industry that has attracted the work of scholars such as Anne Y. Ilinitch, Richard A. D'Aveni, and Arie Y. Lewin who continue in their optimistic quests for "performing economies" or the epistemic communities of equally young scholars like Susan E. Clarke and Gary L. Gaile[16] whose work represents ontological explanations within the framework of the economism of hope rather than political pessimism. However, we should neither be carried away nor misled by the suave but simplistic accounts of the Samuel Huntingtons and Thomas Friedmans of this world and their essentialist theories of absolutist outcomes about globalization and human civilization. There is no need for alarm, though when the alarm bell does go off it is indeed always too late. But we do know that the era of globalization contains so much information and so many attempts that are designed around improving the quality of life, changing it for the better.[17] Sometimes it seems that even in the twenty-first century, our notions of quality of life have not changed as much as they did a century ago within a pessimistic universe.

Perhaps it is more attitudinal than we are willing to accept. It seems, though, that we have yet to completely figure out the best means to achieve the best quality. In other words, Jean-Paul Sartre was wrong when he said that "everything in life has already been figured out"; the question — for him — was "how to live life". Most human beings instinctively know "how" to live life, we just do not know the best way to improve the process of it, and the most telling logic is seen in the amount of time, money, and effort that is devoted to extending life. Or acquainting oneself with the causal factors that promote death as John Earman believes, or the objectivistic arguments by Darwin O. Sawyer, and the intelligent interrogatives of Cornel West where identity is about desire and death; even life after death.[18] Globalization features much in terms of death avoidance and life extension. The extension of life features prominently in all human civilizations from the time of the ancient Chinese and Indians, to the Babylonians, Egyptians, and especially the ancient Greeks. We all want to know how to live longer through religion. That is why many local synagogues, temples, mosques and churches seem recession-proof. It's a big spiritual business — it is about ensuring an everlasting life after all that can be said and could possibly be done about globalization.

GLOBALIZATION AND THE PROBLEM OF RELIGION

The business of globalization is not so spiritual or mythical in the religious sense of the word. Religious globalization involves the commodification of the artifacts and rituals associated with the practice of Hinduism, Judaism, Christianity, and Islam and other worldly religions.[19] Technology-based religion is the watchword of modern religious survival. Even if one visits Roman Catholic churches across the globe today, one would discover Microsoft-based PowerPoint presentations of liturgical services alongside high-resolution images of Christ are created by portable Japanese projectors with high density definition screens and super long-lasting filament bulbs made in India, and plastic casings made in China. But religious globalization is only one aspect of the entire process of globalization.

Like other aspects of globalization, religion is made in the service of some global vision. Religion provides hope for the masses in a limited, periodic, and temporal manner in the same way that other commodities provide instant but restricted satisfaction. It depends on how much time you spend on it. Some people do not need to spend too much time at a religious convention in order to get the message that they want to hear.

Social scientists, especially those brought up on a diet of rational methods and scientific proof, tend not to profess any religious conviction. Religion and religious commodification continue to provide the kind of spiritual food for many who are depressed and in need of more than material wealth, something in place of material wealth. Nevertheless, and despite the presence of amoral, non-religious rationalistic social scientists and despite the infinite number of academic articles and books published since the Enlightenment, people still derive some spiritual sustenance from religion. What we need to know at this point is that while religion has its spiritual dimension, it is very much a big business that needs to consider the bottom line to survive. So religion is a global good available locally for a moderate price of attendance. Free food and drinks are common at religious assemblies.

ABOUT THE GLOBE

When we think about the globe today, we realize that it is totally different from the globe at any other point in geological time. Any activity that human beings have carried out over the past 85,000 years of their evolution would come to naught if the same cosmological instances that destroyed plant and animal life in the Pleistocene Age were to occur as they did sporadically (rather than in one big rush) between 1.8 million to 11,000 years ago. Yet there seems to be so much activity going on today that is seemingly ignorant of the fact that the universe is increasing at an expanding rate and that some stars within our own galaxy are travelling at over 300 km/h through space.

Epistemologically, it is simply too difficult to ponder our entire ontological presence in our daily lives. We cannot all be philosophers. Neither can we all be trench diggers or exotic dancers. But who is to say that any job is superior to another except for the presence of those things called responsibility and power? We study globalization today because of that thing called power. We have to ignore the fact that we are all probably hurtling through space to a point, say some three million light years away, where we will all crash and burn and there will be no semblance of our civilization for posterity. We focus on globalization because it is a series of processes that have come together, not always coherently, and not always completely rationally, to make our world today separate and distinct from any previous worlds or civilizations. Like what appears to be the scientific hypothesis about the ultimate end of our globe as we know it.

There is a politics of globalization because of the nature of man. Globalization is about the nature of man who loves to invent. We are alive in a world that has had a distinguishing characteristic beyond any other living species. It has promoted our dominance of the environment almost exclusively for over 2,500 years in the Western tradition, and even longer if we hark back to the Indian and Chinese versions of the story of our natural inclination to invent. We have more than merely invented images that represent our hopes and desires. If architecture is the celebration of physical and aesthetic values of successive and not just successful periods of civilization, then it is also an invention. Man's ability to invent new things catalysed the information and communications revolutions in the late 1980s and early 1990s. Anything that is invented today is now very quickly transmitted across the globe.

Transportation costs are vastly different from the time of the fabled and romanticized journeys of Marco Polo or the classical inventory of Homer's Odysseus in *The Iliad* and *The Odyssey*.

While invention is a keen factor in our nature, it seems reasonable, perhaps even logical, to assume that our inventions ought to lead us to things that serve us well, things that have function and purpose. Not quite. If we look at the economically most impoverished countries, we will discover that they seem to have the most fabulous aesthetic structures next to the slums that have housed their urban populations for decades since decolonization and national independence. It appears to be true that there is an inverse relationship between economic wealth and aesthetic structures in these countries. The relatively richer countries of the so-called Third World (a most unfortunate name that even the Communists rejected it) are cautious about constructing massively expensive buildings. However, their materially poorer cousins have such fantastic structures as to make the viewer wonder where all the money came from.

This inverse relationship is a deliberate attempt to uplift the human spirit. It appears that man's creations are capable of uplifting the human spirit in ways that constant injections of food and medicines are unable to achieve. This is another invention of man. What relevance then do these structures have in relation to globalization? These uplifting structures — whether they are office blocks, government buildings, or structures representing national icons or legends — are important because they represent hope, progress, and optimism. These are the three buzzwords that keep man alive and motivated. Hope is needed whenever one feels dejected, progress is the sounding board for moving on in life, while optimism allows us to understand why we are going where we appear to be going in the first place. The globalized world allows many more people to achieve in realistic terms what constitutes their versions of hope, progress, and optimism. Perhaps it could be that we have never been able to live on bread alone.

This chapter started with the notion of how human beings and human civilizations have desired to extend life. This is not a defining characteristic of globalization. But what makes human life particularly different in a globalized world is that we now have advanced and complex technologies that are designed not only to extend life. We also use technology to extend the quality of life, improving the ways in which we live life through nutrition, healthcare, physical exercise, and lifestyle choices. The defining features of globalization as we know it today are about sustaining higher levels of quality of life, increasing our hope for a better future through optimism and progress. And human beings achieve this in three main ways: measurement, quantification, and creativity. Because we now have more accurate means of measuring our body of knowledge, we tend to resort to very precise mathematical measurements of our world with the hope that such precision builds on what we already know about ourselves and our environment.

There is a great desire among many social scientists to quantify and measure social changes in the same way that natural scientists endeavour to measure, quantify, and manufacture chemicals in laboratories. Yet once in a while there appears to be a breakthrough — using the scientific method — in paradigms that sustain our epistemological valuation of the world. Breakthroughs are often called thinking "outside-the-box". The scientific method and the methods used in the social sciences do not really allow for thinking creatively because there is a set of assumptions that have to be made before scientific inquiry can proceed. However, we do know that creative genius flows from challenging these assumptions and what has been taken for granted, despite how well that "good" may function and in spite of its use or value in society. So while there has not really been any significant or revolutionary change to the physics of the internal combustion engine, people continue to try to improve and modify it based on prevailing assumptions. This is why the shape and performance of automobiles are restricted and limited (with some exceptions, such as at NASCAR, Daytona, the international Formula One racing circuits). A creative genius will not be held back by the need, for example, to use fossil fuels to power the engine. Or even by having to use the old four/two-stroke engine as the power platform. Globalization helps in the sharing of technological knowledge about different ways of approaching problems.

Globalization is about speeding up the process of sharing knowledge and, ironically, sometimes events such as the release of classified Cold War secrets lead to new discoveries and new breakthroughs, such as the Internet. But the measurement, quantification, and creativity in globalization today is only a small aspect of what we are trying to control. Contrary to Heidegger's belief, technology is not only about the human ability to control the world and the immediate environment. So while the era of globalization may not last as long as the Pleistocene Age, human beings might still be in a position to intensify the value and meaning of life within a brief time span. Perhaps the answer is not to live any longer than we need to; or, alternatively, live much longer than we possibly can, so that we have more time to figure things out.

Perhaps the answer is in limiting the amount of time that we devote to figuring things out, restricting the amount of time that we have devoted to measurement, quantification, and creative thinking. Katzenstein's criticism about the irreversibility of globalization is more profound than it appears. This is because the way forward or the way back may not necessarily constitute the optimal mode of achieving what we want in life. Globalization is indeed a mixed bag of competition and cooperation between individuals, communities, regions, states, NGOs, histories of difference, and languages of technology.

GLOBALIZATION AND AMERICANIZATION

Globalization is not Americanization but many people outside America and inside its walls often mistake the one for the other and not surprisingly. The reason for this is simple: American media networks. These networks not only provide all forms of entertainment but also reality TV, sports, prayer, religion, news, economic predictions, government positions, private sector analyses, and interactive "don't leave your couch" modes of home purchase through late night "infomercials". The secret is to broadcast everything and anything over a 24/7, 365-days period.

The American media is marked by a homologous identity of dispersion and multiculturalism. By this I mean that there are so many different things, so many talking heads, and so much information to simplify and convey that after a while the news becomes real. The autonomy speaks for itself. The major networks are themselves models for foreign news networks who plug into its models of conveyance. This ensures that even old films and outdated messages get re-spun for sale overseas. American media networks offer a plethora of American goods and services that are constantly being targeted at millions of Americans through syndication and copyrights. Their messages are often ones that encompass the American Dream of "hope", "progress" and "optimism".

The American media, in its attempt to remain objective, balanced, and fair in its coverage (and search for profits), often includes and incorporates critiques of its own products and services. Many people continue to think that globalization is Americanization because of the colossal network interface that American media provides for the rest of the world. Otherwise most people who plug into the Internet and to sports and entertainment, efficiently translated into local and native languages of choice, would be unable to associate the kinds of values, mannerisms, and norms that are depicted in American soap operas, Hollywood movies, and serials that are made for cable television. Many Americans know less about the world than the world knows about America.

Not only are American audiences captivated and mimicking the characters in these programmes, they also follow the spin-offs made available through magazines, tabloids, and souvenir items. The entire politics involves and revolves round cults of personality, media hype, individuated demagoguery, and the celebration of gods and stars who can not only be heard but seen to have very specific human qualities. This rash of popular culture, motivated by a sense of achievement and a search for status, is part of the American Dream, and part of what has become the dream of many non-Americans who themselves desire to be part of that dream within their own linguistic idioms. The worldwide reach of Americanization as a product of spectacular production and instantaneous gratification creates a herd-like mentality among its clientele who themselves, once hooked on the experience of the kinds of stories that are told, cannot easily leave or completely disengage. There are stories for everyone and for every occasion. The reasons then, for mistaking American trees for the world's forests, are because the audience often has no choice but to make comparisons. And when they see similarities being produced with a magical larger-than-life quality, it is in human nature to imitate. Imitation, it has been said, is the highest form of flattery. But not all flattery stems from a desire to mimic the "original".

For many decades, "American" values were being promoted over American media and through its networks in the search for ideological dominance over the Soviet Union. With the increasing power of the English language as the lingua franca of science, technology, and now the Internet, we can only guess why this did not happen earlier. In other words, while American television and radio were committed to their often patriotic messages during the Cold War (1955–89), there were other people who were listening. Not all these people were in favour of the Americans. For many years, the guardians of the official French language, for example, have been combating the adoption of American English which to them must sound more hurtful than British English, which does not seem like the hegemonic threat that it was in the eighteenth and nineteenth centuries. However, the French resistance in this case with a small "r" did not result in violence and destruction. Rather, mullahs and other Islamic religious leaders in many non-Western countries were also listening and they were becoming increasingly perplexed as to the imitative behaviour of their own followers. The turning points of course, were the fall of the Shah of Iran and the ensuing Iran-Iraq war. It ought to be said that most were probably less interested in the American entertainment scene than they were probably unhappy with the way in which non-Islamic "values" were being "transmitted" across the world. But the greater the energy used by these religious leaders to suppress information and entertainment from America, the worse the situation.

Then there is the duplicitous side of the American political economy. We can only truly appreciate this fact in hindsight because if someone told you that Saddam Hussein was America's number one enemy in 1977, you would think that person was mad, because he was not — he was working for America. The political economy of duplicity saw evidence of direct American involvement in the Iran-Iraq war in the "desert" diplomacy of former Secretary of State George Schultz:

> It was 20 years ago when Shultz dropped in on a State Department meeting between his top aide and a high-ranking Hussein emissary. Back then the Iraqis, who were fighting a war with Iran, were our new best friends in the Mid-East. Shultz wanted to make it crystal clear that U.S. criticism of the use of chemical weapons was just pabulum for public consumption, meant as a restatement of a "long-standing policy, and not as a pro-Iranian/anti-Iraqi gesture," as Lawrence S. Eagleburger told Hussein's emissary. "Our desire and our actions to prevent an Iranian victory and to continue the progress of our bilateral relations remain undiminished," Eagleburger continued, according to the then highly classified transcript of the meeting.[20]

The politics of American globalization began with an interest in developing its own agenda as a powerful alternative to that of the Soviets. America and its allies in the North Atlantic Treaty Organization (NATO) believed that they had a worthy alternative that ought to be protected and preserved. This ran afoul of those who hated America because of religion, ideology, morals, and cultural norms. The problem really came from American military activity and malfeasance as seen in Hawaii, South Korea, Japan, and Iraq. The problem begins with the kinds of military rituals that are steeped in the "traditions" of its military academies. The pioneering work of Phyllis Turnbull and Kathy Ferguson on the state of the military in Hawaii is only part of a larger politics of domination and abuse as documented in their chapter on "Oh, Say, Can You See?: The Semiotics of the Military in Hawaii" (*Borderlines 10*, University of Minnesota Press, 1998). These scholars predicted the inevitable events in Iraq six years ahead of schedule.

RESISTANCE AND COUNTER-RESISTANCE

Globalization is about opening up spaces that are closed and enclosing spaces that are open. It forces governments to liberalize commercial activities and weakens authoritarian structures of power through the Internet and political rhetoric surrounding international attempts at governance. Globalization is optimism at its best.

Man, as Aristotle believed, is by nature political. And as long as there continues to be an imbalance of power within communities based on tradition, modernization, culture, gender, primordialism, circumstantialism, racism, religion, and wide disparities in socio-economic classes premised on a domestic economy of fossil-fuels; there will be a politics of control, a politics of discord, a politics of resistance, and a politics of subversion that feed into the global reach of globalization. America continues to stand out in the international news media because it has a very large image and its military has enforced that image consistently.

If, as we saw at the beginning of this chapter, globalization is indeed not as irreversible as the econometric pundits would proffer, then we can rest assured even for a little while that there are significant and different kinds of global processes that are concurrent as they are reversible. Katzenstein was right in the sense that having more regional cooperation would lead to better outcomes, a kind of proto-principle in the political science and international relations theory literature. But we must also look further. Hence we also examined the philosophical side of globalization, one that offers criticisms as well as promises of "hope", "progress", and "optimism". We have seen that ancient religions cannot go untouched by the tremendous forces of globalization, but this does not mean that there will be no resistance. When resistance occurs, politics reaps the potential for democracy; but where resistance is absent, politics turns to autocracy.

This introduction covered a wide area of work that constitutes the meaning of globalization and the meaning of America's posture towards globalization. For many scholars globalization represents a compendium in modernity of different voices, different activities and different speeds that impact across neoliberal capitalist states and non-capitalist ones. Globalization is the vehicle on which modernity seeks out new sites to develop, change, and modify. Globalization is the new catchword for modernization into the twenty-first century. But unlike modernization, which was concerned with the patterns of movement to and from and in between traditional societies and modern ones, globalization tends to unite diverse social, cultural, economic, and political dimensions. While modernization was about exploiting local resources, globalization is about deepening the level of exploitation in global terms and across political boundaries. Under globalization, nothing is sacred, and there is nothing that cannot be commodified or commoditized.

Everything created by man can be turned into a good or a service to be sold for profit.

THE CRISIS OF LATE MODERNITY

Globalization is sometimes interpreted and criticized as the triumphalist phase of capitalism, "a neoliberal apology by another name"[21] with a case for military deglobalization as Robert Nye suggested in 2001. However, the U.S. congressional approval for the sale of weapons to Indonesia in the fall of 2005 makes Nye's arguments sound more like Republican foreign policy[22] than where Nye would nominally commit his ideas. Also, the recent theoretical developments in global measurements have relegated Douglas Kellner's critical theory of globalization to a position of prodigious theoretical lamentation than when he first mooted it in 2003.[23] On the other hand, if globalization is defined in terms of the expansion of monetary instruments, as Michael Pettis suggests, then it seems like it might never go out of style.[24] But then, that was what they said about colonialism in the eighteenth and nineteenth centuries. Yet we cannot ignore the fact that globalization suggests on the one hand the crossing of frontiers and the transformation of substance into relation, yet on the other hand names the reinstatement of substance and identity at the level of the "globe" itself.[25] These definitions go beyond the initial evolutionary structuralist view of global institutions postulated by Rochester, Birkinshaw, Morrison, Hulland, and Modelski in the first decade after the Cold War.[26]

While the crisis in political theory that was resurrected in the debate between Isaac and McClure in the 1990s truthfully continues within the larger moral debates of the discipline, other disciplines within the social sciences and humanities are similarly facing increasing agonistic challenges within and across the globalized world. Concerned with problems of world identity within its own discipline, insecure scholars have regressed on appreciating the impact of globalization.[27]

The development of globalization itself was no mere accident of fate. The rise of neoliberal global institutions was a direct result of the old colonial division of labour and the relatively crude economics that drove their extraction of surpluses from the developing world of their colonies and the creation of markets in these colonies themselves. Therefore the question of globalization is not only historical and economic but also political and moral. The question of the moral value of the actions of the old colonial powers of Great Britain, France, the Netherlands, and to a lesser extent, Germany are key to understanding the position and impact of globalization on states in late modernity as articulated by Wallerstein, Torres, and others.[28]

The extent and depth of globalization's processes are mediated by two main components as discussed in the subsequent chapters. The two main mediating conditions are speed and time. Globalization is about speeding up human activities at a pace that has never been previously thought possible. This is part of the reason why globalization is worth studying in all its different varieties. The neoliberal capitalist world order is likened to a "Ship of Fools" floating on a sea that is depthless and unexplored. Neoliberal capitalism flows across political and cultural boundaries with urgency and purpose. This is why there are different schools of thought when it comes to the meaning of globalization. It defies definition. Edward Said's view of the globe was articulated by the discursive pronouncements of Orientalists keen to make their mark on the exotic East. Said believed that there were pockets of known resistance all across the Orientalized world that sought to challenge modernity's tempo, demands, and pressures that were multiplied and conveyed through globalization of goods and services that are designed for the masses and the elites. More so, these products are designed for the masses to feel like elites and for the elites to feel that they are part of the masses. International terrorism and piracy are mere setbacks to the power of globalization. 9/11 has heightened the level of conservatism and the conservation of private values in public spaces. Terrorism will abate and modernity's military machines will seek out these pockets of disgruntled and disenfranchised terrorists with glee and zealousness.

Is there a crisis of modernity embedded in the vehicle of globalization? Certainly, but the crisis is neither economic as Wallerstein and Jameson believe, nor civilizational as Huntington has proclaimed. The crisis of modernity is no longer likely to emerge within Marxist class contradictions. Neither is this crisis looming for international trade unionism which no longer exists as a worldwide fellowship. The crisis of modernity will not come from religion or politicized society but rather, from the loss of nerve among men. The crisis of modernity is worthy of a book-length argument but for now it seems that as long as the patriarchal neoliberal capitalist world system continues to function, this crisis will be averted to a point when the profit motif has exhausted itself. The speed and timing of the goods of globalization will force a greater disparity between the richest rich and the poorest poor. The middle classes will resolve along the lines of self-perception and continue to view themselves according to the upper or lower classes that they feel a part of. Lefebvre's view of globalization is contained in the physical architectural forms, between modernity and post-modernity, between function and form, substance and style. This kind of globalization will cure the tendency for middle-class fractionalism. In other words, the sweet sauces of global goods will distract the largest working classes from fulfilling their Marxian heritage. This might not necessarily be a bad thing.

For those who need a deeper handle on globalization, refer to Katzenstein's excellent work on global political economy, security, and culture. The subsequent chapters identify and illustrate the themes and paradoxes in the politics of American globalization. But more importantly, globalization is not a phenomenon restricted to American politics, culture, and economics. Globalization is a world phenomenon. Human beings experience globalization's processes through different rates of torque, dissimilar push and pull factors. The processes of globalization's many faces is an intractable mixture of ethnic and religious communities, political institutions, state actors, NGOs, politicians, journalists, financial analysts, economists, peasants, CEOs, consumers and producers, capitalists and socialists within the neoliberal world order of modernity. Globalization is unevenly mediated by technocrats, innovators, and IT specialists. Americans are a significant part of the processes, no less "prisoner[s] of the passage" (Foucault [1965] 1988, p. 11) on the global *Ship of Fools*.

What then, is the meaning of culture if power is dependent on money and wealth? What is the point of attaching value to authority if it is transient? If securities can be worth billions in the first hour of trading and lose most of their value by the day's end, are we inflicting a new kind of financial terror on ourselves? Have we been fighting the wrong wars since the dawn of being? The problem with today's generation of leaders is that they are all raised on a diet of excellence in logical thinking to the point that they are unable to sense danger. After all, "zoogles are not all boogles" as Nassim Nicholas Taleb argues in *The Black Swan: The Impact of the Highly Improbable* (Random House, 2007) where "a black swan is relative to knowledge". We have embarked on an international glossary of terms that undermines as it de-legitimizes the structures that are critical to our survival in late modernity.

Notes

1. James S. Romm, *Herodotus* (New Haven, CT: Yale University Press, 1998).
2. J. Peter Euben, *The Tragedy of Political Theory: The Road Not Taken* (Princeton, NJ: Princeton University Press, 1990).
3. Could it be called the Huk War of Independence like the American War of Independence? The answer is "no" because the Huks lost their war in Central Luzon while the Americans won the war against the British. Had the British

won the war in its largest colony, America would probably be a very different place today. One man's terrorist is another man's freedom fighter.

4. Gerakan Aceh Merdeka (GAM) has direct links with separatists from the Pattani United Liberation Organization (PULO), Gerakan Mujahideen Islam Pattani (GMIP), and some indirect links with Kumpulan Mujahiden Malaysia (KMM).

5. Robert H. Kupperman, Debra van Opstal, and David Williamson, Jr., "Terror, the Strategic Tool: Response and Control", *Annals of the American Academy of Political and Social Science* 463 (1982): 24–38.

6. Luciana Parisi, "Information Trading and Symbiotic Micropolitics", *Social Text* 22, no. 3 (Fall 2004): 25–49.

7. Joseph S. Nye, Jr., Philip D. Zelikow, and David C. King, *Why People Don't Trust Government* (Harvard University Press, 1997).

8. Morley Segal, "The Freedom of Information Act and Political Science Research", *PS* 2, no. 3 (1969): 315–20; see also, Jack P. Geise, "Political Liberty and Free Action", *Polity* 18, no. 1 (1985): 47–69; and Alasdair Roberts, "Structural Pluralism and the Right to Information", *University of Toronto Law Journal* 51, no. 3 (2001): 243–71.

9. Robert Young, "A Specious Paradox", *Philosophy and Phenomenological Research* 35, no. 2 (1974): 268–70.

10. If the word "vicissitude" was more popular and more easy to pronounce by the majority of people in the market for books on globalization, it could better be used to accurately to describe the nature of globalization in modernity.

11. During the British Empire, the eyes of the world were on Whitehall, the old name for the seat of British colonial control. Some political scientists working in the Commonwealth would not be able to tell you what Whitehall is, but they would be able to tell you what was recently said by a White House spokesman and how it affects the global economy.

12. See U.S. Supreme Court case number 290 U.S. 534, at 545 (1934). See also, *Anderson v. Celebrezze*, U.S. Supreme Court Case number 460 U.S. 780, at 794–95 (1983).

13. Darius Rejali, *Torture and Democracy* (Princeton University Press, 2007).

14. Peter J. Katzenstein, "Regionalism in Comparative Perspective", *Arena Working Papers* 1 (1996).

15. Guillermo A. Calvo and Enrique G. Mendoza, "Capital-Markets Crises and Economic Collapse in Emerging Markets: An Informational-Frictions Approach", *American Economic Review* 90, no. 2 (2000): 59. See also D. Gale Johnson, "Population, Food, and Knowledge", *American Economic Review* 90, no. 1 (2000): 1–14; and Philippe Jorion, and William N. Goetzmann, "Global Stock Markets in the Twentieth Century", *Journal of Finance* 54, no. 3 (1999): 953–80.

16. See Anne Y. Ilinitch, Richard A. D'Aveni, and Arie Y. Lewin, "New Organizational Forms and Strategies for Managing in Hypercompetitive Environments",

Organization Science 7, no. 3 (1996): 211–20; and Susan E. Clarke, and Gary L. Gaile, "Local Politics in a Global Era: Thinking Locally, Acting Globally", *Annals of the American Academy of Political and Social Science* 551 (1997): 28–43.

17 This is illustrated, for example, by Oded Stark, "Altruism and the Quality of Life", *American Economic Review* 79, no. 2 (1989): 86–90. See also, for comparison, N.F.R. Crafts, "Some Dimensions of the 'Quality of Life' during the British Industrial Revolution", *Economic History Review* 50, no. 4 (1997): 617–39. There are alternative notions of the meaning of the "quality of life" according to social science and clinical surveys. However, most of the academic work revolves round the assumption that quality of life estimates usually make the assumption that the people involved are "normal" and not physically, emotionally, or otherwise challenged. See for example, Sarah Rosenfield, "Factors Contributing to the Subjective Quality of Life of the Chronic Mentally Ill", *Journal of Health and Social Behavior* 33, no. 4 (1992): 299–315. This article raises further questions such as whether indeed such notions as "normal" and "quality" can ever be anything but subjective and hence reconcilable within the idioms that are provided by the processes of globalization.

18 John Earman, "Causation: A Matter of Life and Death", *Journal of Philosophy* 73, no. 1 (1976): 5–25; Darwin O. Sawyer, "Public Attitudes Toward Life and Death", *Public Opinion Quarterly* 46, no. 4 (1982): 521–33; and Cornel West, "A Matter of Life and Death", *October* 61 (1992): 20–23.

19 Bernard S. Jackson, "The Prophet and the Law in Early Judaism and the New Testament", *Cardozo Studies in Law and Literature* 4, no. 2 (1992): 123–66; Charles Liebman and Bernard Susser, "Judaism and Jewishness in the Jewish State", *Annals of the American Academy of Political and Social Science* 555 (1998): 15–25; Gidon Levy and Udi Adiv, "The Jew The State Thinks is an Arab", *Journal of Palestine Studies* 13, no. 2 (1984): 176–78; Bernard Harrison, "Judaism", *Annals of the American Academy of Political and Social Science* 256 (1948): 25–35; Louis Bolce and Gerald de Maio, "The Anti-Christian Fundamentalist Factor in Contemporary Politics", *Public Opinion Quarterly* 63, no. 4 (1999): 508–42; Mark Juergensmeyer, "Christian Violence in America", *Annals of the American Academy of Political and Social Science* 558 (1998): 88–100; J.M. Spieser, "The Representation of Christ in the Apses of Early Christian Churches", *Gesta* 37, no. 1 (1998): 63–73; Richard Werbner, "The Suffering Body: Passion and Ritual Allegory in Christian Encounters", *Journal of Southern African Studies* 23, no. 2 (1997): 311–24; Matthew C. Moen, "The Evolving Politics of the Christian Right", *PS: Political Science and Politics* 29, no. 3 (1996): 461–64; Mary-Jane Deeb, "Militant Islam and the Politics of Redemption," *Annals of the American Academy of Political and Social Science* 524 (1992): 52–65; Anita M. Weiss, "Women's Position in Pakistan: Socio-cultural Effects of Islamization", *Asian Survey* 25, no. 8 (1985): 863–80; or a rather simple summation by Bernard Lewis, "Islam and

Liberal Democracy: A Historical Overview", *Journal of Democracy* 7, no. 2 (1996): 52–63.

[20] Robert Scheer, "The U.S. Winked at Hussein's Evil", *Los Angeles Times*, 30 December 2003.

[21] Robert C. Dash, "Globalization: For Whom and for What?" *Latin American Perspectives* 25, no. 6 (1998): 52–54.

[22] Joseph S. Nye, Jr., "Military Deglobalization", *Foreign Policy* 122 (2001): 82–83.

[23] Douglas Kellner, "Theorizing Globalization", *Sociological Theory* 20, no. 3 (2002): 285–305.

[24] Michael Pettis, "Will Globalization Go Bankrupt?" *Foreign Policy* 126 (2001): 52–59.

[25] Marc Redfield, "Introduction: Theory, Globalization, Cultural Studies, and the Remains of the University", *Diacritics* 31, no. 3 (2001): 4.

[26] See for example, J. Martin Rochester, "Global Policy and the Future of the United Nations", *Journal of Peace Research* 27, no. 2 (1990): 141–54; Julian Birkinshaw; Allen Morrison; John Hulland, "Structural and Competitive Determinants of a Global Integration Strategy", *Strategic Management Journal* 16, no. 8 (1995): 637–55; and George Modelski, "Evolutionary Paradigm for Global Politics", *International Studies Quarterly* 40, no. 3 (1996): 321–42.

[27] Bruce Mazlish, "Comparing Global History to World History", *Journal of Interdisciplinary History* 28, no. 3 (1998): 385–95. See also, Joan Wallach Scott, "History in Crisis: The Others' Side of the Story", *American Historical Review* 94, no. 3 (1989): 680–92.

[28] See for example, Immanuel M. Wallerstein, "After Developmentalism and Globalization, What?" *Social Forces* 83, no. 3 (2005): 1263–78; and Carlos A. Torres, "Globalization and Comparative Education in the World System", *Comparative Education Review* 45, no. 4 (2001): iii–x.

2

CULTURAL AMERICA AND THE GLOBALIZATION OF (IM)PERFECTION

THE GLOBALIZATION OF (IM)PERFECTION

Foucault was concerned with authoritarianism in Western cultures and societies. He criticized the embedded structures of authoritarian politics serving the wealthiest minorities. His criticisms made him unpopular among politicians and conservative critics. With the exception of the Academy, Foucault was demonized by the establishment both in many European and U.S. cities and became the target of homophobia and xenophobia.

The deification of Foucault or demonization of his work is only part of the picture of his philosophy. Foucault was as imperfect a man as he was diabolically precise as a cultural historian and an intellectual.[1] In 1996, Reid asked whether Foucault was even concerned about "willingly spreading HIV" in his desire for sado-masochism among his partners of the underground sex clubs that he visited.[2] Foucault's visits to America are a reminder of human imperfections, regardless of social and economic status, regardless of intellect. Attendance at the best universities, whatever that might mean, does not make the student a better person.

Humanity desires perfection as it portrays imperfection. If our perfections are celebrated in our conjoint successes as human beings, then there is much reason to celebrate. Some of humanity's achievements can be summarized in: Locke's *Two Treatises on Government* (1689) and the right to overthrow rogue governments; the declaration of the first *Ten Amendments to the U.S.*

Constitution as the Bill of Rights (1789); Wilberforce's maiden parliamentary speech against the slave trade (1789); Jean Barnard Foucault's invention of the rotation of the earth in 1851 and Jean Leon Foucault's invention of the gyroscope in 1852; Wollstonecraft's *A Vindication of the Rights of Woman* (1792); the founding of the Royal Society for the Prevention of Cruelty to Animals (the *Martin Act* of 1822); Dicey's popular *Law of the Constitution* (1895); Einstein's discoveries from 1905 till his death in 1955 in Princeton, NJ; the Wright brothers' activities in the early 1900s; the discovery of air-conditioning in the 1920s; Focke's and Sikorsky's invention of the helicopter in 1936 and 1939 respectively; the invention of the pacemaker in 1957; Biro's invention of the ballpoint pen in 1944; mass produced color televisions (1951–53); Tomlinson's invention of email in 1972; the development of the personal computer in the late 1970s, and the discovery of the World Wide Web in the late 1980s are only a few examples of success stories in human civilization that celebrate possibilities for human perfection in creativity.

But our impetus for perfection through creativity appears shrouded in the moral ambiguity of human imperfection: Jefferson, U.S. Ambassador to France, and his affair with his slave's sister in Paris before the Bastille fell in 1789; the U.S. Supreme Court decision in *Brown v. Board of Education of Topeka* (1954) that separate educational amenities for ethnic minorities were inherently unequal; Nixon's resignation in the Watergate scandal under the threat of impeachment and subsequent pardon by his former Vice-President Gerald Ford; English soccer hooliganism of the late 1980s; the 1992 Los Angeles riots that followed when four policemen were acquitted of beating Rodney King; the kidnapping and rape of a 12-year-old Okinawa girl by U.S. Marines in 1991; U.S. financial speculator George Soros' conviction of insider trading and €2.2 million (US$2.58 million) fine in 2002; and the abuse and torture of Iraqi prisoners of war in Abu Ghraib by Charles Graner and Lynndie England, both U.S. Army reservists in the 372nd Military Police unit in 2003 are only a few stories that momentarily shocked the world.

Human perfection is inseparable from its imperfections. The globalization of humanity's best successes appears with its worst excesses. Foucault's ignorance as a man cannot be separated from his brilliance as a philosopher. He said, perhaps somewhat ironically, that "Our civilization has created the most complex system of knowledge, the most sophisticated structures of power: What has this kind of knowledge, this type of power made of us? In what way are those fundamental experiences of madness, suffering, death, crime, desire, and individuality connected, even if we are not aware of it, with knowledge and power?"[3]

THE POWER OF U.S. GLOBALIZATION

In the eighteenth and nineteenth centuries, while the European colonial masters were entangled in different traditional diplomatic, cultural, and religious differences, America was quietly expanding its sovereign political power not in the least in terms of the physical geography of the contiguous United States. No one could possibly have forecasted the kind of future impact that the simple purchases modelled on the Louisiana Purchase from France would have had in the twentieth and twenty-first centuries' global economy. Consequently, the European product and manufacturing bases were too embroiled in nationalist tensions over a wide range of European made products that came under such powerful arrangements as the European Coal and Steel Community. European business concerns were continually torn by local demands for protection with overarching needs for creating an economic and political entity that would benefit all of Europe and not some parts of its developed Western states. The end of World War II saw a torn and divided Europe with devastated cultural egos and emaciated economic structures. American military technology and economic power helped rebuild war-torn Europe and this process continued deep into the late 1950s as the world divided ideologically between the United States and the USSR.

While Western Europe during the Cold War days was very much dependent on American military technology as R.D. Norton notes in his paper on "Industrial Policy and American Renewal"[4] and combat troop deployment in the face of the Soviet bear,[5] the European manufacturers and MNCs still had access to an entire continent of resources from the Low Countries, the Benelux economic confederation, the Seine, the Rhine, the Danube, and the Mediterranean coastal areas. However, Western Europe during the Cold War was neither a single nor a united entity, and it was militarily dependent on NATO. The United States on the other hand, in pursuing its strategic defence policies abroad in Europe, the Mediterranean, Africa, the Middle East, and the Asia-Pacific, also had access to an entire continent of resources that belonged to a single political entity, that is, the United States of America. Since 1945, America has increasingly established itself as the principle architect of neoliberal capitalism. This was in spite of the propagandistic politics of the Soviet regime, as illustrated by Vojtech Mastny's award-winning book, *The Cold War and Soviet Insecurity* (1998) and Martin Sicker's *The Bear and the Lion: Soviet Imperialism and Iran* (Praeger, 1988). Meanwhile, America helped rebuild Japanese and South Korean cities from their war-torn gloom until they ironically began competing with American consumer goods and services in less than forty years' time as Hugh Patrick's influential work, *The*

Financial Development of Japan, Korea, and Taiwan: Growth, Repression, and Liberalization (Oxford, 1994) illustrates. This is similar to the mobilization of the military and civilian forces by Minos in Thucydides's *History of the Peloponnesian War* who built a great navy to master the Grecian Sea and to command Cyclades and enslave the Carians in the old customary ways of the Locraines and Acarnanians and the greatest parts of the Peloponnesus.[6]

By the late twentieth century, when the Cold War came to an end, American capitalist experiments overseas in Europe and the Far East culminated in a powerful U.S.-centric nexus of advanced economic production. The American product manufacturing base that was highly advanced during the munitions factory era of the 1940s would serve it well in the post-war reconstruction era. The Americans made the shift from Fordist to post-Fordist and just-in-time production at an incredible rate. American-made goods and services ranged from experimental research to manufacturing and financial services, advertising, media services, and telecommunications infrastructure. America led the world in terms of its ownership of the World Wide Web, that twentieth century invention by American scientists headquartered at RAND, Santa Monica, California, that was initially designed for American military communications during the Cold War. Despite these fantastic achievements, American capital brings with its process of neoliberalism some contradictory patterns.

America is the richest country in the world with some of the poorest people. Ironically, America seems to be one of the most politically peaceful countries on earth but has inherited a modern history of sustained and bloody violence on American soil and overseas across the world. The lighter side of American democracy appears to have an ugly side that is so much less appealing. The modern political history of American politics runs a parallel with a "sterile field of cares and ignorance, among the mirages of knowledge, amid the unreason of the world" (Foucault [1965] 1988, p. 12).

POVERTY AND ETHNICITY

The level of manufacturing rose dramatically by the end of the 1960s in the face of Vietnam and as a groundswell against a backdrop of free love, communal living, drugs, and flower power. Pro-socialist academics came under interrogation by FBI agents while those academics with socialist leanings continued to challenge America's hawkish moves in Southeast Asia, ostensibly to prevent the Domino Theory from being realized. The American war effort catalysed the sluggish American economy by the early 1970s as the poverty rate was reduced to about one in ten Americans. However, this did not take into account the population increases since 1958. By the time of the OPEC-induced oil crisis, about 23 million Americans were considered poor. What did the social sciences do with regard to the problem of poor Americans? It was only when Lyndon B. Johnson's administration raised the problem of poverty as part of its domestic presidential campaign that behavioural American social science paid attention. Several pioneering institutes were established around poverty, such as the Institute for Research on Poverty in 1966 at the University of Wisconsin-Madison. Social science research helped document and analyse the problem of poverty and linked it with the larger problem of scarcity and unequal economic distribution within the United States. By the end of the 1970s and the beginning of the 1980s, more Americans went under the poverty line. Was there a link between American moves to globalize their domestic economy, with poverty malfeasance and homeless persons? The reality might have been that the over-burdened welfare state system was developing into an unmanageable behemoth. Not surprisingly, a recent national survey by a conference of mayors indicated the following:

> Overall, requests for emergency food assistance jumped by 17 per cent this year and requests for shelter increased by 13 per cent, according to the 25-city survey by the U.S. Conference of Mayors. On average, 14 per cent of requests for food aid and 30 per cent of requests for shelter went unmet. The annual survey pointed to unemployment and lack of affordable housing as the leading causes of hunger and homelessness. "The survey underscores the impact the economy has had on everyday Americans," said conference president, Mayor James A. Garner of Hempstead, N.Y.[7]

This means that while the American economy appears to be making an upward beat, the number of problems surrounding the concept of poverty and unemployment continue to dominate discussions within what can be called a welfare state mentality. The more handouts that are given, the more hands that will be reaching out for more. The dilemma is similar to a Charles Dickens novel like *Bleak House*, upsized onto the manifolds of America's great industrial cities and post-industrial culture. So while social science continues to gradually figure ways and means out of social problems, the nature of these problems thickens. Not by the decade or the year. Neither by the month nor the week. Not even the hour nor the minute. But by the second and millisecond. Not surprisingly, then, the malaise within behavioural social science continues to be echoed by such writers as Piven in the foreword to one of the most influential and certainly the most important studies on welfare in America, by Sanford Schram. In the book, *Words of Welfare: The Poverty of Social Science and the Social Science of Poverty* (1995), Piven introduces the main argument very coherently:

> Despite large amounts of federal funding to support social science research on the causes of poverty, little progress has been made in reducing poverty. In fact, it appears to have worsened dramatically in recent years. Part of the reason for this, argues Sanford Schram, is that policy analysis has come to serve the needs of the state at the expense of its citizens. In the case of welfare policy in particular, analysis is often geared toward managing poverty rather than trying to lessen it, with a focus on controlling the behavior of "the poor". Moreover, research on poverty and welfare dependency is frequently based on questionable assumptions about the economic structures of late capitalist societies, thus neglecting the importance of perspective in social science research.[8]

Schram's book went on to win the 1995 American Political Science Association's (APSA) Michael Harrington Award but the problems that the book raises continue to persist. Schram's book is only one of many intelligent responses by social scientists who are genuinely concerned with changing the system. But it is difficult to change a system that appears to deliver both good and evil goods and services, and where the pluses of globalization sometimes appear to outweigh the minuses. Where sometimes it appears that America needs to have a percentage of its population living under the poverty bracket as if to show that in a land of great opportunity, sometimes it takes more than a desire to raise yourself up by the bootstraps, especially when the prognostications of non-partisan research centres like the Washington-based Urban Institute makes arguments like "American Indian, Hispanic, and black students have little more than a 50–50 chance of finishing high school with a diploma. Graduation rates for Whites and Asians are about 25 percentage points higher" (*Urban Institute*, 2000).

Clearly, the social sciences were doing something about the problem of poverty while simultaneously serving as a social voice of warning to America. But like most advice from social scientists, the warnings have been left unheeded. It seemed all the federal government was doing was casting pearls after swine and throwing good money after poorly thought-out policies and misconceived ideas about poverty control and eradication, which were clearly not the answer. On hindsight, however, it always seems easier to challenge the past with the clarity of the present. Nevertheless, Americans became increasingly aware of the situation of poverty as the mass media took over the need to inform and perhaps educate the public about the problem of the poor, and the problem of the poorest poor which by the mid-1980s at the height of Reaganomics and the Star Wars programme rose to almost 30 million. How about the period just before 9/11? The U.S. Census Bureau, for example, stated that the nation's official poverty rate rose from 11.7 per cent in 2001 to 12.1 per cent in 2002, while "median household money income declined 1.1 per cent in real terms from 2001 to US$42,409 in 2002". The Institute for Research on Poverty at the University of Wisconsin-Madison argues that in 2002, 34.6 million people or 12.1 per cent of the population were poor by the official measure of poverty. Social scientists are also aware that those living at and under the poverty line and are single parents or children, are always the hardest hit because their levels of resistance against common social diseases is low, they often hold multiple menial jobs where they are likely to be exploited, and they are probably more prone to mental, physical, emotional and sexual abuse. Married families tend to be more able to withstand a loss of a breadwinner or the loss of a job better than single-parent families in the poverty trap.

Some believe that by 9/11, approximately 1.5 American children out of ten lived in poverty. This is ironic as Osama Bin Laden and his terrorists attacked the World Trade Center (WTC) in New York because it represented the symbol of world capitalism. The terrorists attacked the WTC because it represented successful capitalism. It is ironic because it seems very clear that successful capitalism — the material success that Osama and his cronies are so envious of — comes at a very high price. American neoliberal globalization means that America's political leaders seem prepared to have an increasingly large proportion of America's youth and adult citizens live at or under the poverty line. If we look at the state of American globalization and its impact on the ethnic divide, the data is even more revealing. For example, Song argues that,

> Among the racial and ethnic groups, blacks and Hispanics suffered particularly high rate of poverty (24 per cent and 23 per cent, respectively), about three times higher than the rate for non-Hispanic whites in 1999 (8 per cent). The poverty rate for Asians and Pacific Islanders was 11 per cent.[9]

The differentiated social structure of poverty appears to have hit hardest those whose own generational and ethnic history was longest associated with American growth.

It appears that at least since 1945, two clear processes have increasingly emerged as supporting American globalization through its domestic economy: (1) the presence of an impoverished underclass of 8–12 per cent of the population; and (2) the presence of ethnic enclaves whose co-ethnics are at times represented through a politics of tokenism. We see a token minority representing all other minorities in children's television programming. We see the presence of an ethnic and cultural showcase that is part of America's secret recipe of success. This was clearly demonstrated by the cultural historian, Michael Kammen's work, *In the Past Lane: Historical Perspectives on American Culture* (Oxford, 1998) or Cornel West's intellectually persuasive arguments.[10] We also see an America that is intolerant of public personalities who at one point are loved by millions but at another point are vilified by the same, such as O.J. Simpson, Martha Stewart, Michael Jackson, and George W. Bush. Bush was unable to explain his initial hesitance to disclose an incredibly timed sale of stock worth US$848,560 in the Dallas-based Harken Energy Corporation while sitting on the Board of Directors "shortly before it was announced that Harken Corporation had very poor quarterly showing" (*US News and World Report*, 1992; Paul Krugman, *New York Times*, 7 July 2002; Arianna Huffington, *Pigs At the Trough*, 2003).

THE SPOILS OF SUCCESSFUL GLOBALIZATION

America had won the Cold War. It had become the world's only military and economic superpower. It had the largest number of the genuinely richest people on earth, not as a per capita measure but by sheer numbers. Yet, at the twenty-first century turnpike, America was looking at a worsening poverty situation among its own citizens.

Earlier, we hinted at the presence of two secrets to America's success in globalization. Firstly, the presence of a constant underclass of poor persons, and secondly, an ethnic and cultural showcase of political tokens representing the liberal ideal of different images. However, there is a third secret to America's success. In 1945, US$100 could buy you property and furniture to furnish your newly acquired property. But most workers would take months to earn this amount. When we adjust this for inflation, the US$100 in 1945 dollars is worth US$1,034.44 today. Most Americans, based on current GDP per capita estimates, are able to earn this within a month. But it can hardly buy you a complete set of furniture let alone property. The secret is in the fact that America must keep the dollar inflating at an increasing rate. It can never let it down. The moment that deflationary pressures appear is the moment the American Dream will disappear. This is why America, as the world's largest and most powerful neoliberal economy, needs to be propped up by as many capitalist countries and markets as possible. Otherwise it could begin an economic downturn from which it might never recover.

That is why Americans are indeed the world's largest debtors, because they manage to export their proprietary and ideological belief system overseas. It is about creating a complex web that shows all about a highly confident climate for investment, domestic spending, retail, manufacturing, construction, and financial services. And statistical social science has provided the means for calculating such confidence in terms of productivity, wealth acquisition, and related items such as the producer price index (PPI) and the consumer price index (CPI). We look at the CPI here since it is the index that reflects the cost of consumer choices for most Americans, and by extension, many non-Americans. According to the U.S. Bureau of Labor, the CPI

> is a measure of the average change over time in the prices paid by urban consumers for a market basket of consumer goods and services. The CPI represents all goods and services purchased for consumption by the reference population (known as CPI-U or CPI-W). The Bureau of Labor Statistics has classified all expenditure items into more than 200 categories, arranged into eight major groups.

The major consumer items, according to the bureau, includes an entire range of what the average American consumer, from the U.S. President to a U.S. janitor is likely to consume: breakfast cereal, milk, coffee, chicken, wine, fuel oil, bedroom furniture, men's shirts and sweaters, women's dresses, jewellery, new vehicles, airline fares, gasoline, motor vehicle insurance, prescription drugs and medical supplies, physicians' services, eyeglasses and eyecare, hospital services, televisions, cable television, pets and pet products, sports equipment, admissions, college tuition, postage, telephone services, computer software and accessories, tobacco and smoking products, haircuts and other personal services, and funeral expenses.

Does the CPI reflect reality? In a sense it does because it shows the relative changes in prices over time for a given place. However, the CPI cannot be used to illustrate differences in prices and the cost of living between points on the capitalist globe. There are other measures such as the Cost of Living Index and the "quality of life surveys" in the social sciences that try to provide measures of reality. Apart from its normal function of illustrating the costs that consumers are willing to bear based on their consumption patterns, the CPI is useful for illustrating another known but often not mentioned point. The CPI represents 87 per cent of the U.S. population. This means that the poor are naturally left out of this representative statistic because they are indirect consumers. The poor are consumers in the sense of being insufficiently important to be included in the statistics. The data will therefore continue to reflect the needs and wants of those who can afford to spend, even on borrowed time (since all money has time value) and is a self-fulfilling prophecy. This is because the CPI is often used by federal, local and other regulatory bodies in their profiling of costs. The CPI is also considered an important variable by market analysts in their predictions of economic health. Also, it reflects what Madisonian democratic theory has been warning us of all along: that the tyranny of the majority will enslave those who are in the "minors".

MATERIAL CONSUMPTION

Does the wide variety and range of goods that are generated for consumers mean that Americans are spoiled for choice? In a very grave sense, the answer is yes, because consumer choices provide a sense of the kind of globalization that is being exported to the rest of the world. The Bureau of Labor's range of goods and services also illustrates what kinds of goods are consumed elsewhere in modernity. It is a reflection of the kinds of goods and services that are in fact necessarily consumed elsewhere in the capitalist world from Athens (Ohio) to Athens (Greece), Tokyo to Trinidad, Boston to the Bahamas, and Paris (Texas) to Paris (France). While most Americans are living lives in which they are spoiled for choice for food, medicines, consumer durables, and automobiles, most people on the planet are living below the poverty line. All this talk of poverty is depressing. Yet America needs to keep hope alive, and to maintain cultural icons who represent the American way. It comes to no one's surprise that the 2004 Miss America, the global ambassador of American culture and values, has a graduate degree from an American university. It is even less surprising that her favourite food is McDonald's extra-value meal. In 2001, the author of *Reefer Madness*, Eric Schlosser, introduced *Fast Food Nation* where, among other things, he claims that Americans "spent about $6 billion on fast food" in 1970 and this amount rose to "more than $110 billion" in three decades and, hence, more than the amount of money that is spent on "higher education, personal computers, computer software, or new cars".[11] This is indeed important because American fast food has been a major force of its globalization strategy. While Schlosser's book may make its reader want to rethink eating fast food, the concern here is with rethinking the course of American globalization and how such powerful MNCs such as KFC, Coke, McDonald's, and MTV are in the game of global domination as several media pictures from American television portray them. And now we turn from the politics of fast food to the politics of pet food.

PET FOOD

The American pet food industry was worth US$11 billion in 2001 (*Animal Protection Institute*, 29 January 2002). This is almost the amount of funds that have been devoted under the Stewart B. McKinney Homeless Assistance Act of 1987, in which the U.S. Congress "recognized the need to supplement 'mainstream' federally funded housing and human services programs with funding that was specifically targeted to assist homeless people. Over US$11 billion in McKinney funds have been appropriated since then, and billions more have been provided through other federal, state, and local programs and benefits" (*Homelessness: Programs and the People They Serve*, December 1999). Homeless persons are likely to be non-Hispanic Whites (41 per cent) and African Americans (40 per cent), 11 per cent Hispanics, 8 per cent Native Americans (Ibid.). It is interesting to note that about half of all homeless persons have never been married and the other half have been married at least once but the marriage has ended in separation or divorce, with at least 56 per cent remaining in the same communities where they were first domiciled or had friends or relatives.

The GDP per capita for Latin America was US$3,385 in 2002. There are approximately 454.7 million Latin Americans. The amount of money spent by Americans on the pet food industry in a single year is about 75 per cent of the combined GNP of Argentina, Brazil, Chile, Colombia, Ecuador, Mexico, Peru, Uruguay, and Venezuela. That is to say that the US$11 billion pet food industry draws a startling comparison when compared to the combined populations of nine other sovereign countries, people who live just south of the United States. The US$11 billion industry supported 60 million pet dogs and 75 million pet cats in 2003 (*Pet Food Institute*, 14 April 2004). This means that most American households have at least one pet. The pet food industry is nothing when compared to the other spin-offs from pet ownership in America. For example, the 1998–2001 American Pet Association Polls of 17,121 pet owners in February 2003 revealed several interesting facts about consumer behaviour that could only happen in such an advanced, post-industrial country as the United States. Most pet owners bought Christmas gifts for their pets and celebrated their pets' birthdays by way of the purchase of a gift, a special meal, or a new toy. At least half of the American pet owners surveyed believed that they were more attached to their pets than other human beings. This included the 67 per cent of pet owners who allowed their cats to sleep anywhere they want including their master/mistress' beds. This may not seem consequential to you except when you realize that there are also 3.5 million homeless people in America with almost 1.35 million of the homeless being children (*Urban Institute*, 2000).

If a forty-pound bag of the cheapest generic dog food costs US$10 with approximately 68 million dogs in the United States, and if American pet dogs consume on average one bag a month, we are looking at US$680 million spent on dog food alone. Don't even consider the costs of getting rid of dog waste in public places and private homes, and forget about the fact that on average each dog owner is likely to spend US$196 on veterinary medicine and pet clinics in a single year. There are more cat owners than dog owners in America, and although cats are self-cleaning, they do consume food and need veterinary attention which itself costs the average cat owner US$104 per year (*The Humane Society of the United States*, 2004). While most Americans were surfing hundreds of channels through pay-per-view and satellite TV, most Africans were trying to make ends meet, and the highest paid Indonesian civil servant in the heady days of former President Suharto made US$400 per month in the late 1980s. The lowest paid Indonesian was paid about US$13 per month as a volcano-watcher. This means that Americans spent more at the vet than the poorest Indonesian civil servant earns in a year.

In contrast, imagine a country where there are 16 million sport utility vehicles (SUVs) that are designed for off-road use but only 5 per cent of that total is actually used for off-road functions. For example, Ford Motors reports that over 80 per cent of its SUVs have never even been taken off-road. This means that in the United States, urban density has reached enormous proportions and has resulted in cramped spaces for everyone: Drivers competing with huge, gasoline-guzzling, fuel-inefficient and over-sized SUVs that are really not designed for use in the city most of the time. Thousands die each year from car crashes but if the crash involves an SUV and a non-SUV, the chances of the non-SUV driver surviving that crash is reduced further. The imaginary country is, of course, very real and there are rather morbid statistics to prove the dangers involved because of the SUV overpopulation. The Detroit Project, which is an anti-SUV lobby, argues that massive SUVs such as the Chevrolet Tahoe "kill 122 people for every million models on the road" while a Japanese car such as the Honda Accord "kills 21 for every million on the road" and that "injuries in SUV-related accidents are more severe". Even if these statistics were only 50 per cent true we would have a very severe situation on hand in American city streets. So why are there so many SUVs on the road despite the strong lobby against this and despite the many problems that are associated with SUVs in accident situations? Part of the reason is in the desire among SUV consumers for "up-sizing" consumer products. Americans think big. Size apparently is a factor in image building. If you win a lottery or inherit a windfall, or suddenly turn into a professional athlete or a popular MTV singer, then you are not the average consumer. And if you did make it big you would not want to buy the cheapest most fuel-efficient car or the lowest cost foreign import. As a trendsetter, your public would expect you to represent the larger-than-life image presented over media broadcasts into everyday life. Hence, you would probably buy the biggest SUV available on the market. But most people in the United States are not professional athletes, nor come from wealthy families, or possess some stunning ability to outlast, outlive, and outsmart everyone else in their chosen industry.

The average American consumer is unable to make all the big purchases that movie stars, Harvard MBAs, and wealthy Wall Street types can make. However, the average consumer — who feeds into that giant machine called globalization — may have the same aspirations as these wealthy icons of consumerism. If we all cannot be like California State Governor Arnold Schwarzenegger, we can at least own a Hummer/Humvee (or two, three, four, or five) and pretend to be like him. But in terms of urban cultural trends, Schwarzeneger is only one of thousands of possible icons of consumerism who symbolize the veritable success stories that more ordinary citizens clamour for. Consumer culture is driven by marketing and advertising revenues.[12]

Also, whether you are wealthy or poor in America, the advertising is going to hit you sooner or later. Upper class (old money), upper-middle class (the newly rich), middle class Americans (the majority class), and lower class Americans all watch the same advertisements on television. And while their pocketbooks might not be able to manage a new car or a second home at a fancy address, their hopes and aspirations are limitless. It is part of the American Dream. It does not matter that for every successful millionaire there are over a million failures. It does not matter that some of these images that are broadcast over television are mind-bending constructions of reality which no one can truly afford and those who can, can't afford the time. The American Dream is quite different from the passions of the Corcyraeans who desired to rob other people of their dreams by blocking out the light for any other dream to occur through their ambassadors and auxiliaries in that Athenian summer.[13] People often forget that the reason it is called the American Dream is because of the second part of the phrase, and not the optimistic adverbial that can somehow magically modify a dream into a reality. So back to the advertisements. In terms of SUV advertising, the budget in 1990, again according to the Detroit Project, was US$172.5 million. A decade later, this amount rose to a whopping US$1.51 billion. And you thought that the US$11 billion that was slated to help the poor was meaningful. The power behind American-made products is in national identity. In the post 9/11 era, it has become even more important to outwardly display the national colours. This means that one's patriotism cannot be in question when the nation is under attack. What better way to reflect that patriotic cause than by buying American? Combined with the aggressive marketing strategies of GM, Ford, and Chrysler, buying big is a win-win situation in the face of any war overseas. The profits are enormous. For example:

> In 1998, GM, Ford and DaimlerChrysler earned US$2.8 billion, US$6.7 billion and US$6.47 billion respectively, for a total of US$15.97 billion. On February 25, 1999, Ford Motor Company unveiled its newest and biggest SUV yet: the Ford Excursion. The Excursion, which is not classified as a light truck, is intended to compete with the Chevy Suburban, which has long been the "King Kong" of the passenger vehicle market. Each Excursion is expected to sell for US$45,000 to US$50,000, and earn a profit of US$12,000 to US$20,000. The technology exists to make SUVs and other light trucks more efficient, but automakers have failed to prioritize fuel efficiency in the design of their vehicles. Passenger trucks have been getting bigger and heavier culminating in the 19-foot 3-ton Ford Excursion that was released this year. The result of investing in body building and not in efficiency technology is that light truck fuel efficiency has actually declined in recent years (*Public Interest Research Groups*, 2004).

Despite the fact that most American-made cars have parts made all over the world and that most of the workers of these parts do not even speak American English does not seem to matter. Because if you are American, you need to show that you are American by buying American. And America is always associated with the word "big". But if you ever get a chance to drive that Ford Excursion, and feel the power behind the wheel of the largest most powerful SUV in the world, you might be tempted to show how American you can be.

In 2000–2001, Americans spent about US$120 billion on improvements and repairs to their homes (*Austrade*, Australian Government, 13 April 2004). Americans also drank more beer, more wine, and smoked more cigarettes than all of Southeast Asia combined. American fruits and vegetables that are disposed off in bumper harvests could feed millions of starvation-level people in Africa. The total combined disposable wealth that Americans spent on SUVs alone would be sufficient to keep a small African country like Namibia and larger ones like the Sudan and Congo afloat for an entire fiscal year. American pharmaceuticals produce enough legal drugs to keep entire South Asian nations like Nepal and Bangladesh sedated for months. The number of illegal immigrants that the United States supports in the underground economy is sufficient to run small banana republics out of business.

PORNOGRAPHY AND GUNS

>Americans spend more money at strip clubs than at Broadway, regional theatres and orchestra performances combined. The industry has mushroomed since the 70s, when a federal study found that it was worth little more than US$10 million. Now the US leads the world in pornography; about 211 new films are produced every week. Los Angeles is the centre of the film boom and many of those in the trade are otherwise respectable citizens. Nina Hartley, a porn star, told Schlosser: "You'd be surprised how many producers and manufacturers are Republicans." The majority of women in the films earn about $400 a scene. At the moment, there is a surplus of women in California hoping to enter the industry. The internet has provided a fresh and profitable outlet. In 1997 about 22,000 porn websites existed; the number is now closer to 300,000 and growing (*Guardian Unlimited*, 2003).

In 1999, the U.S. pornographic industry was worth a ballpark figure of US$1–3 billion dollars. This is a very conservative estimate. For example, Eric Schlosser thinks that Americans spend at least US$8 billion in pornography, but in 2001 Schlosser said that Frank Rich of the *New York Times Magazine* estimated that revenues from pornography were much higher and amounted to at least US$10 billion.[14]

It is virtually impossible to gauge the specific value of the underground pornographic industry. U.S. pornography — as the sale and purchase of human sexuality and the gross exploitation of men, women, and children — continues to play an important part in the American global economy. It represents different things to different people. For the moral majority proponents, American pornography is Satan on earth. For the American Muslims and Jews, pornogaphy is the evil of man expressed on human kind. But for many people, it is the solace by which they can overtly or if necessarily, secretly, derive some degree of escapism and satisfaction from consumption. For the politician who is about to be elected, pornography is sinful and is the gross exploitation of sex workers, and many who stand for re-election know the value of keeping silent on such matters, as long as pornography remains restricted to certain districts of the city, away from influencing the urban youth, and within control of the city's urban cops.

There are different explanations in the reports of crime, prostitution, and pornography in American cities. Some believe that the workers are to be blamed for their individual choices as much as the johns and the pimps. But some social scientists believe that the reason for this underclass of people remaining trapped in this vicious cycle of poverty and pornography is a result of a larger, highly complex social problem of crime, underworld bosses, gangsters, illegal drug trafficking, and drug abuse that continues to embed itself within each successive generation of people.

The US$3–5 billion pornographic industry has effectively and very efficiently used technology to its fullest advantage. It would seem that any American parent or any other parent in modernity would be hard-pressed to control the movement of pornography over the Internet, despite raids, stings, and arrests by Interpol, the British constabulary, the FBI, and the various branches of U.S. police enforcement units in the United States and (primarily Western) Europe, "where madmen and madness become major figures in their ambiguity: Menace and mockery, the dizzying unreason of the world, and the feeble ridicule of men" (Foucault [1965] 1988, p. 13). The pornographic industry is also highly sensitive to market demand, secretive where it has to be, and open where it can be. U.S. pornography is highly adaptive to other world societies too. While the pornographic empires of Hugh Hefner and Larry Flynt may be on the decline in terms of *Playboy*, *Penthouse*, and *Hustler*, many other modes of exporting American pornography continue to emerge. There is even a sub-black market for the black market that imitates and copies, ironically, the already illegal copies of pornography on video, DVDs, and VCDs in Asia (for example).

The American public as a whole seems to be able to tolerate the extremes of free speech and the right to bear arms. America seems willing to provide simultaneous support for the intrepid criticism of a new breed of social and political critic in the names of Michael Moore, Eric Schlosser, and even former Republican columnist, Arianna Huffington. American politics seem to accept the extent to which the relatively porous boundaries between conservative politics and liberal ones sometimes overlap, crossover or even get mixed up. It would seem that the only thing that American globalization and its economic, political, social and cultural processes fear is death, though not completely. America cannot simply legislate between the fine lines that are drawn between satire, freedom of speech, freedom of expression, the right to publish, the right to voice opinion, and the right to bear arms without consequences. Up till now, for example, the academic jury is disunited in its analyses of the impact of the "Brady Bill":

> On November 30, 1993, the *Brady Handgun Violence Prevention Act* was enacted, amending the Gun Control Act of 1968. The Brady Law imposed as an interim measure a waiting period of 5 days before a licensed importer, manufacturer, or dealer may sell, deliver, or transfer a handgun to an unlicensed individual. The waiting period applies only in states without an acceptable alternate system of conducting background checks on handgun purchasers. The interim provisions of the Brady law became effective on February 28, 1994, and ceased to apply on November 30, 1998. While the interim provisions of the Brady law apply only to handguns, the permanent provisions of the Brady law apply to all firearms.[15]

All U.S. presidents so far have disagreed among themselves over the interpretation of the Brady Act. The Right to Bear Arms is for all intents and purposes an anachronistic law in American modernity. The *Brady Act* (1993) clearly helped reveal that the National Rifle Association's vested interests and activities over the "gun and ammunition" political economy it supports and advocates was vulnerable and not as politically invincible as once believed. These people are responsible for promoting an environment of weapon ownership among citizens, aliens, felons, and psychotics. Despite the informative work of satirist Michael Moore in his well-researched documentary, *Bowling for Columbine* (2003), the politically charged gun debate has ironically been supported by people like Charlton Heston who seem immune to the urgency of an issue that has resulted in the deaths of thousands of Americans from gun violence, gun-related crime, and gun-related accidents.

SUMMARY

This chapter has illustrated the complexities of America's rise to the top of the capitalist heap; in a sense it is in praise of the folly of capitalism. It has demonstrated the startling contradictions and complementarity of economic, social, and political norms that have emerged over the last sixty years of the American century. America refuses to allow the rise of alternative hegemonic powers that might challenge its privileged status. While Americans want true and genuine peace in the Middle East, the political system does not allow a sufficient continuity of policies between Republican and Democratic presidents, despite the presence of a perennially powerful Jewish lobby.

Max Weber introduced the concept of the "bureaucratic iron cage" in the early 1900s. The "iron cage" syndrome works this way: for every bureau that is collapsed in the drive towards administrative efficiency, there are other bureaus that will have to be created in its place. When one bureau is dissolved, others will have to be created to take over the function it plays. This trend continues till there is a complex mass of bureaus that exist to map out and control every aspect and dimension of human society in modernity. The new Department of Homeland Security (DHS) will take at least another two years for its staffers to settle in and discover their actual jobs. This is the latest Cabinet-level department to be created in the wake of 9/11. There are many bureaus in the DHS and one such example is the National Incident Management System (NIMS). Other examples of bureaus within the DHS are the Science and Technology Directorate, the Analytic Services Incorporated (ANSER), and the Homeland Security Institute (HSI), a Federally Funded Research and Development Center (FFRDC). The NIMS bureau performs the function of standardizing reporting procedures and the management of incident protocols for all levels of state and society (*DHS Website*, 2004). The growth of the bureaucratic machine will continue until every eventuality stemming from the nature of man can be anticipated and prevented, circumvented, or re-invented. It would appear at some level that technology is the key, and the solution, to these problems. But technology as it stands in late modernity today is still far behind human intelligence and the human capacity for civilized behaviour and uncivilized destruction. In addition, uneven levels and pockets of economic development across the globe mean that there will always be a ready and willing market where problems are resolved through the creation of such administrative structures. Ironically, this is because for all we know about previous and current civilizations, we still know very little about ourselves and the nature of man. Perhaps philosophy and political theory have the answer. But then again, perhaps not. This is because the nature of man is unpredictable.

The unpredictability of man in modernity gives rise to the concept of a series of administrative structures that serve to function as ways and means of controlling man and his actions in modernity. The *Ship of Fools* that Foucault mentions needs such iron cages. These cages act as centres for structuring society and for controlling behaviour. In the case of the DHS and its bureaus, the iron cage grows because there are simply too many abnormal fools running around the vessel, our metaphorical *Ship of Fools* in modernity, and trying to destroy it by running it aground. Ostensibly, these people do not share the norms and values of the larger majority who wish and desire a stable and peaceful life.

Life for these terrorists on the *Ship of Fools* revolves round personal sacrifice of innocent men, women, and children. It is ostensibly about the difference in norms but in reality it is also about self-hate and a desire for destruction. The desire for destroying the world as they know it stems from the evil side of nature that rises from the heart of the terrorist. No one really knows whether it is purely ideological, religious, or political. We know that it is substantively all these components that are mixed in a potent and explosive cocktail. Therefore, the resources that could otherwise be used to manage poverty or increase welfare benefits are now necessarily diverted towards the iron cage of counter-terrorism. Encountering the terrorism of modernity demands deeper and greater administrative measures for anticipating, out-thinking, and out-strategizing the intelligence and operational networks of Al-Qaeda and the Jemaah Islamiah.

But there will be more groups as we proceed. This is only a slice of what appears to be a pattern of terror that traces its roots to the barbarians at the gate. This means that funds that would otherwise be spent on education and poverty will now be transferred towards national security, which in terms of military defence spending was already a multi-trillion U.S. dollar economy on its own.

The existing contradictions of the extremes of wealth and poverty within a world-class capitalist system are the secret of America's success when complemented by political structures and social norms that help steer greater confidence among people who believe in themselves and continue to be fascinated by America and the politics of American globalization. The Nathaniel Ropes Professor of Political Economy at Harvard University's Department of Economics, Alberto Alesina, and his colleague, Edward Glaeser, the former Paul Sack Associate Professor of Political Economy, quote the *World Values Survey* where one of the many interesting findings is that

> sixty per cent of Americans believe that the poor are "lazy" [while] only 26 per cent of Europeans hold this belief.... It seems easier for White middle class Americans to consider the poor less worthy of government support if they think of them as different. To put it crudely, but candidly, indifference comes easily if the poor are assumed to be mostly Black. This is more difficult in Norway where rich and poor are White, often blond and tall.[16]

Of course the co-authors offer more empirical support for their claims than what can be presented here, but one cannot be easily convinced of their essentialist and reductionist approach in their "social scientific method". It is unclear how they figure the jump from the "perception of values over poverty" and correlate this with racism and "Blackness". Therefore, it seems that for these co-authors to suggest such a correlation might require much more empirical work than merely economistic hypothesizing.

However (and this is where their main concern lies), I can believe scholars who argue that the U.S. welfare state is much less generous than that in Europe, and that the reason for such generosity in Europe is because of the culture of pluralistic politics, as we will visit towards the end of the chapter on "War" in this book. Pluralism involves the creation of a polity over time that engulfs the entry and exit of different and competing interest groups, activist groups, specialist and expert groups with a view to enhancing creativity through overlapping layers of interest within society. Pluralism American-style demands that each group and each member respects the presence and the existence of other groups. Therefore there is a rights' argument to be made about the nature of pluralism because it is only through a shared belief in the respect for the individual and the community to be different can such pluralism work. Yet there are many problems with such an idealistic political persuasion, as seen in the existence of racist and sexist groups that resort to political violence to achieve their ends.

Nevertheless, the pluralistic political culture is made possible by the process of proportional representation where minorities will have a greater chance of being represented in the political process. On the other hand, the plural American political culture built on neoliberal capitalism is not as fermented as the older European version of pluralism. This is not to say that the Europeans have a superior welfare system and, like the *Narrenschiff*, that their colonial policies were only about "carrying their insane cargo from town to town" (Foucault [1965] 1988, p. 8). Or that there are significant political gains to be made from adopting a more European-type pluralistic political culture. The problems are different for both cases. It seems that neither the European pluralistic political culture nor the less fermented American plural political culture present real alternatives to the liberal, libertarian, or communitarian citizen.

Also, we can now understand why the problem of racism within the pluralistic culture of America is naturally reflected in its legal history since the forced migration and sale of the first African slaves in the early seventeenth century to the establishment of what came to be called the Jim Crow laws and, eventually, the prevalence of public common sense that culminated in formal civil rights legislation of the mid-1960s. But by no means is the story of primordialism and the essentialist attachment to race over.

The fear is that if the ISR *World Values Survey* is indeed reflective of current trends, then we can say that racism and the welfare state is here to stay for a longer time than socialists, communists, and liberals would care to admit. This leads us to believe that perhaps a clearer distinction might be made between those who support the idea of precision in the social sciences, and (as distinct from) those who support the normative challenges that make some sense (but not much) of the public's hallucinations "in Thierry Bouts's *Hell*, with the nakedness of the damned" (Foucault [1965] 1988, p. 21). What is desired in this book is a greater understanding of globalization through an examination of the American model simply because America is a global power with many humanitarian and sympathetic dimensions. The American *oeuvre* is not overly limited or shackled by the mistakes and problems created by the military and the CIA as shall be seen in the subsequent chapters.

It is very important that we do not consider America to be as ominous and damned as Thierry Bouts' *Hell*. Neither can Nietzsche's view of a super powerful being be adequately applied to American politics. Foucault was describing modernity writ large, and Nietzsche was interested in restoring the faith to a people that had been misplaced by medieval Christianity. Foucault was warning us about the hallucinatory effects of engaging in potentially dangerous exercises that can stem from an immoral view of being human and living in humanity. Nietzsche was warning us about the death of a god that was no longer useful; the death of a god that had died as if to spite the rise of the global marketplace. This is why it is possible today to continue to be materially successful without advocating any one religious view, or espousing any single religious doctrine no matter how ancient, how proven, or how convincing.

Americanization is a thing of the past. It is a thing of the past because there is no single board room in which all the CEOs of American MNCs sit together to plan and strategize the domination of the world. Militarily, America knows that it cannot ride roughshod over competing cultural and economic paradigms. It cannot convert the world by force even it wanted to do so. Those sceptics who believe that American militarism is an uncontainable indication of its desire for global supremacy fail to remember that much of the American military motif has been done in response to potential dangers. Here lies the problem. Because American governments have tended to be reactive rather than proactive up till 1945, it can no longer allow for another Pearl Harbor to occur before something is done about it. It can no longer allow for another 9/11 before congressional hearings discover that the intelligence services were correct and had played their part. The problem for the rest of the world is that American foreign policy in its proactive mode is becoming increasingly paranoid and when strategy is modelled on paranoia, mistakes are made. This is why even though America had illegally invaded the autocracy of Saddam Hussein, it was right in stopping the ethnic pogroms of Saddam in the Middle East. But America was wrong in misleading its people, and its allies in the United Kingdom and the Asia-Pacific, with the search for weapons of mass destruction. Until today, there are no signs of WMD. This is why America seems provocative and evocative. It provokes those who do not share its ideological values and evokes others to embrace them. Does America use the threat of power to convince? Yes it does, but not in the way that the old colonial masters used to employ. America is not a colonizer and the world, led by the American people, and guided by the philosophy of John Locke, should ensure that it does not become one. This is the new order of things.

America cannot invade Cuba despite its being a huge thorn on its front yard. America continues to retain the title of Heavy Weight Champion of the World not because it is the best at everything but because Americans believe that they can do everything to the best of their ability. There is a tremendous level of self-confidence among American business leaders and political leaders. Their confidence seems to cover as many bases of the global neoliberal world order as is humanly possible. Many who convert to the American Dream of hope, progress, and optimism cannot and do not want to leave.

What fascinates many views of America from the outside is that despite the complexity of American bureaucratic apparatuses, despite the widening gap between American politicians and American voters, despite the differences within American cultural communities, America continues to function as a powerful and united entity. It moves onwards and forwards. Americanization may be dead, but American leadership on the global stage is very much alive.

American modernity is fascinating because it seems to be able to drive the world economy at a speed and pace that no other civilization or community or nation has ever done previously. The British experiment with colonialism attempted to achieve this global dominance but failed because the strategy was unilateral. The resources and profits that were gleaned from its colonies were directed inwards to reward the Crown. The rest of the surplus value extracted from the British colonies across the world was redirected towards stabilizing the Empire and controlling its dissidents. America has surpassed

British history of global control because it provides in-built opportunities in ways that no other benign hegemon, least of all the former Soviet Union, could provide. America is a fascinating phantasm of hope, optimism, and progress because its political ideology of neoliberal democracy seduces and subsumes American citizens and non-American foreigners. It is the seductive effect of American neoliberalism that is paving the way forward as a model for other powerful states in the making, such as China and India. Will America give up without a fight if its place at the top of the economic pyramid is challenged? According to neoliberal theory, it should not give up at all. In fact, the America that supports the importance of free trade would certainly welcome competition.

We live in a world where most people born after 1965 have heard of America and Americans, though this is not true the other way round. Is this not the litmus test of a true and genuine global hegemon where other people and societies have to study your country, and not the other way round? The political and economic models that America has proposed to the world however have not been returned without criticism as we see in the WTO or the IMF, or even the World Bank. The United States is, however, able and willing to support causes that further the American ideals of life and liberty as long as its national interests are not violated. Friend can turn into foe overnight. The loyal are rewarded with economic investments, the disloyal left to suffer till they have learnt their lessons. Is America all about brute force? Not quite. This is because America seems to respect the rights of American citizens to challenge the very fundamentals of its own philosophy of being in modernity. America continues to grow because it is the land of incredible opportunity. For every terrorist that wants to bring America down, there are hundreds of thousands who want to make America their own home.

For every terrorist who thinks that America is an evil satanic dictatorship, there are millions who perceive it as a haven for political refugees and those prophets who are not welcome in their own lands. It would seem that most people would like a slice of the American pie. The world was watching when the British handed over their oldest colony of Hong Kong to China under its last governor Chris Patten. The world also saw how many Chinese Hongkongers who had served faithfully in the name of Great Britain were denied entry into the United Kingdom despite being full-fledged citizens. The old adage about one's word has taken on a new and different meaning simply because there are insufficient resources to maintain the ideals of a socialist past.

BBC World reported in late August 2004 that Scotland Yard (otherwise known as The Metropolitan Police Service) was trying to resolve the problem of crime in Greater London. The report stated that persons of Indian origin made up 4 per cent of the population but were involved in 16 per cent of the crimes. The report also mentioned the street along which there were many famous "curry houses". How is America different in this respect? What measures have American local government implemented to prevent such racial profiling? Does America have an equivalent story of the inability of police to curb crime in the cities? How many of us must fall victim to these facts of urban life before something is done permanently about it? The perversity of crime and the pervasiveness of ethnic hatred is a phenomenon that has come to engulf the modern world. It is up to individual communities to police themselves and to remain vigilant over the possibility of disruptive actions against their cultural and social norms and values. It is too late already if one is going to wait for scholars to create models of articulating public cooperation. It is too late already if communities and individuals wait for the state to create corridors of trust and self-confidence. The problem of poverty is something that is globally shared. China hopes to reduce its problem of poverty by 2015. But it will fail without economic investments. These investments will not flow smoothly if China continues its ideological diatribe against democracy and positive democratic values. China, India, and any other trading partner of the United States must work in closer cooperation with the states that support freedom. The freedom of the individual and the freedom for creativity is no one's copyright.

America is fascinating because there are pockets of success at the community level that become model communities to be emulated across America. Some do not even have a distinctly physical base such as "The March of Dimes: Walk America" that tries to save the lives of young babies and children. There are similar instances and examples in the United Kingdom too and I am sure that readers will be able to make connections with these realities. The important point is that America is a globally exciting place because it happens to be one of the best places for energetic growth in the world today. In spite of the problems, there is still ample space and time for any individual or community to develop. The United Kingdom unfortunately lost this chance when it could not protect its colonial possessions in 1939. The age of Great Britain has long gone and is very unlikely to return. America is in a favourable position to positively create spaces and sites of increasing prosperity without brute force. America is today's model for the future. But the American model is made up of different parts. Some are Japanese, some Korean, others are Made in the Czech Republic and China, each contributing some useful part, but each bringing its own cultural, monetary, and terror-filled past. We do not wish to blame any state for all the sins in the world; we just want each state to bear the burden of their own.

Notes

1. Since not all historians might wish to use the word "intellectual" and not all intellectuals are cultural historians.
2. Roddey Reid, "Foucault in America", *Cultural Critique* 35 (1996): 179–211.
3. Michel Foucault, "Politics and Reason," *Stanford University Tanner Lectures on Human Values*, 10 October and 16 October 1979. See also Allan Megill, "Foucault, Structuralism, and the Ends of History", *Journal of Modern History* 51, no. 3 (1979): 451–503.
4. R.D. Norton, "Industrial Policy and American Renewal", *Journal of Economic Literature* 24, no. 1 (1986): 1–40.
5. Read for example, Uri Ra'Anan, "Soviet Strategic Doctrine and the Soviet-American Global Contest", *Annals of the American Academy of Political and Social Science* 457 (1981): 8–17; Ali Farazmand, "Globalization and Public Administration", *Public Administration Review* 59, no. 6 (1999): 509–22; Robert L. Pfaltzgraff, Jr., "Emerging Global Security Environment", *Annals of the American Academy of Political and Social Science* 517 (1991): 10–24.
6. Thomas Hobbes (trans., with notes and introduction by David Greme), *Thucydides' The Peloponnesian War* (Chicago, IL: University of Chicago Press, 1959), "The First Book": Sect. 4-13, pp. 3–9.
7. Sewell Chan, "Survey Indicates More Go Hungry, Homeless Aid Lacking as Greater Demands Conflict With Improving Economy", *Washington Post*, 19 December 2003, A11.
8. Sanford Schram, *Words of Welfare: The Poverty of Social Science and the Social Science of Poverty* (University of Minnesota Press, 1995).
9. Xue Song, "American Poverty and Welfare Reform", *Perspectives* 2, no. 6 (2001).
10. Readers may wish, as an interesting alternative to the cultural history of Kammen, a more philosophical approach as suggested by R. Fred Wacker, "Assimilation and Cultural Pluralism in American Social Thought", *Phylon* 40, no. 4 (1979): 325–33. See also, the cultural politics of difference in Cornel West, *Keeping Faith: Philosophy and Race in America* (NY: Routledge, 1993).
11. Kathryn Eastburn, "American McHistory — Eric Schlosser's *Fast Food Nation* is About More than Just Burgers and Fries", *Baltimore City Paper Online*, 28 February–6 March 2001; and "Americans are Obsessed with Fast Food: The Dark Side of the All-American Meal", *CBS News*, 31 January 2002.
12. "Arnold Schwarzenegger was sworn in as the 38th Governor of California on 17 November 2003. His landslide election as the state's chief executive follows a distinguished career in business and entertainment". However, this has not

helped California's economic woes in recent years. Governor Schwarzenegger also came under criticism for owning several gas-guzzling SUVs (Humvees) which contradicted his own policy on the environment. The governor said in his 2003 campaign that he was planning to retrofit one of his five Hummers to a hybrid hydrogen engine but did not achieve this by Earth Day 2004. See "The Governor's Verbal Gas" in *Los Angeles Times*, 7 July 2007. See also <http://www.governor.ca.gov/state/govsite/gov_pressroom_main.jsp>.

13 Hobbes, *Thucydides' The Peloponnesian War*, "The Third Book": Sect. 85, p. 207.

14 See also Eric Schlosser, *Reefer Madness and Other Tales from the American Underground* (London: Penguin Books, 2003), p. 269, fn. 112; Duncan Campbell, "With Pot and Porn Outstripping Corn, America's Black Economy is Flying High — Illegal Migrants Provide the Muscle for US Black Market", *Guardian Unlimited*, 2 May 2003.

15 "Implementation of Permanent Provisions of the Brady Handgun Violence Prevention Act", Department of Treasury, Bureau of Alcohol, Tobacco and Fire Arms, ATF News, 29 October 1998.

16 The distribution and management of the survey data is directed by Ronald Inglehart at the Institute for Social Research of the University of Michigan, Alberto Alesina, and Edward Glaeser, *Fighting Poverty in the US and Europe: A World of Difference* (Oxford University Press, 2004).

3

ASIA

Imagine an underground passageway that is two metres wide with windows full of goods stacked up to the top of the corridor that the back walls are totally hidden. A bustling two-way movement of buyers, sellers, investors, tourists, terrorists, gun runners, ordinary decent families, police, military personnel, diplomats, government bureaucrats, politicians, peasants living under the poverty line, slum dwellers, and homeless persons serves as a channel for the exchange of trade, commerce, ideas, sorrow, emotion, and technology: this is the connection between the politics of globalization between America and Asia. It is about a fantastic journey, full of life and death, and surrounding a definitively impervious lantern that gives off the light of hope, optimism, and progress.

This situation is well illustrated in particular by J. Lodge Gillespie's romantic tropes in the "rhetoric and reality" of America in Southeast Asia after the Pacific War. His work helps connect readers with the rediscovery of the fact that the complexities of domestic U.S. economic influence have increased tremendously since the 1960s.[1] The empirical evidence about the economic influence is overwhelming. China and India, for example, have bought trillions of U.S. treasury bonds and keep holding these large volumes as a security against the future of their own currencies and economies. All Western gasoline consuming states, including the OECD, are intimately linked to U.S. oil consumption and international oil policy. The United States is Southeast Asia's biggest trade partner after China and India. Asian stocks are indelibly linked to U.S. stock markets that a hint or a turn of phrase by the Chairman of the U.S. Federal Reserve Bank (the Fed) has an immediate and multiplier effect on these markets in Singapore, Bangkok, Jakarta, Sydney,

Kuala Lumpur, Hong Kong, Tokyo, Seoul, and New Delhi. Another deep area of influence in 2008 is the training and development programmes of indigenous Southeast Asian Special Forces. And a third area is illustrated in technological hardware and software. Communications hardware keeps changing with urban planning strategies to improve and develop connections, for example, between airports and their delivery sites.

THE POWER OF THE AIRLINE BUSINESS IN ASIA

The power of the American and European airline industries are so apparently seamless that there have been no other major competitors to their virtual monopoly since the end of the Soviet empire in 1989. Even during the Cold War, Soviet-built airliners did not perform as well nor were as serviceable as those built by American and European consortiums. Until today, the powerful American and European airliners that interconnect the world as they speed up the processes of globalization continue to dominate. There are no real competitors from Japan, Africa, the Middle East, Asia, or Latin America.

Within the United States, the physical limitations of the hub-and-spoke systems that form the basic infrastructure of the American airline industry today had its fundamentals in airport planning and design in the 1950s. A decade after World War II, American airfields began demilitarizing their war-time functions and were converted from short grasspatch airfields into long, multiple runways, high-grade gravel tarmacs, and new airport lounges that included amenities like those found in the city centres. Additionally, these new runways could take on the weight and intensity of jet-propelled aircraft that became particularly popular from 1959. The hub-and-spoke system illustrated its usefulness in the mid-1970s. This system was designed to meet the demands of higher passenger volumes and set in place a stable yet competitive environment that also saw the lowering of costs of passenger tickets across the United States relative to the time and place of departure and arrival. The hub-and-spoke system subsequently demanded that shorter haul aircraft were needed to transport their passengers from the spoke cities to the hub airports across hundreds of kilometres which saw the realization of authentic non-stop travel as we expect and demand as air travellers today. Americans, Europeans, Asians, and virtually any other air traveller across the globe are in a position to enjoy the utility of non-stop air travel today because of these innovations in communications technology. Here, we recall Heidegger's definition of technology as involving the ability of man to control his environment through artificial means, and therefore does not have to merely be limited to the stereotypical metaphor of technology as necessarily computer-based innovations but entire strategies of change.

However, the technology applied in the American airline industry in the mid-1970s compared to today's technology makes it somewhat of a misnomer to define today's short-haul airplanes in terms of the planes of yesteryear. This is because short-haul aircraft today are more powerful, fuel efficient, much faster, more comfortable, safer, and can carry a higher passenger load than their predecessors. While the basic design of the Boeing, McDonnell-Douglas, and Lockheed (and their European competitors such as Airbus Industries) aircraft have not changed dramatically since 1971, the absolute volume of passenger traffic demanded the rise of a new kind of air travel within the contiguous United States and Hawaii. This demand was met by the use of low-cost frill-free carriers that could fly directly from city to city rather than through the hub-and-spoke system. Thus, it was only communications technology that has enabled an apparently anachronistic practice from the 1970s to reappear as a solution in the 1990s.

The globalization of communications technology and the theoretical dynamics behind new systems have served as a model for European and Asian modes of travel. The American hub-and-spoke system has therefore been circumvented by the use of more powerful and efficient, lower cost, multiple short-haul airline flights on small to medium-sized aircraft. The demand for such aircraft continues to add to the employment possibilities for American job seekers. By the early 2000s, such Asian countries as Singapore, Malaysia, Thailand, and Indonesia had also begun their push towards the use of these shorter, low-cost high-turnaround domestic airlines. The long learning curve used in America and Europe has enabled a much shorter learning curve to be applied in Asia with the basic tenet being the concept of open skies. The strategy of low-cost carriers requires faster turnaround and keeping the planes in the air as much as possible over shorter distances across the densely populated Asian cities. Airlines are only one source of multiple passageways in modernity.

There are many other forms of multiplying the effect of these passageways criss-crossing American and Asian cities. For example, the airline flights from New York to Singapore in Southeast Asia, and from Chicago to Chengdu in China are increasingly mediated by cheap airfares, better service, more value-added quality, low-cost bus fares, and intercity train systems. These multiple passageways are also catalysed by information and communications exchanges. Singapore Airlines (SIA) for example, has a 49 per cent stake in Tiger Air, a low-cost carrier which is in partnership with the European-based RyanAir. The decisions made usually come from the very top of the business structure in Singapore and often involve the politicians themselves. For example, when many SIA pilots resigned after wage negotiations broke down in early 2004, the former Senior Minister (SM) Lee Kuan Yew had to resolve the issue. Lee had been in power ever since the days of the old Malaysia-Singapore Airways (MSA), TWA, Pan-American, and the British Overseas Airline Corporation (BOAC), and has outlived all these enterprises.

Singapore's contribution to the international airline business is Singapore Airlines. This is the only Asian-based MNC in the world that has proven beyond doubt that it is indeed the global leader in safety and quality service. Other airlines use SIA as the global standard. Indeed, there are two main pillars of SIA's success. One is the fact that the fleet is kept young and planes are considered old before they are even five years in service. The young fleet is also the best fleet that money can buy. SIA makes money out of leasing or selling ageing aircraft with many more years of serviceable life to other airlines. The second pillar of its success is the Singapore Girl. For years the tagline was that SIA was a "great way to fly". As one of the most profitable MNCs and the only Asian standard that has become the global standard, SIA promoted safe, comfortable, and luxurious pampering by glamorous, young cabin crew. While other airlines were locked in wage disputes and union rights, SIA was making waves by providing the kind of service that no other airline in history had ever witnessed.

The onset of the globalizing airline industry was fraught with failure. The American and West European airlines had a clear advantage and head start at the end of World War II. When Malaysia-Singapore Airlines (MSA) eventually split into SIA and Malaysian Airlines (MAS), SIA came out tops in profitability and success while MAS was not so successful. MAS began with the same fleet as SIA but the latter had much more to prove, given the fact that Singapore was only five years into being a new sovereign state. MAS on the other hand rested on its laurels and did not quite make the cut despite massive government injections. MAS is now not as widely known as SIA which has outperformed every American and European airline in history in terms of profits, service, and safety. Part of the success of SIA and the less than successful results of MAS might be attributed to the ways in which Singapore and Malaysia faced the challenges of globalization from the West.

LEGITIMIZING SPECIAL FORCES IN SOUTHEAST ASIA

This section focuses on the special forces of several Southeast Asian states and their responses to globalization into the second decade of the twenty-first century. In the U.S. Global War on Terror, also known as the Long War, a significant emphasis has been placed on the duties and responsibilities of the special forces. This decision after 9/11 and the failure of the CIA and other government intelligence agencies to resolve the problems of terrorist anticipation and counter-intelligence operations have gravely affected the conduct of training, the strategies, and the tactics of special forces in Southeast Asia. The reason for the focus on the special forces is because they represent the highest concentration of highly skilled soldiers whose jobs are often unknown, whose identities are secret, and whose lives are always at stake even during training and especially during operations. Much of the capabilities of these special force units are dependent on the level of political support in terms of budget and the location of the units themselves in terms of the military hierarchy of command and control. Special force units cannot come under too many layers of administrative control otherwise they will be unable to function effectively. Another problem facing special force units in Asia and America is that when these units come under attachment to the line or regular units, the line/regular unit commanders are unable to deploy them effectively. A third set of problems is that the closed identities of these soldiers make it difficult for the state or for governments to monitor the activities of such highly-trained personnel. And as the various United States Special Operations Command units have proven in Vietnam, Cambodia, Iran, Iraq, and Afghanistan, there is always room for improvement. The U.S. Special Forces schools exert the greatest influence over the foreign validation and special skills training for Indonesia, the Philippines, Singapore, and Thailand. While the indigenous special force units of Southeast Asia certainly train with European and Middle Eastern special force units, it is only the United States that has the wherewithal to conduct in-depth and meaningful training and operations in the actual field and in the simulated classroom, anywhere in the world.

Special forces units in Southeast Asia have a long and intertwining history that dates back to the time of the colonial era. Because of the small numbers of European and American citizens in Southeast Asia who were available for special forces training at the end of the war, the old colonial powers were forced to rely on indigenous, homegrown recruits into the forerunners of these elite units. Hence it became a traditional pattern for local indigenous commanders to be trained in the Netherlands, the United Kingdom, France, or the United States as the case may be. There were also regional and local issues of politics and sovereignty that complicated the development and growth of these units such as the relationship between Singapore and Malaysia, the Philippine claim over the Malaysian state of Sabah, and the insurgencies in the southern Philippines and southern Thailand by Muslim separatists. Cutting across the political divide were issues that became politicized such as ethnicity, religion, and class. The politicization of ethnicity, religion, and class is partially due to the colonial experience and partly due to the demands of the indigenous people. The problem of communism was also a significant political ideology that shaped the initial special forces development in the earlier stages of globalization. Special forces in Southeast Asia are critical because they represent the best means of directly challenging the problems of terrorism that globalization has inadvertently catalysed in this part of the world. Security over the international sea lanes, especially the Strait of Malacca, is critical. Such international shipping lanes are critical for the transportation of neoliberal capitalist oil tankers, VLCCs, and other commercial vessels. A terrorist attack or even local pirate disturbances create pockets of vulnerability and disrupt trade and commercial vessels passing through these international waters. If not kept in check, these soft targets will provide the perfect position to leverage wider scale attacks on the populated cities in the region.

The relationship between Singapore and Malaysia has been politically undulating. There are territorial disputes and differences that date to the time when both were colonies of Great Britain. Malaysia has complained about Singapore's close links with Israel. Singapore was unhappy with the backtracking of the Malaysian political leadership over issues confronting the two countries. When Singapore's then Deputy Prime Minister Lee Hsien Loong visited Taipei before becoming Prime Minister, he received a stern warning from the People's Republic of China. Malaysia's Deputy Prime Minister took advantage of the situation to advise Malaysians not to antagonize China's sovereign policy. Singapore is the only country in the world that has had (until late 2010) another country's railway near the middle of its city centre, at Tanjong Pagar. The railway land and tracks run all the way up through the centre of the island to Woodlands in the north of Singapore where it joins the old Singapore-Malaysia Causeway. There it joins the main railway line in Johor that goes all the way up to Bangkok and potentially Beijing. All that land belongs to the Malaysian Government. Up till December 1997, the Malaysian Navy, Tentera Laut DiRaja Malaysia (TLDM), occupied the Woodlands Naval Base (KD Malaya) that it used for recruit training. However, in 2002, Malaysian leaders accused Singapore of being "poor neighbours" because "they (Singapore) deliberately increased the rate for the lease for the naval base in Woodlands that we were forced to vacate and we vacated without being paid even a *sen*".² In fact, Singapore offered the Malaysian Government the option of an alternative location in the vicinity for a fee of S$500,000 for as long as the TLDM would need it despite the building cost to the Ministry of Defence of about S$50 million (US$33 million) in 1991 dollars. In 1981, Lee Kuan Yew explained to then Malaysian Prime Minister Mahathir that the TLDM could use the facilities for as long as it wanted. This gesture was extended by Singapore Prime Minister Goh Chok Tong in September 1992 in order to forge closer ties with Malaysia.

Malaysia and Indonesia held mass military exercises close to the Singapore border on 9 August 1991 (Singapore's National Day). Codenamed Malindo Darsasa, the combined arms exercise was of concern because it was held in Kota Tinggi, which is 20 kilometres from the Singapore-Malaysia border. Indonesia and Malaysia used paratroopers in the joint-exercise that lasted from 29 July to 11 August 1991, and did not make diplomatic matters any easier. This is because paratroopers and other airborne elements are considered elite attack units and not defensive ones. Therefore when Malaysia and Singapore leaders make strategic plans, they must always consider the security aspect of globalization. Singapore's leaders prefer to use the "package deal" approach in their negotiations while Malaysian ones have shown to prefer the "single issue" approach. The strained ties between Singapore and Malaysia occasionally find comic relief such as in Mahathir's suggestion to build a crooked bridge or a scenic bridge in place of the century-old Causeway. There are also territorial disputes over Pedra Branca (the Portuguese name for what the Malaysians call Pulau Batu Putih); Malaysian water; Indonesian sand; and Malaysian airspace. There are also competing claims by other Southeast Asian states and China over the Spratly Islands and other parts of the South China Sea. One school of thought is the security complex theory that might be used to explain the Southeast Asian situation. However, it is tempting to add that the other dimensions of globalization such as norms, values, culture, and religion would require a modified theory that could be called a graduated security complex.

Malaysia has consistently been an outspoken member of the Organization of the Islamic Conference (OIC) and is a strong believer in ummah or universal Islamic brotherhood. Before 9/11, Bali, and Madrid, Malaysia's foreign policy output was highly inflammatory against the United States and highly anti-Semitic. However, after Prime Minister Abdullah Badawi took over in October 2003, there was a significant reduction of the political rhetoric against Americans and against Jews by Malaysia's top leaders. And his Islam

Hadhari or moderate Islam, appears to be more than just window-dressing but a positive policy decision. But there are certain situations that remain in the minds of the Malaysian political leaders. For example, Singapore drew the indignation of Malaysia when it invited Israeli President Chaim Herzog for an official visit in 1984, and much earlier when it deployed Israeli Defence Force consultants to train the Singapore Armed Forces (SAF) in the early days of its formation in the post-1965 era.

The current Prime Minister of Singapore, Lee Hsien Loong, believes that the country is a steadfast ally of the United States and will remain as such as long as America does not "interfere" with Singapore's domestic politics. When Lee Kuan Yew was still Prime Minister in 1988, (First Secretary) Mason Hendrickson, an American diplomat stationed in Singapore was asked to surrender his credentials to the President of Singapore and then deported because he interfered in local politics. A similar-ranked Singaporean diplomat was deported from Washington, D.C. in retaliation by the U.S. Government. Singapore posted him to Japan and promoted him. Singapore has squared its position very clearly when it comes to security issues in globalization. There were more pressing and serious issues in Singapore's modern history, such as the Laju incident in January 1974 when terrorists from the Japanese Red Army attacked the Shell oil refinery complex on Pulau Bukom, an island off Singapore. Four SAF commandos were involved in the operation. On 29 March 1991, SIA flight SQ117 was hijacked. The SAF commandos rescued over 100 people on board and killed all the terrorists with no injuries to the commandos, all in less than one minute.

In 1997, due to the challenges of globalization, the mass media, greater public awareness, and the change in special force weapons and tactics across the world, there is a different kind of exposure. The old days of secrecy of the special forces units across Asia and America are gone. There is greater openness and willingness to talk about the nature of special force units in Singapore, Malaysia, Indonesia, Thailand, and the Philippines. Singapore's largest daily newspaper, the *Straits Times*, for example, once carried a special report on the Special Operations Force, and elite unit or set of units within the elite commando unit.[3] Recently the Singapore Minister for Defence moved in Parliament an amendment to the SAF Act in order to enable the Singapore Armed Forces to be deployed "in aid of civilian authorities for specified purposes or specific events … with regards to terrorist attacks in Singapore, threats to visiting dignitaries, damage or disruption to the operation of key civilian installations" and, in classic Singapore style, "the bill will not involve the government in any extra financial expenditure".[4] In preparing its security in the face of globalization, it is not surprising that the nature of the administrative culture in Singapore moves towards legitimizing the activities of the SAF with civilian authorities. This is not something new in Southeast Asia. Under Indonesian presidents Sukarno and Suharto, the Indonesian armed forces, ABRI and now the TNI, are centred on the principle of *dwifungsi* or dual function of the armed forces in society:

> The Indonesian military has a Dual Function in its roles — firstly to ensure peace and stability of the country (defenders of the country/nation) and secondly as a social-political force in national development. This is how the military has legitimized its position in the government.⁵

The dual role of the TNI is to (1) secure the peace and national order and (2) to maintain power and state control in terms of internal security and national defence. The doctrine therefore allows the military to hold positions in government. Hence all Indonesian citizens have a right to participate in government. The doctrine is central to the political ideology of *pancasila* [middle path] proposed by General Nasution and widely used by Suharto from 1966 to 1998. One of the longest established units that has witnessed and participated in the transformation of Indonesia from a left-leaning republic (for a brief period under Sukarno), through Suharto's authoritarianism, and now the democratic transition, has been the Komando Pasukan Khusus (KOPASUS), TNI's special forces unit that was established in 1952. It has had a long period of service during which it has confronted communists, conducted the bombing of MacDonald House in Singapore, taken part in other aspects of *Konfrontasi* (Confrontation policy) in the Malaysian states of Sabah and Sarawak, and Brunei (before its independence in 1988). KOPASUS has been accused of committing human rights abuses and other atrocities in East Timor (Timor Leste). These allegations were raised by different NGOs and human rights organizations and began ostensibly when Indonesia annexed East Timor in 1975. Formerly known as Portuguese Timor, the mainly Roman Catholic populated island became a sovereign state in 2002. KOPASUS is also reported to have been involved in covert operations in other parts of Southeast Asia, as well as within Indonesia itself in Aceh (northern-most province of Sumatra), the three provinces in Papua (Irian Jaya), and in most of the major Indonesian cities. While there have been many limitations placed on KOPASUS because of its alleged operational track record, many of its senior officers wear special skills qualification badges that show they were trained in the United States. KOPASUS has the single most experienced number of special forces personnel who took part in every major conflict in Southeast Asia except for the Vietnam War. While KOPASUS has been vilified by civilian organizations in the past, it has simultaneously gained the respect of professional members of the special forces of other Asian states mainly because of what they have done and what they have shown they are capable of achieving.

Although Indonesia spends only 3–4 per cent of its GDP on the military, a significant proportion of the military budget goes towards Westernization and modernization of their equipment. For example they used to deploy the U.S.-made Skyhawk attack fighters but updated their arsenal to the American-made Northrop Tiger attack fighters, the French Mirages, the European-made Hawk Trainers, and the American Fighting Falcons. Unlike the Thai and Malaysian Air Forces who support their own military special forces, the Indonesians tend to spend much less on their support aircraft when compared to Singapore, Malaysia, and Thailand. It is more discernible, however, to see that changes in top-level commanders often result in changes in purchasing contracts from Western arms manufacturers. This is clearer in Malaysia and Thailand, given the strange differences in weapon systems platforms that keep popping up every three to four years. Why would the purchasing commanders buy completely different sets of equipment from Scandinavian, European, Russian, and American arms dealers when there are compatibility issues? There are many other reasons for new equipment to be incompatible with old equipment, such as technology upgrades, lack of existing spares, end of product life, et cetera. However, reports of commanders of purchasing units and budget departments receiving kick-backs for certain tenders are more than anecdotal. For example, according to Transparency International, Thailand's ranking has fallen in their 2006 index of corruption and received 3.6 out of 10 in the 2006 Corruption Perceptions Index (CPI) while Singapore was the top scorer with over 9 out of 10 for being the least corrupt. "Indonesia came in 143rd out of 179 on transparency in the 2007 rankings according to the Transparency International Corruption Perception Index. The score is compiled by a neutral organization using expert methods to unravel how locals perceive corruption among politicians and public officials. Singapore's score is, like Sweden's, at No. 4."[6]

The case of Thai military corruption is linked to the level of systemic corruption in its structures of governance. However, there are many citizens who believe that the military is not corrupt and that politicians are the ones who are. However, the Thai courts and local Thai newspapers have proven otherwise.[7] In other words, the idea that a corrupt military can be fixed or resolved is only a dream if the larger governmental administrative apparatus itself is not fixed. But the level of corruption among some senior members of the establishment is not easy to prove. Those who believe, for example, that former police general and Prime Minister, Thaksin Shinawatra, is corrupt have not had an easy time bringing him and his family up on corruption charges or pinning these on him even if he was ever convicted of the allegations.

In the case of the Philippines, however, there are certain instances where the level of corruption is so great that it becomes hard not to notice:

> "There is a lot of unhappiness in the region about corruption in the armed forces of the Philippines and the chronic inability of the armed forces to deal with its internal security issues," Abuza said.
>
> The Philippines' military is often compared with those of other countries in the region, like Indonesia's, in terms of corruption. But the comparison ends quickly.
>
> Unlike Indonesia, which overthrew the Suharto dictatorship only six years ago, the Philippines has been free for almost two decades of its late dictator, Ferdinand Marcos, who virtually made the military his private army.[8]

The suggestion here is that despite having rid itself of Marcos twenty-two years ago, the level of corruption continues to remain at an alarmingly high level. This is despite the fact that the Philippine Armed Forces have no real regional role to play in Southeast Asia and their greatest contribution is the occasional quelling of the Islamic insurgency in the south. This is a sad turn of events since both Thailand and the Philippines in particular have been receiving U.S. military aid for decades. The Philippines has had a long and very close military relationship with the United States, more than any other Southeast Asian nation. The United States used to occupy Subic Naval Base and Clarke Air Force Base as its forward line of defence during the Cold War. Like their counterparts in Southeast Asia, the Philippines has a wide range of special forces units across all armed services. Like Thailand and Indonesia, the Philippines special forces also are heavily involved in politics. The Philippines special forces culture, however, tends to involve subaltern officers (up to the rank of lieutenant colonel) from different cohorts of the armed forces academies who launch sporadic and limited takeovers of cities (such as the Makati incidents) or buildings from which they make various demands. The usual reason that motivates them is systemic corruption. While the Thai coups are often well planned and orchestrated, the Philippines ones appear to be much less so. One exception is the case of the insubordinate, rebellious maverick senior officer called Gregorio "Gringo" Honasan. Colonel Honasan was the deeply respected military leader who precipitated the downfall of Marcos just hours before the 1986 EDSA People Power revolution took place.

The culture of the Philippines shows that unless the people are involved at the mass level as well as the Catholic Church, no coup is likely to succeed. The Philippine Army itself does not support coups led by junior officers out to make a quick impression or an immediate impact as various coup attempts against Philippine presidents have shown. However, the Philippine special forces are certainly not lacking in military experience or operational capability. For many decades various special force units have combated Muslim rebels in the southern island of Mindanao and throughout the archipelago. Like Indonesia, the Philippines encounters the obstacle of providing security across thousands of islands and islets from where insurgents and other terrorists can easily conduct their operations. Notable Philippine special force units include the Philippine Special Warfare Group modelled after the U.S. Navy SEALS; the airborne delivered Special Forces Regiment (created from scratch by Fidel Ramos in the late 1950s); the Philippine scout rangers of the First Scout Ranger Regiment who were drawn from the famous Philippine Division — the distinguished regular infantry division in the old United States Army; the Light Reaction Battalion; and the Marine Force Recon Regiment. There are other special force units in the police and coastguards. All the aforementioned special force units come under Army SOCOM, or Special Operations Command, and follow a very similar order of battle as their U.S. counterparts.

In the case of Thailand, many if not most senior military commanders, especially from the 1st and 3rd Army groups, have been trained in the United States. However, the Thai case is differentiated from the Indonesian one because of the eighteen military coups and counter-coups since 1932. The most recent coup was in September 2006 that removed the democratically-elected civilian government of Thaksin Shinawatra on the basis of alleged corruption. The United States has not made overt attempts at taking sides over the recent coup although there have been some calls for sanctions against the military junta, the Chairman of the Council for National Security, General Sonthi Boonyaratkalin, and Prime Minister General Surayud Chulanont within Bangkok and from the United States. Former Thai Prime Minister Thaksin Shinawatra appealed to the Thai people after Sonthi's Council for National Security (CNS) installed Assets Examinations Committee (AEC) froze most of his (Thaksin's) wealth through his new Internet website. The nature of globalization today is even more interesting because since the coup, Thaksin and his wife Khunying Potjaman Shinawatra have been seen in Singapore but work out of London and he has made several investment decisions overseas such as the Manchester City Football Club. The interconnectedness of the Web is further demonstrated by the fact that the AEC has been able to freeze most of Thaksin's family wealth. This was achieved by hiring specialist forensic accountants to uncover Thaksin's hidden wealth in Thailand and the rest of the world.

The global interconnectedness can be traced back to early 2006 when Singapore's Asia investment arm, Temasek Holdings, invested US$1.9 billion in Shin Corp, which is a giant Thai telecommunications company. The coup plotters under Sonthi accused Thaksin of abusing his power as prime minister by corruptly enriching his own family from the sale of Shin Corp to Temasek in which he avoided taxes. The public outcry and demonstrations came to a head when he was in New York and the coup plotters took over by surprise in a bloodless coup. Thaksin is now in self-exile and refusing to return to face charges brought up against him and his family by the police and the attorney-general. Diplomatic relations between Bangkok and Singapore remain cool.

There are several threads that tie the security aspects of globalization across several Southeast Asian states. One clear aspect is the fact that many military officers and non-commissioned officers from the special forces in Indonesia, the Philippines, Malaysia, Singapore, and Thailand have trained in the United States and have cooperated at various levels of command, control, communications, and computing technology. Joint operations through bilateral and multilateral exercises — sometimes through the Five Power Defense Arrangements (FPDA) and 1951 Treaty signed by Australia, New Zealand and the United States (ANZUS) — are commonly held annually and biennially. Joint exercises by members of ASEAN are also common. Also, the nature of the graduated security complex in Southeast Asia is such that all military operations and exercises tend to involve one other Asian state. Often it involves an external military power. Sometimes problems arise because of the intensity of such exercises as seen in Malindo Darsasa and when Malaysia pulled out of a FPDA joint exercise several years ago. The post–Cold War, post-9/11 eras have demonstrated how the "fixity" of security arrangements is contingent on global economic and political change. The faster the world globalizes, the quicker the security arrangements have to adapt to the new forces that often restrict and curtail military budgets as well as determine military expenditure. Globalization has demonstrated that the indigenous special force units in Southeast Asia tend to use one another, the United States, and several European counterparts to test and accredit their professional abilities and skills. The greatest security challenges that globalization will bring in the future will come from within the region (such as Indonesia's intention to build nuclear power reactors) and from outside the region (if China decides to finally beef up its air force and naval influence in the region).

TWO STRUCTURES OF AUTHORITY: SINGAPORE AND MALAYSIA

Malaysia and Singapore have some similar public policies and administrative regulations such as: building construction policy, housing policy, land transport policy, traffic control systems, and the use of international standards for healthcare policy. The similarities in policies and regulations are a testament to intertwining social, cultural, and economic histories.

Singapore approached globalization's challenges very differently from Malaysia. It was because Singapore was ejected from Malaysia in 1965 without anything but those people who wished to remain in Singapore, and the country was forced to make very dramatic, calculated risks about its political and economic future. Singapore decided, at the behest of economic planner Goh Keng Swee, to take the MNC route in the early 1970s when the rest of Asia was torn between agricultural self-sufficiency and ideologically determined foreign investments. The Singapore economic gamble proved an overnight success. Malaysia on the other hand became more politically stable because of the implementation of the New Economic Policy (NEP) which was basically to ensure that the *bumiputra* (sons of the soil) were not left out of the economic race. However, this created a crutch mentality and reduced the productivity levels of many Malaysian workers. "Mahathir Mohamad has been criticizing the Malay community in news media ... for lagging behind ethnic Chinese and Indians, despite three decades of affirmative action for Malays in jobs, access to credit and education. Mahathir says Malays take privileges for granted, creating a crutch mentality."[9] Despite the apparent setbacks of affirmative action through the NEP and later the National Development Policy (NDP), Malaysia's choice of globalization strategies did work and the nation rapidly became one of the fastest growing newly industrializing economies of the world that began to marginalize many of its agricultural workers, at least from the Second Malaysian Plan.[10]

SINGAPORE AND GLOBALIZATION: SUCCESSFUL POWER, AUTHORITY, AND LEGITIMACY

The word *abang* in Malay refers to the older brother and *adik* as the younger one. For many years Malaysian political leaders assumed the unofficial view that Malaysia was to play the role of the *abang*, but Singapore's political leaders had never accepted the role of *adik*. It is possible that these metaphorical familial labels could be reversed if we use different yardsticks of performance, such as GDP per capita. Nevertheless, there are many reasons why Singapore and Malaysia are successful capitalist countries and each competes against the other for U.S. and other world investments — like two brothers tied together by blood ties, but quarrelling periodically — and sometimes the competition spills over into the political realm:

> Even Malaysia's first prime minister, the gentle Tunku Abdul Rahman, saw separation as punishment for an unruly child. If Singapore continued to misbehave, he told the British High Commissioner then, Kuala Lumpur could always cut off its water. Others have spoken of Malaysia-Singapore relations as an abang-adik (big brother-small brother) relationship. When they say Singapore is "insensitive", they mean it isn't deferential. When they say it is "aggressive", they mean it doesn't know its place…"Ungrateful", "insincere", "unmindful of history" — all these descriptions bear no relation to Singapore's acts of commission or omission, but have everything to do with its refusal to be the dutiful younger brother/illegitimate child/mistress, or any other subordinate family position that catches Kuala Lumpur's fancy.[11]

Singapore and the United States share many similar views on the global balance of power. Singapore supported the U.S. invasion of Iraq (illegal by UN standards) when most other Southeast Asian countries considered the event both illegal and a precursor to further American global interventionism. One clear model of "intervention the other way" into the global arena is the case of the global company Singapore Airlines. The following section examines one of the economic narratives that contributed to the successful globalization of the Singapore economy under its first prime minister since its independence.

Singapore's efficiency and international success is attributable to a tightly run, carefully controlled society, depoliticized polity from 1959 to the middle of 2004. The incremental political liberalization of Singapore began taking shape some time after the 1997 Asian financial crisis — following Deputy Prime Minister Lee Hsien Loong's announcement about Singapore's financial liberalization back then — it became clear from the experiences of other Southeast Asian states that in order for any single sovereign state to survive well, it had to adapt to the various demands of globalization by opening up rather than shutting down or implementing capital controls.

At one point in Malaysia's recent history under Mahathir, Malaysia adopted a "Look East" policy (although this was really about using Japan as an economic model and attracting Japanese investments in the heady 1980s). However, that model failed to bear fruit. Nevertheless, Mahathir's reaction to the 1997 Asian financial crisis in what he called his "*kampung* economics" was indeed the correct medicine for the Malaysian ringgit. He pegged the ringgit and introduced other capital controls in order to safeguard the value of the Malaysian currency. Singapore's own sound financial fundamentals and lower exposure because it had tied the Singapore dollar to a basket of other international currencies, was left almost but not totally unscathed by the speculative attacks that saw the fall of the Thai baht and a crash of dominoes that impacted the rest of the world.

On hindsight it is always easier to analyse the financial crisis that globalization and its interconnectedness brought onto Southeast Asia, but the crisis saw the death of many businesses and the end of many small, medium and large enterprises across Asia. What began as a currency crisis rapidly deteriorated into a financial crisis. Mahathir blamed George Soros for speculating and preying on weaker Asian currencies. Indonesia broke into riots and looting. The crisis also ended the long authoritarianism of Suharto and ushered in a difficult period of democratic transition that began ostensibly in 1998. Ten years hence, Indonesia has not Balkanized as some political scientists believed it would, but has overcome the worst effects of the Asian financial crisis.

Singapore is known for periodically implementing controversial domestic policies in its effort to make the entire nation globalization-ready or perhaps globalization-adaptive. For example, the island state manages its traffic situation with an iron hand calculated to reap a big profit at the same time. Singapore is the most expensive place to buy a motorcar in the world, and Malaysia is not very much cheaper. The Singapore Government collects billions of dollars in several main ways: (1) income and business taxes; (2) Certificates of Entitlement (COE) that allow a person to legally purchase a car; (3) what used to be for many years a 150 per cent tax on imported cars (none are manufactured in Singapore), and the ten-year age limit that is placed on the lifespan of each COE. The lifespan of cars can be extended but at a cost. So if you need a car for more than ten years, you have got to keep buying one at least once every decade. The reason given for implementing the ten-year limit for each COE was because it was supposed to keep the car population young and therefore reduce the possibility of mechanical failure and the problems associated with older cars. However, this policy has not shifted with the changes and improvements in vehicle technology. Singapore also has a three-quarter tank rule on cars travelling to Malaysia, the world's first Electronic Road Pricing (ERP) system, a world class international airport, a meticulously clean and artificially green city, and a highly efficient mass mover of people called the Mass Rapid Transit (MRT) system which is a cross between the San Francisco-Oakland Bay Area Rapid Transit (BART) and Hong Kong's Mass Transit Railway (MTR) but cleaner, more efficient, and as secure as the BART or the MTR.

The three-quarter tank rule requires Singapore-registered cars to have at least that much petrol in their tanks before entering Malaysia. This was ostensibly implemented at the request of Malaysians living in the southernmost state of Johor that lies adjacent to Singapore. Singaporeans who filled up their tanks on the Malaysian (Johor state) side were accused by Malaysian groups in Johor of pushing up the cost of living in that state. However, the three-quarter tank rule also protects Singapore's monopoly over the retail gasoline market made up of Esso-Mobil (Exxon-Mobil), Shell, Caltex, and Singapore Petroleum Company (SPC). The companies often seem to raise and lower their prices at distinctly similar times. But whether the prices are higher or lower, the Singaporean car owner ends up paying. After years of authoritarian control into the psyche of most Singaporeans through its powerful bureaucratic apparatus, the government has said that it does not want to interfere with the price mechanism despite allegations of cartel-like pricing (by these oil companies) over the Internet and in the local coffee shops. The arena for control over the domestic retail market narrowed recently when British Petroleum (BP) announced its withdrawal from the retail oil sector in early 2004, and had its retail outlets bought over by SPC. This means that there are now only four players in Singapore's petroleum retail market. In addition to these players are six major energy companies, including SPC, viz., Singapore Power; PowerSeraya; PowerSenoko; Tuas Power; PowerGas. In the first quarter of 2007, an article appeared in the Singapore financial daily, the *Business Times*, that announced the diversification of the energy companies. Some have said that the retail market in Singapore is too small to make a profit and vulnerable, given the recent 1997 Asian financial crisis. But it must be remembered that the local retail trade is only part of the largest petrochemical industry in Southeast Asia and one of the largest in the world refining at close to 1.4 million barrels per day. The competition from India and Malaysia is limited and underdeveloped.

SINGAPORE AIRLINES: A GENUINE GLOBAL SUCCESS STORY OF POWER, AUTHORITY AND LEGITIMACY

There are several reasons why SIA has become such a global success. The first reason is that the fleet is never ageing and is always kept young. This has kept the planes relatively more safe and in better shape than older aircraft. The assumption here is that the older the aircraft the more likelihood of a breakdown which might endanger lives. The second secret of SIA's success is that the cabin crew, especially the Singapore Girl, is always kept young, or at least, youthful. Whoever was the first executive to decide on the kind of "soft-focus service" from beautiful Asian girls could not have imagined the extent to which he had made a brilliant business decision way back in the mid-1970s. The classic Singapore Girl today no longer comes from Singapore alone. The airline trawls the Southeast Asian and Asian region to bring on board young potential stewardesses to work with the best airline in the world.

The powerful image of the Singapore Girl is so unique that no other airline has been able to imitate, innovate, and improve on the product. Many have tried but some part of their organization or business will falter. Singapore Airlines has extended its global reach and share of the world markets by having a high level of quality control over flight staff and ground staff as well.

Ever since its inception, SIA has been a major purchaser of Boeing aircraft, especially the very popular 747-series "Jumbo Jet", the 737-series, 777-series, and the new 787-series at the cost of billions of American dollars. SIA took delivery of the world's first Airbus A380. Airbus recently successfully landed its gigantic jetliner at Changi International Airport and has agreed to pay costs on delayed deliveries to its global customers. Despite Airbus' strategic achievements, SIA continues to remain a big investor in Boeing, the former Seattle-based company. Singapore also remains one of Boeing's largest and most credit-worthy customers. SIA had become the "best airline" in the world with the right blend of local administrative expertise and primarily American technology. This meant that Singaporeans and foreigners had big stakes in SIA as the national carrier reaped hundreds of millions of dollars worth in profits in the best global success story of airline management in modernity. This also meant that SIA was a national resource and was being carefully watched by its competitors and the government that had created it. In late 1980, the Singapore Airlines Pilots' Association (SIAPA) began a "work-to-rule", peaceful "strike action" after being unable to agree with their newly minted collective agreement. SIA was considered a national resource in the local economy, and SIAPA was eventually de-registered in 1981. The local papers reported that fifteen leaders were charged with commencing illegal industrial action and convicted. It continues to be illegal to initiate industrial strike action in Singapore today.

Some twenty-four years later, a replay of the events of 1980 emerged but this time with a different set of pilots. This time, Lee Kuan Yew powerfully challenged the pilots that he did not want to do them in, but won't allow them to do Singapore in. The implication in 2004 was that someone in ALPA-S, the local pilots' union, had been covertly muddying up the waters through illegal back-door negotiations and was about "to do Singapore in", to destroy the nation. This person was singled out by (the former Senior Minister) Minister Mentor Lee Kuan Yew for instigating trouble between ALPA-S and the old SIA management. After several months of public and private negotiations, the matter was resolved between the new ALPA-S union leadership led by a less truculent man, an SIA pilot named Mok Hin Choon, who was willing to work closely and with full cooperation with the new management team. At the end of the strained relations between the pilots' union and their senior management, the local newspaper, the *Straits Times*, reported wage increases for SIA staff, while some of their top-flight senior managers ended up working for the other Singapore airline, Tiger Air.

The "mud-raker" or instigator singled out by Lee Kuan Yew was a former SIA pilot named Ryan Goh, a Malaysian citizen with permanent residency (PR) in Singapore and PR status in Australia.[12] Because of the incident, Goh was considered an undesirable resident by Home Affairs Minister Wong Kan Seng. Pilot Goh's appeal to have his Singapore PR status reactivated after it was revoked so that he could continue working for SIA was turned down. He moved to Australia. However, there was no move on the part of ALPA-S or other SIA pilots to defend Goh in any public manner. Perhaps this might have indicated that Goh himself did not have any support from the pilots themselves or the pilots who supported Goh withdrew when they sensed danger, suggesting that the camaraderie among SIA pilots is not as seamless and unproblematic as some observers might have thought. This raises the question of how Lee Kuan Yew was able to quickly pinpoint that one man was behind it all.

There were many significant players in the creation of SIA as a global company, such as J.Y.M. Pillay and his team who were some of the primary architects of SIA's surging global success story. It is unlikely that 1,600 airline pilots can "do Singapore in". On the other hand, SIA has a very good reputation to uphold. The treatment of its entire staff must continue to reflect the global standards that it has set for the airline industry worldwide. For example, pilots should be paid fair salaries, comparable to those of other top global carriers. The operating theory for global success is that one should not under-pay some people in order to over-pay others. Otherwise, when people feel shortchanged, you could get bad press. There is a gulf of difference between labour union management in the United States and the ones in Singapore. The global position of Singapore Airlines continues to signify its importance as an employer of thousands of Singaporeans and foreigners locally and overseas and the state is unlikely to fudge issues with any union within the SIA Group that infringes or tests the limits of its state-determined boundaries of labour action.

SIA is such a global communications and hospitality industry that it has American airliners, European airplanes, French champagne, Asian cuisine, foreign-based pilots, and its secret weapon, the "Singapore Girl". The exotification of Asian women has been a useful strategy for increasing the profits of SIA which run in excess of US$600 million in spite of the Asian financial crisis. While this concept has not been the single most important variable in determining SIA's profits, it has become part and parcel of the image of service and quality that SIA's customers have become familiar with. In terms of the politics of the body, the concept has reaped material benefits by presenting images of a smiling, slender, gentle, caring, but voiceless Asian woman in haute couture providing service that was touted by Batey Ads as "A Great Way to Fly". Their hair, nails, and make-up have certain regulatory standards to meet. The dress code is itself an extension of the grooming courses that they have to take while in training. Crew members are employed on five-year contracts that are renewable pending assessment reports. SIA crew who become pregnant are not allowed to fly but may apply to return to the company two years after they give birth. However, it used to be rare to see female flight attendants aged forty and above, with the exception of some in-flight supervisors. European and American airline MNCs have difficulties sacking crew who do not maintain their youthful figures or who are considered "too old" or "overweight" to remain in service because of the strong emphasis on workers' rights. SIA's policy of contract renewal for their flight stewardesses is clearly established from the start, so the crews know what they are getting into.

SIA cabin crew showed their mettle in at least two situations. One was in 1991 on SQ117 when the airliner was hijacked by four Pakistani terrorists who were subsequently killed by members of the elite SAF Commando unit without harming passengers or crew. A second instance was a result of pilot error. On 31 October 2000, SQ6 crashed on take-off killing seventy-nine passengers and three crew members. The conduct of the cabin crew under pressure in both cases were admirable, to say the least. Ironically, the Singapore Girl image is one that now includes women who are not from Singapore but instead from Japan, Korea, Malaysia, and India. Can the global traveller really tell the difference? The customers keep ranking SIA as the best airline in the world and there are three reasons for this: quality of service, efficiency, and safety record. The trick here is to sell off the planes before they show signs of ageing and to keep the crew young and agile. Therefore, a legitimate company like SIA could not possibly join the fray of the low-cost, frills-free airline industry because it would eradicate its hard-won premium for world class travel.

GLOBAL EDUCATION: POWER, AUTHORITY AND LEGITIMACY

Asia has learnt much from America by creating opportunities for its young and old people to take advantage of American educational opportunities. There are many instances and examples of how Asians have learnt from American educational modernity and benefited from these experiences. American educational systems have been emulated and modified all over the world and have even had a tremendous impact on the conservative Western European educational systems. Asian elites are often trained at American universities and work in American business enterprises regardless of historical affiliation, economic ideology, or political ideology. This phenomenon is illustrated in South Korea, Thailand, and the Philippines, economic allies such as Singapore and Japan, critics of America like Malaysia and Indonesia, the authoritarian military junta in Myanmar, Communist China, former adversaries such as Vietnam, and former British colonies such as New Zealand and Australia. These elite graduates from American universities and those who graduate from American military colleges and universities return with some knowledge about America and with some idea about the American way of life, perhaps even the American Dream. Their influence eventually trickles down and percolates into their own indigenous or national communities.

Asia has therefore a blend of historical educational systems introduced indigenously and from first contact with Portuguese, Spanish, Dutch, and British colonialism. The massive changes to Asian education systems and their inherited biases from the colonial period were interrupted by the outbreak of World War II. This was the major turning point for the region. It saw the rise of postcolonial nationalism all across the region and the world that would persist through the Korean War, the Vietnam War, the Cold War, the Gulf Wars, and 9/11. The synchronous adjustments made within the national Asian systems of education over 200 years of modernization have had an uneven effect on the relationship between these countries and the Western world. The unevenness of the educational experience with English as the language of science and technology, and of communications and information, would mean that those countries with scholars trained in the English-speaking world would potentially possess the advantage over other nations in Asia with regard to the pressures to globalize. However, the case of the Philippines is a clear exception as analysed in Rappa and Wee in *Language Policy and Modernity in Southeast Asia* (2006).

There are other factors that have helped or hindered Asian responses to modernity and towards globalization. A significant factor is the presence of the U.S. military in the region as a countervailing force against major forms of aggression. While the U.S. presence is a clear deterrent in the post-9/11 era, it was not always a welcomed presence in the Indian Ocean or the Pacific Rim. And while the U.S. presence in Southeast Asia itself has had a tremendous but silent effect on curtailing potential flashpoints and tensions within the region as seen in Korea and the Taiwan Straits. Naturally, there are also other languages that have had a significant impact on the region through foreign education systems such as French and Dutch, but these languages are themselves not as widely accepted across the world as English. The business of education in Asia is highly political because it involves factors of national policy, local community, cultural norms, and rising expectations of the voting public. The tension will continue to exist between foreign talented skills and local talented skills.

Education is a serious business in Singapore and this issue ranks high on the national agenda, alongside economic performance, defence, and security. Singapore is a clear beneficiary of the American military presence in the Pacific and its benign hegemonic role in the region. The likelihood of war breaking out between China and the island of Taiwan for example, is dependent on Washington, Beijing, and Taipei's diplomatic conferencing abilities. Southeast Asian economic stability will suffer from an East Asia that is turned into another Middle East.

GLOBAL POLICY ON SINGAPOREANS AND THE FERTILITY PROBLEMS

The population policies of the 1970s and 1980s were ironically so successful to the point that they caused a negative impact on Singaporean fertility. In 2004 for example, the total fertility rate (TFR) was 1.26, thereby forcing new approaches to understanding the fertility process as a package of problems rather than an isolated policy issue. Singapore has tried for decades to solve this problem. It has tried to persuade people from Hong Kong, China, India and elsewhere to settle in Singapore, but only with mixed results. The results are mixed because Singapore Chinese and Chinese nationals, while sharing similar ethnic ancestries, are very different communities and are totally different but in name. Some Singaporeans of Chinese ethnicity whose ancestors lived, worked, and died defending Singapore are adamant about making it clear that they are Singaporean, not from China. While many ethnic Chinese nationals have settled well and adjusted to life in Singapore, a small fraction have resorted to crime and policy abuse.

Nevertheless, many Chinese nationals moonlight in Singapore on tourist visas which they extend every few months or weeks depending on their case. There continue to be complaints in the local newspapers about the social behaviour of the Chinese nationals. Perhaps this might change over time. It used to be easy to spot a former Chinese national in Singapore from their accent, attire, and mannerisms. Now it is not so easy to identify them except for their accent. But their children sound and act totally Singaporean. So this means that in one generation, Singapore is able to create a Singaporean from a single ethnic-based identity. Very soon, there will be less value placed on these differences.

In a straw poll of Singaporeans over a week in December 2007, a total of 350 people were asked two questions. The first question was: "Are you Singaporean" and the second was: "Have Singaporeans accepted China Chinese migrants into Singapore society?" Of these, 150 kept quiet or had no response. Out of these 150, 92 were Singaporean (mainly Chinese), 17 expatriates from Western countries (including 2 Chinese Australians in the expatriate group), 11 Chinese nationals, Malaysians (3), and Indian nationals (27). Out of the 200 respondents, 30 per cent were non-Chinese Singaporeans (Indians, Malays, and Eurasians) while 70 per cent were Chinese Singaporeans.

Some 79 per cent of the 200 said that the Chinese nationals have not been accepted into Singapore society, 15 per cent said they have been accepted, while 6 per cent said both yes and no. Most of the respondents who reported that the Chinese migrants had not been accepted by Singaporeans also cited unsolicited reasons for this situation: anti-social behaviour, lack of respect for Singaporeans, and the prospect of losing their jobs (to Chinese migrants). The most interesting unsolicited response came from a Malay-Muslim Singaporean respondent who said that the Chinese were not accepted by Singaporeans and added that her brother was working in China and was better treated by the Chinese over there. The results of the straw poll, which are not statistically representative, does gives some insight into the attitudes of Singaporeans on the street. Nevertheless, it is also known that many Chinese nationals would prefer to move to Canada or the United States. In other words, the cultural resistance from some Singaporeans towards Chinese migrants and the greater perceived attractiveness of the United States or Canada suggests that the supply of suitable migrants might be low. If the situation is as dire as the straw poll suggests, then the migrant policy, while a good one, is a necessary but not sufficient strategy. Also, the state should conduct a separate and elaborate poll to ascertain the value of the policy.

The question that Singaporeans have to ask themselves is whether or not they wish to have a larger population of Singaporeans that will bring in many benefits, or remain with the status quo of not replacing themselves along fertility lines. They have to ask whether they are willing to accept the current policies of integrating former Chinese and Indian nationals into Singapore society. The danger is that one day "local" Singaporeans may only make up a minority of all the citizens. This will magnify the problem of security and defence as well as political control. It will also mean that Singapore may lose control over its own economy.

Part of the solution to Singapore's fertility problems is to encourage more Singaporeans to marry foreigners (without severely antagonizing current customary and traditional practices and preferences). This part involves a mindset change among Singaporeans. America possesses many positive qualities that can easily be emulated by Asia, and one of these models is that of the cultural melting pot of people.

THE BIG RED ONE: ASIA'S LARGEST FOREIGN INVESTOR

America is Asia's biggest foreign investor outside the region. America has had its hand in the political and economic pies of Japan, South Korea, Vietnam, the Philippines, Thailand, Malaysia, Singapore, Brunei, Indonesia, Australia, New Zealand, China, Taiwan, India, Nepal, Bangladesh, Pakistan, Sri Lanka, and virtually the entire Pacific Rim which the U.S. Seventh Fleet seems to claim like its own backyard swimming pool. America, when compared to the rest of the world, has another comparative advantage. The United States has "a relative abundance of educated, skilled workers, and a relative scarcity of educated, unskilled workers. This is suggested by the fact that U.S. exports embody a much higher ratio of skilled labor to unskilled labor than its imports or manufacturing production for domestic consumption".[13]

The richer America gets, the more people want to get something out of it. Take the case of the Organization of Petroleum Exporting Countries (OPEC) for example. When OPEC decided to command a higher premium on its barrels of "black gold", it restricted supply to create an artificial rise in prices in 1973. The oligopolistic nature of the oil industry through its corporatist cartels controlled the global oil industry and the nations that were most dependent on them, namely Japan, South Korea, Singapore, and all the Western European countries. This was indeed a bad time since it was at the height of the Cold War with the Soviet Union. America did not need the additional pressure from the oil states. After World War I, the United States was the world's largest producer of oil with close to 70 per cent of the world market share. When faced with the pending shortage of oil reserves, the CIA staged a coup in 1953 in Iran and returned the Shah of Iran to power. During the Cold War, the United States also produced sufficient quantities of oil and natural gas from the Gulf of Mexico and its other oil fields in Oklahoma, Texas, and Southern Florida to run most of its economy modestly with fewer cars and more efficient use of fossil fuels. However, a drastic supply cut would have crippled the growth of America's urban population and limited the completion of its complex system of interstate highways, and most importantly, the military industrial complex.

If we read Edward Said's seminal work, *Orientalism* (Vintage, 1979) correctly, we would consider the Middle Eastern states back then as being part of the Near East, at least historically. Despite such historical knowledge and cultural critique, there continues to be much ignorance about the complexities of the Middle East, such that America is not capable of full comprehension. The neoliberal capitalist world order has been supported by the reasoning and rationale of the Federal Power Act (1920), the functions of the Federal Energy Regulatory Commission (FERC), the U.S. Department of Energy, and the U.S. Nuclear Regulatory Commission (NRC).

The complexity of political and economic consequences on businesses never fails to surprise. Although it was a fact that American MNCs were hardest hit by the OPEC-induced recession, all these MNCs had to do was to dispose of their least profitable overseas assets. The MNCs would then concentrate on the diversification of the local product base. "Clearly, for OPEC as a whole, the quota system offers higher collective revenue, but the gains among members are quite disparate. For the most part, the small producers such as Gabon, Algeria, Qatar, Indonesia, and Nigeria benefit significantly ... because of the enormousness of the Saudi reserve base, when Saudi Arabia matches cheating, it is producing reserves it would otherwise produce in the distant future".[14]

Singapore was particularly hard hit by the OPEC oil crisis in 1973. As a struggling Southeast Asian economy that was seeing the vestiges of American defeat as a total and a complete rout in Vietnam, the genuine economic and financial architects of Singapore, namely Goh Keng Swee and Hon Sui Sen, were particularly interested in making the Singapore economy work. As a result there was a shift in emphasis towards diversifying the kind of MNCs from Western Europe and America such as Rollei, Texas Instruments, DuPont, Hewlett-Packard, Phillips, and expanding the capacity of Mobil. But Singapore was alone in this quest. While some Malaysian politicians of the period hoped for Singapore to fail after it was forced out of the Federation of Malaysia in 1965, the converse became history. But the magnitude of Singapore's success was attributed to an alignment with Western countries, especially the United States, and it was perceived negatively especially by Muslim-dominant countries such as Malaysia and Indonesia, with their masses of poverty-stricken citizens at that point in time. Singapore's success was in its ability to attract MNCs when the other countries in the region were debating the advantages and disadvantages of import substituted investments (ISI). In addition, Singapore's secret use of Israeli consultants for its fledgling army worsened the relationship with its Southeast Asian neighbours and increased the level of suspicion of the Muslim-dominant states. While Singapore adopted a policy of trading with any country regardless of political ideology, Malaysia and Indonesia did not think that the use of American economic know-how and Israeli military tactics was a step towards building ASEAN brotherhood.

This chapter examines why America is important to Asia in terms of the historical complications that have arisen over the deep American military and economic interests in Asia. America has a special and close relationship with many Asian nations, especially now in the post–Cold War, post-9/11 era where its dominance as the international military hegemony and to a certain extent, economic hegemony, continues to be visited on different Asian constituencies for different reasons.

WHAT HAUNTS AMERICA IN ASIA

America has a long and complex modern history with Asia. Much blood has been spilled on both sides. Take the Vietnam War for example. When a country's soldiers go to war, they have to be professionally and psychologically prepared. American soldiers were not. Most were draftees. Apart from the ideological ill-preparedness, once the President committed American citizen-soldiers to the fight, there should have been complete moral and social support. There was not. American liberalism, with its great respect for differences of opinion and democratic divergence, threw up a range of conflicting ideals which ended in widespread protests at Bowling Green University, the University of California, and the University of Hawaii at Manoa. Look at successful wars that ended quickly. They all had the complete support of the public. This was not the case in Vietnam.

Vietnam was a sullen war that continues to be fought by the ghosts of idealistic patriots whose own people did not support them. When they returned to their homes in the inner cities, middle class suburbia, the American West, and the Deep South, there were no parades or celebrations. By way of comparison, there were thousands of American soldiers killed in action against the Japanese forces during World War II, many of whom remain unaccounted for till today. Some of their own sons, those who were old enough to have children, went on to die in Korea and in Vietnam. There have been at least 5,000 to 8,000 American soldiers who have gone missing since the end of the Vietnam War. Close to 60,000 Americans are now dead or missing in Asia in the ideological cause of democracy. During the Vietnam War alone, America had devoted over 2.5 million soldiers and civilians. This may be seen in the history of U.S. warfare in Asia described for example, by Michael Maclear, *The Ten Thousand Day War: Vietnam, 1945–1975* (St. Martin's Press, 1981), and more recently by Peter S. Kindsvatter in *American Soldiers: Ground Combat in the World Wars, Korea, and Vietnam* (University Press of Kansas, 2003).

There are also signs that Asia is turning increasingly towards American and Western ideals of freedom and democracy as seen in Kazuo Kawai's *Japan's American Interlude* (University of Chicago Press, 1960), Elizabeth J. Perry's *Challenging the Mandate of Heaven: Social Protest and State Power in China* (M.E. Sharpe, 2001) and Bill Robinson's objective analysis in *Promoting Polyarchy: Globalization, US Intervention, and Hegemony* (Cambridge University Press, 1996).

Asia's discomfort was most clearly demonstrated by the North Vietnamese during the Vietnam War. However, since the end of the Vietnam War where Americans at home received mixed signals about Americans overseas in the paddy fields, American foreign policy towards the region (known by the Department of State as part of "East Asia") has been mixed. By this I mean that American foreign policy was dominated by ideological interests and the need to stem the influence of two kinds of communisms. One was the Soviet-supported motif adopted by Ho Chi Minh and the North Vietnamese, and the other kind derived from Mao Zedong that led the way to the punishment "of both good and evil" supporters of their respective regimes.

The ideological subdivisions in World War II were politically overt and caused severe tension between the Soviets and the Chinese across their Eurasian borders, with limited skirmishes and exchanges of small arms fire. However, these subdivisions did not mean that it would make the ideological problem any less simple for the United States. At some level, the Department of Defense (DOD) and the Department of State (DOS) (i.e. the US Ministry of Foreign Affairs) were — as institutional competitors — unable to take advantage of the Sino-Soviet divide and manipulate it for their own benefit. One clear dividend was the new level of rapprochement that was achieved when Richard Nixon made his historic visit to China. This forestalled China's own interests in reclaiming Taiwan by force which itself was being indirectly supported by the United States and some of its allies. When Mao Zedong died on 9 September 1976, a new era of modernization was gradually unleashed and raised the stakes between the United States and China, again in terms of committing to its role as a dominant land power in the East while trying to break through the rudimentary and inchoate policies and politics of Mao's widow and the other members of the Gang of Four. The two-year window known as the era of deMaoization[15] that began ostensibly after 1978, saw the PRC endeavouring to adjust to the problem of political succession, while strongman Deng Xiaopeng continued to solidify his position and quash his enemies within the Chinese Communist Party, the grassroots cadres, and the People's Liberation Army (PLA). This was anticipated in Peter R. Moody Jr.'s *Opposition and Dissent in Contemporary China* (Hoover Institution, 1977). The internal crisis in China in the 1980s saw greater American predominance in establishing itself militarily in a more entrenched manner than ever before. American warships and entire fleets roam international ports of call with limited local resistance. Its nuclear-powered aircraft carriers are designed to theoretically travel without stopping for two decades. These behemoths of the ocean are only restricted by the need to replenish the basic necessities for human consumption, and by the mental well-being of the crew. For these reasons, the globalized world of consumption would expect a significantly different variety of goods and services such as DVDs, PC CD-ROM games, and other technologically based products that would never have been thought of by sailors in the nineteenth century. This makes one wonder about the sort of goods and services that might be provided over the next half century.

The rise of Reaganomics would also result in the depletion and bankrupting of the Soviet military budget through the Star Wars programme. No one even knew that Star Wars might not work. The important point is the chase to end the Cold War came suddenly. Gorbachev's unfortunate twinned policies of *glasnost* and *perestroika* resulted in the internal exposure of a deeply corrupt and inefficient system within the Soviet Union and its Soviet satellite republics across Europe and Asia. Therefore, the politics of American globalization was achieved in a hurry very much by non-Americans themselves who, in their own attempts to compete with the superpower, failed to live up to the ideological and practical extent of their economics. The end of the Cold War and Bush Sr.'s announcement of the new world order in 1990 unleashed the hope of having freer trade now that the command economy had proven itself unproductive and irrelevant for the progressive economics of the twentieth century.

However, Bush's new world order did not see any dramatic increase in free trade in Asia even by 1999, a decade after the Cold War had ended. The Asian Free Trade Agreement (AFTA) is still standing as a possible ideal goal for the future but the responses from Southeast Asian countries, for example, have been mixed. At a more dangerous level, the North Koreans continue to expect special treatment from the United States. The communist North is also vilified by the continuing American military presence in the South. There was a great possibility for a limited but destructive war emerging in the Korean peninsula as the North Korean harvest failed and its ageing political leadership went through a difficult period covering up the death of Kim Il Sung in 1994. Policy analysts at RAND were concerned as far back as 1989 about Kim's preparation for nuclear war with the South. There is a continuing need for American executive intervention in North Korea as seen in June 1994 and August 2003 when North Korea felt that it was under threat from Western imperialist powers, notably the United States, because of its ideological beliefs that must appear problematic, if not totally anachronistic, to some of its left-wing critics within the controlling political party.

The Chinese themselves desire American wealth and support for the old Most Favoured Nation (MFN) status. The Chinese Communist Party (CCP) wants the wealth without the responsibilities that are attached to democratization. The CCP and the top leadership's actions during the Tiananmen Square episode is a case in point. Depending on your point of view and your perspective, it might have been a massacre, a pro-democracy movement, a class-struggle, a counter-revolutionary struggle, an act of sabotage, or the work of terrorists. Again, depending on where you ground your political values and ideological vantage point, it would appear that Tiananmen in 1989 was an overt act of state control and intimidation against a political movement designed to weaken the CCP. Naturally, the next big place to democratize is communist China, and despite the academic and political rhetoric about the One China Policy, it seems very clear that Taiwan is a sovereign and independent country on its own with a visibly different set of values and principles since it thwarted Mao's intention to complete the People's War in 1955. However, whether or not the United States will interfere with Taiwanese or Chinese sovereignty seems moot now. On the one hand, the United States officially recognizes only China. On the other hand, it has sent its fleet into the straits again. There appear to be mixed signals coming from the United States and this is where Americans might become embroiled in another hot war if it does indeed break out. A third perspective presents itself in terms of the literature on brinkmanship and the extent to which each side might be bluffing through the mobilization of military and paramilitary units along their coastlines.

The view from Asia is one of a political balancing act between and among three capital cities, two in Asia, one in North America. The Chinese have believed for a long time that Taiwan, the last frontier and renegade since the People's War of Liberation in 1949, will eventually be reunited with the mainland. Beijing fears that if it backs down on the Taiwan issue, the island will become an entrenched bastion of democracy for overseas and local Chinese democrats who have now tasted the fresh and variegated fruit of Western neoliberal capitalism. Should ASEAN intervene? Are economic sanctions from the United States signposted along the road to Chinese democratization and capitalism? Lee Kuan Yew, Minister Mentor of Singapore, has argued forcibly for the inevitability of China's rise to power through its manufacturing base. He has argued that the twenty-first century is the Pacific Century and that the motor behind Asian resurgence is China.

DISCOMFITURE WITH AMERICA

Despite the widespread discomfort with American presence throughout Asia and in spite of its winning the Cold War without firing a single shot, there continue to be deeply held anti-American sentiments in Asia. On a lighter note, its allies, such as Singapore — a republic without republican values — would periodically lay down the law against American interference. For example, the deportation of Mason Hendrickson mentioned earlier.[16] Singapore under Prime Minister Lee Hsien Loong will be no less tough, despite the third prime minister's jocular demeanour and diplomacy. In Malaysia, the federal government in Kuala Lumpur vehemently rejected American claims in 2003 about a clandestine meeting of Al-Qaeda related operatives in its capital Kuala Lumpur that was alleged to have occurred before the 9/11 terrorist attacks. The United States later agreed that the meeting did not take place. Social scientists from top-notch universities in America have found difficulties penetrating and understanding Malaysian politics and culture. There is bureaucratic resistance and foot-dragging because the political masters, especially when Mahathir was in charge, were anti-American in many ways. For example, when he was in power, Mahathir launched his "Look East Policy" which was designed to emulate Japanese methods of teamwork and values as opposed to Western and American norms of trade unionist activism. While visiting the leader of the National Justice Party (now a fledgling opposition party in Malaysia), the former U.S. Vice-President Al Gore antagonized Malaysia's incumbent leaders. Al Gore is neither known for a John F. Kennedy–like charisma or possessing the wit and stature of Ronald Reagan, however, he certainly was able to ruffle Malaysian cabinet ministers' feathers:

> Among nations suffering economic crisis, we continue to hear calls for democracy in many languages, "People Power", "Doi Moi", "Reformasi", Mr. Gore said at a dinner that included Malaysia's top leadership. "We hear them today — right here, right now — among the brave people of Malaysia." The speech stunned and infuriated Malaysian government officials. So tense has the political situation been in Kuala Lumpur over the last few months that using the word "reformasi" in public has landed many protesters in prison. "It's the most disgusting speech I have ever heard in my life," said the trade minister, Rafidah Aziz, a close ally of Prime Minister Mahathir bin Mohamad. "I hope I never live to hear another one from anyone like that." "There are narrow-minded people in this world," she said, "but certainly that reflects an unabashed intervention into local affairs" (*International Herald Tribune*, 1998).

Much to the chagrin of the dominant local political climate, Gore praised the Reformasi supporters of the imprisoned former Malaysian Deputy Prime Minister Anwar Ibrahim.[17] In Malaysia, it is not considered appropriate behaviour when you are a visitor in someone's home to criticize that person's home from within his house. This is considered taboo in Malaysia, as it was in Singapore's "Hendrickson Affair". What is interesting is that no other American leader who was actually in Malaysia has criticized it openly.[18]

Gore's comments unleashed a torrent of outrage from indignant politicians and newspapers amid charges that he was interfering in Malaysian affairs. Prime Minister Mahathir Mohamad described Gore's remarks as "disrespectful" and "offensive". Foreign Minister Abdullah Ahmad Badawi branded the remarks "unwarranted", "provocative", and "abhorrent". Saying that the United States would be responsible for any "rupture" in Malaysia's multiracial harmony, he accused Gore of supporting a "form of terrorism".

> [Ambassador] John Malott defended Gore on Friday, saying he only called for democracy and was not inciting people to violence.... Malaysia could not be called a democracy just because it held elections. "Democracy is not simply having elections," he said. "Stalin held elections. Even Hitler held elections".[19]

Gore drew attention from the local and regional media because of the Anwar case. Anwar was a young, highly capable and rational political leader and former Deputy President of the largest race-based political party in Malaysia called UMNO. The United Malays National Organization (UMNO) is *primus inter pares* in the National Front (NF). The NF, also known as the Barisan Nasional (BN), is the political umbrella for all the other dominant political parties that have ruled the Federation since 1971. The BN was the creation of ethnic riots in 13 May 1969 after a state of emergency had been declared because of fighting between Malays and Chinese. Malaysia has not seen such massive and widespread riots since those heady days of ethnic chauvinism and communist insurgents. Anwar was spotted by Mahathir when he was a student activist. Because of Anwar's background in Islamic Studies, he was very capable of swinging the right-wing Malay ground towards the moderate centre UMNO party. Anwar was also marginalized from UMNO at the onset because of his radical views and hence reminded Mahathir very much of himself when he first started his political career in the 1960s.

Unlike Mahathir, who was professionally trained as a medical doctor at the University of Malaya in Singapore, Anwar Ibrahim had a humanities background with a specialization in Islamic Studies that made him more in touch with the people, the *ummah*, or the universal brotherhood of Muslims. He became like the hero in one of Chinua Achebe's novels, *A Man of the People*. Or perhaps like one of the anti-heroes in *A Hundred Years of Solitude*. However, critics and ordinary people alike are divided over what really happened in terms of his sacking. Some say that he was sacked because he was planning to unseat Mahathir. This would have been considered an act of gross ungratefulness in Malaysian politics. Another argument involves a counter-factual suggestion that it was about political revenge by powerful politicians, much more senior in age and experience than Anwar, but who were passed over during Anwar's meteoric rise to power. The official reason for Anwar being sentenced to six years imprisonment was because he had committed sodomy, a crime in Malaysia.

In 2003, Prime Minister Mahathir Mohamad made more anti-Semitic remarks. Mahathir said that the Jews were behind 9/11. However, he defended his remarks by saying that they were taken out of context and that he meant no offence by saying that Jews ruled the world. In his speech at the fifty-six member Organization of the Islamic Conference (OIC), Mahathir said, "Jews rule the world by proxy. They get others to fight and die for them" (*CNN*, 2003; *BBC*, 2003; *IHT*, 2003). He said that Muslims had achieved "nothing" in their fifty years of struggle against Israel, citing the fact that Jews had invented powerful ideological arguments like socialism, communism, human rights, and democracy. As a result, Mahathir said, Jews "gained control of the most powerful countries and they, this tiny community, have become a world power". He expressed surprise that over a billion Muslims could be held at bay by only "a few million Jews". Naturally, the speech drew a mixed bag of responses. The OIC members gave him a standing ovation. But the United States, Europe, Israel, and Australia regretted his statement:

> "Prime Minister Mahathir's bluster and polarizing rhetoric are not new", a senior [White House] administration official said. "But his most recent hate-filled remarks further cement his legacy of outrageous and misguided public statements. We urge leaders of all faiths to publicly condemn these vile statements" (*CNN*, 2003).

The United Kingdom's Foreign Office contacted Malaysia's High Commissioner, Mohammed Dato Abdul Aziz, and "expressed concern" over Prime Minister Mahathir's comments in his speech:

> It's unfortunate that Mahathir chose to make these remarks which we regard as unacceptable. It's particularly regrettable that some of his positive and welcome messages, such as negotiation being the right path to peace and the futility of terrorism, have been obscured and overshadowed by racist remarks (*CNN*, 2003).

Known for his powerful rhetoric, confrontational remarks, and provocative leadership, Mahathir has shown himself to be a wily politician who had held on to power for over twenty-two years, until he transferred power to his deputy, Abdullah Badawi[20] in October 2003. This makes him Asia's second longest serving prime minister. Because there are no term limits to Malaysia's form of democratic governance, Mahathir had served continuously as prime minister over five U.S. presidential administrations from the time of Jimmy Carter to George W. Bush. If one were to include the time he had spent in politics, including the time he served in the Dewan (Malaysian federal Parliament), one would have to include three more U.S. presidential administrations: those of Lyndon B. Johnson, Richard M. Nixon, and Gerald R. Ford. In his two decades as prime minister, Mahathir antagonized many heads of government and is not known to be a man who minces his words but better known for his "rationalistic" economic policies.

Apart from his lack of cultural sensitivity, Mahathir has been known for making very persuasive arguments. For example, when most democracy-inclined Asian countries were looking towards the U.S. economy and Western MNCs for economic development, Mahathir told his public to look eastwards towards Japan (and then later, China but in a limited sense). His "*kampung* economics" or village economics resulted in his rejection of the IMF aid package that was offered with several strings attached during the 1997–98 Asian currency crisis. If he had not pegged the Malaysian ringgit and had followed IMF suggestions, the Malaysian economy would have been in turmoil and started a deep downward spiral towards economic depression. But whether or not Mahathir's "*kampung* economics" was a result of his wariness of the IMF as being controlled by the United States is another matter. Mahathir was not alone. For example, in late April 2004, the Acting Managing Director of the IMF Anne Krueger herself mentioned before a joint IMF–World Bank meeting that the IMF "may have contributed in some instances to insufficient spending on infrastructure, at least in the short run".[21]

However, after Mahathir handed power over to Badawi, the Malaysian bureaucrats and senior politicians quickly turned away and began re-aligning themselves with the new crew. Indeed Mahathir's eventual scathing attacks on Badawi in 2006 and 2007 brought him little support either from his old party or from his own supporters. After Mahathir stepped down from power he lost his political ground. Pak Lah (Badawi) who is not known for openly criticizing anyone severely in public, gave Mahathir's rantings and ravings a wide berth. But eventually he did imply that it was Mahathir's economic policies and big spending that resulted in the massive debt from construction projects in and around KL. Americans watched silently as they saw Mahathir fall from power and fall from grace until he was hospitalized. After he recovered from his illness, he went on the attack again, saying that without the NEP and later, the NDP, the *bumiputra* would fall behind all other ethnic categories. In 2007, some estimates suggest that about 9 out of every 100 *bumiputra* lived below the poverty line as compared to 4 out of every 100 non-*bumiputra*. He continued to imply that the Malays have developed a crutch mentality and the fact that they make up a large majority of the Malaysian population would mean that if the NDP and future affirmative action programmes were removed, the country might slip into riots again as it did in the mid-1960s that eventually led to the implementation of the NEP in 1971.

"Asia's discomfort with America" can be summed up in terms of what is perceived as the politics of interference by a global hegemonic power.

THE OTHER WAY AROUND: THE POLITICAL PARADOX

When we talk about American globalization in Asia, we are really referring to a political paradox. This political paradox allows for a minority of people who have bothered, to vote consecutive governments into power while most of the silent majority (might have) made it to limited protests, remained apathetic, or were consumed by their own struggles.

> ...the US is basically a one-party state — the business party with two factions, Democrats and Republicans. Most of the population seems to agree. A very high percentage, sometimes passing 80%, believe that the

government serves "the few and the special interests," not "the people". In the contested 2000 election, about 75% regarded it as mostly a farce having nothing to do with them, a game played by rich contributors, party bosses, and the public relations industry, which trained candidates to say mostly meaningless things that might pick up some votes. This was BEFORE the actual election, with the accusations of fraud and selection of Bush with a minority of the popular vote.[22]

While many may not agree with the socialist politics of Noam Chomsky, he does make an interesting point about the support that the American people really have for their government. The 2000 presidential election was clearly a result of institutional lethargy backed by a conservative Republican Supreme Court. That is how Bush came to be in charge. While Chomsky's influence is a direct result of his work at MIT in linguistics, his politics is not entirely convincing because it does not appear to answer many of the questions that are raised by American liberals. However, he does have a point with regard to representative politics and reality. It seems that the American people's lethargic attitude towards the government has resulted in the government doing whatever it thinks best anyway. And this affects the nature of its global presence everywhere in the world.

America cannot help but interfere in politics overseas and in this case, in the politics of Asia. It appears that the kind of liberalism exported by American government is the kind that needs to engage with the people and their communities. It is the kind of ideological politics that is universalistic in nature, where the standards of value and morality are clearly defined by those in power. It is particularly distressing for Asian countries that have their own traditions, rights and wrongs, moral belief systems, and customary practices. American government overseas is often, though not always, insensitive to the practices of foreigners in their own land. It is also about punishment. It is about punishing the unconvinced until they are converted. American government is often unable to accept the fact that there are people whose ideas and value systems are different from those of the Western democratic tradition. This is more than ironic; it is a political paradox.

The first part of the paradox is the fact that American government overseas is aggressive to the point of bullying smaller nations. The United States has conducted wide scale offensive, defensive, retrograde, and covert military operations throughout Asia and the Pacific. The USAF are capable of attacking any point in the world, let alone Asia, at the behest of the commander-in-chief. The U.S. Army has more continuous combat military experience in Southeast Asia than any other land or amphibious army in the world and any other time in history. The U.S. Navy has virtual control of all international waters (let alone Asia and the Pacific) and continues to move freely to dominate and control without hindrance or challenge since 1989. America dominates most of the world without necessarily controlling all of it all of the time. U.S. Government is therefore for all intents and purposes hegemonic and supreme. Such military dominance cannot find a conventional adversary. This is why the terrorists are so successful. Conventional warfare is unable to fight terrorism. Nuclear warfare is way out of the ballpark. Such military dominance also finds that many smaller nations react with fear, hatred, and suspicion. Many nations with large Islamic populations, such as Malaysia, Indonesia, and China, pose potential problems for anti-terrorist organizations. Such military power is often reciprocated with political platitudes and rhetoric that arise out of feelings of fear for the safety of their own country. No country in Asia wants to be branded another Iraq because no one can stop the invading power of an American military attack.

The second part of the paradox is that Americans have elected successive American presidents who all share some common ground when it comes to foreign policy. In effect, the old adage about Democratic presidents being doves and Republicans being more hawkish is completely untrue. There is very little evidence to support ideological differences between Democratic or Republican presidents. This leaves us with over 200 years of data that will prove beyond reasonable doubt that U.S. presidents are generally hawkish on foreign policy and doves on domestic policy. This might be why they score well on foreign policy initiatives that are relatively more removed from the average Joe Smith and Jane Doe than are domestic ones which directly affect these citizens. So far we have a situation where America dominates militarily through the threat of inflicting political violence. We also have a situation where political party ideologies are generally irrelevant to the formulation of foreign policy and where U.S. presidents are fairly consistent in pursuing their foreign policies regardless of party differences.

Now comes the interesting part of the paradox: the people. They are the ones who have elected these presidents and these governments which have generated these politics of fear and control. The American people, however, often do not support the kinds of policies that have emitted from successive U.S. presidencies. The American people are often against the kinds of atrocities committed by Americans on locals overseas and committed on Americans by locals overseas. In fact, voter turnout for most American elections is low. A majority of about 35–43 per cent do not support what the American government is doing overseas. Naturally, right-wing Americans might tend to believe that whatever the government does is best for the country. But they are in a minority of about 8–13 per cent. On the other hand are Americans who actively oppose American intervention wherever and however it might be executed throughout the world. Therefore the political paradox arises because most Americans do not support most of the different kinds of U.S. government policies overseas, because most Americans do not go to the polls. There are, of course, various reasons for this, though a discussion of this issue is not the scope of this book. The political paradox arises because most Americans do not support the kinds of policies that are implemented overseas but have to pay the price for being American. Ordinary American citizens continue to be targets for kidnappers, terrorists, blackmailers, and fundamentalists because of the kinds of foreign policies that are promulgated by American governments supported by a minority of Americans. This is why Americans seem to believe in one thing but their government appears to do something else.

American foreign policy is shaped and influenced by think-tanks such as RAND, independent social scientists, military advisers, the American media, and covert operations by the CIA. This does not mean that there has always been a coordinated and singular mission for all Asian countries and the rest of the world. The U.S. system of government and politics is built on checks and balances of power and interlocking institutional validation. The framers of the Constitution had intended this system of checks and balances to prevent the kind of absolutist abuse that featured in King George's England. They wanted to circumvent the authority of dynasties with monarchs who had ruled by fear and complete subjectivity. This is why American political institutions tend to compete for influence over the public domain rather than complement one another. In competing for power, there is a clear and added advantage of showing independently how objective and productive one can be with limited resources in a given time frame. This is very unlike the British system where senior administrative servants with years of cumulative experience slowly percolate ideas downwards from their political masters and upwards towards them; they do not compete for influence over one another. Rather, the British system involves behind the scenes discussions and agreements among the top civil service heads who often have the same Oxonian educational background and whose families have met at the same clubs for generations. The American system desires creativity out of competition while the British system tries to instil discipline and creativity through what that famous English philosopher Edmund Burke called the "wisdom of the ages". The wisdom of the ages involves incremental and gradual decision-making that is based on careful and logical deduction from as many possible views sharing their knowledge at the same time. The American system involves independently creating different subsystems that have to discover their own means of achieving the mission. This is why American policy in Asia and the rest of the world sometimes appears inchoate or contradictory. This is why there appear to be different systems of management handling different situations rather than a singular whole. The problem for America was that after 9/11, this old method of institutional independence was seen to be theoretically weak, especially in terms of intelligence-gathering and analysis. Although in theory such a system ought to be superior and produce different and creative points of view, when push came to shove the American method did not produce the kinds of results that were intended. Hence, the creation of the DHS and its various integrative bureaus that connect intelligence, security, political, legal, research, and civil society groups. Critics of the new political institutionalism and supporters of the philosophy of the founding fathers believe that it is executive malfeasance that has led to the inability to react rather than the institutions themselves. For example, through the congressional deliberations and meetings on the matter of 9/11, many felt that sufficient intelligence and early warning was presented to Bush for him to act but he failed. If you had listened to the testimony of Condoleezza Rice, Bush's national security adviser, you might have wondered what exactly was done and why was it done in such a manner. The President defended his position by stating that the intelligence reports were not specific enough to act on.

The problem of political institutionalism or executive disorder and the creation of new departments are not of particular concern here. Rather, the key is for Americans to realize that their overseas identities are being determined by a minority of people who bother to vote and participate fully in the American political process. Americans are also politically apathetic and while one set of demonstrations are raised over one issue, the matter soon fizzles out of social memory except for social scientists to analyse years later.

OIL

It is hard to understand why some people earnestly believe that the United States is interested in the Middle East for altruistic reasons such as human rights or non-oil trade. American troops were not trying to keep the peace in the Sudan, the Republic of Congo, East Timor, or Kashmir. The reason is because these places do not produce sufficient quantities of oil for export to make them sufficiently attractive and worth the trouble of establishing diplomatic relations, economic, social and cultural exchanges, and military assistance. Inasmuch as the United States is interested in preventing war from breaking out between China and Taiwan because of the gross amount of investments that it has in both countries, there is a similar reason why the Middle East peace process appears to be a never-ending story. A country's foreign policy is always dictated by its national interest. And the national interest of America's MNCs and Military Industrial Complex that control much of American life is "oil". We should recall at this point that the *Ship of Fools* metaphor suggests that the only reason why the United States is so interested in the Middle East is oil. Oil sustains American neoliberal globalization. Democracy, protecting Israel, ensuring the safety of Americans, or promoting free trade or world peace are only secondary objectives. The U.S. State Department knows full well that without oil, the entire U.S. economy will collapse, and the American Dream will implode. This is a fact. The two Gulf Wars were ostensibly about removing dictators like Saddam Hussein (the Shah of Iran and his troops committed similar atrocities when they were in power). The real reasons are the oil fields beneath Basra in Southern Iraq. Some analysts say it is between 5–7 per cent of total world production per day. Others say the figures are much higher, perhaps high enough to solve American oil problems for the next quarter of a century. There are also sufficient oil and natural gas reserves in that region to make anyone want to invest in a stable and democratic Iraq. For example, in his story that begins with the death of a *Ship of the Desert*, John Cassidy argues that:

> With the exception of its Southern neighbor, Saudi Arabia, Iraq has more oil buried underneath it than any country in the world: a hundred and twelve billion barrels in confirmed reserves ... more than six hundred wells, which produce three streams of crude: Basra Regular, Basra Medium, and Basra Heavy. The oil is trapped at such high pressure that when a well is drilled it gushes out by itself, so there is no need for the "nodding donkeys".[23]

American national interest in the Middle East, or in the Straits of Malacca or in China and Taiwan, is really about protecting America and Americans. These and many other places serve as important and strategic locations for ensuring the smooth flow of American goods and services. So the main reason why America seems to be everywhere is because it is safeguarding the American way of life, perhaps the American Dream, and certainly not merely for human rights assistance or aid for natural disasters. Is there anything wrong with possessing such overt and Machiavellian stratagems? Not if America remains a benign hegemony that truly believes in free trade and not the new protectionism disguised as free trade.

THE FIGHT AGAINST TERROR

There are compelling reasons to believe that there are significant terrorist networks in the Southeast Asian region, South Asia, and the Middle East where the hatred of Americans and Jews appears to be most severe. However, the U.S. Department of State in February 2004 also believed that there were strong indications of a fundamentalist Islamic presence in China. While Chinese Muslims are a minority, the numbers are not insignificant. It is not inconceivable to consider that out of the twenty million Chinese Muslims, a handful of fundamentalists may be easily linked to acts of terror and terrorist training. Twenty million is about the population of Malaysia which is in turn about the size of New Mexico. For example, even as far removed as China was from the Middle East, the voice of the Islamic Association of China could be heard: "Islam advocates peace and more than 20 million Chinese Muslims love peace and oppose war" (*Times of India*, 22 March 2003). Clearly this was not only a kind of resistance against the wrongful American invasion that went against UN resolutions and the UN Security Council, the resistance also reflected a move by the Islamic Association of China to establish a political connection with other Muslims across the globe who shared the same sentiment. Not surprisingly, the U.S. State Department also fears that from among the 20 million members that the Islamic Association of China claims to represent are a minority group of right-wing fundamentalists who support aggressive action against the United States and its allies.

China has undergone rapid changes in state and society since deMaoization and the implementation of the four modernizations. The end of the Cold War left China without its sometime ally, the USSR. The end of the Cold War weakened international socialism. Chinese communism has succeeded because it is socialism with Chinese characteristics. The adaptive Chinese strategy of having pockets of capitalist development was not a clever reconstitution of its political ideology to suit global capitalist pressures, but a realist reaction from having no choice at all. China was thus forced to recognize that the United States was now the clear ideological victor. As the world's most populous nation and the ideological adversary of the United States, it would now be expected to make concessions at some level. As a result, China has indeed become a little less inscrutable and has made moves to impress upon the United States that it is more of a friend, and at the worst, not an enemy. The United States has "rewarded" China several times with most favoured nation (MFN) status along with millions of dollars of investments. Many Chinese of the younger generation in the larger cities, such as Shanghai, Guangzhou, Nanjing, and Jinan have begun to mimic American popular culture.

American globalization in China is therefore looming on the horizon as a kind of counter-culture that the state authorities are keeping an eye on. At the same time, the strength and value of the greenback as an international currency benchmark in the post-Bretton Woods era has grown from strength to strength in China since the end of the Mao era. Chinese authorities are beginning to realize the value of American English and an American university education. Many Chinese see the value of the green card as a ticket out of poverty. Despite the severe setbacks of 9/11 and the anxieties with global terrorism, America is still attractive to foreign migrants. This is part of the power of American global politics. The day that America is no longer attractive enough for people to want to migrate to is the day that marks the end of the American era. This happened to Italy in the fifteenth century. It began in France and the United Kingdom in the twentieth century. It might happen to America in the twenty-first century. There are over 600 cities in China and one can imagine that each of those cities, with millions of people, are potential targets for some kind of international fast food chain in the classic style of the McDonald's Corporation.

Furthermore, the Chinese authorities have cracked down on Chinese Muslims. Whether or not this was politically motivated is not the question; it definitely was. The question is what kind of politics were involved in motivating the police attacks and the state intervention. The issue of Islamic terrorism takes on different avenues of interpretation. Often, innocent Muslims might be victimized and the point remains about the quid pro quo of it all:

> ... a group of young men kneel together for evening prayers ... from the Koran ... The men, all Turkic-speaking Uighurs, cannot worship at any of Shanghai's half-dozen mosques, as they would risk being spotted by undercover police informants searching for suspected Islamic militants (United Press International, 2002).

We see that the United States is indeed considered an important nation for China, and the Chinese authorities have gone out of their way to display resolve. But the question remains whether the state authorities can see the forest of innocence for the trees of the guilty in the case of the Uighur:

> ... Following the Sept. 11 attacks in the United States, China launched a major offensive in Xinjiang, sending soldiers into the region's cities and towns to close mosques and arrest scores of suspected separatists ... Uighurs ... have been the main target — mosques have been closed down, Islamic clergy have been detained, and Uighur books have been

> burnt ... Thousands of young Muslim men fled to other regions ... such as Tajikistan and Kyrgyzstan, slipping out through China's porous mountain borders. In January, China published a lengthy report alleging the East Turkestan Islamic Movement [ETIM] ... had received money, weapons and training from Osama bin Laden's al-Qaeda... "Jailing community leaders and intellectuals on trumped up 'state secrets' charges and repressing Uighur culture has nothing to do with combating 'terrorism,'" Amnesty said. It is a systematic denial of basic human rights ... the U.S. State Department said it had added the ETIM to its list of terrorist organizations and agreed to freeze the group's assets (United Press International, 2002).

Here again we see the power of American liberalism in the argument being made by Amnesty International. While the Chinese state is eager to display a strong anti-terrorist stand, the way it has gone about making such a stand has made it appear rather duplicitous. Amnesty International saw the human rights violations coming, as it is indeed a very thin and perhaps even vague line between what these militant Chinese groups do and what they are perceived to be doing. China takes its sovereignty very seriously, as do all other states in the globalized world. Subversion is a very serious threat to state security and it becomes very difficult for any state authority to prove the extent and depth of subversion since the normal laws of evidence do not seem to apply to those hoping to overthrow legitimate governments. However, it was not just the Chinese authorities who were working on the anti-terrorist aspect. Apart from the Chinese intelligence reports and police reports about these activities, the Americans had their hand in this pie too:

> Less than a week later, the U.S. embassy in Beijing said for the first time it had evidence that the group was planning terrorist attacks on foreign embassies and interests in Bishkek, the capital of Kyrgyzstan. "We have evidence that the ETIM have been planning attacks against U.S. interests abroad," a U.S. embassy spokeswoman told UPI, refusing to comment on the apparent shift in policy. China's foreign ministry in Beijing refused a request to answer specific questions from UPI about the U.S. allegations against the ETIM, but instead issued a brief statement welcoming last week's decision (United Press International, 2002).

The changes and twists and turns in American policy indicate that the top people do not always know what they are doing and hence the answer, like China, is to hide behind the iron curtain of bureaucratic secrecy. This means that the information will eventually be leaked in some other way. So the next step for the state is, naturally, to offer even more rhetoric about how two ideological enemies are actually capable of cooperation:

> "China is prepared to make joint efforts, enhance mutual consultations and deepen bilateral co-operation with the US in the fight against terrorism," the foreign ministry statement said ... the U.S. State Department's listing of the ETIM as a terrorist group means Xinjiang's struggling liberation movement is now fighting a war on two fronts: one at home, against the Chinese government's repressive policies, and the other overseas, to win back the support of the international community. "We are completely shocked by the U.S. allegations," he said ... To date, neither government has provided verifiable proof of a link between bin Laden and the separatists in Xinjiang, though U.S.-led forces in Afghanistan did capture Chinese Muslims fighting with the Taliban ... Hasan Mahsum, the ETIM's leader and China's most-wanted fugitive, denied allegations that his group had ties with bin Laden and al-Qaeda during an interview with Radio Free Asia in January. But the existence of such a group has apparently been enough to convince the Bush administration, and Uighurs say they fear the U.S. move will further sanction China to crush any remaining peaceful dissent. "We are fighting for our freedom, not for the overthrow of Western governments," said Tusin. "Our anger is not directed against the U.S. and the international community, but against the Chinese government" (United Press International, 2002).

It should also be noted that with the loss of over US$8 billion worth of oil reserves when the Shah of Iran fell to Islamic "revolutionaries" in 1979, the United States decided that an alternative pipeline to the Russian oil fields would be the most viable alternative. Therefore the war in Afghanistan is also about oil and not merely about the search for Osama. Perhaps the Uighurs were too politically embattled or naive to understand the connection with oil. The Chinese authorities are not as duplicitous as their war on their "own citizens" appears. After all, since the ETIM has openly declared a war against the Chinese Government, it has given the state no other choice but to do whatever it can to prevent the overthrow. No other secessionist movement in China has worked for so many dynasties. It seems unlikely that the ETIM, even with Amnesty's soft power help, is likely to succeed. Amnesty officials are themselves considered suspects within the intelligence game because they are clearly not asking the rebels/freedom fighters to lay down their weapons. Despite the expression of American diplomatic concerns, the ETIM rebels appear to have done what Osama had done many years before when, ironically, he was trained by the Americans themselves. They have gone underground. Going underground in a globalized world means that they can surface almost anywhere in the world and at any time through almost any one. The amount of resources that would be needed by China and America to stage a specific war would erode the value of economic investments in China from American sources.

Writers like Lowell Dittmer may claim that the biggest problem of globalization in East Asia is the problem of regionalism, and while internationally influential scholars like Katzenstein might tend to agree with the importance of the regionalization thesis, the question for America in particular remains to be one of commitment and cultural sensitivity to the local labour and social practices.

AMERICA AND THE ASIAN CURRENCY CRISIS: A DEEPER EXPLANATION

The U.S. sub-prime loan market continues to wreak havoc as Americans reject the political solution to what is essentially an economic problem. The U.S. dollar is likely to slide downwards until 2010. Alan Greenspan, the former foremost chairman of the Federal Reserve Board believes that all the indications of a U.S. recession are on the cards. China and India have both bought massive amounts of U.S. government bonds. The world's economies are deeply tied to the American one. If America goes down, so will many people and many jobs across the world. That is the underbelly of globalization. Yet sometimes the problem arises outside the United States.

Indeed, most Asians are unlikely to link America to the 1997 Asian currency crisis except for what is perceived as a controlling role that America has over the IMF, and the ways in which the IMF tried to influence the economies that were affected. But there was much more involved. For almost a decade before the currency crisis (sometimes called the financial crisis), the Thai economy was experiencing high single-digit economic growth. Unethical and greedy currency speculators, noticing the structural weaknesses in the Thai system, began making deep speculative attacks on the Thai baht that forced the military-led government to float the currency on the international market. This further exposed the softness of the currency. The speculative attacks reaped huge profits for the American based speculators who left the Thai Government vulnerable except for a quickly put together IMF aid package that helped stem the currency's free fall in value. The crisis in Thailand revealed that the construction industry had been financially over-extended and currency speculators' attempts to make a quick dollar resulted in catalysing what could have been contained at the national level. However, the level of corruption prevented an earlier diagnosis that could have thwarted the problem. The crisis in Thailand reached such dramatic proportions because of the speculative attacks from the outside and because of the unbridled greed and corruption on the inside. Speculative attacks were not limited to the baht but were also aimed at the Hong Kong dollar, the Indonesian rupiah, the Malaysian ringgit, and even the Philippine peso. While the South Korean won and the Singapore dollar remained relatively unscathed because of their sound economic fundamentals compared to the other Asian countries, the currency crisis spearheaded by the currency speculators also put strong pressure on these two countries' economies.

Also, the close connection between Asian currencies and the U.S. dollar meant that any changes in financial movements in any of the Asian stock exchanges would bear an impact on other bourses in the region. The crisis exposed the weak structural defects in the local banking and financial structures that were themselves caught in a heated race to develop faster growth with limited financial liberalization. More importantly, the financial crisis caused panic and shrank foreign investments costing billions of U.S. dollars which undermined investor confidence in the region. The result was obvious. Southeast Asian share markets went into a recessionary spiral that lasted for almost six months as hundreds of thousands lost their jobs. The economic disparities between the richest rich and the poorest poor also increased in Indonesia, South Korea, Malaysia, Thailand, and the Philippines, reflecting the kinds of income differentials experienced by so-called "First World" nations under a recessionary climate. However, the remarkable economic growth of the fastest growing region in the world — East Asia and Southeast Asia — meant that these countries had achieved in ten years what it took the West decades to achieve. The financial crisis had severe political implications. Thai Prime Minister at that time, General Chavalit Yongchaiyudh was forced to step down and dissolve his Cabinet because of his inability, inter alia, to steer the country out of the recession in sufficient time. Most evidently, the crisis saw the end of the authoritarian rule of Indonesian President Suharto who had governed since the mid-1960s and who had personally overseen the rapid modernization of Indonesia, especially Java, the annexation of Timor in 1975, and the forced migration of ethnic communities across its 17,000 islands.

Timor, for example, was a former colony of the mercantilist colonial power of the Portuguese and made a self-declaration of independence from Lisbon on 28 November 1975. The Portuguese could do nothing. However, Suharto's troops — some of whom were allegedly involved in the "false" declaration of independence — illegally invaded and occupied the island. The UN, the United States, and Portugal were unable to prevent the atrocities that were to develop. Over the next two decades from 1976 to 1996, over a quarter of a million individuals were allegedly tortured and killed by Indonesian armed forces. On 30 August 1999, a UN-sponsored referendum unseated the dictatorial stranglehold of Suharto as the Timorese voted unanimously for independence, this time from the Indonesian colonizers. However, Indonesia, under successor-elected presidents since Suharto fell from power in 1998, continued a pogrom of violence to prevent political independence from Jakarta. Despite the atrocities allegedly committed by the soldiers of recent presidential contender Indonesian General Wiranto, the former Indonesian colony of "East Timor" was finally recognized worldwide as an independent and sovereign state on 20 May 2002.

It is interesting how the United States showed an exceptional level of disinterest in this situation. Perhaps the main reason is that Timor does not pose a direct threat to the United States, nor perhaps ever will. Neither does it interest the United States in economic terms. Or perhaps it is the State Department's tacit recognition of what might have been considered to fall under the Portuguese sphere of influence up till 1975. Wiranto had been commander of the troops in the final days of Suharto's regime and also served under B.J. Habibie and Abdurrahman Wahid.[24] As the former military chief of Indonesia, Wiranto has said that he would not accept personal or legal responsibility for any crimes committed by his troops in East Timor. General Wiranto,

> was proud of his record, and would not resign his cabinet post because that might be interpreted as an admission of guilt. *The Straits Times* said, however, that the general had left open the possibility that he might resign if the Indonesian president demanded it on his return from overseas. Last week President Abdurrahman Wahid called for Wiranto's resignation after a government report blaming him for atrocities in East Timor. Indonesia's human rights commission recommended that he and five other senior generals be prosecuted for their involvement in the violence that followed last year's referendum on independence, in which at least 250 people died .... The president has said that he intends to pardon Wiranto even if he is found guilty of human rights abuses.... The president also confirmed that he had no intention of seeing the general imprisoned. He said, "I will pardon him. For the past several years we have been good friends, despite whatever he has done in the past" (*BBC News*, 8 January 2000).

Wiranto won Golkar's initial nomination for president easily even though he was:

> indicted for crimes against humanity in neighboring East Timor ...Wiranto's victory is expected to cause concern in the United States and other Western nations. *The Washington Post* reported in January that the US has put Wiranto and others accused of crimes in East Timor on a visa watch list that could bar them from entering the country. United Nations–funded prosecutors in East Timor indicted Wiranto last year over the Indonesian army-backed militia bloodshed during the territory's bloody breakaway from Jakarta in 1999.... "Monas Square did not become a second Tiananmen Square ... and for that the people have to thank him." The general's last public office was as security minister under [former] president Abdurrahman Wahid ... [who] sacked him in 2000 in what was seen at the time as a successful attempt to reduce the influence of the powerful military over the government. Wiranto launched a high-profile campaign for the Golkar nomination, flying to numerous speaking engagements across the archipelago and sometimes crooning to the crowds. He has issued a CD of his love songs. With 91.8 million votes counted so far from the general election, Golkar is set to replace President Megawati Sukarnoputri's Indonesian Democratic Party of Struggle (PDI-P) as the largest parliamentary party.[25]

The impact of Wiranto on the United States was one that most Americans probably did not even realize. Following the other Asian bourses like the Hang Seng, the Stock Exchange of Singapore, the Kuala Lumpur Stock Exchange, and the Nikkei, the Dow (in America) plunged about 8 per cent while the New York Stock Exchange was forced to suspend trading based on biased consumer sentiment and fears that the Asian economies might go into remission and collapse. This would mean that the over-extended banking loans by Japanese investors would cause the collapse of many companies in Japan that were trying to ride the East Asian and Southeast Asian economic wave to get out of their own economic doldrums. It was as if the wave collapsed right under them before even reaching its peak.

During the Asian currency crisis, Alan Greenspan argued for the important role that the IMF had to play in the face of stiff resistance from members of Congress from Republicans and Democrats alike. Greenspan said that "the IMF's role is to create 'a platform' for the reconstruction of market confidence in Asia".[26] Despite the work of pro-IMF supporters such as Greenspan, IMF apologists, and academic neoliberals who preferred to defend the IMF's so-called "market liberalization" policies, the failure of the IMF as an international organization speaks for itself.[27] The IMF almost, as Stiglitz argued, brought the world economy into a global meltdown. The IMF clearly displayed its inadequacy as an international organization. A compelling loss of the IMF's reputation was a result of its own agenda to impose its own brand of liberal economic "theory". If Malaysia had accepted the IMF's financial aid package and financial changes to its national financial system, it would have been a disaster for Malaysia and many other Southeast Asian countries. The paper by Makin, for example, suggested that "the recent financial crises of East Asia and other emerging financial economies have exposed major structural weaknesses in their banking sectors and financial systems, which have acted as the major conduits of foreign savings" (Makin 1999, p. 678). He went on to suggest that there was a need for such countries to follow rigorous international banking standards. If this had indeed been the case, the IMF's "aid package" and "political agenda" would have worsened the Asian financial crisis and made the recovery process last even longer. Doubts about the validity of the IMF in Asia also fuelled anti-American sentiment to a certain extent since the IMF is seen to be largely controlled by the United States.[28] A more convincing argument was made about the crisis by Henry Laurence, in his paper on "Financial System Reform and the Currency Crisis in East Asia".[29] One of his main conclusions, given the time that the paper was published, is understandable and makes sense.

The ongoing experience of Japan illustrates the political difficulties of reforming a financial system. Finance, more than any other sector, is liable to be closely interwoven with political control and therefore may be the hardest sector of all to liberalize. An absence of external pressures — for example, as can be inflicted either by speculative currency attack or the IMF — has meant that both Japan and China have been slower to undertake real reform than they should have been (Laurence 1999, p. 371).

What domestic bank in the West does not have structural problems? It is clear that in the Asian case, financial speculators like George Soros manipulated the weaknesses in the system to their advantage without considering the ethical impact on the entire economy. Rather than solve the problems as Makin and others in the minority have suggested, they would have made the recovery from the financial crisis a much longer and more difficult process. During the Clinton administration, U.S. "bargain hunters" who were "purchasing Asian enterprises fed sentiments hostile to Washington".[30] Do we really have to invoke Joseph Stiglitz's analysis of the Asian financial crisis to explain the level of idealism and ignorance in Makin's defence of the IMF? No matter how sound the financial structure might be, as often is the case, all it takes is for one person to demolish the entire structure.

Take the case of the oldest merchant bank in the United Kingdom. In 1995, the unethical and deceitful activities of a relatively unknown trader named Nicholas Leeson led to the demise of a world-renowned bank. Leeson was a 25-year-old Londoner with no real trading experience in Asia. He worked in Singapore at what is known as an unseated company called Baring Futures (Singapore) Pte Ltd. According to the *Final Report of the Bank of England* on this matter, the collapse of the oldest British merchant bank was a result of unauthorized work performed by Leeson in Singapore. Like other rogue traders, Leeson covered up his massive debts by creating the impression of confidence through false accounts, in a way that was similar to "the politics of the unethical" that led to the filing for Chapter 11 in the Enron case. Leeson also took advantage of an organizational restructuring of the parent company with the establishment of the Baring Investment Group. The reason for the collapse of the oldest British merchant bank was a simple one: the absence of supervision.

The bank should not have allowed Leeson to manage the whole operation unsupervised. Leeson was both the chief trader and head of settlements. It is the story of financial risk gone awry. The case shows a special kind of risk that speculators are willing to take regardless of the possibility of failure and the impact of such failure on the larger economy. Barings Bank had a very "sound" system that had worked for centuries. Formerly known as Baring Brothers and Company, it was founded in 1762 during the time of the philosophical Enlightenment in England. The bank collapsed on 26 February 1995. This is represented in "the false punishment of a false solution, but by its own virtue it brings to light the real problems which can then be truly resolved. It conceals beneath error the secret enterprise of truth" (Foucault [1965] 1988, p. 32).

On the topic of banks supervision, Singapore's Senior Minister Goh Chok Tong said in a *BBC* television interview in July 2007:

> We were worried...The crisis took on a very mega proportion when a few weeks later on, there was a currency meltdown — the Korean won, Malaysian ringgit, Indonesian rupiah ... very tragic for Indonesia....When the crisis came about, all of us were focused on resolving our problems and, of course, the Asian Tigers lost credibility. We became overnight the Asian Kittens, not the Asian Tigers. But at the same time, I was very happy that the countries which were less hit were rallying together to help the countries which were very badly hit. When Thailand was hit, Singapore, amongst others, pledged US$1 billion as part of a line of credit to be extended by the IMF.... when the crisis hit us, we widened the band for the Singapore dollar to fluctuate within. That made the

Singapore dollar more flexible. Of course, we have learnt from the crisis that we have to have better corporate governance. So the supervision of banks is better. But instead of just seeing banks from the point of a regulator, with a lot of regulations, we moved into disclosure-based supervision. In other words, we require banks to be more transparent. Let the market decide and the transparency of information is very important for the market players.... make sure that banks do not over lend, do not have a huge non-performing loans portfolio."... now [in 2007 there is] more trade between ASEAN countries and China and increasingly, there will be more trade between some of us in Southeast Asia and India. The trade between Singapore and India, for example, has gone up. This is so not only in the absolute sense but also in the relative sense. In other words, if you take trade between Singapore, Southeast Asia and China as a proportion of our total trade and compare it with the percentage of our trade with US, our trade with China has gone up. China is a very important factor. It's like a huge elephant getting into a swimming pool. So, it's going to displace other swimmers in the swimming pool. (*BBC TV*, July 2007)

Asia's response to the problem of globalization is a mixed bag of competitive economic policies, political will, futurism, and economic idealism that appears to make the states in this region not much different from other states in modernity. But there is a difference. The next section looks at the enterprising relations between America and some Asian countries. While all Asian countries deserve attention in this globalized world, these countries in particular seem to be of political and economic importance to the US: China, Japan, Malaysia, and Thailand.

CHINA AND THE UNITED STATES

Because China has about the same geographical land size as the contiguous United States, it produces the potential for a similar if not greater amount of current and potential natural resources as Vaclav Smil argues in "China's Energy and Resource Uses: Continuity and Change".[31]

China remained relatively unscathed during the 1997–98 currency crisis because it lagged behind the Tiger Economies in the capitalist rat-race for wealth. This had two main implications. Firstly, Chinese leaders could sit back and observe how the other Asian countries and the IMF scrambled to resolve the problems created by George Soros and other currency speculators, and secondly, it created a context in which investors, now wary of the Tiger Economies, were willing to look elsewhere in Asia where, for example, land

and labour costs were so minimal it would be inconceivable not to think about investing in China.

But China has political problems and foreigners are not always aware of the economic and cultural norms that govern Chinese business practices there, as seen in the Singapore case in Suzhou.[32] The transfer of software and economic modeling based on the Singapore experience was a US$13 billion investment. Singapore continues to be the sixth major investor in the Chinese mainland's city of Liaoning with over US$818 million invested (*Straits Times*, 21 April 2004). And the US continues to be the single largest investor in China.

China has been pursuing a very interesting course of propping up its foreign currency reserves by bulk-purchasing long-term U.S. government bonds. After Japan, China is the second largest purchaser of U.S. treasury bonds, which has become a major reason for the inflating U.S. deficit. Some financial analysts argue that a sudden stoppage of Chinese bond-buying would force U.S. interest rates upwards, although this was not verbalized by former Federal Reserve Chairman Alan Greenspan.

The Chinese are making a lot of sense by buying into stronger currencies through bond issues in Europe, Asia, and the United States with a threefold intention. Firstly, it gives the Chinese renminbi an external form of validation since it is currently not convertible in the ordinary sense of the word. Such validation results in strengthening the potential power of the renminbi or yuan, and increases investor confidence that its currency is potentially worth "that much" or "that little" in terms of its present exchange rate of about 8.28 yuan to the U.S. dollar. The second advantage of the Chinese bond-buying spree is that it prepares the currency for a strong beginning when officials finally decide that it can be floated internationally. However, it is unlikely that the State Administration of Foreign Exchange will press for floating it internationally in the near future since China continues to benefit from pegging the yuan at its current rate, which gives it complete control over its future rather than being left to the global pressures of currency movements in, for example, a given basket of currencies. The third advantage of the Chinese strategy is that China now has massive foreign exchange reserves of the greenback totalling close to US$450 billion in the second quarter of 2004. This means that American taxpayers will continue to bear the risk of being over-extended to Chinese purchases and over-exposed to the possibility of China's sudden stoppage of its buying spree — which would cause great inflationary pressures on the U.S. domestic economy.

The authoritarian structure of the Chinese economy — with its pocketful of capitalist enclaves along the coast and in Shenzhen, Suzhou, Hong Kong, and Shanghai — will allow it to use political coercion, military force, and economic instruments to keep the cost of labour low. This means that rather than China becoming a huge market for foreign countries, the country will use its position as a late economic developer to make the world a place for Chinese goods. This situation will improve as investment, technology, and capital continues to flow into the country. The CCP is also observing very closely Hong Kong's constitutional development in terms of this pocket of capitalism under Chinese communism (*Straits Times*, 26 April 2004). Recall that China remained virtually unscathed during the 1997–98 Asian currency crisis because it was simply not sufficiently plugged into the system. But not everything in the Chinese economy is completely in the hands of its financial controllers. Increasing globalization and higher levels of investments from the United States and Europe will force its local workers to demand better wages for higher productivity. China's high single-digit growth rates are a typical reflection of a rapidly industrializing economy and do not necessarily project the potential for economic growth in the long run.

There are also the negative effects of capitalist development in a country that is already so demographically large that "corruption" is a normal way of life. It is not only in China but all over the world wherever people gather to live and work in communities. Call it "business networks", "*guanxi*" or "interpersonal relationships", or "economic culture" as detailed, for instance, by Yadong Luo in *Guanxi and Business* (University of Hawaii Press, 2000), it is still a form of corruption at the end of the day. Capitalism will only catalyse the forms of corruption present in the Chinese state and society and bring it to a different level. The lack of a tradition of clear regulatory laws governing business practices and the absence of liberal economic principles mean that much of what really goes on in the Chinese economy is not accounted or properly audited and this means a lack of control for a country that has survived for generations on central control. A director of an international merchant bank said that the reason why the United States cannot stop China or Japan from soaking up U.S. long-term government bonds, that is, the treasury bonds in particular, is simply because of the free market and a possible hedge against China's own intention to float its currency in several years. When the currency is eventually floated, there will be a fall in the value of the yuan and having a large amount of reserves would help reduce the impact of a loss in value. However, one remains very sceptical about the soaking up of such large amounts of Treasury bonds by a country that does not emulate the kind of liberal democratic values that are espoused by Americans and the U.S. Government while still wanting to benefit from liberal capitalism in any event.

More recently, there have been many reports in the local and foreign press about corruption and failed investments with Chinese partners. The China Aviation Oil (Singapore) scandal is another clear example of the dangers of investing in China. China presents a potential goldmine for savvy investors, but those who are merely relying on technocratic expertise and rational arguments such as the Singapore officials in the Suzhou project should realize that the Chinese are smart businesspersons. America hopes to convert China into a glowing market of over a billion people for both economic and political reasons. But the Chinese know this too. For several years, China began soaking up trillions of U.S. dollars to shore up the value of the renminbi. China sold more U.S. treasury bonds in April 2007, which to economists is a sign that China is ready to diversify its forex reserves because of the sale of close to US$6 billion worth of T-bonds, reducing the volume held to about US$412 billion. The GDP of China compared to the rest of Southeast Asia and America and the West is still very low. For example, the per capita GDP of each Chinese worker is currently less than 8 per cent of the per capita GDP of a Singapore worker. However, a small percentage increase in economic growth of the Chinese economy means a disproportionately large increase in total trade. The question now is whether Chinese investors are willing to go large, and where, and when.

INDIA AND THE UNITED STATES

While China poses the best challenge in terms of culture, language, and economic potential, India seems to come third to all these variables, with Southeast Asia as the best second option. This is because India continues to be plagued by corruption, political scandals, bureaucratic inefficiency, massive poverty, ethnocratism, and a failure to take advantage of the fact that it has been the world's largest democracy for the longest time among all other developing countries. India has also failed to stem the tide of its best professionals and most creative artists leaving for the United States and Western Europe despite the acrimonious (ethnic and racial) xenophobia in these older liberal democratic states. The Hindu nationalist party in its decade of power failed to complete its globalization project. This has been the greatest election upheaval since Indian independence. The ethnonationalistic politicking of the Vajpayee government is on the demise, and the rise of Sonya Gandhi's Congress Party, ostensibly through the new Indian President, has turned the tables on the possibilities for continuing

Hindu revivalism in the political and cultural history of modern India. The forestalling of Hindu revivalism has not solved other problems that continue to haunt the subcontinent. India has a highly charged racial and religious political culture where it is said that everyone has a political opinion, from the rich Bollywood moguls who produce hundreds of movies a year for the world's largest movie-going audience to the poorest homeless peasant roaming the Indian countryside. During the Cold War, India leaned towards the USSR, or as some Indian scholars would argue, India was politically more independent when it came to political relations with the United States during the Cold War.

Nevertheless, the post-Cold War era has seen India being increasingly recognized as a regional player and a rising world economy. The Indian economy is also plagued by acts of god which make emergency responses to such disasters difficult given the size of its population and complex cultural systems. While many Indian ethnic nationalists see the work of the current Hindu nationalist Bharathiya Janata Party (BJP) led by former Prime Minister Vajpayee in a positive vein, there are some who would disagree with the economic prospects of India's future ability to provide jobs for one of the fastest growing populations in the world. There are deep-set problems in agriculture and local commercial enterprises that are sometimes drawn into the political forays between Indian Muslims and Indian Hindus who constitute the largest religious and ethnic communities in the country. The bourgeoning middle classes have split their support for Vajpayee's failed bid to return to office, and the rural-based peasants' political scepticism has triumphed. This is because they are the ones on the ground who are most likely to feel the immediate impact of negative consumer sentiment in the markets or suffer from a lack of proper national policy on disaster relief. Disaster relief is another Indian policy that is more talked about than operationalized. This is understandable given the limited resources and the resulting value of human life in the world's second largest population. Successive Indian governments have found it difficult to reform its ancient and fragmented agricultural systems and land policies.

Over the years, Americans have made ostensible donations to the country in cash and in kind but this is insufficient and difficult to track. Because it is such a large country where there are more poor people for every working person, corruption is a significant factor in getting things done. It is not so much that people are unwilling to work and in fact they are most willing, but the problem is that there is simply not enough work to go around. Indian scientists, engineers, and computer programmers woo the world with their expertise and while Southeast Asian and American corporations outsource their backroom activities to India's cities. Investing in India is a good way to make money for the major corporations because labour laws are weak and labour is cheap. Naturally, India's main economic competitor for FDI is China, with whom it has had several border clashes. India's current annual FDI is only US$3 billion, about 5 per cent of the amount that China gets every year. India has also often been touted as the world's largest democracy. However this ideological situation has not led to consistently smooth political relations with the United States. Rather, India is indeed a breeding ground for the kind of liberal differences that Americans take so seriously. "Oblivion", it is said, "falls upon the world navigated by the free slaves of the *Ship of Fools*" (Foucault [1965] 1988, p. 34). The political power of freed rural peasants living the life of economic slavery has helped shift the political mandate to govern the world's largest democracy to the alliance between left-wing splinter parties and Gandhi's dynastic Congress.

While liberalism in America has seen the marginalization and virtual wiping-out of socialist political parties, including the Communist Party of America, especially after McCarthyism, the reverse appears to be true of India. Perhaps the large rural and urban poor make a suitable breeding ground for egalitarian-sounding socialist and other left-leaning parties.

India offers a fantastic array of investment opportunities for greedy capitalists because of its high level of first-rate engineers, computer professionals, and emphasis on information technology. Unlike China, which has a different set of problems, India has a complex and complicated history of rising ethnic nationalism and religious intolerance between Hindus and Muslims. Mosques and temples will continue to be burnt and accusations and blame will continue to be hurled at both parties to the problem.

India is also burdened with the illegal but very subtle caste structure that stratifies Indian society across cultural, religious, and social norms. India is also known to reject MNCs that are not culturally sensitive to its needs as seen in the marketing problems of McDonald's Corporation in India and Coke's subsidiary in India, Hindustan Coca-Cola Beverages (HCCB). McDonald's has perhaps found its nemesis in India because its basic product is the beef burger patty. In India, the cow has been considered for millennia as a sacred animal and not for making into beef patties. It is amazing to think that McDonald's (with its reputation for fast food serving up beef hamburgers as a main value meal) had not carefully considered this while trying to force open a new market where millions are vegetarian. Because of the value of the fast food industry in the United States, and because money always draws attention, there are pending lawsuits against the corporation about allegations of concealing the use of animal extracts in their french fries:

> McDonald's reiterated that the french fries it served in India did not contain any animal extracts. "McDonald's India would like to assure you that French fries in India are a 100 percent vegetarian product and do not contain any beef or animal extract of whatsoever kind," the company said in an advertisement in a newspaper on Saturday. The Press Trust of India quoted McDonalds Delhi Managing Director Vikram Bakshi as saying that all McDonald outlets were open in Delhi after taking "necessary precautions". Earlier this week a vegetarian lawyer and native Indian, Harish Bharti, filed suit against McDonalds in the United States accusing it of "secretly" lacing its French fries with beef fat. A report on the case appeared in a leading Indian newspaper on Friday, stirring protests and attacks on the fast-food chain. "The cow is sacred to Indians. Foreign firms have made a habit of dumping things here without any regard to feelings of people," Goel said. (Indian Express Newspapers [Bombay], 2001)

The beverage giant Coke did not have the extent of the problems that McDonald's of India will have to do battle with for a long time to come. However, HCCB's own marketing secret reveals the nature of such MNC operations on the shop-floor by providing bottles of Coke as the international and national alternative to popular beverages such as tea and Pepsi-Cola. The consumption of tea in India, for example, is an important and traditional pastime. If one can get past these problems, one can access the wide variety and huge potential for investment, but control and constant monitoring is essential for the capitalist to take advantage of the huge labour pool. India is likely to see a net outflow of its best and brightest citizens to the United States and the United Kingdom where there are a growing number of diasporic Indian communities.

There is also increasing sentiment in India in terms of improving investments and companies like Coca-Cola, McDonald's, and Ford who were among the first to invest significantly in India in the post–Cold War era. They are more likely than not to benefit from their pioneer status, if the rupee does not go into another currency tailspin or get bogged in financial doldrums because of currency mismanagement, bureaucratic red tape, and systemic corruption. Renewed investor confidence in such companies as Reliance Industries and the Indian Oil Corporation are positive harbingers for the emerging Indian market. But the political mandate awarded to Congress is limited by a forestalling of alternatives to Sonya Gandhi's party. This does not in any way lessen the burden on the ethno-nationalist and ethno-religious politics that have divided and continue to split India. It is doubtful that Congress and the communists will be able to increase the voices of the political masses that have put them in power once again.

JAPAN AND THE UNITED STATES

The "liberal democratic" politics of Japan continue to experience deep links with the United States in order to discover new ways of making Japan's economy work. But there are also important political linkages between the politicians of both countries. In the third year of the Junichiro Koizumi administration, members of the Liberal Democratic Party such as Shinzo Abe and Tetsuzo Fuyushiba of the New Komeito Party hoped to foster better relations with Washington (*Straits Times*, 26 April 2004). Meanwhile, political negotiations were going on to effectively deploy a USN Aegis-equipped destroyer with the SM3 radar system to the Sea of Japan "to jointly counter any missile threat. Plans call for radar information obtained in Japan to be passed on to the United States in real time" (*Asahi Shimbun*, 22 April 2004).

Like China, Japan is the other significant macro-economic beneficiary from taking up trillions of yen worth of U.S. treasury bonds. Japan is taking advantage of the free market to increase its stake in the United States and this will either cause increased investor confidence in the long-term economic power of the United States, or if the critics have their way, will cause inflationary pressures on the U.S. economy if Japan were to abruptly stop buying. The primary beneficiaries in the international (read U.S.) bond markets are the governments, central banks, merchant banks, and offshore banks. The major secondary beneficiaries would be the MNCs, while the major losers will be the U.S. taxpayers should the demand for bonds fall dramatically.

Both China and Japan have mimicked each other in terms of large-volume buying of bonds, but while China appears to benefit from its action, Japan seems to be only just keeping afloat. Part of the reason for China's high economic growth over the last ten years is due to the rapid and widespread industrialization and movement of FDI into what is supposed to be the largest single consumer market in the world. However, Japan is still suffering from a long hangover since the 1990 economic growth bubble was burst because of a lack of significant controls over the banking sector, the volume of bad loans, and Japanese companies having over-extended themselves. At the national level, Japan also incurred a higher deficit because of the First Gulf War, which was supposed to have boosted the world economy (the United

States, Japan and their economic allies in particular) but this was thwarted by the Asian currency crisis.

Let us now move to Japanese popular culture within Japan and examine the extent of influence that American popular culture has on this Asian country. The idea of mimicry has clearly been seen in Japanese innovation and technology. More Japanese teenagers are sporting dyed blond hair, wearing the clothing and imitating the mannerisms of American Hispanics and African Americans from South Central Los Angeles and the Bronx. "Let us not be surprised to find it actually prowling through the streets" (Foucault [1965] 1988, p. 36). But the imitative culture is also not a one-way street. Like the multiple passages between America and Asia that we described above, American entertainment and media have themselves begun mimicking Asian motifs as clearly illustrated in the movies by the late but acclaimed Japanese film director Akira Kurosawa, especially in his final film with the postmodern bent. There are many reasons to believe that the Japanese economy will bounce back, especially with modified versions of what has come to be called the "flying geese" theories of regional development through Japanese FDI. This was in a manner similar to when West Germany was supposed to be the engine of growth for the European Community during the last five to eight years of the Cold War until the Federal Republic of Germany was stymied for some time by the social costs of political reunification with the German Democratic Republic (Communist East Germany).[33]

Japanese women have also come under increasing pressure to conform to traditional values that have been patriarchal for centuries. There is a desire among Japanese men for women to return to their traditional roles in late modernity despite advances in women's rights and feminist theory in Japan. However, if we read the map of Japanese political culture correctly, we will be able to recognize the differences between the younger generation of those in their teens to twenties, and those in their thirties and forties. While the older generation of Japanese women has its social and personal roles figured out, those in the youngest have not. Japan has one of the world's highest literacy rates and most comprehensive system of education in the world. This means that the younger generations are more willing to explore the world on their own — for example through the Internet and travel — rather than merely accept their fate according to custom and traditional family practices.

Like other places that have achieved high levels of material success, Japanese women are now more willing to challenge what has been "accepted gender practice and function" for centuries. This is causing a downward pressure on Japan's relatively homogenous social structure. Japanese popular culture is a mixture of both locally inspired cults of personality in fantasy worlds and the importation of America's MTV culture. The blend that results is one where Japanese pop idols are powerful influences in their own right and bear the trademarks of an imitative and innovative popular culture.

These popular icons — whether they are real or anime or a mixture of reality in anime — have reversed the unidirectional manner of the American MTV culture and created their own unique innovations that are doing two things: (1) defining the uniqueness of their own popular culture; and (2) influencing American popular culture and other forms of Asian popular culture in Taiwan, Korea, Singapore, and China. At the aesthetic level, there are certain cues involved in the kind of export J-pop culture to America and the rest of the world. These include (1) a rejection of the idea that hard work will lead to employment stability; (2) a nihilistic view of a world in which only superheroes are able to compete across a moral terrain out of which there is never a clear winner; (3) feelings of disenfranchisement with the establishment and rejection of traditional gendered roles; (4) the centrality of materialism but the failure of it to satisfy individuals; and (5) a rejection of the traditional Japanese view of honour/dishonour in favour of individual differences such as "dating gaijin" rather than locals. While these artifacts of Japanese popular modernity are indeed reflected in many aspects of urban cultures across the globe, the high value of the Japanese yen and the superior performance of the Japanese economy from 1970 to 1990 had created a large amount of relative wealth that has trickled downwards and across Japanese middle class society. Young Japanese middle class citizens are enjoying the benefits of the products and services created by the Japanese workers from their parents' generation. However, Japan as a whole is becoming increasingly dependent on the United States for its future economic survival. Also, the reported changes in political culture and social changes are not sweeping Japan as once believed.[34]

The Americans were there at the right time and the right place. The history of Japanese militarism in the early twentieth century had ostensibly launched Japan into the modern period. But the forced modernization of Japan through a fine balance between a strong military cabinet and weak, non-military, traditional leadership resulted in greater damage to the region and to Japan itself. The wartime Cabinet exhausted its own resources in its attempt to create the Greater East Asian Co-Prosperity Sphere. This made Japan invade China, occupy Mongolia, and rape the rest of Southeast Asia. It was the acute and double military debacle in Hawaii and the Philippines that drew America deeply into the political and economic fray of Southeast Asia rather than South Asia, which remained at that point in time the colonial purview of Britain's falling empire in the East. The creation of conditions of conflict by Japan ironically resulted in America's benefit in the longer term.[35] American support for the Japanese economy also engulfed its security dimension as seen in U.S. support in the 1970s and 1980s.[36] This was the period where it became increasingly clear to members of the House of Congress and the U.S. Senate that Japan, rather than being a mere relic from the Pacific War with a highly skilled and homogenous workforce, was in reality a strategic economic partner for American globalization and security in the tension-filled days of the Cold War with the USSR.

Thus it was more than merely being the victor victorious at the end of the war in the Pacific, or MacArthur's political rhetoric in Japan and Korea. The depth of America's links with Asia runs deep, for example to the time of Japanese reconstruction from 1946–56 in the vulnerable first ten years of the fledgling Japanese economy. This gave American investors and overseas administrators first-hand experience in dealing with rebuilding, in the case of Japan, an entire economy from the ground upwards that had been decimated by the war.[37]

America also has the highest number of scholars and research scientists in research and development compared to any other post-industrial country in the world. Only Japan came close but since the Japanese bubble burst in 1990, the Japanese brand of teamwork and company loyalty has had to undergo radical changes in its system of social and business values. Japan needs to address its status from an international player to reassess its role as a regional economic giant.

MALAYSIA AND THE UNITED STATES

Malaysia's Prime Minister Abdullah Ahmad Badawi wrote a letter to U.S. President George Bush Jr. and other leaders of the UN Security Council and the Group of Four most powerful states in April 2004. Abdullah Badawi presented Malaysia's position on the meeting among Islamic states with a focus on the Iraqi and Palestinian issues. This is in contrast to the pronouncements of former Malaysian Prime Minister Mahathir Mohamad who never lifted an olive branch or any other kind of peaceful twig to the United States. Recall Mahathir's reaction when former U.S. Vice President Dan Quayle during his visit to the Malaysian federal capital, Kuala Lumpur in the early 1990s, lambasted Malaysia's human rights record and questioned its democratic record. Mahathir accused America of being dominated by Jews. He again said in 2003 that America was indeed being run and manipulated by a small number of Jews who control everything from finance and broadcasting, to journalism and the print media. The powerful Jewish lobby was accused by the former Prime Minister of being the problem behind the Palestinian Question. However, the events of 9/11 prompted the new Prime Minister who took over in October 2003, after fresh and clean elections, to extend the palm of cooperation and friendship. This resulted in both countries seeking and offering intelligence-sharing strategies with U.S. intelligence networks and through regular and legal American diplomatic channels.

The Bali bombing and reports of Al-Qaeda operatives and clandestine meetings in Indonesian and Malaysian cities have not boded well for the relationship between these predominantly Muslim countries and the U.S. hegemony. The arrest of the ageing Islamic cleric Abu Bakar Bashir and his incarceration and subsequent trial soon after the Bali bombing of a nightclub in the Kuta Beach area — now left out of the "best beach resorts" programme on the Discovery Channel — was a keen move by Indonesian authorities. Whenever a crisis erupts, the elite Indonesian and Malaysian anti-terrorist forces are often sandbagged by a rush of emotion from genuine and peaceful followers of the faith and public threats and bombings from Muslim extremists with underground arms caches from Yala Province in southern Thailand, Kelantan in Malaysia's northern territories, to Jogjakarta in Java. Little wonder that American embassies in the region bear a similar architectural face to its embassies elsewhere in the world, architecture that gives the impression of "Fortress America" (overseas edition).

THAILAND AND THE UNITED STATES

The structure of Thai society is best understood as a pyramid. At the top of the structure are the King and the royal family. They are considered very sacred and are supremely respected even when issues of politics arise. It is not uncommon for the King to summon political leaders in order to encourage them to resolve their differences.

A second tier consists of the ruling elite. The elite are made up of Thai people who may be of Chinese descent and run many of the top companies within the country. For a traditional Asian society, Thailand is interesting because many of its top CEOs and corporate leaders are women. This is different from other Asian countries, and many Western countries, where the CEOs and top executives are usually men. The ruling elite comprises the highest military commanders within the Thai Army and the Thai Police, "in the precise sense that the classical epoch gave to it — that is the totality of measures which make work possible and necessary for all those who could not live without it" (Foucault [1965] 1988, p. 46). The reason for their dominance in politics is because of the combat power backing that they possess.

Since the end of the Pacific War, the dominant role of the military has not meant that there has been a clear and hierarchical politics among the generals themselves. In fact, since the absolutist King abdicated in favour of a constitutional monarchy, Thailand has experienced seventeen bloodless coups. However, the infighting has been contained predominantly within the military and the political parties and their supporters. The poor have remained mostly outside this realm of politics. The only exception to this political model is in the southern provinces where there are militant Islamic enclaves, many based in northern Malaysia, who are fighting for a separate state. This has been the case most significantly since the end of the Cold War. During the Cold War, there was greater news focus and media attention to the problems of communist insurgents and the activities of the Communist Party of Thailand and the Communist Party of Malaya. In the past, the peasant rebellions and insurrections in the south were primarily sporadic and politically motivated by religion or by ideology. However, these forms of political violence were marginal to the larger corporate and business aspects of the Thai economy.

The third tier of Thai society's pyramid is made up of the peasant workers who are themselves predominantly engaged in Thailand's agricultural sector. Rice continues to dominate as the main export of the country and Thailand is in fact the world's largest rice producer. While globalization has created a widening middle class of nouveau riche workers, the predominantly peasant farmers continue to bear the brunt of economic fallout and downturns. Like in all capitalist societies, these are the people who are hardest hit and most frequently sacrificed in terms of having to suffer the indignities of having no food, no home, or no jobs. Nevertheless, the problem of globalization in Thailand has spawned a deep, affective fissure between the minority elite industrial upper class and the majority peasant farmers and unskilled labourers who work for a pittance of what a waged salary worker earns in Bangkok. The reason Thailand has many social problems with globalization is because it embraced globalization with welcome arms in all possible areas of the economy.

The Thai people are known to be gentle and gracious in their demeanour as described by Orientalist perspectives of those who wish to believe in the exotification of Asian women, men, and children. However, the reality is furthest from such images: a Thai garment worker from northern Chiang Mai once said that life is cheap in Thailand. Thai culture seems to have been damaged by globalization inasmuch as it has damaged itself because of the nature of its traditional practices.

The concept of gift giving, for example, is taken to extremes when there is much wealth or riches to be attained. Corruption and the human flesh trade are worth billions of Thai baht every year. The politicians, police, army, and bureaucracy are involved with all kinds of corrupt practices. In a large sense, corruption is a way of life in a very overt sense in Thailand unlike America where corruption is considered something to be embarrassed about and is usually hidden from public view. This does not mean that Americans are any less prone to corrupt behaviour than Thai people. Rather, it is the rich and the super rich who tend to be corrupt. Most people in America and Thailand are indeed not corrupt and live by simple but strict moral codes of decency, honesty, and integrity, but this is often not the case in Thai corporate culture or American corporate culture. Corruption is very much a large part of the process and experience of globalization for the elite in both countries. There is really very little that trickles down to the majority poor.

Corruption in Thailand is also clearly at the root of its tourism industry where ignorant and impoverished Thai people are drawn into a swirling pool of drugs, sex, pornography, and pedophilia in places such as Patpong Streets 1 and 2 in Bangkok, Pattaya, and Hat Yai in Thailand's south. These are the markers that indicate to us the similarity between these Thai cities and those described by Foucault in *Madness and Civilization*:

> no doubt like the "decree of the *Parlement* dated 1606 ordered the beggars of Paris to be whipped in the public square [like the American prostitute caught in Tehran in the 1990s]" branded on the shoulder, shorn and then driven from the city (Foucault [1965] 1988, p. 47).

Globalization appears as a very large neon light to which many poor people, young men and young women, are drawn towards with the prospect of getting a job and earning enough money to send back to the villages. However, these simple folks are often ignorant of the entire vertical and horizontal efficiency of underground networks. However, such a cultural infestation ought to be understood against the backdrop of the major inadequacies of international organizations such as the IMF. Two books stand out as powerful indictments of the global and local structures of politics and globalization. One is by the Nobel Prize winner in economics, Joseph Stiglitz, on *Globalization and Its Discontents* (W.W. Norton 2002) and the other is a neo-Waltzian argument intricately made by another award-winning writer and Yale Professor of Law,

Amy L. Chua, in *World On Fire: How Exporting Free Market Democracy Breeds Ethnic Hatred and Global Instability* (Doubleday 2003).

A new Thai Rak Thai party that emerges out of the ashes of Thaksin's old TRT could draw from a bank of 288 experienced former MPs. While over 100 key MPs in the former Thai Rak Thai [Thais Love Thais] political party have been banned by the military junta from holding office till 2012, this is unlikely to weaken the power base created by Thaksin in his two terms as Prime Minister since he once had the direct support of over sixteen million Thai votes. However, since the Election Commission is appointed by the military junta, their new party might not receive approval and the banned political leaders would be under scrutiny if they were to influence Thai politics by proxy. The junta made it difficult for Thaksin to return, saying initially that if he did return they could not guarantee his safety. Then the Prime Minister who displaced him said that he would personally guarantee Thaksin's return. If the former Prime Minister and his wife return to Thailand they would have to face police charges made in their absence for the purchase of an empty piece of valuable land worth billions of Thai baht that Thaksin's wife, Khunying Potjaman, allegedly won in an open bidding. According to the interpretation of the law by the current regime, family members of the prime minister cannot benefit from the office that he holds. Nevertheless, Thaksin filed a lawsuit against Thailand's Assets Scrutiny Committee (ASC). The ASC froze over US$2.1 billion of Thaksin's assets for which he is seeking compensation of US$1.7 billion from the ASC. The ASC members were given a new lease of life for another year till the middle of 2008. Thaksin's personal financial value has fallen from Forbes' list of the world's richest people since the asset freeze and his estimated worth is only about US$250 million since his purchase of Manchester City Football Club. The British authorities are themselves investigating the sale of the football club to Thaksin. Meanwhile the direct threats to the military junta were momentarily deflected by thousands of anti-coup protesters who marched to the house of the President of the Privy Council, Prem Tinsulanonda. By July 2009, Thaksin's "remote-control" politics from undisclosed locations overseas had waned significantly. Meanwhile, the incumbent Prime Minister Abhisit Vejjajiva has survived the disruption of an ASEAN summit; massive demonstrations in Bangkok; the H1N1 bird flu pandemic; and continuing calls for his resignation. Nevertheless, Abhisit has survived much longer than Samak Sundravej and Somchai Wongsawat.

A professional politician, Abhisit is a "product" of globalization. He was born in England in 1964 and educated at Chulalongkorn University and Oxford University. He taught at the Royal Military Academy (Chulachomklao) and at Thammasat University. However, Abhisit does not have the background of a Thai military general. His rise to power was through the backing of his political party and the business elite in Bangkok.

Thai military politics is very interesting because the structure of the Thai Army is very similar to the U.S. military yet the power of civilian control over the military is totally unlike the American model. The rise and fall of military commanders is tied to two main cohorts from the Armed Forces Preparatory School, and it is clear that almost three decades of Thai politics is tied to the graduates of these two warring cohorts. Unlike in the United States where the Constitution is taken very seriously not only by the civilian population but by the American professional military personnel, in Thailand, the Constitution is often used to serve the political purposes of those who can assume power. This is why there have been over eighteen coups in Thailand since the end of absolute monarchy in 1932. The September 2006 coup is just as complex as previous coups. Ironically, Thaksin did not think much of the fact that Surayud Chulanont was very close to Prem Tinsulanonda and appointed Surayud supreme commander himself in 2003. On the advice of the King, Surayud, like Prem before him was appointed to the Privy Council. Meanwhile Surayud and Prem were grooming Sonthi Boonratlin for higher military command. As a result of Thaksin's trust in his senior-most officers, Sonthi was able to launch the bloodless coup with the guidance of Prem and then appointed his old commander, Surayud, to be the Prime Minister. In the case of a military junta, the prime minister holds less power than the head of the junta which was now called the Council for National Security. Sonthi believed that he had to act because he was aware, as late as January 2006, that there were rumours that Thaksin had intended to remove him from his post as army commander to a less influential one, which would have been effectively a demotion.

Unlike the Indonesian case under Suharto who masterminded the frequent change of the top generals, Thaksin was basically a businessman. Even as a police general, he did not rise up through the officer class like Prem, Surayud, and Sonthi had. Thaksin was closer in style to former Prime Minister Chuan Leekpai than previous army commanders who became prime ministers. Thaksin was therefore not really clued into the military culture, even though he did receive good intelligence reports. But his greatest flaw was to think that democracy would remain in Thailand and that his overwhelming victory at the 2003 polls would guarantee him at least another term in office. The hunger for political power by Thai generals is well known. One reason is that the system that has been created is so enmeshed in money politics that it has become impossible to change the nature of Thai politics. Short of another

1932 revolution, the Thai political culture is likely to remain in the forseeable future. The King remains as the third and perhaps most important pillar in Thailand's political culture. Revered by Thais like a god, the Thai King appears to the Thai people as their saviour and is beyond reproach. Although the present King has been on the throne for over sixty years, he has never been associated with coercion or undermining any regime. In fact, he is perceived to be the person who is holding Thailand together. Yet all generals no matter how lustful for power or how corrupt, have to bow before His Majesty. Thais are not allowed to stand before their King and have to remain below him. The King has survived all the military coups and political upheavals all these decades if only to protect the well-being and safety of the Thai people.

The demonstrations and challenges to the junta by different groups and organizations have disrupted the economy every week since the September 2006 coup. Such sustained demonstrations show that many Thai citizens are unhappy with the coup plotters, the military junta, and current government. The appreciating Thai baht if not kept in check will make the country's exports increasingly expensive and turn more investors away to Vietnam and even Cambodia.

THE BUSINESS OF MAKING MONEY IN ASIA

Investment opportunities in Asia abound for the Americans with information technology and communications skills who are young enough and possess sufficient drive and determination to work in places that are as foreign as any other place on earth. Many have gone to Asia to begin work in their youth but have never left and have started families and social networks. There are Americans in Asia who are in fact more Asian than the Asians themselves. The long-time *kama'aina* or long-staying expatriates, serve as valuable contact points for quick launches into the local Asian marketplaces and they know exactly what one needs to do in order to survive. And with the low cost of travel these days, it becomes much less problematic to make last-minute changes to any itinerary. American investors need more than quick routes deep into emerging Asian markets.

Those Americans who want to make money in Asia often watch very carefully the kinds of programmes that are aired over various Asian broadcast networks from CNBC, Star News Network, CNA, Sun TV, Zee TV, HKTV-B, The Nine Network, and others from the Asia-Pacific capital cities of Astana, Auckland, Baku, Bandar Seri Begawan, Bangkok, Canberra, Colombo, Dhaka, Dili, Islamabad, Jakarta, Kabul, Katmandu, Kuala Lumpur, Male, Manila, Nandy, New Delhi, Port Moresby, Seoul, Singapore, Sri Jayewardenepura

Kotte, Taipei, Thimpu, and Tokyo. The money-making entertainment programmes from many of these far-flung cities have a very distinct identity that is based on local and native or even regional languages but with very clear grandiose, Hollywood-style glamour.

V.S. Naipaul may be considered by some as a great Indian, Trinidad-born novelist with keen observations about life, but being more colonial in his mannerisms than the colonials themselves, Naipaul did make at least one astute observation. He noted the idea of the way in which Asians and Africans like to mimic their former colonial masters, as seen in his brilliant *The Mimic Men* (Vintage 2001). Naipaul's observation is similar to that imposed by Homi Bhabha's interstitial evaluation of "mimic man" but whose work is so densely sordid that it defeats plain language users from understanding whatever he might have to say, lost in ambivalence as he illustrates so well in "Of Mimicry and Man" in his *The Location of Culture* (Routledge 1994). Yet when one goes back to read him again, former impressions of ambivalence transform into highly intelligent literary hieroglyphics that has become the style that characterizes Bhabha's work. The idea of mimicry is not limited to the Hong Kong or Taiwanese entertainment field that ranges from reality TV to soaps that are more extreme than *Days of Our Lives* or *Peyton Place*.

The mimicry between Asia and America is incredible. The Western images along the streets of Singapore, Bangkok, Kuala Lumpur, and Tokyo make one think that one could be in the United States. However, there are clear differences in the local customs in terms of business practices, interpersonal networks, and the recent history of MNC organizational behaviour. Japan is too expensive for any one person to want to invest in in a big way. It is better nowadays to have a Japanese product that is made anywhere else but in Japan. However, Japanese innovation and creativity continue to be the main source of potential for the only country in Asia to have made it to the G-7, and in that sense claims recognition and status. China is a great place to invest in if you can get by the language barrier. As a business executive intent on making money in China, it would be a great disadvantage not to know the language. Labour costs are low, but there are certain distinct features about *guanxi* (relationships) and Chinese business practices that the intrepid executive ought to know before foraying into what will become the world's largest consumer market for low-value, low-yield but high volume domestic consumer products. The answer is not so much to make it in China for sale elsewhere in the world, but to make it in China for sale in China. This is, however, harder to achieve than it seems. India, on the other hand, which had significantly lower FDI than China, has the clear advantage of having close to 289 million professionals who also speak the language of globalization.

The high levels of literacy make India a very promising place to be for the capitalist willing to immerse in a deep and ancient culture with one of the fastest growing economies in South Asia since 9/11. As a result of the large number of English-speakers, there continue to be many firms that have decided to outsource their back-room operations to this country. Outsourcing currently makes up 2–5 per cent of foreign income earned by local Indian nationals. At this point in modernity, there are at least seven countries in South Asia and the word "Indian" is more about national identity than ethnic identity. India is also relatively politically stable, a country where freedom of speech and the expression of such liberties are taken seriously. There are also many more languages spoken in India compared to China, where Putonghua gets you most places with ease. Both Indian and Chinese bureaucracies are full of red tape and tend to present problems for new investors and very often more red tape is created in trying to rid the apparatus of old red tape. Levels of corruption that might hinder business practices are high in both countries.

The Southeast Asian markets represent another set of valuable regional sites for investments where labour costs are relatively lower than in Europe and several inroads have already been made in terms of manufacturing, banking and financial services, telecommunications, information technology, and tourism. Although Southeast Asia is gradually pricing itself out of the low-wage labour market when compared to Latin America, India, Africa, and China, it continues to make up for this with highly-skilled and hardworking labour who appear to be very zealous about the language of globalization.

The business of making money in Asia works on a simple principle. This is the principle that revolves round the question of what can you bring into Asia to benefit both investor and the invested? The principle of business in Asia involves producing a good or service that is both cheap and functional that everyone needs every business quarter because it has a limited but value-laden lifespan. Examples include printers and toner, toothbrushes and cosmetics, computer hardware and software, pharmaceuticals, food, and apparel. Perhaps with the exception of Japan, the rest of Asia does not possess a sufficient critical mass of experts in research and development to ensure a constant supply of creative products and services. Nevertheless, the edge that Asia has is in its wide markets, lower wage and start-up costs, and weak trade unions. Asian markets are also beginning to open up and become accustomed to the capitalist goods and services of neoliberal lifestyles so well embedded in Western European cities and all across America. Another advantage that Asia has is its ability to innovate through reverse engineering and discovering alternative ways of acquiring product intelligence and consumer market knowledge and know-how. The possibility of developing Asian markets is a tremendous pull factor in attracting worldwide investments, if and only if the United States continues to assert its presence as a benign military and economic hegemony in the Asia-Pacific region. And if Asia can survive the weight and the pull-down effects of the 2008 American recession.

Notes

1. J. Lodge Gillespie, Jr., "Rhetoric and Reality: Corporate America's Perceptions of Southeast Asia, 1950–1961", *Business History Review* 68, no. 3 (1994): 325–63. By way of a quick comparison, and a reminder of the earlier propagandistic nature of Americanism in Southeast Asia in the 1950s and 1960s, see Kenneth T. Young, "Asia and America at the Crossroads", *Annals of the American Academy of Political and Social Science* 384 (1969): 53–65; and contrast this with the work of Richard F. Doner, "Approaches to the Politics of Economic Growth in Southeast Asia", *Journal of Asian Studies* 50, no. 4 (1991): 818–49; and Susan M. Collins, Barry P. Bosworth, and Dani Rodrik, "Economic Growth in East Asia: Accumulation versus Assimilation", *Brookings Papers on Economic Activity* 2 (1996): 135–203.
2. See Bernama, 30 December 2002.
3. There are many other special force units in Singapore including the Republic of Singapore Navy's Naval Diving Unit, which conducted diving operations when Silkair flight MI185 crashed in December 1997. That tragedy killed over 100 passengers and crew, including a well-known Singapore Eurasian model, Bonnie Hicks.
4. *Singapore Armed Forces (Amendment) Bill* 12/2007.
5. ABRI, 1998; TNI, 2007.
6. Antonio L. Rappa, "Cutting off the Nose to Spite the Face", *Business Times*, 22 November 2007.
7. Antonio L. Rappa, "Thai Military Culture in Late Modernity", paper presented at the 10th Thai Khadi Research Institute, Thammasat University, 9–11 January, 2008, Bangkok, Thailand.
8. See Carlos H. Conde, "Corruption Troubles Philippine Military", *International Herald Tribune*, Thursday, 26 May 2005.
9. *Voice of America News*, 18 June 2002.
10. See especially, P. Ramasamy, *Plantation, Labour, Unions, Capital and the State in Peninsular Malaysia* (New York: Oxford University Press, 1994), for an important old school reminder of the structuralist views of merchant capitalism in his excellent study of marginalized Malaysian plantation workers.
11. Janadas Devan, "Abang, Adik will Simply not Play Little Brother", *Straits Times*, 27 July 2003.

12 The idea of "PR" or permanent residency "status" is important for some lawyers, interpreters of the law, and political analysts and politicians. For them, a person with citizenship of one country but PR in another is not someone who is completely loyal to her or his own national identity since the award of PR usually indicates long-term stay elsewhere other than one's place of domicile. Hence a person with PR in another country may choose to emigrate there rather than remain in the original country of domicile. There are different interpretations of PR, including the associated idea that PR has become an important tool in globalization that is used to attract and reward certain types of residents who are perceived as being an asset or a benefit to the host country.

13 Frederic L. Pryor, "The Impact of Foreign Trade on the Employment of Unskilled U.S. Workers: Some New Evidence", *Southern Economic Journal* 65, no. 3 (1999): 472–92.

14 James M. Griffin, and Weiwen Xiong, "The Incentive to Cheat: An Empirical Analysis of OPEC", *Journal of Law and Economics* 40, no. 2 (1997): 289–316.

15 Francesco Sisci, "La démaoization de la Chine", *Le Grand Soir: Asiatimes*, 10 Novembre 2002.

16 Rafael X. Zahralddin-Aravena, "Chile and Singapore: The Individual and the Collective, A Comparison", *Emory International Law Review* 12, no. 2 (1998): fn. 153.

17 *Reformasi* is the Malay word for "reform" and is the battle-cry for the supporters of the National Justice Party that was founded by Anwar supporters, including his wife Wan Aziza.

18 See for example, BBC News, 23 November 1998; and *The New Republic*, 7 December 1998.

19 See BBC News, 23 November 1998.

20 Abdullah Badawi is the man who replaced Anwar Ibrahim who was jailed for allegedly sodomizing his former family driver, Azizan Abu Bakar. Anwar believes that he was framed by his former boss, Mahathir Mohamad.

21 See also, Anne O. Krueger, "Meant Well, Tried Little, Failed Much: Policy Reforms in Emerging Market Economies", *Roundtable Lecture at the Economic Honors Society*, New York University, New York, IMF, 23 March 2004; and "IMF/World Bank Report Calls for Urgent Action on Poverty Reduction by All Countries", Press Release No. 04/85, 22 April 2004.

22 Noam Chomsky, "An Interview with Noam Chomsky", *ZMagazine*, 2 January 2004.

23 In a "Letter from Iraq", see John Cassidy, "Beneath the Sand: Can a Shattered Country be Rebuilt with Oil?" *New Yorker*, 11 May 2004.

24 Habibie, a German-trained engineer, was the interim President who served under Suharto and made his mark as Minister for Technology. As an Indonesian Vice-President in Suharto's Cabinet, Habibie was constitutionally appointed President after Suharto but was rejected by the MPR.

25 "Monas" is an acronym for *monumen nasional* or the National Monument in central Jakarta. See "Ex-military Chief Wins Suharto Party Nomination", Agence France-Presse, 21 April 2004.
26 See *Wall Street Journal*, 12 February 1998.
27 Tony Makin, "Preventing Financial Crises in East Asia", *Asian Survey* 39, no. 4 (1999): 668–78.
28 Robert A. Scalapino, "The United States and Asia in 1998", *Asian Survey* 39, no. 1 (1999): 1.
29 Henry Laurence, "Financial System Reform and the Currency Crisis in East Asia", *Asian Survey* 39, no. 2 (1999): 348–73.
30 Scalapino, "The United States and Asia", p. 2.
31 Vaclav Smil, "China's Energy and Resource Uses: Continuity and Change", *China Quarterly* 156 (1998): 935.
32 John W. Thomas, "Institutional Innovation and the Prospects for Transference. Part I: Transferring Singaporean Institutions to Suzhou, China", draft paper, Harvard University Kennedy School of Government, 20 September 2001. See also, John W. Thomas and Lim Siong Guan, "Using Markets to Govern Better in Singapore," draft paper, Harvard University Kennedy School of Government, 15 August 2001, written for the Kennedy School of Government's Visions of Governance in the 21st Century project.
33 With reference to the "flying geese" theories, see the compelling and interesting but outdated paper by Martin Hart-Landsberg and Paul Burkett, "Contradictions of Capitalist Industrialization in East Asia: A Critique of 'Flying Geese' Theories of Development", *Economic Geography* 74, no. 2 (1998): 87–110.
34 For further reading, consider the useful but outdated book by Edwin O. Reischauer and Marius B. Jansen, eds., *The Japanese Today: Change and Continuity* (MA: Harvard University Press, 1995) as a basis for understanding Japan; the creative work of Delores Martinez, ed., *The Worlds of Japanese Popular Culture: Gender, Shifting Boundaries and Global Culture* (Cambridge: Cambridge University Press, 1998); the interesting counter-impressionistic argument made by Yoshio Sugimoto, *An Introduction to Japanese Society* (Cambridge: Cambridge University Press, 2002); and the terse but comprehensive work by Mark Schilling, *The Encyclopedia of Japanese Pop Culture* (NY: Weatherhill Publications, 1997).
35 Peter J. Katzenstein, Robert O. Keohane, and Stephen D. Krasner, "International Organizations and the Study of World Politics", *International Organization* 52, no. 4 (1998): 652.
36 This was clearly the case in terms of Foreign Assistance. See, for example, William J. Long, "Nonproliferation as a Goal of Japanese Foreign Assistance", *Asian Survey* 39, no. 2 (1999): 328–47; and Dennis T. Yasutomo, "Why Aid? Japan as an Aid Great Power", *Pacific Affairs* 62, no. 4 (1989–90): 490–503. See also, John O'Loughlin; Luc Anselin, "Geo-Economic Competition and Trade Bloc Formation: United States, German, and Japanese Exports, 1968–1992", *The Journal of Economic Geography* 72, no. 2 (1996): 131–60; Brian Woodall,

"The Logic of Collusive Action: The Political Roots of Japan's Dango System", *Comparative Politics* 25, no. 3 (1993): 297–312; Roger W. Bowen, "Japan's Foreign Policy", *PS: Political Science and Politics* 25, no. 1 (1992): 57–73; and a more outdated but intuitive argument in Takashi Inoguchi, "Japan's Response to the Gulf Crisis: An Analytic Overview", *Journal of Japanese Studies* 17, no. 2 (1991): 257–73.

37   Errol A. Henderson, "Neoidealism and the Democratic Peace", *The Journal of Peace Research* 36, no. 2 (1999): 206.

4

MONEY

Consuela: "Very soon, you are going to be rich"
Joe: "And that's not gonna break my heart"[1]

Money legitimizes life in late modernity. Money empowers, authorizes, and legitimizes people. Money motivates, inspires, and stimulates us to do things we would otherwise not do. There is an old realist adage in political science: power is the ability of A to get B to do something B would otherwise not do. If money can make people do things they ordinarily would not do, then we can assume that money is power. In 1651, Thomas Hobbes asserted that the impression of power is power. It follows then that the impression of money (or possession thereof) is power. People who give the impression of wealth — dressing in expensive clothes, driving expensive cars, or wearing expensive watches — are often assumed to be wealthy. This has resulted in an unhealthy "respect" for superficial wealth and the appearance of wealth. People all over the world treat those with greater wealth in a superficially nicer manner. However, it is not a simple matter of giving people the impression of wealth.

Giving people and strangers the impression of wealth, otherwise known as "keeping up with the Jones's" is difficult and expensive to maintain. And money is at the root of this problem. Even the Christian Bible has a saying that the "love for money is the root of all evil" (I Tim: 6:10). Note that it does not say that money itself is the root of evil. We will understand why later. The influence that money has over people in late modernity harks back to the primordial past of civilization and currency. When we claim that money makes people do things they would otherwise not do, we are not simply referring to a willingness to rob a bank, or take a bribe, or deal drugs. We are also referring to individuals who risk life and limb just for a small monetary reward. People will do really stupid things just to win a small money bet. But does money bring happiness? The nouveau riche sportsmen of the NBA, NFL, NHL, and European soccer clubs, for example, seem to think so. At least the images that viewers and consumers in late modernity are fed daily and nightly in the mass media seem to suggest that material wealth, with all the trappings of conspicuous consumption, brings happiness.

Before the financial crisis of 2008 hit hard, Colleen Walsh of the *Harvard Gazette* reported on charitable prosocial contributions and discovered in her research that people were happier if they spent money on others. But that was in April 2008. Perhaps now that several banks have sunk and many more businesses have filed Chapter 11, people are unlikely to be as prosocial as Walsh's report suggests. Money has time value and exhibits characteristics of an international public good. Money is time-dependent but has no intrinsic value. So money on its own is nothing without the sentiment of human value perpetuated with its use. Money has value if we attach value to it. That is why, " 'The love of money is the root of all evils' and there are some who, pursuing it, have wandered away from the faith and so given their souls any number of fatal wounds."[2] If money is about power and all power is political, then political science must indeed be the most important of all the sciences, as Aristotle argued over two millennia ago.

By and large it is hard to believe that most people would not accept money if they could get away with it. Surveys do not really tell you the truth. No one wants to sound like they are unethical. Respondents are more likely to say that they would do the right thing. Deep down inside we have all been branded. Superficial branding are the markers of wealth. People want to be treated well. And many believe that wearing the right clothes and shoes or being seen with the right company gets you better treatment. Time after time I am told by students who have been working in the corporate world that it is "who you know rather than what you know that gets you ahead". Getting ahead means happiness. And the shortcut to happiness, we moderns believe, is money. That is the tricky part. People assume that money can buy happiness. This seems a logical, if materialistic view, looking at the level of greed that is intensifying around the world these days. But the ethicists may not agree. If I have a shot at being rich, says the man in the street, why not? I could always use my wealth to help the poor, making worthy donations, educate orphans, and establish an institution to promote peace in the Middle East, for example. Who could possibly disagree with the prospect of help through money? Well, Pierpaolo Barbieri, for one, has very great ideals and would disagree with the idea of monetized prizes:

There is consensus among the liberal elites that the American education system is a fundamentally flawed one, and that it requires sweeping reform. Nevertheless, I dissent from the Crimson Staff in their endorsement of monetary incentives for New York City schools that serve communities with a high proportion of low-income Latino or black students. Doubtless, many of the students from such disadvantaged backgrounds need help to stay in school and focus on their studies, which are eventually what will give them a chance at better circumstances. But paying the way forward will not pave the way forward. Throwing money at high school students with good test scores is a simplistic answer that alters the ideals of education, sending a terrible message to students everywhere. The state provides free education because, as a society, we choose to cultivate love for learning. Though many may argue that there are instrumental benefits behind it, learning should not be pegged with money, even if many of these students will grow up to be Wall Street investment bankers. Parents are free to incentivize their sons and daughters however they choose, but to give money without stipulation of how it can be used is far from a scholarship for excellence; it's an invitation for careless spending that sends the message that money is the direct reward of learning. But it's not, and it shouldn't be. Better opportunities for the future are the prize, not just cash. If we regret the circumstances that have led this country to the brink when it comes to public education, we should not condone measures that give up on every value behind education: If we want our youth to grow up with the right values, we should not support giving monetary prizes to students who achieve outstanding test scores.[3]

But what exactly are these right values? Even book prizes cost money. Would it be better to pervert the true value of money by cloaking it in a gift? Indeed, what better motivation than making good clean money from being intelligent. However, the reasons why liberal elites believe that America's educational structure is fundamentally flawed and is in need of reform have little to do with money as reward for scholastic achievements among impoverished students. Rewarding outstanding students with money is what America does best. Is that not much better than forcing someone into the drug trade or aiding and abetting terrorists into e-Jihad or encouraging self-radicalization? The next narrative is about political intrigue, at the heart of which is money. And ill-gotten wealth is the point of our next story.

Imagine a place so steeped in the tropics that it offers only heat exhaustion, malaria, yellow fever, and other tropical illnesses and diseases; a place so backward that for many years visiting seafarers believed that ghosts would consume and engulf people with a fatal fever from the swamps. Yet such a place attracted no less than what was to become a series of political and economic intrigues that involved the youngest president of the United States (he was forty-three years old when he took the oath of office), several Wall Street financiers, foreign experts, and ex-military specialists. Ironically, the case resulted in the creation of a new country, with its own national boundaries. And the CIA was not even involved (but only because it had not yet been established in those days). This country even had a film that was shot entirely on its location between the Atlantic Ocean and the Pacific Ocean. This place is the Republic of Panama.

The Panama Canal was a result of the creative economics and the executive political will of the earlier American capitalists at the turn of the nineteenth and twentieth centuries. Neil Postman believes that in order to save our future we need to build a bridge to the eighteenth century. He is half right. What Postman neglects to reconcile are the existing problems within modern cosmopolitan societies today. The problems of poverty, hunger, and the burden of state welfare systems continue to afflict the advanced post-industrial economies of the West. The roots of these economies are deeply embedded in the Industrial Revolution, but the speed and pace of modernization has resulted in an incomplete understanding of the economic lessons that were themselves partially understood. Modernity possesses and cannot be dispossessed of information overload, and is consequently faced with too little time to understand the real value of the information being gathered. One lesson from the past was that the bourgeoning Western economies on which America had modelled itself were not designed to help the masses but to enrich the elites. This was the economic history that Nietzsche had warned us about in "Nietzsche's Preface to Constitutionalism", an article published in the *Journal of Politics* in 1963. In anticipating Postman's book by at least thirty-six years, Kariel argues that:

> We are distinguished, [Nietzsche] reasoned, by our capacity to remember the past, to recollect our past action. We are distinctively historical beings, as animals are not. Our experience, more properly, our consciousness of our experience — distinguishes us. And it rests upon us like a burden. Our consciousness of our past, our conscious knowledge, is our curse. Fully to take the past into conscious account — indeed, fully to take the future into conscious account — confounds all action. Full knowledge of the past, full knowledge of the future (including our inescapable death), produces either delirium or paralysis. Thus history, experience, consciousness, intellectual awareness, rational knowledge — all these are enemies of life. If we favor life we have no choice but to repress these (Kariel 1963, p. 217).[4]

We need to build the bridges to the eighteenth century but ones that are strong enough for us to return. But in building these bridges we seem to be merely going over previous ground, and the seeds of the end of modernity as we know it today are so deeply embedded in the economic structures of Western societies that the full awareness of the present and a complete awareness of the future, as Kariel anticipates, will end in a consciousness about our own proximity to death. As Kariel should full well know, by about now.

The story of successful capitalism is therefore a long and twisted narrative that begins and ends with personalities. There was no real strategy of global economic dominance on the part of the United States. The driving force and motivation during the Westward expansion towards California and against the Native Americans, the Spanish, British, and French territorial possessions was the story of a seemingly unstoppable machine. Guided by the Monroe Doctrine and Manifest Destiny, the early Americans decided that they would be guided by shear synergistic economic conquest rather than by the classical economic theories of Adam Smith and his contemporaries. Indeed, it was the rejection by the early settlers of such "classics" that made the growing American economy particularly robust and its war machine particularly confident, not so much of success, but of the possibility of failure. The Panama Canal is a case in illustration that represented an imbalanced mix of political intrigue, Wall Street financing, stubborn determination, and a relentless physical geography. It was a good enemy to go up against. And I would like to argue that the likely company of politicians, economic czars, lawyers, and ex-military men came together in a perfect concoction to establish what was to become a truly genuine American MNC.

This chapter explores and tries to make sense out of the successful capitalist narratives of several American CEOs. For every success story that one encounters, there are millions of failed stories that never see the light of day. The reason for the focus on capitalism's success is two-fold. The first reason is that it gives us a sense of optimism. Perhaps for those who are believers, success stories motivate us to some higher plane. The second reason is that these successful MNCs and their successful leaders are themselves a product of failed chances. Not all of them were born with a silver spoon. Many rise from humble economic backgrounds. In reading success one must also read with peripheral vision. One must be willing and able to understand that globalization is not about a movement to make everyone richer and much better off than the day before. Demographic research and the ethnographic record, for example, have shown clearly that there are problems of calculating what poverty, wealth, or financial costs really mean.

THEORY AND CAPITALISM

Classical laissez-faire economic theory involves two main assumptions. The first assumes that there are limited resources that are in demand. The second assumption is that these resources are potentially exchangeable by trade through a market mechanism. Economic models designed on the work of the Irish political economists developed a priori distinctions about absolute advantage and comparative advantage. Both forms of economic advantage revolve around the concept of production and the efficiency of production, that such goods can be produced from limited resources and that the production process can be sustained to support trade and the economy. But for any one economy to grow, it has to take part in market exchange in order to satisfy a range of unlimited wants. One of classical economic theory's endowments to modern economic theory was the idea of unlimited wants outstripping limited resources.

Different aspects of demand and supply economic theory occupied the theorists of the Enlightenment era and the ensuing Industrial Revolution. The early theories such as Condillac's theory of commercial governance, Condorcet's theorem, Adam Smith's *Wealth of Nations*, Ricardian economics, and Malthus's work were too difficult and too complex for most ordinary people in the days leading to mercantilism. These early economic models were not immediately or directly helpful to ordinary folk except perhaps for providing simple economic models that could explain market functions and market competition. Classical economic theory seemed purely reserved for erudition and the work of the classical and neoclassical economists. But people still understood how economics worked. They did not necessarily have the language to express their knowledge and experience but they were able to make quotidian sense of living with economics and early business practices. Part of the reason for this intuitive trait of economics and the apparently natural extension from man's social interaction came from the work-life routine. The early merchants, craftsmen, apprentices, traders, their guilds, and virtually anyone who participated in economic markets had some form of understanding of economics. Different parts of the economy were understood by different people. These were simple aspects of economic thought like the meaning of currency, the value of money, simple interest calculation, estimating stock values, the price mechanism, early state regulators, and the fact that money has time-value. Nevertheless, the models in theory and the theory in practice have come together to form what we understand as modern economic theory. These include some convincing models that help us understand business, society, and capitalist culture in practice such as the Pareto effect, the Nash solution, the backward-bending leisure curve, the Lorenz curve, the concept of reciprocity, marginal utility theory, Giffen goods, bargaining, and negotiation theory.

We have learnt different and compelling notions of capitalist economic theory from Smith, Pareto, Samuelson, Keynes, Milton, Reich, Stiglitz, Kahneman, Granger, Merton, Lucas, and many others. Economic theory as we understand it today is particularly interesting because it builds on successive models of interpreting the business and economic world. It would appear that the ideal models that were created about the concept of markets, producers, households, consumers, the meaning of the firm, the meaning of technology, and the different types of market seem to suggest that economics as a discipline has learnt well from itself. The positivist or behavioural method particularly characterizes modern economics today. This is why many economic philosophers believe that the highest point of economic theory lies in mathematical formulae that go beyond the reach of most ordinary people who are not schooled in such languages and vocabularies.

There are two main problems with modern economic theory. The first problem is that most of its models are in fact idealized versions of the world that cannot be easily applied to real world situations. In the case where the explanatory models are used to explain economic relationships in real world settings, we discover that the contexts in which these explanations present themselves are so simple that the facts do not seem to fit theory. For example, graduate students in economics may have to study the General Equilibrium Theory of a capitalist market economy. To many scholars, this general theory is very appealing, convincing, and elegant. It has clear mathematical definitions and economic explanations of its constituent components. An excellent combination of mathematical logic and economic relevance. But because there are potentially so many different variables that constitute a real capitalist market, it becomes virtually impossible to isolate the independent variable. But perhaps that was not one's intention. Perhaps, for example, one wanted to understand how a simple market economy worked, then the best picture that an economic theorist could give you would in fact be very limited. She or he would present you with idealized versions of two models: the perfect market mechanism and the imperfect market mechanism. Under the first, one would recount the basic assumptions of perfect knowledge, perfect competition, and perfect labour and resource allocation. In the second model, one would hold some or several of these assumptions constant and use proxies to determine the performance of a given good X or Y, or a given household A or B, or a production centre, or a specific type of technology's performance under perfect and imperfect competition. Therefore what the questioner received was not a perfect and imperfect model explaining economic reality but two perfect or idealized models given to explain imperfect reality. Therefore we can conclude that economic theory can be exciting and captivating only if one understands the kind of vocabulary used and the language that carries its signs and symbols. Hence, at an advanced level, one could introduce different kinds of ideal states that seem to reflect or mirror the reality of capitalism such as welfare economics, international trade theory, convergence theory, and of course, the neoclassical work of Vilfredo Pareto and the various careers and disciples that he has created along the way since the late 1800s and the rise of modernity in the wake of the Industrial Revolution.

We do not have to go far to get a glimpse of the kinds of economic theories that have become the signs and symbols of modernity. For every age of modernity, there has been specific and different economic models and schools of economic thought. And each and every age seems to have had a different personality, perhaps even a Nobel Prize laureate in economics, at the centre of some new paradigm of economic thought. One could say that someone like Bill Gates fits the picture of the kind of personality that has come to dominate the meaning of an economic paradigm such as the PC revolution, despite what his detractors might say against him. From him we have more modern applications in economic markets and virtual economic markets such as e-Bay on the Internet. The culmination of man's natural inclination to invent and to market goods and services by building on past experiences have led to the creation of Wi-Fi wireless platforms for PC notebooks that provide users robustness or flexibility, PC notebooks that digitally record, store, and transmit data through secured domains, and more ergonomic, intelligent, simple yet powerful personal computers from Apple.

AMERICAN CAPITALISM IN MODERNITY

When it comes to American capitalism we need to ask ourselves this question: "Do all the MNCs and CEOs of America depend on in-depth knowledge of Pareto economics or post-Keynesian theory in order to make a profit?" Why study when you can pay someone to do it right? If we examine the MNCs that have grown up indigenously in the United States, we would find that there are very few economists and even fewer, if any at all, economic theorists, on their payroll. Why is this?

One reason is that economics is an extension of human nature's need to control the environment in the same way that Heidegger believed that technology was about controlling man's environment. Therefore, economics ought to be a vital technological tool for controlling the environment and the intention of the MNCs was to dominate the capitalist and business environment with the aim of achieving monopolistic status. Yet economic theories about capitalism, the ideology that won the Cold War, do not seem to feature centrally in the modern MNC.

Perhaps this is because one does not need to have a Nobel laureate in economics to make rational market decisions. Any economics graduate should be able to effectively use the latest economic models to run specific algorithms to determine the best possible outcome of a given problem. There is another reason why one does not have to be an economics genius or be mathematically brilliant to determine when to make a stock purchase. Perhaps the greatest difficulty that confronts economics as a discipline and economists as practitioners of their science is that they seem to come up with different predictions all the time for any one given problem. This is not the same as saying that one should do the direct opposite of the economic predictors and one would come out on top. There is a higher problem with economics in terms of economic philosophy which has tended to take a backseat in the modern universities across the globe. No one teaches economic philosophy. If it has been taught at the university, chances are that it would have been taught as a political ideology in the political science classrooms of the 1980s and 1990s. Perhaps this is where the problem lies. There is demand in modernity for straight and simple answers to the kinds of tricky situations that are delivered by life in this age. As such, the General Theory of Equilibrium involves recognition of a larger philosophical belief in a unified and balanced universe in which all things tend towards a symmetrical cadence, in a sense then, as an extension of the biology of man. Nevertheless, the latest research in economic theory revolves around econometric modelling, the use of algebraic formulae in computing market imperfections, applied economics, mapping of financial markets and stock indices, and computer programmes that can track historical trends of market indicators, top-performing investments, and non-performing markets. This is where the economic modelling in modernity seems to be best employed: in the business of market analyses and prediction.

It would seem that the great Western philosophers buried the treasure of the knowledge deep in complex and convoluted arguments that would take several lifetimes to distil. Some of the buried continental treasure continues to be researched by scholars interested in the aesthetic value, I think, more than making some practical link to Kantian critiques in support of the Enlightenment. Kant's own contribution to economic thought was highly metaphysical. He believed that it was interpretation that creates the good rather than the good creating the interpretation. This would explain why there are many possible interpretations of an imagined or real concept across native speakers of the same language domain. But because Kant was so difficult to distil, his contemporaries interested in classical economics could not devote too much time to unravelling his transcendentalism and therefore a highly complex and abstract view of experience, subjectivity, and reality.

Nietzsche was more interested in warning us moderns about what we term modernity and the dangers of event-filled historicism (and the doctrines that remind us of the importance of the so-called Wisdom of the Ages) rather than delving in perceiving and understanding economic models in modernity. Heidegger had something interesting to warn us about the dangers of technology. And he passed this message onto Arendt who squandered it on meaningful and accessible political theory. She demystified political philosophy, gave access to many, and lost some degree of the intrigue that had captivated scholars for the preceding 500 years. However, there is an overlap of arguments about whether Arendt herself was a political philosopher or a political theorist. It appears to me that she was more of a political theorist with training in political philosophy, a training system that she rejected in her work and experience of modernity, not in the least because of Heidegger's influence. But the world of these political philosophers and political theorists was one that was caught up with the great social, economic, and cultural fractures of the time. It was an economic world that was limited and to an extent misdirected by the long staying power of European metaphysicians. Knowledge, both economic and political, continued to reassert itself in Hegelian terms of a dualistic universe, one that was set for the arrival of positivist social and political science where emphasis and appeal presented itself in terms of phenomena and explanatory models that were "applied", "practical", and "directed".

Most Americans, however, are less interested in the high abstraction of metaphysical theory and post-metaphysical speculation. Most Americans eventually came to accept the kind of neopragmatism that was associated with the observations of Thomas Paine and John Dewey. Ordinary American people were willing to settle for a much lower benchmark that explained economic life in simple terms. This benchmark is easily seen though not easily attainable. This currency involves making money work for you. So students who seem disinterested in philosophy and theory courses and embarking on a pragmatic treadmill will eventually discover that they are unable to keep up with the spinning and the speed. That is when they will rediscover the importance of reflecting on the ancient and medieval texts. By then it might be too late. Yet armed with such knowledge, we should be able to avoid our minds becoming like the stories about Panama and acquire some kind of knowledge as best we can. Because an intimate knowledge of how money works is the real basis of MNC power.

The case of Panama, the first genuine American MNC, is not such an unusual story that it stands out as a model for emulation. Rather, Panama seems to suggest a pattern among developing areas that would otherwise remain unused, infertile, perhaps even as dysfunctional as some of the crew on the *Ship of Fools*. But simply because places like Panama have been developed and its utility has been proven does not imply that it is a perfect story of success.

BUILDING CONFIDENCE

Accumulation theory details the fact that in order for a business strategy to work, there ought to be a unity of different aspects of the process (Jessop 1990, pp. 198–99; Rappa 2001, pp. 5–16). Any growth model requires arrangements, negotiations, and businesslike understanding between and among parties that intend to build a better society and perhaps a better world. The rise of the United States as an economic hegemony reveals certain stories of successful capitalism that has been built on effective negotiations between politicians and business persons. The net effect of their work might be severely criticized as "collusion" at one end of the spectrum or "business acumen" at the other. It can be seen that some aspects of building the organizational culture for American MNCs were born out of the Panama Canal (1870–1914). This involved a significant degree of collusion between the chief executive, Wall Street bankers and lawyers, and military men willing to do the dirty work of construction and coercion.

A nicer way of putting this would be the creation of a better understanding between government, businesses, and the army. In physical terms, the idea of linking the Atlantic and Pacific Oceans goes back to the time of the Holy Roman Empire, but a series of failures over almost four centuries resulted in the sale of the "site" by the French to the United States. While Ulysses S. Grant and William McKinley were the first two U.S. Presidents who were involved in this project, it was the youthful Theodore Roosevelt who pushed the canal works through after McKinley was assassinated. However, it was actually William H. Taft who saw the longest amount of digging work done on the project while the political scientist and war president, Woodrow Wilson, finally saw its proper end. It was a strange idea because of the immensity of the task but a functional one because if the idea could be achieved, communications would significantly be improved and the political returns would become enormous. It can therefore be argued that there was no collusion but instead the President was acting out of national interest and a deep desire to entrench U.S. sovereignty.

Nevertheless, there was some degree of back-room dealing and secret meetings that enabled the United States to take possession of the Canal Zone from Colombia through a third-party agreement with a Frenchman designated to help out with the political processes required for eventual congressional approval. The back room political deal resulted in much hatred and antagonism toward the United States but it seemed that only nature kept taking the lives of the construction crews through malaria and yellow fever. Nevertheless, the American MNCs such as the McClintic-Marshall Company, which was involved in the project, learnt much from the inept French attempts at creating a canal that was sufficiently wide and deep to allow ocean-going ships to pass through from the Pacific to the Atlantic and vice versa.

There were also other secret deals in Wall Street that enabled the canal's completion. The completion of the canal was interrupted by the advent of World War I. Ironically, thousands of local inhabitants who were desirous of work and seeking employment anywhere they could find it would eventually die in the zone from various causes. And American workers died on the project that was operated and managed by former officers who received their professional military training from the U.S. Corps of Engineers. This means that they had the expertise for moving and building roads and bridges, had knowledge of the use of explosives, and had practical training in war and peace-time operations. This position of using former army officers ties in with anti-Marxist state theories of disciplining and controlling the police, military, and other coercive state elements (Jessop 1990, p. 279). The notion of control extends beyond the experience of labels. Hence military experience of individuals now converted to civilian occupations does not lessen the value of having shared those experiences in the first place.

The story of the Panama Canal is rationally described by David McCullough's *Path Between The Seas: The Creation of the Panama Canal, 1870–1914* (Simon & Schuster 1978); Ulrich Keller, *The Building of the Panama Canal in Historic Photographs* (Dover 1984); and Ovidio Diaz Espino's *How Wall Street Created a Nation: J.P. Morgan, Teddy Roosevelt, and the Panama Canal* (New York: Four Walls Eight Windows, 2001). The creation of the Republic of Panama was the result of American neocolonialism and the strong-arm tactics of U.S. President Theodore Roosevelt. In fact, Espino's intriguing book about the Panama Canal details the political duplicity, rhetoric, wheeling and dealing, and the gun-boat diplomacy that involved Theodore Roosevelt (the fifth cousin of the Great Depression Democratic President, Franklin D. Roosevelt); J.P. Morgan (the financier himself and not the corporation that took on his name); the Wall Street law firm, Sullivan and Cromwell; Philippe Bunau-Varilla; Charles P. Taft (the brother of the future president who was

U.S. Secretary of War); and Douglas Robinson (Roosevelt's brother-in-law) who helped finance the project.

Theodore Roosevelt believed in speaking softly and carrying a big stick. This does not mean that he was particularly any more powerful because of this style of leadership, but it does remind one of the kinds of political leaders who also used such a method. In other words, the leadership style required of politicians in charge of large economies does not necessarily have to be tied to their political ideologies. Roosevelt introduced many progressive policies that liberated America from its relatively insular, Western European–bound thinking. After all, America was still fighting to survive as a nation within a world where the United Kingdom and France were still considered Great Powers. Ironically, Roosevelt did not like the railroads and the stranglehold they had over large parts of the contiguous United States.

But Roosevelt's policies would prove too progressive for many Americans and he failed to get re-elected even after being shot in the chest (this was before term limits were imposed on the executive branch of the U.S. Government, i.e. the President of the United States of America).[5] A Nobel Peace Prize–winner himself, Roosevelt believed that he would greatly expand the powers of the executive. This president believed that while one should not break the law, one ought to certainly go to the fullest extent of doing what the law would not expressly forbid. Perhaps because Roosevelt was a Republican president (though he switched to the Progressive label after the war) he appeared to have the "right" political ideals to move American liberal capitalism in ways that a Democratic president could not. See for example, the arguments put forward by writers like Edmund Morris, *The Rise of Theodore Roosevelt* (Ballantine 1980) and Nathan Miller's *Theodore Roosevelt* (Perennial 1994).

And ultimately, perhaps not by design or executive fault, American taxpayers paid the price. This was because, as the famous journalist Pulitzer discovered, it was scandalous how American taxpayers had not even known that they had paid ten times the amount of money for a piece of property that was worth only US$4 million in 1914 dollars.[6] That is equivalent to about US$0.75 billion in 2005. The Panama Canal, Theodore Roosevelt and (what is known in political science as) the rise of the "Imperial Presidency", Wall Street, and "foreigners" set the basis for this chapter on the political power of American MNCs.

OUTSOURCING

Outsourcing is not new. It is a business technique like putting old wine in new wineskins. Outsourcing involves moving the more expensive "parts" and aspects of American businesses to someplace cheaper. Yet there seems to be a current trend in modernity where there is a need to label old activities with new names such as "convergence", "conveyance", "prospecting", "head-hunting", "downsizing", "right-sizing", "matrix", "flat hierarchy", "insourcing", and "outsourcing", for example. Outsourcing for U.S. corporations is worth anywhere between US$58 billion to US$75 billion annually in savings.

Since the 1990s, at least ostensibly after the end of the Cold War, there was a rise in the need to outsource less productive sections of businesses. However, over the past three years, the tide appears to have changed. The current backlash against business process outsourcing (BPO) might be attributed to a section of America interested in supporting xenophobic tendencies. American xenophobia, catalysed by the tragedy of 9/11 and the public beheading of an innocent American hostage in Iraq, is going to get much worse before it sinks even lower. Most Americans are not xenophobic, but those who do fear foreigners tend to direct their hatred towards them because they believe these foreigners are stealing American jobs.

Yet capitalist states appear to be able to survive the vagaries of neoliberalism very well through regulatory policy and a firm knowledge of the extra or external economic arena as Jessop argues poignantly in *State Theory*.[7] For example, many U.S. businesses feel that the best bet is with foreign labour for several reasons. Firstly, they are not paid in U.S. dollars and are not domiciled (and hence not a burden on the U.S. domestic economy) in the United States. While Jessop's own brand of neoMarxism does not tally with the kind of critique that Sartre and others presented, his complex theories of descriptive capitalist accumulation strategies continue to make intellectual sense. Furthermore, because these workers are not living in America, the company does not have to worry about the high cost of medical insurance, cost-of-living allowances, income tax deductions, U.S. laws and Immigration and Naturalization Service (INS) regulations governing foreign work permits, the problem of legal aliens becoming illegal aliens, cultural shock, and 401K pension schemes. These foreigners are therefore not eligible under U.S. law for medical, dental, and other benefits. And so the companies do not have to and are certainly not obligated to resolve these social expectations of life in modernity. Also, foreign outsourced labour does not have to be unionized.

Some pundits believe that outsourcing is a good thing for consumers and citizens alike. They say it is good for consumers because the lower costs enjoyed from BPO mean a cheaper product and the savings are then passed on directly to the consumer base. Furthermore, they maintain, while jobs are lost in the United States, they result in higher employment levels overall which in turn mean a more profitable company or MNC that can then hire more locals to do more technically-demanding jobs at higher wages.

The problem with this argument is that it is false and misleading. MNCs exist for one purpose — to make money for their shareholders. As long as the MNC can find a better, cheaper, and more productive way of producing goods over a shorter time span, it will continue to do so. Lower costs are often not passed on to the consumer, and the citizens who need the lost jobs are often not the ones who are the same consumers of the given product. Nor are they able to fill the promised, more technically-demanding jobs at higher wages. This means that on average, outsourcing is good for the macroeconomy, MNC shareholders, its board, and less so for others. In fact, when more operations are moved overseas, the MNCs' tax profiles are lowered significantly. The United States Uncle Sam cannot tax these productive MNCs anyway and the potential incidence of tax on such businesses may be lost for good.

Let us put some relevant numbers together to support this argument. Various risk analysts estimate the total projected costs of outsourcing by U.S.-based MNCs, where the MNC is headquartered in any one of the fifty states, including Hawaii and Alaska, to fall within a range. That range of numbers *ceteris paribus* looks like this: between 200,000 and 500,000 new jobs created overseas; between US$1.5 billion to US$25 billion over the next five to eight years.[8] True, the numbers are insignificant when compared to the revenues that could be derived from insourcing back room operations, and others. However, taking the lower end of US$1.5 billion, this would amount to much more money than most average American workers would receive in any given U.S. state during a non-inflationary year, perhaps with the exception of Alaska, Hawaii, Illinois, New York, North Carolina, and Texas.

And, if we took just one half of the lower range of jobs created (that is, 100,000 new jobs created), while the numbers represent an average, and a small one at that, the value derived from such numbers would not be something to scoff at during an election year. Also, outsourcing versus insourcing does not create more jobs for locals and foreigners alike. Supporters of outsourcing rationalize: the "if you move MNC jobs overseas you will create new jobs back home" argument really ought to be read as "let's hire foreigners to do the jobs locals could do because they're cheaper and less troublesome". So why should U.S. MNCs cut back on outsourcing? Because there are totally employable Americans who are willing and able to do these jobs at equally competitive salaries without resorting to aggressive trade union tactics. It is merely a matter of where the MNCs want to put their money and how much of a bottom line the management is thinking about.

This reminds us of the kind of neoGramscian theories that effectively mapped out the nature of the capitalist bottom line. In addition, readers can pursue the powerful arguments made by Niklas Luhmann, Michael Mann, and especially Ernest Mandel's *Late Capitalism* (1975). The desire and greed for wealth has resulted in a fall in offspring in developed countries with the exception of the United States. We are aware that part of the reason for the graying populations of post-industrial countries is due to the fact that many people perceive having children as being an economic burden. If a primary purpose of marriage is to have children, then many younger people seem to be putting this socially constructed arrangement off because having a family means that one cannot spend all one earns on oneself. Apart from the United States, other developed nations are falling deep into the fertility trap where their most precious resource — their citizens — is not meeting their quota of offspring. This is the bottom line of fertility: there will be fewer younger people to support a larger number of older persons over the next twenty-five to fifty years.

One clear problem that besets modernity's advanced post-industrial societies is that the fertility problem knows no national boundaries. The replacement level of citizens who make up these countries keeps falling. Total fertility rate (TFR) is down. With some exception to the United States, the rest of the developed world has failed in trying to raise the TFR to 2.1 for every woman of child-bearing years. It would also appear that it becomes increasingly more difficult to raise the level the closer one gets to the 2.1 threshold, which can be explained by Pareto's law where 80 per cent effort might be able to achieve at best outcome, a 20 per cent increase towards the target level.

Thus far, the literature on ageing indicates that pro-natalist policies have not worked comprehensively. Those policies that have worked are too deeply buried under other kinds of social policy that it becomes difficult to isolate the independent variable. But trying to isolate the independent variable in the case of pro-natalist policies is like trying to predict who might win the 2008 U.S. presidential elections. It is a needle in a haystack; everyone knows that it is in there somewhere but no one can safely say where it might be. The United States is an exceptional case because of its liberal immigration policies that do not discriminate against ethnic ancestry as found in other countries. This means that people continue to find America an attractive place that is suitable to raise a family. Policymakers outside the United States are searching for different methods and modes of resolving the issue of ageing by changing essentialist and patriarchal policies, modifying in-migration laws, and giving bonuses and perks to those they want to produce more children. The economic bottom line is that the economies with the larger number of younger people might be the ones that survive late modernity.

A CONVERGENCE THEORY OF POVERTY

There is a cautionary note from the *Global Monitoring Report 2004* that most developing countries will fail to meet their poverty reduction targets, even those projected for as late as the next decade. This finding is not surprising because as neoMarxist theory tells us, there will continue to be a widening gap between the rich and the poor, between the haves and the have nots. As global population increases at an increasing rate, especially in the developing countries, there will be more people who need employment, and hence more people in competition for potentially the same amount of occupations that are available.

The widening gap between the impoverished and the richest rich in countries (regardless of GNP per capita) will continue unabated. This is because there are significant indications from all financial sectors, business trend projections, and government policy analyses that the poor are here to stay.

Most poor persons will be unable to get back on the capitalist beltway to life, liberty, and the pursuit of happiness. This is because of their hand-to-mouth existence and because they are likely to fall through the social safety net and hit the ground running from all the social pressures that keep them down there: illegal drug abuse, alcoholism, welfare dependency, racism, gambling debts, incarceration, prostitution, homelessness, demoralized attitudes towards neoliberal capitalism, and the neuroses and psychoses that prevent their minds from pulling themselves up by the bootstraps. Very often the poor are just poor because of bad luck, that catch-all phrase exhibiting a category for those who are born at the wrong time, in the wrong place, and for the wrong reasons. Even the World Bank and IMF have projected dismal views of the future for the next decade.[9]

It seems that neoliberal capitalism requires a certain quota of poverty to exist at the bottom of the achievement-oriented society. Such societies can only do so much for the luckless who cannot seem to possibly recover despite aid to them. This is what I call the "convergence theory of poverty". The operating principle here is that capitalist societies need many more poor and impoverished persons as a complement to the wealth and power of a few. The disparity between the two is concordant with the images and metaphors of ontological perceptions of being. In other words, human beings living under the so-called aegis of modernity are self-prescribed units that buy into the images created by the international mass media to the point that these images, however inaccurate, however sketchy or however partial, become the reality of the message that is being revealed. People believe in statistical support of poverty because the image of poverty exists as an important function of world capitalist domination.

Could it be that the ideological nature of capitalism requires the presence of the poor? And that for the minority rich to remain in their wealth, there has to be a poor underclass of persons who simply cannot achieve or fit into any other part of the political and social system that they are branded outcasts from the onset?

Poverty is converging across all centres of capitalist development. Perhaps Marx was right about the owners of the factors of production being callous authoritarian controllers of the "have nots". While he was certainly wrong about the historical determinism of revolution arising out of the internal contradictions between the base and the superstructure, he was quite right that there would be problems within capitalist societies that display great differences of wealth between the rich and the poor, between the workers and the owners of these workers.

No "real" Marxist or "socialist" revolution is on the cards for America's future. But even if it did arrive later in American modernity, the poor will doubtless become cannon fodder for the movers and shakers of neoliberal global capitalism. So who are these movers and shakers and what kinds of salaries and bonuses do they expect to motivate them to higher levels of capitalist creativity? The next section examines with some empirical data the kind of expectations and results that the best American CEOs have achieved in recent years. This harks back to the wonderful quote from Thucydides' *History of the Peloponnesian War* where it is said that "we use riches rather for opportunities of action than for verbal contestation, and hold it not a shame to confess poverty but not to have avoided it."[10] This means that we should not even be worried about using wealth to promote wealth while simultaneously having had previously experienced the depression and obstacle of poverty and its deep and dark cavern of remorse and regret. No one owes the impoverished a living, and successful CEOs continue to realize this as a reality throughout their lives. Capitalism and the neoliberal international economic system as we understand it today provides a deep and unending series of traps that serve to weaken and complicate honest and earnest attempts at accumulating capital. There is not an individual alive today who can remain secure with a total belief in the capitalist oeuvre. This is because the commitment to capitalism does not ensure or guarantee anything more than one's participation in the global traits of greed and avarice.

Capitalism is both theory and practice in one, and cannot and should not be understood as being separable into sophia and praxis, or any other Hegelian form of dualistic world view. It cannot be understood outside theory. In a throwback to the great thinkers of the Enlightenment, it becomes clear that capitalism is neutral in the sense of being callous and unfeeling. It is like that old and famous poem by James Shirley called *Death the Leveller*. It is an end where one will experience the total transformation of one's own biological matter as it is dispensed outwardly into the cosmos until the initial energy that exists is nothing that resembles the original mass. We are all moving towards that nothingness and will eventually have nothing to prove our existence, let alone the achievements that we think we might have made in this single life. In a sense, there is a great degree of nothingness in capitalism and awaiting capitalists. A certain quality makes capitalists as a whole very driven and pragmatic people, unwilling and unbending to give much personal time to the study of political philosophy or the classics of economic theory as those espoused by the great Irish political economists. Perhaps if they did make space and time for such study there would be much fewer capitalists alive and well today. Thus in order for the convergence theory to work, capitalism must work and Marxian economics must fail. So here is a clear epistemological path, even if only temporarily grounded, at this stage in late modernity.

CEO HAVEN

If you consider yourself a true American capitalist, then you would want to be part of the top-range CEO Haven that resounds with stories of successful American Dreams. But for every successful CEO raking in huge corporate bonuses, there are stories of CEOs involved in corporate scandals, abusing executive privilege by taking personal flights on the company jet, and fully paid vacations overseas on company expense in order to evade personal taxes and paying Uncle Sam.

When Ellen Smith, a writer for the Associated Press, claimed that the "the highest paid executives collectively enjoyed $30.9 million",[11] I did not believe this because it seemed that the figure was too small. While Smith was correct in arguing that the perks for American CEOs were clear to the public, she did not pursue the matter sufficiently. For example, the CEO of Goldman Sachs, Hank Paulson, received US$21.4 million in fiscal year 2003 that was almost twice his fiscal year 2002 pay (which was a whopping

US$12.1 million) excluding the US$5 million bonus for that year.[12] The headline news of such achievements drives and motivates capitalists to go to extremes in order to achieve top-notch status. Much has to be sacrificed. Unfortunately, this often involves breaking the law. Because capitalists are by nature very impatient with their own personal goals and often mix their personal goals with their corporate ability to achieve those goals, most forget that it takes most successful CEOs decades to get to where they are. The top earners in corporate America earn more than the U.S. President could even think about making in two consecutive terms in office.

The youngest CEOs at the very top have a median age range of 38–43. Most have graduate training in business. Some are legally trained while others have degrees from prestigious Ivy League universities which, as we all know, are crucial for making network connections. The public is drawn to both the stories of success and failure of the CEOs. There is much applause and support for those on the ascent while those who fall quickly see their celebrity status disappear and their erstwhile colleagues scamper for cover from all forms of government agencies. Unlike many other countries, the anti-trust culture in the United States is very strong and the public are often willing supporters of condemning corporate monopolistic culture even as they are sometimes ready to invest directly and quietly in these giants themselves. A true capitalist CEO who desires to be part of American CEO Haven has to be able to walk the tightrope between shady deals that lead to financial perdition and ethical ones that can often lead to dismal returns to stockholders.

The problem for the people at the top is how to negotiate modes of going to the fullest extent of what the law does not expressly forbid, as Theodore Roosevelt did, without breaking it. But because shareholders and other greedy executives are often impatient to consider the magnitude of their personal wants and business objectives, they are willing to remain quiet and to elect CEOs who are both able and willing to bend the law to their own advantage. As long as people benefit within the neoliberal capitalist culture of corporate America, they will remain silent. If they feel that they have not benefited sufficiently, they will complain, and sometimes such complaints results in the fall of very highly placed public officials and corporate executives. Most shareholders are often not aware of the wheeling and dealing exercises of their CEOs. Most only want a CEO who will take their company to new and profitable heights regardless of the consequences to the environment, the customer base, or the people working towards the bottom line.

However, there are many pitfalls along the way because for every honest business person on Wall Street, there are people who are watching and waiting for that honesty to dissipate into insurance fraud, tax evasion, backroom deals, abuse of company expenses, falsification of internal audit processes, and insider trading. The *New York Post* reported on 27 April 2004 that a Long Island software manufacturer, Computer Associates, had finally conceded its faulty accounting procedures that claimed US$2.2 billion in sales in 2000 and 2001. Legal suits were raised against Sanjay Kumar and his accomplices who posted negative results in order to collect US$1.1 billion in bonuses. Securities and Exchange Commission (SEC) investigators revealed discrepancies that eventually resulted in the demotion of CEO Sanjay Kumar, and an indictment by state prosecutors who were getting help from whistle blower Ira Zar, the ex-CFO of Computer Associates who admitted to accounting fraud. The IRS is sufficiently capable of monitoring the lifestyles of these people even long after they have served their prison sentences to ensure that whatever profits that could possibly be recouped would be done so in the most expeditious manner.

The money that is thrown at the capitalist "big boys" is so dazzling that it makes the decision-making process of many top-flight executives seem to be all about the business of business risk. "Do I or don't I?" "How much is it worth and how much can I get away with?" American MNCs are not alone in the SEC investigations. Recently, China Life became the target of an SEC insurance probe into its IPO in New York and Hong Kong.[13] China Life is the largest assurance company in China and the probe will slow down the intention of gaining greater investments to speed up the growth of its local and foreign markets. There might be irregularities and omissions in the conduct of China Life's daily core businesses, as reported in the *Financial Times* of London. Most recently, Reuters reported a loss of Fourth Quarter profits for China Life. No mention was made of the SEC probes of 2004.[14]

The view from above is sometimes cloudy, confusing, and misleading. However, there are moves and ways forward that might be contentious but will bring in more money to the company than a tropical storm brings rain to the Panamanian jungle. But for those who are able to stay on that tightrope and see through the clouds, without getting on the wrong side of the SEC, DEA, FBI, or private investigators, the bonuses and benefits are amazing. Not as amazing as the amount of money that Amazon.com CEO makes a year (in spite of the incredible success of his company over the past decade), but often better than his entire composite stock options in the company. The benefits and bonuses can only go upwards with the right CEO, in spite of gloomy business conditions.[15] Oftentimes, the salaries of these high-flying CEOs contain such buffers as to be virtually recession-proof. The top achievers in CEO Haven who can stay ethical and clean in their business deals stand to make the most money over time and to keep it even if the company's profits swan-dive. This is because it seems that these men (90 per cent of the top 15 per cent of all capitalist achievers in this patriarchal world are men) get incredible amounts of money even when the company is doing poorly and has gone completely into the red. There is an even more interesting story to tell about the very top capitalist achievers. According to *Forbes*, the highest paid American CEOs in 2002 were all men. Most had graduate training in business and related fields or at least useful ones like law and accounting. Most had been at the job for at least ten years. And most were in their mid to late sixties. In other words, CEOs right at the top do not appear overnight, nor does it take only a few years to make it to CEO Haven. The norm for achieving top-flight CEO-ship is between fifteen to thirty-five years on the job and to be in charge as a CEO. The crème de la crème include Reuben Mark (Colgate-Palmolive), George David (United Technologies), Richard S. Fuld Jr. (Lehman Brothers),[16] Henry R. Silverman (Cendant),[17] Dwight C. Schar (NVR), Lawrence Ellison (Oracle), Richard M. Kovacevich (Wells Fargo), Howard Solomon (Forest Labs), James E. Cayne (Bear Stearns), and Todd S. Nelson (Apollo-Education Group). These were only in the 2002 cohort. They are very wealthy men even in 2005.[18]

According to Forbes, the worst performer in their analysis was Richard A. Manoogian who has been the CEO of Masco for thirty-six years. His six-year average compensation amounted to nothing less than US$13,023,626, according to Masco's books. Another CEO who received an F-grade from *Forbes* was Stephen F. Bollenbach, the eight-year-long CEO of Hilton Hotels, whose six-year average compensation was US$6,339,279. As for Michael D. Eisner, the CEO of Walt Disney for twenty years, his six-year average compensation was a fantasy world amount of US$121,170,940.[19] This is why the salaries of these high-flying CEOs contain such buffers as to be virtually recession-proof because no one else can fill their august positions given the political sensitivities of removing a CEO who knows too much, or of replacing one to whom the political fortunes and life-long careers are indelibly tied to.

The successful MNC must have capable drivers who always think only in the best interests of the company and not themselves. This matter is best illustrated in CitiGroup's current setting aside of US$6 billion towards legal costs in the pending law suits in the Enron case where the securities corporation engaged in shady deals that drove the company from dazzling and meteoric heights of capitalists' fantasy to the dustbin of the dotcoms. Another MNC characteristic is "drive and passion" for the company that equals long-term rewards, at least most of the time. The MNC must always outlive its CEOs and executive management. The business must go on in spite of the cracks that set in or in case of unforeseen circumstances. The people want their goods. Or they will take their money elsewhere. CEOs' successes, however, sometimes take their toll. Perhaps it seems just a little too ironic for the CEO of a fast food MNC who promoted healthier forms of fast food (like an expanded salad range) to die of a heart attack at a fast food convention. While Jim Cantalupo's company, McDonald's Corporation, was making one-and-a-half times more than the previous financial year,

> CEO...Jim Cantalupo ... died of a heart attack while in Florida for a McDonald's convention, was replaced by the fast-food chain's 43-year-old president and chief operating officer, Charlie Bell. Bell paid tribute to Cantalupo in a news release accompanying McDonald's quarterly earnings report as "an incredibly inspiring and passionate leader" and said he is committed to strengthening McDonald's and "continuing the momentum that began under Jim's leadership." Net income for the first three months of the year was US$511.5 million, or 40 US cents per share, compared with US$327.4 million, or 26 US cents per share, for the same period a year ago. That matched the consensus estimate of analysts surveyed by Thomson First Call. Revenue was US$4.4 billion, up 16 per cent from US$3.8 billion a year earlier.[20]

It is sad to think that the amount of wealth we accumulate, like the Egyptian pharaohs who had only one really big project, can never be taken with us when we die. All the good deeds that Cantalupo did for the poor and the needy in his lifetime had done nothing to extend the brevity that was his life. This is why capitalism is about greed and avarice, and not about being nice. One thing is for sure, as the CEO of McDonalds, Cantalupo left a certain legacy that was politically relevant and socially necessary:

> McDonald's premium salad range was one of several innovations introduced in the US by [Jim] Cantalupo that drove sales and helped give McDonald's a healthier image in the face of rising concerns over obesity... Charlie Bell, the 43-year-old Australian appointed chief executive within hours of Cantalupo's death after a heart attack on April 19, pledged to continue the momentum of the changes begun by his predecessor ... McDonald's had served 2.3m more customers during the first quarter compared with last year, the equivalent of adding 1,500 restaurants, but had added only 100 restaurants in the past 12 months.[21]

The new CEO was appointed within hours of the old CEO's death. But Bell himself stepped down in late 2004 to fight cancer, and died two months later. Skinner took over Bell's job and has remained at the helm ever since. Skinner was paid bonuses of almost US$9 million in early 2007 for his performance.

The MNC must outlive its CEO and improve on what the CEO has done in order to continue to satisfy the legal requirements of its faceless shareholders. The heads of America's 500 biggest companies received an aggregate 8 per cent pay increase in fiscal year 2003 and as a group, their total compensation amounted to US$3.3 billion versus US$3.1 billion in fiscal year 2002.[22] While the remuneration in CEO Haven is more money than ordinary folk will make in a thousand lifetimes, what is startling is the vulgar continuity of the process, and the willingness for some to be sad in one frame, and happy in the next.

HOPE: BACKGROUNDS THAT WORK?

Many of the top financial MNCs since the writing of the first edition of this book have closed down. Some of the worst hit include the now defunct Lehman Brothers and the recently rescued AIG. Lehman Brothers filed Chapter 11 in late 2008.

But let's consider the person right at the top who pulls the team together and who make the politics of American globalization work the way it does. These are people who have usually gone through the right education system, possess the right values, and have an instinctive feel for taking the right business risk. What does it mean to be a successful CEO? Can we rely on a summary of their background interests to chart a course of understanding about the way commercial politics works? Were it possible, it would be interesting to create a clone distilled from the background of these CEOs to create a super CEO. Not possible. Nevertheless, some brief background notes on America's top CEOs is instructive to understand the power that motivates neoliberal corporate America. As we have seen, the right education and connections do not always work. The original brothers Lehman must be turning in their graves now, for example.

Top on the list is Reuben Mark who has been CEO of Colgate-Palmolive for twenty years and with the company for over forty-three years. *Forbes* ranks this 65-year-old man as number one in the category of "Household & Personal Products". Mark was educated at Middlebury College BA in 1960 and holds a Harvard MBA dating back to 1963. He urged Colgate to help rebuild a school in Harlem and actually used to do community volunteer work on Manhattan island till he moved to his Greenwich, Connecticut home.[23] According to *Business Week*, "He rode a motorcycle ... hunts game birds ... and wants his company to be the superstar, not him".[24] Mark's total compensation package was US$148 million.[25]

Number two on the list is George David. For the past ten years, George David has been CEO of United Technologies (UTX) and worked for the company for almost thirty-one years. David, who was ranked number one under "Conglomerates", was educated at Harvard and holds an MBA from the University of Virginia's Darden Graduate School of Business Administration. According to *CNNMoney*,

> George David runs a company so diversified it makes products as small as air conditioners along with products as complex as the military's Blackhawk helicopters. With 155,000 employees worldwide, United Technologies has held its course and managed an impressive 28 billion dollars in revenue. Since David took over in 1994, the operating profit margin has jumped from 4 per cent to 14 per cent.[26]

David also believes in voluntary service, having served in the United Way in Hartford and in the American Red Cross. David's total compensation package was US$70.5 million.[27]

Richard S. Fuld Jr. was 58 years old with degrees from Colorado and NYU's Stern Business School. Fuld also chaired Lehman Brothers Executive Committee. He used to chair the Mt. Sinai Children's Center Foundation. His total compensation package according to *Forbes* was US$67.7 million.[28] A few years ago, Fuld Jr., was number three on the list of the top CEOs. Fuld received close to half a billion U.S. dollars since he began working at Lehman in 1993 right up till late 2007. By 2008 Fuld was punched in the face at the Lehman Brothers Gymnasium when news broke about Lehman's bankruptcy. He was blaming everyone, apparently, rather than taking the blame himself as the CEO.

Henry R. Silverman was CEO of Cendant (CD) for almost one-and-a-half decades in the same company that he founded. *Forbes* ranked this 63-year-old executive number one in the "Hotels, Restaurants & Leisure Education" industry. He holds degrees from Williams College and is a Juris Doctor from the University of Pennsylvania. Silverman has made significant contributions to various buildings, scholarships, professorships, and other academic activities at the University of Pennsylvania. He was also awarded honours for his public crusade against discrimination by the U.S. Hispanic Chamber of Commerce. The State of New York Governor's Office nominated

Silverman to the Board of Commissioners of The Port Authority of New York and New Jersey.[29] A Yankees fan, Silverman, "is a study in contrasts. Formal, almost aristocratic in his bearing, he favors monogrammed shirts and a plush office that's sprinkled with Georgian antiques. But his speech is blunt, with a manner more like a street fighter than the prep school-educated son of privilege".[30] His total declared direct shares at Cendant tallied up to eight million in the summer of 2003 and his total compensation package according to *Forbes* was US$60.0 million.[31] In 2005 it was decided by the Cendant Board to break up the company into its four main interests. By summer 2006, the break-up was sealed. CEO Silverman was rewarded with a severance package of US$62.53 million plus another US$50 million from the real estate subsidiary of Cendant that became known as Realogy Corp.

The next one on the list is Dwight C. Schar. He was CEO of NVR for eighteen years, and worked with the company for a total of thirty-five years so far. When he was 62 years old, *Forbes* ranked him number one in "Construction". Educated at Ashland University, Schar stepped down as CEO in the summer of 2005. At 67 years old in 2009, Schar is chairman of the executive committee of NVR.

Schar was a former teacher whose story is a kind of latter day rags-to-riches narrative. He worked his way up very quickly and astutely made the right political moves that finally ended in his taking over the company itself. He was one of a 100 business persons who were part of the Northern Virginia Roundtable that represented the heart of the economic force of Republicanism in the state.[32] While the roundtable was not really a pressure group, it certainly acted as a lobbying community of business-minded individuals who support political causes that put business as a top priority.

Over the years, Schar demonstrated that he was most capable at political networking. Apart from his political contributions in cash and kind that led him to become George Bush's finance chair for the state of Virginia, Schar made other commitments. He contributed to the local university, children's groups, youth groups and teen groups, and a cancer society.

Schar is known to be a generous donor to the causes in which he strongly believes. He and some of his friends also expressed their passion for the Redskins when they got together to make a controlling bid for that team.[33] Schar is now considered a minority owner of the team:

> The Redskins completed the sale of a minority stake in the club, to Dwight C. Schar, Robert Rothman and Fred Smith. Their purchase of about 20 per cent of the Redskins for a little over $200 million — with no say over operations — put the total value of the organization at over $1 billion.[34]

NVR is now found across eleven states and its total sales approximate US$3.7 billion.[35] Schar's total compensation package according to *Forbes* was US$58.1 million.[36]

Lawrence J. Ellison is the co-founder and CEO of Oracle and has remained at the helm for over thirty years. Ellison was born in 1944 and was appointed CEO and director in 1977. He was also company president from 1978 to 1996. Ellison said,

> NT will earn more, but Windows CE may become the world's most ubiquitous operating system. And in each case, Microsoft is using its desktop monopoly and predatory tactics to … control the standards, eliminate competing access points, lock consumers into Microsoft products, and purchase competing technologies. With over $12 billion of monopoly profits in the bank, there are few markets Microsoft can't dominate. But it doesn't stop there. Microsoft is now aggressively moving to use its monopoly power to control online content. As more and more Americans come online, the ability of Microsoft to favor its own content will have profound cultural, societal, consumer and economic implications. For your news go to MSNBC™; for financial services go to Microsoft Investor™; for travel services go to Microsoft Expedia™; for retail shopping go to the Microsoft Plaza™; to buy a car go to Microsoft Carpoint™; and to buy or sell a house go Microsoft Home Advisor™.[37]

Of course, not all of Ellison's predictions have come true, but they were certainly believable back then. It has always been Ellison's (and Oracle's) dream to be number one. Not surprisingly, Ellison is a close friend of Apple's Steve Jobs. While Jobs has had the most difficult of all the backgrounds in the sense that he was orphaned at a young age, and, like Gates and others, dropped out of college and hence took a big risk, Jobs is not on the rich CEO list. His own net worth of US$1 billion puts him very far behind his friend Ellison and others. Ellison received a compensation package of US$1 million in FY 2008.

One person that has eluded both Oracle's Ellison and Apple's Jobs is Bill Gates. Perhaps one of the most influential men on earth, Gates allowed Jobs to cut an Internet browser deal years ago that would save Apple. Bill Gates is just a cut above the rest. Always one step forward. Constantly just one move ahead. Consider his 1999 book, *Business @ the Speed of Thought*. Gates and his wife Melinda have donated over US$23.8 billion to charities on education and learning. After all, that is Microsoft's core business. Bill Gates is also one of the most controversial political figures in corporate America. He is like an almost indispensable interactive wood-carpenter of the twenty-first century. The majority of Americans and non-Americans worldwide use his sophisticated source codes and platforms to do work. The kind of work really does not matter since it is mostly done on Microsoft. When I was in graduate school, there was a strong movement against using Microsoft and IBM PCs. Many of us had no choice but to churn out term papers and finals on typewriters or Apple derivatives. What was political in the corporate world of computing software somehow travelled down to us all and not surprisingly. While many people actually learn to use a computer on old Apple II models, most end up with a PC.

The strong movement against Microsoft and the PC ended in a division of hardware between the PC cluster and the Mac cluster. The rest is history. We now return to the CEOs who depend on the work of Ellison, Jobs, and Gates.

Ellison, like Jobs and Gates, does not have the benefit of any college degree, or a fancy graduate school MBA. This might be the reason why they made it so far. Perhaps it was because they were not tainted by the education system, and indeed created a system apart. Perhaps it can be said in American popular culture that the "nerds" do control the globalized, computing world. Ellison was ranked number one by *Forbes* in "Software & Services". For a man who taught himself all he needs to know, he earns a total compensation package of US$40.6 million.[38] *Forbes 400* cited him in 2001 as the third richest person in America with US$58 billion, while the second richest person was Bill Gates of Microsoft Corporation at US$63 billion, and the ninth richest was Michael Dell of Dell Computers, whose gross wealth is estimated at US$16 billion. Bill Gates has been the richest man in America from 1993–2003. But if Sam Walton of Wal-Mart were still around, according to *Forbes 400*, he would be worth about twice as much as Bill Gates. Sam Walton was born 29 March 1918 and died in 1992.

There are other top-notch CEOs, like Richard M. Kovacevich (Wells Fargo), who was educated at Stanford and receives a total compensation package of US$37.8 million.[39] Listed also as one of the most powerful individuals in America, Howard Solomon was born on 12 August 1927 in New York. Solomon is the CEO of Forest Labs.[40] This 76-year-old has degrees from CUNY and a Juris Doctorate from Yale. Solomon commands a compensation package of US$36.1 million.[41] A Republican-supporter of the Bush campaign, James E. Cayne is the CEO of Bear Stearns, 70 years old, and like Ellison, has no degrees but commands a total compensation package of US$33.9 million.[42] Bear Stearns had twenty offices around the world and 10,574 people on its payroll in 2002. The diversified financial company had benefited significantly over the border wars between New Jersey and New

York, receiving tax incentives to stay on in New York and politically outwitting successive New York politicians, including the venerable Rudy Giuliani.[43] By 2009 this situation had changed dramatically.

The tenth-best-compensated CEO was a former executive vice president and faculty member of the University of Utah. Todd S. Nelson, CEO of Apollo-Education Group. He has degrees from Brigham Young University and University of Nevada at Las Vegas (UNLV) and is worth US$32.8 million.[44] Running an MNC in America or at least from an American city with worldwide connections is not like building the Panama Canal. The tasks are now more urgent, with seemingly limitless possibilities, intense rivalry and competition, and limited resources. And the U.S. President does not usually directly intervene to help out. There are some clear characteristics that all American CEOs share that make them the wealthy capitalists that they are today. All are willing to put in more energy than what they perceive are their nearest competitors by industry. All have a high degree of focus on making a simple mission spectacular. Each has a specific inner ear that makes them very sensitive to potential changes in taste and market moods. They enable themselves with knowledge from the best people in the world for the job. They fight to get the best technical expertise and administrative managers to creatively contribute to the product. Being a successful CEO in America involves dedication and ethics. They know exactly where the boundaries lie, and understand the political and organizational semantics of what the law does not expressly forbid them from doing. Being ethical is the way forward because if you do the right thing you remain on the job in a way that makes you outlast your competitors who might fall by the wayside because of moments of intense greed. Successful American CEOs never see failure as a step back but a process and opportunity for renewal.

PROGRESS: TRUTH AND FALSITY

> I always say that I landed on Omaha Beach, but I don't tell people that it was six weeks after the contested landing.[45]

The U.S. economy is built on images of truth and falsity. These truths and falsehoods are complicated by a wide and deep and immense range of statistics and mathematical permutations from specialists in such highly specialized fields that sometimes no one understands what they are talking about. For example, high wages often mean low levels of employment for the average worker in the United States, but low unemployment during critical election years may result in lower wages across the board for most middle class and lower class workers. But, as the World Values Survey claims, 60 per cent of Americans think that the poor are lazy. One might deduce from this finding that when you start getting lower wages, and perhaps when you finally lose your job, you might become one of the poor. And if you are considered one of the poor, then people are going to think, six out of ten times, that you are a lazy American. So, as the old saying goes, "get a job!" But how much of our self worth or dignity should we be willing to lose when faced with occupational or career changes?

The images of truth and reality and the gap between the two becomes more complex and confusing when we add oil to the fire or salt to the open wound: the ideological belief in individualism and the truism of achievement through hard work and personal sacrifice only worsens the self esteem of those who are indeed out of work and out of energy but full of responsibilities and commitments made during gainful employment. Therefore, it is one thing for academics and IMF managers to say that we ought to liberalize financial structures when the MNC that used to employ 250,000 Americans now only employs 2,000 because it makes more sense and a fist full of dollars to outsource or relocate backroom operations to several other countries. This is despite the fact that standards may be compromised, where cost-of-living is low, and where the CEO and the entire board can have their permanent offices in tax shelters where the sun shines all year round rather than in gloomy tax-burdened cities of snow, sleet, rain, and unionized strikes.

Most locals who lose their jobs to the backroom operators overseas are very unlikely to be employable. This is because new jobs will be created locally but for different purposes and with different skills requirements. But is a cost-cutting MNC likely to send those who have recently been made jobless for training and upgrading?

CONCLUSION: OPTIMISM

The political economy of the United States of America has a profound financial, social, cultural, and political influence on the process of globalization throughout the world. Anyone alive today probably knows more about America than the next nearest sovereign country to their own home nation. The ideals of Pax Americana and the American Business Dream are tantamount to the capitalist perfectionism of perfecting the U.S.-led neoliberal international economic system. American MNCs and their CEOs are powerful machines whose personal drive and ambition cannot be easily or summarily curtailed, moderated, or circumvented in any series of academic discourses. But while scholars try to pin down their epistemological success stories, they themselves get caught in the economic rat race of research grant applications, research funding from government and private sources, and the fight against those bureaucrats who control the masses with their hypocritical use of regulations while hiding their own agendas for self-reward, self-promotion, and self-aggrandizement with the camouflage of neutrality and language of rationality — as if people did not know they were mostly undeserving. Yet this is nothing compared to the level of trickery and machination that goes into making profits in what Fredric Jameson has called the "cultural logic of late capitalism".

How powerful are American MNCs? They are as powerful as their CEOs make them. There are specific characteristics in the background of the top performing CEOs but one must not mistake the difference between imitation and substantive drive. As we have seen, imitative behaviour and the idea of the mimic man as described by Homi Bhabha and V.S. Naipaul, indicate a shallow copying of an original perception or impression with the view to achieving the same status and dignity of these origins. Going to the same schools and clubs, and having the same hobbies as these CEOs, does not make one likely to be as successful as they are. Rather, the politics of globalization in America demands, and indeed requires, CEOs who are as dissimilar as possible. The key ingredient to their wealth is networking with a focus.

If you discover that your networking costs are more than your entertainment budget can withstand in any given year, something is not going right. Successful politics requires a certain disjunction, a rejection of the road well taken and is similar to the advice found in these titles: Robert D. Kaplan's *Warrior Politics: Why Leadership Requires a Pagan Ethos* (Vintage 2003); the monastic-like life choices presented in the case study by Robert B. Catell, Kenny Moore, and Glenn Rifkin's *The CEO and the Monk: One Company's Journey to Profit and Purpose* (John Wiley and Sons 2004); the inspirational logic of Laurie Beth Jones's *Jesus CEO: Using Ancient Wisdom for Visionary Leadership* (Hyperion 1996); or, one book that I have not read but seems to be getting a lot of publicity and positive reviews, Eric Yaverbaum's *Leadership Secrets of the World's Most Successful CEOs: 100 Top Executives Reveal the Management Strategies That Made Their Companies Great* (Dearborn Trade Publishing 2004).

Max Weber may have made many erroneous arguments but one thing he did get right was that work defines life. But people work for different reasons. Most are unwilling to work without pay. But can money buy happiness in the end? The answer is quite clear. It cannot. But it can purchase temporary respite from suffering; it can gain relief for others in pain; and money, as Cyndi Lauper said in 1984, changes everything. Sometimes the changes are bad; at other times, the changes are good. Take the current economic crisis that the world is experiencing. There are three solutions that the experts have come up with. One is to bail out existing companies on the verge of bankruptcy. Another is to extend loan periods and forego interest payments. And the third is for the Fed to cut interest rates. Note that all these solutions involve money.

Money has time value and exhibits characteristics of an international public good. But it has no intrinsic value. A trillion, billion U.S. dollars on planet Mars is worthless. So money on its own is nothing without the sentiment of human value perpetuated with its use. Money is also a store of future value. But therein lies its volatility. If we miscalculate the future value of money, we risk loss. If we undervalue it, we risk profit. In the case of the sub-prime crisis, it can be attributed to three conditions: Throwing good money after bad; taking long-term unsecured risks; and allowing greed to determine the value placed on money. Money is a universal good that can be traded as currency in late modernity. Perhaps the answer to this growing worldwide recession is to increase liquidity so that companies can borrow more from banks, or so that banks would be more willing to lend to companies and individuals. The banks are currently unwilling to extend loans because of the greater risks incurred through interbank borrowing, but if there were greater liquidity in the market and the Fed cuts interest rates, then the loans will be more forthcoming. Since the entire economy is in a recession, one need not worry about inflationary pressures. This solution may sound simple and unsophisticated but at least it makes sense. For all the sophisticated tools and complex mathematical models used on Wall Street, for all their econometric rhetoric and technical expertise, there is nothing to show for their financial terrorism and greed that led to the crisis. Not even a fist full of dollars.

Notes

[1] *A Fist Full of Dollars* (1964).
[2] I Timothy 6:10.
[3] Pierpaolo Barbieri, "Dissenting Opinion: Paying the Way Forward — Monetary Incentives Pervert the Ideal of Education", *Harvard Crimson*, 18 October 2007.
[4] Henry S. Kariel, "Nietzsche's Preface to Constitutionalism", *Journal of Politics* 25, no. 2 (1963): 211–25.
[5] This is similar to the shooting in the chest of Taiwanese President Chen Shui Bian in the 2004 election in Taipei. Chen, however, went on to win the election.
[6] Ovidio Diaz Espino, *How Wall Street Created a Nation: JP Morgan, Teddy Roosevelt, and the Panama Canal* (NY: Four Walls Eight Windows, 2001), p. 6.

7   Bob Jessop, *State Theory: Putting Capitalist States in their Place* (University Park, PA: Pennsylvania State University Press, 1990), pp. 309–10.
8   My own estimates from various business risk companies, interviews with bankers, and interviews with shareholders of American companies.
9   "IMF/World Bank Report Calls for Urgent Action on Poverty Reduction by All Countries", *Press Release No. 04/85*, 22 April 2004.
10 Thomas Hobbes (trans., with notes and introduction by David Greme), Thucydides' *The Peloponnesian War* (Chicago, IL: University of Chicago Press, 1959), "The Second Book": Sect. 40, 111.
11 Ellen Smith, "Perks for American CEOs Alive and Well", *Associated Press/Halifax Herald Ltd*, 24 April 2004.
12 Jenny Anderson, "Goldman Sachs CEO Paulson Joins JP Morgan Boss in Big Bucks Club", *New York Post*, 25 February 2004, p. 33.
13 According to FT's London sources, "The [American] SEC, looking at the circumstances surrounding the IPO, does not comment on individual investigations. An SEC inquiry becomes formal if investigators believe the case should go further and they gain powers to compel the delivery of evidence after a vote of the agency's five commissioners." See, "China Life Confirms It is the Target of SEC Probe", *Financial Times*, 28 April 2004.
14 Reuters, 25 March 2009.
15 Stephen Lynch, "Bankers Pay Headed Up: Survey", *New York Post*, 13 September 2003, p. 22; See "The Best Performers", *BusinessWeek Online*, 5 April 2004; and "Something Ventured, Something Gained", *CIO Magazine*, 15 April 2004. See also the television quote by Paul Solman, "Starting in 1998, when Enron's stock began to defy gravity, CEO Ken Lay exercised options on hundreds of occasions, pocketing over $200 million in gains. His successor, Jeffrey Skilling, exercised more than $100 million worth of options, many of them just before the company tanked. But why were executives given such huge options grants to begin with? According to Graef Crystal, it's because companies treated stock options as if they weren't an expense, didn't cost their companies a dime", in "Sharing the Wealth", *PBS Online News Hour*, 6 January 2003.
16 According to the Lehman Brothers' website, the "history of Lehman Brothers parallels the growth of the United States and its energetic drive toward prosperity and international prominence. What would evolve into a global financial entity began as a general store in the American South. Henry Lehman, an immigrant from Germany, opened his small shop in the city of Montgomery, Alabama in 1844. Six years later, he was joined by brothers Emanuel and Mayer, and they named the business Lehman Brothers", and it is located at the prestigious address: 745, Seventh Ave., New York, NY 10019. See <http://www.lehman.com> for details.
17 The Cendant Corporation describes itself as "one of the foremost providers of travel and real estate services in the world; one of the world's largest hotel franchisors, the world's largest vacation ownership organization, and one of

166 Globalization: Power, Authority, and Legitimacy in Late Modernity

the world's largest car rental operators; the world's largest real estate brokerage franchisor, one of the largest retail mortgage originators in the US, and the world's largest provider of outsourced corporate employee relocation services; the franchisor of the second-largest tax preparation service in the US and leading providers of travel information processing services worldwide." See <http://www.cendant.com> for details.

[18] Data on the most recent wealth estimates accumulated by the latest cohort of top ten CEOs was not available before going to press.

[19] 2004 Forbes.com Inc.

[20] Dave Carpenter, "McDonald's Earnings Increase 56 per cent", *New York Post*, 27 April 2004.

[21] Neil Buckley, "Cantalupo Recipe Rewards McD's", *Financial Times*, 28 April 2004.

[22] 2004 Forbes.com Inc.

[23] See also "Colgate-Palmolive Co. — They Put a Smile on Your Face", *Corporate Board Member Magazine*, September/October 2002.

[24] Nanette Byrnes et al. "Reuben Mark — Colgate-Palmolive", *BusinessWeek Online*, 23 September 2002.

[25] 2004 Forbes.com Inc.

[26] "George David, United Technologies, CEO and Chairman", *CNNMoney*, 20 June 2003.

[27] *Forbes* defines total *compensation* package as "… total compensation as salary and bonus; 'other' compensation includes vested restricted stock grants, and 'stock gains', the value realized from exercising stock options during the just-concluded fiscal year". See 2004 Forbes.com Inc.

[28] 2004 Forbes.com Inc.

[29] George E. Pataki, *Office of the Governor of the US State of New York*, 2004.

[30] Amy Barrett, Stephanie Anderson Forest, and Tom Lowry, "Henry Silverman's Long Road Back — He's Fighting to Restore Cendant's Reputation", *BusinessWeek Online*, 28 February 2000.

[31] 2004 Forbes.com Inc.

[32] Virginia Business Online, June 2001.

[33] "Redskins Report: Notes, Quotes, Anecdotes", *CBS Sportsline.com*, 28 August 2003.

[34] "Back to Washington", *St. Petersburg Times*, 8 January 2004.

[35] Kenneth Bredemeier, "Rebuilding a Fortune: After the Early 1990s Bust, NVR Chief Dwight Schar has Revived his Company, Bought Part of the Redskins, and has Built Many Houses", *Washington Post*, 1 March 2004, E01.

[36] 2004 Forbes.com Inc.

[37] Lawrence J. Ellison, "Competition in the Digital Age: Beyond the Browser Wars", *Statement of Chairman and CEO of Oracle Corporation before the US Senate Committee on the Judiciary*, 23 July 1998.

38 2004 Forbes.com Inc. In 2009, Forbes.com cited Bill Gates as the richest person in America with US$58 billion falling by US$18 billion to US$40 billion. Lawrence Ellison net worth in 2009 was US$22.5 billion. The price for "entry" into this elite club of global billionaires remains unchanged at US$1.3 billion.
39 2004 Forbes.com Inc.
40 Robert Steyer, "Mixed Picture at Forest Labs", TheStreet.com, 20 April 2004.
41 2004 Forbes.com Inc.
42 2004 Forbes.com Inc.
43 Charles V. Bagli, "Mayor Rejects New Deal for Bear Stearns Jobs", *New York Times*, 6 January 2003.
44 2004 Forbes.com Inc.
45 Henry A. Kissinger, Thayer Award Speech, *USMA West Point*, 13 September 2000.

5

TERRORISM

There was a time when the idea of the reign of terror was limited to the French Revolution of the eighteenth century. These days, terrorism can be anything, any place, and anyone. Terrorism is fundamentally and inherently political. It is violence and the threat of violence, used and directed in pursuit of or in service of a political aim. This definition underscores clearly the other fundamental characteristic of terrorism: that it is planned, calculated, and a systematic act.

Terrorism is not difficult to define. It is just hard to predict. Terrorism is about point of view (perspective). It involves subjectivity and moral suasion. Indeed, the word "terrorism" derives from the French Revolution's "regime de la terreur". It refers to the desire for a restoration of order and the execution of traitors. The reign of terror referred to a revolutionary state of affairs that degraded into anti-monarchical demonstrations. The belief was that the terrorist was a freedom fighter who was being suppressed by the absolute powers of the monarch. This indeed was the case when one considers the end of the absolute Thai monarchy in 1932 and the devolution of power to Parliament and the military in reality. Seven years later the National Socialists seized sufficient power to launch the most comprehensive and tactically brilliant war. If not for its diabolical ideology, the National Socialists would probably have garnered more support. If not for its megalomaniacal leader, the National Socialists would have changed the face of Germany in a more meaningful way than the bestial manner in which the Nazis executed power and terrorized the new-found European innocence. Indeed, the Nazis as well as the Japanese for their atrocities in China during the Nanking massacre for example, could well be regarded as the state-sponsored terrorists de rigueur.

By the end of the Vietnam War, the concept of terrorism was then made even more complex with the ideological determinants of neoMarxism and neoMaoism. A new form of terrorism emerged in the 1980s that represented the frustrations of the new left and the neoMarxist beliefs of socialist Europe. This was made worse by the failures in Southeast Asia and the Middle East where Islamic fundamentalism had taken root.

By the 1990s, new forms of terrorism had already demonstrated itself despite the eventual weakening and demise of the old guard IRA-style killings and assassinations. The new terrorists would make their mark by flying their victims and themselves into their targets. The old-fashioned way of survival has given way to suicide terrorism where demands that are not met are not necessarily a bad thing for the terrorists. All the terrorists have to do, as a bright young student once said, is to get it right the first time. Counter-terrorist units have to get it right all the time.

There has been an incredible level of conceptual and practical dovetailing vis-à-vis the old terrorism and the new terrorism. One of the characteristics of the new terrorism is the lack of distinction among its choice of targets. The terrorist attacks of the 1990s such as the 1993 World Trade Center (WTC) bombings in New York, the 1995 Tokyo Sarin gas attack, 1996 Oklahoma City bombing, and the 2001 bombing of the WTC again clearly demonstrate that striking fear among the innocent was more important than making an ideological or moral point. While there is a religious dimension in the new terrorism, it is also clear that religion has taken on a secondary importance when it comes to the choice of targets. Terrorists of the new age do not care who their victims are. More importantly, the new terrorism invokes a natural fate or tendency towards fatalism. There is nothing to fear in death because that is simply the gateway to eternity. The following passage speaks about a different kind of prominence and a different kind of terror.

> My fellow Americans ... We pray that peoples of all faiths, all races, all nations, may have their great human needs satisfied; that those now denied opportunity shall come to enjoy it to the full; that all who yearn for freedom may experience its spiritual blessings; that those who have freedom will understand, also, its heavy responsibilities; that all who are insensitive to the needs of others will learn charity; that the scourges of poverty, disease and ignorance will be made to disappear from the earth, and that, in the goodness of time, all peoples will come to live together in a peace guaranteed by the binding force of mutual respect and love (*Public Papers of the Presidents*, Dwight D. Eisenhower, 1960, pp. 1035–40).

Terrorism gives meaning and purpose to terrorists who have lost faith in man; they want to bring everything down. There are no second demonstrations for the suicide bomber. The "ism" in terrorism means that it is ideological. Terrorism is an extension of human nature across the physical environment. It has thus become a natural thing for men to kill other men for proprietary rights. It is about bravado and egotism. Terrorism used to be a masculine thing. It is now, under the age of terrorism, a genderless thing. Terrorism involves the venting of aggression and frustration essential to being human. But that which is greater than terrorism is war. War is terrorism by the state. The state is greater than war and war than terrorism because it controls and determines human nature.

However, the problem with war is that like fire, it is a good slave but a poor master. And hence war can lead to the destruction of the state. The state must therefore always remain in control of war and the potential for war. Like the pyramids of Egypt, war is symbolized by life and death. But in the late modern world, the soldier no longer lives a life that is separate from other forms of public and personal life. For example, soldiers can incur debt and gain credit, and perform all other tasks that are common to civilian members of the American public. But there is an important difference in being a soldier, and that is the threat of death.

The relationship between the state, the individual, and military service should be given careful consideration in the politics of American globalization because of the global presence that the American military possesses. Withdrawing troops from a region a decade after the end of the Cold War is purely late symbolism. The Bush administration's announcement in summer 2004 about withdrawing 70,000 troops worldwide is really a redeployment exercise. *Pax Americana* cannot continue without the presence of American military technology and hardware in terms of its current global distribution. Like Hermocrates, the son of Hermon who proudly announced in our continuing story of the Peloponnesian War as it relates to war in modernity:

> I am therefore of opinion that dismayed with this reckoning, they will either not put over at all from Corcyra, or whilst they spend time deliberating and in sending out to explore how many and in what place we are, the season will be lost and winter come; or deterred by our unlooked-for opposition, they will give over the voyage. And the rather for that as I hear the man of most experienced amongst their commanders hath the charge against his will and would take a light occasion to return if he saw any considerable stop by us in the way. And

I am very sure we should be voiced amongst them to the utmost. And as the reports are so are men's minds; and they fear more such as they will hear will begin with them than such as give out that they will no more but defend themselves, because then they think the danger equal. Which would now be the case of the Athenians (Hobbes 1959, "The Sixth Book", Sect. 34, 398).

The presence of active and inactive performativity was anticipated in the strategic considerations of the battles that constitute the vicious cycle of militarism in any age. This reality, based on the essentialist nature of an unchanging and warlike masculinity, demands that proper attention be paid with the full regard to prior diplomatic and civilian agreements that have constituted realpolitik. A post-modern reflexivity is not an option for those who seek to dominate and benefit from such dominance. This harks back to the realist balance of power theory that dictates a close watch be kept continuously on one's adversaries as one keeps an eye on one's enemies. After all, an interpolation of the passage above suggests that the enemy of my enemy's enemy is my enemy. Once America had decided to take the lead in the war after the attack and massacre at Pearl Harbor in World War II, there was no way but forward as any other would invite a power vacuum that would be filled with adversaries. The cutbacks on military spending from the Cold War days in relative terms have resulted in the increase in the confidence levels of terrorist cellular networks all over the world. These networks themselves keep a vigilant lookout to "how many and in what place we are" and plan very carefully now that much of their conventional tactical methods have been disrupted and exposed. The propensity for terror constitutes a major half of the other side of man. It is the half that needs to be disciplined and controlled. It is the half that when exposed to the natural elements will, as Shakespeare wrote, "cry havoc, and let loose the dogs of war"; that the evil and untrustworthy side of man would become so great and so powerful a force that once released would become untamable, intractable, and therefore dangerous. As Hobbes reminds us,

> Where everything from every place grieved them; and fear and astonishment the greatest that ever they were in, beset them round. For they were not only grieved for the loss which both every man in particular and the whole city sustained of every man of arms, horsemen, and serviceable men, the like whereof they saw was not left, but seeing that they neither had galleys in their haven nor money in their treasury nor furniture in their galleys, were even desperate at the present of their

> safety; and thought the enemy out of Sicily would come forthwith with their fleet to Peiraeus, especially after the vanquishing of so great a navy, and that the enemy here would surely now, with double preparation in every kind, press them to the utmost by sea and land and be aided therein by their revolting confederates. (Hobbes 1959, "The Eighth Book", Sect. 1, 504)

As long as there continues to be an imbalance of power within communities based on tradition, modernization, culture, gender, primordialism, circumstantialism, racism, religion, fossil fuels, and socio-economic class there will be a politics of control, a politics of discord, a politics of resistance, and a politics of subversion that feed into the global reach of American globalization. One has to be careful that the political power of those who are in charge does not go to their heads. No one would know about the horrors of uncommitted criminals holding high positions and beyond the reach of most ordinary citizens. This is especially true in military organizations where the prospect of civilian intervention is buffered by military "standard operating procedures" (SOP). Witness the horrifying, tragic images over the Internet and through CNN and the BBC about Iraqi prisoners of war.

> At Bethleham, violent madwomen were chained by the ankles to the wall of a long gallery; their only garment was a homespun dress. At another hospital in Bethnal Green, a woman subject to violent seizures was placed in a pigsty, feet and fists bound; when the crisis had passed she was tied to her bed, covered only by a blanket; when she was allowed to take a few steps, an iron bar was placed between her legs, attached by rings to her ankles and by a short chain to handcuffs. (Foucault [1965] 1988, pp. 69–70)

This is terrorism.

The hope, optimism, and progress of American globalization in modernity have never escaped the tragedy of its political paradox that has cost American lives since World War I. The American public has more access to information today because of technological advances, which has led to the political intensification of its tragic history in modernity.

AMERICA'S GLOBAL REACH: THE TERROR WITHIN OR THE TERRORIST WITHOUT?

When the mullahs took over Iran in the insurrection led by Ayatollah Khomeini and his militant clerics, the cycle of violence continued under the name of a different god, in place of the capitalist one.[2] Over ten different nations sold arms to both sides of the Iran-Iraq War including the Soviet Union, France, Israel, and the United States. And now Iraq has been invaded by the United States and its allies. The UN under Kofi Annan vehemently opposed the Bush-led invasion. The United States still owes the UN money. The reasons for the non-payments are political and politically motivated. Despite being in arrears, American presidents have continued to ensure they have a global reach even without UN support. While the UN flounders on matters such as the PRC and Taiwan, the United States has continued with its support for Taiwan. The basis for the U.S.-Taiwan relationship lies in the military provisions under the Taiwan Relations Act (1979) that empowers the United States to assume a military position in the event of a PRC attack on the island. The United States has also continued its policy of free arms trade to Taiwan and other East Asian countries. America's military cannot continue its global reach without interfering in the politics of foreign governments, and many foreign government elites welcome the U.S. presence in their region.

One example is Singapore. In 2004, for example, the Singapore prime minister had three meetings with George W. Bush. Singapore has for a long time officially maintained a fifteen-man American logistics unit on the island state. Singapore has often hosted U.S. naval aircraft carriers in its naturally deep harbour, much to the chagrin of Muslim-dominant countries such as Malaysia and Indonesia. The American interest in East Asia, which comes under the U.S. Pacific Command, is overtly welcomed by its allies in the region — Singapore, South Korea, and Japan. Yet there have been widespread protests by opponents in these countries, with the exception of Singapore, against American military presence. Since the U.S. pullout from Clarke Airbase and Subic Naval Base in the Philippines, the United States had at first increased its naval presence in the South China Sea, then reduced it, and then sent in the fleet again. Why does the United States need such a global presence and how is this achieved?

The answer is simple. America's global reach is tied to a global vision. Not the one proclaimed by Bush in 1990 but an earlier ideal that goes back to 1960.[3] In order to enjoy the universal freedom that Eisenhower used in his 1960 speech, it has to be imposed on others who do not believe in it. Or so it would appear. Let us look at global reach some 4,500 years ago when there was a thriving civilization in Egypt. Before the desert sands engulfed the pyramids, the land surrounding it was fertile, green, and arable. It was the best land that the Nile offered. Exactly ten miles (16 kilometres) from the centre of modern Cairo are the pyramids. Most archaeologists and research scientists think that the pyramids were created for symbolic purposes; that the ancient Egyptians believed that their pharaoh was a god who had perfect control over the rising and setting of the sun. That the sun rose and set at the behest of the pharaoh and the death of the pharaoh would mean doom for the sun which they knew was crucial for the growing of crops in the Nile Valley. Therefore, the resting place of the king would allow his spirit to symbolically raise the sun each day. This is of course a spurious correlation as we understand it today. It cannot be accepted except as a kind of fateful belief of the Egyptians in that era. Other researchers believe that the pyramids were created out of a cosmic necessity, that the mathematical accuracy involved in the construction of the pyramids was itself a reflection of the presence of higher cosmological beings who guided the Egyptians.

The largest pyramid itself is built from over two million slabs of about a tonne each. The ancient Egyptians were capable artisans who had hewn these huge slabs of limestone and emplaced them with such geometrical precision that they could withstand twenty-three centuries of erosion, and worse still, 2,300 years of human civilization. Yet these pyramids were built to serve a higher and more perfect purpose. That purpose, some modern researchers believe, involved astronomical calculations with regard to the position of the stars in the Milky Way, the galaxy to which earth belongs. While the researchers were right about the symbolism of the pyramids, other deductions about the purpose and function of these ancient tombs are possible. The pyramids were more than symbolic places for the pharaoh to ensure the rising and falling of the sun each day. They were more than mere cosmological monuments to their dead king writ large across the universe. These monuments were created to celebrate the power of Egyptian kings over all men. They were a celebration of conquest over other men and other civilizations.

The U.S. presence in East Asia provides an interesting study in comparison to the limited global reach of the ancient Egyptians. Take Taiwan for example. This island is home to the descendants and familial relatives of the Kuomintang (KMT) members and those who escaped Mao's putsch in 1949. Despite being an avid supporter of the U.S. presence in China in the 1930s before the Pacific War, the KMT had been riddled with political corruption. Nevertheless, there continues to remain important strategic reasons for the U.S. support of the democratic enclave of Taiwan. The United States will continue to use its relationship with Taiwan as an alternative China in case Sino-U.S. relations turn sour. The PRC has fired live artillery rounds across the Taiwan Straits several times since Mao called off an invasion of the island in the 1950s. It was only the U.S. military presence in the region, in

Okinawa, Tokyo, and the Philippines in the 1970s and 1980s, that prevented a pro-Maoist attack to complete the Chinese Revolution's unfinished business. However, there are two main items on the agenda. Firstly, the pyramidal relationship between the People's Liberation Army, the Chinese Communist Party, and the people continues to serve as the basis of "socialism with Chinese characteristics". Secondly, China is under pressure from the United States and some other countries to float the yuan, which will result in making the PRC's exports more expensive than the current fixed amount of US$1 to 8.28 PRC yuan. Because of the nature of Chinese politics that has evolved in its modern history, China will have no doubts about invading Taiwan if it continues with its former President Chen Shui Bian's political platform of "independence" and "democratic" rhetoric. Taiwan is the fly in the Chinese ointment. And America will doubtlessly use the island as a staging area should it come to war.

The Russians are unlikely to help the Chinese. The 2001 Sino-Russo agreement is merely an instrument on paper that is an agreement to remain non-enemies for the time being until both countries sort out their finances. Besides, it has never been in the U.S. strategic interest for any Sino-Russo accords to materialize. This would potentially cut off one half of the U.S. Pacific Command and result in the reconfiguration of NATO and perhaps even the newly-formed European Union that was launched on 1 May 2004 in Dublin. The Indians have a 1,370 kilometre long disputed border with China. What is interesting here is that both the Chinese and the Indians use Russian-made, Soviet era weapons and are reported to spend close to US$100 billion annually on their large land armies. In other words, if China were to invade Taiwan, it would give the countries surrounding it an opportunity to resolve many historical differences with the country. China does not currently have the resources to defend its long borders from Russian or Indian incursion and has to configure all these in terms of any military calculus. The Taiwanese, on the other hand, continue to bait and annoy the Chinese PRC leaders with their calls for greater democracy. Internally, China has reneged on the Hong Kong mini-Constitution with regard to the terms of the appointment of the chief executive of the Hong Kong Special Administrative Region (a post formerly held by a pro-China, shipping capitalist, Tung Chee Hwa, who has now been replaced by Donald Tsang). As a result, China has come under economic and political pressure from the United States, the United Kingdom, and other interests in this former British colony to make the required changes. But China merely told them to keep out of its internal politics.[4]

PYRAMIDS AS SYMBOLS OF SUPERIOR POWER

The pyramids were reminders of man's mortality, about life and death. For the early Egyptians, the earth was the centre of the universe and the pyramids were the central symbol of superior power. Egypt was the superpower of its day. The ancient Egyptian cities were among the most brilliant and most civilized places on earth. The pyramids were a reminder to all travellers visiting the centre of the universe of the supreme power of the pharaoh over all men, and over life and death. These symbols were built to last. Despite the evil and horrific values of the Nazis, they did not destroy the pyramids. Neither did the Italians or the British during World War II. For these old armies, the pyramids were a respite from the horrors of the war and represented a sacred place built on values of honour and glory. The pyramids were also the symbols of war.

By the time of the Yom Kippur War and the Six-Day War, both Israeli and Arab military machines did not destroy the pyramids. It is as if these lifeless stones possess some kind of spiritual power for the posterity of mankind. Perhaps, as symbols of war, these ancient tombs present a startling reminder to men about their own mortality and brevity of life. If Eisenhower's speech had been engraved in the Rosetta Stone, it would have been just as appropriate a universal creed, a freedom expressed in the artisans who built the pyramids as nationalist sentiment increased in ancient Egypt.

It would seem that Eisenhower's idealism would perhaps never come true as long as we have war. Many hope that American globalization will bring with it peaceful overtures of a Keynesian-like exchange of goods and services, greater markets, innovative products, and functional commodities at low prices. Better to trade than to war. As we have seen in Eisenhower's speech, "those now denied opportunity shall come to enjoy it to the full; that all who yearn for freedom may experience its spiritual blessings; that those who have freedom will understand".

Yet Americans seem to want to have peace so earnestly that they are willing to go to war to get it. Look at Korea, Vietnam, Iran-Iraq, the Cold War and the arms race, the proxy wars between the former superpowers, the First Gulf War, and over a decade later, the Second Gulf War. Now look at the war on terrorism. As far back as 2002, "The U.S. State Department ... named the Philippines, Indonesia, and Malaysia as 'potential Al Qaeda hubs'" (Desker and Ramakrishna 2002, p. 162). In other countries, many operatives now considered "terrorists" were ironically trained by the Americans and their various special forces during the Cold War. The century now is the playing out of the vestiges of the Cold War, and of 9/11, where former allies, foreign military special forces, and other paramilitary units trained by Americans have refused to lay down their arms.

This is similar to the Malayan People's Anti-Japanese Army in 1945 that refused to surrender their weapons and turned towards communism as they led a jungle-based military campaign against the former British colonies of Malaya and Singapore while operating from covert bases along the Thai-Malaysian border. Soldiers who were supplied with weapons and training to suit one purpose cannot easily be told to lay down their weapons after hostilities are over or after the political victory has been achieved, because they who were trained to kill and assassinate always need an enemy. The process of war is a deep and penetrating part of globalization.

Unlike our modern buildings in a post-9/11 world, no one feels threatened by the Egyptian pyramids in the sense that terrorists had been threatened by the presence of the twin towers of the World Trade Center in New York pre-9/11. The pyramids are political symbols of death, power, and tragedy. The pyramids are huge sand castles that have ironically long survived the immediate threats to the Egyptian dynasties. We do not make them like we used to anymore. The globalized world today, created by neoliberal capitalist energy generators called MNCs, has built non-permanent structures that remain unprotected and vulnerable to the enemies within and the enemies without. There is something else, a different and more ominous structure that has existed intact and in perfect condition as a relic from the Cold War. It continues to dominate the directional frontiers of all kinds of science, and kinds of experimental technology from physical matter to the manipulation of nano-matter and the artificial creation of genetic codes through mutation. These structures have become so embedded in the American way of life and constitute such a great portion of the American Dream that the silent anti-war protesters of the 1960s have all but remembered them as distant and dissatisfying memories of victories that were never achieved and pyrrhic battles that were never won.

THE MILITARY INDUSTRIAL COMPLEX

The military-industrial complex (MIC) comprises a huge interstate network of military bases, security structures, and affiliated industries that have been created to fulfill their complementary needs. The MIC serves three main constituencies: the 'name of the people', 'big business', and the 'military establishment'.

> ...the US is basically a one-party state — the business party with two factions, Democrats and Republicans. Most of the population seems to

agree. A very high percentage, sometimes passing 80%, believe that the government serves "the few and the special interests," not "the people". In the contested 2000 election, about 75% regarded it as mostly a farce having nothing to do with them, a game played by rich contributors, party bosses, and the public relations industry, which trained candidates to say mostly meaningless things that might pick up some votes. This was BEFORE the actual election, with the accusations of fraud and selection of Bush with a minority of the popular vote.[5]

The natural evolution of American politics has resulted in the gross engulfment of the American polity by the military industrial complex. As we have seen in the previous chapter, a minority of the population directs the majority thinking; the minority popular vote therefore determines the outcomes for the majority of American citizens. This was what Madison had cautioned his peers and the American people in the *Federalist Paper Number 51*. He called it the "tyranny-of-the-minority", the minority that wields so much power as to be able to control the rest of society through its social, cultural and political institutions. And if the Madisonian man was indeed angelic, and not a financial terrorist, there would be no need for government. We would perhaps even be able to accept a kind of anarcho-syndicalist politics that was the entire rave in the early twentieth century. The MIC is made up of a pyramidal structure of military academies that come under the direct control of the Office of the Secretary of Defense. These are the civilian structures that control the military units. Each year, the Department of Defense (DOD) (that comes under the direct purview of the Office of the Secretary of Defense) devotes close to US$1 billion to academic institutions that are involved in military-type research, an amount that is larger than most sovereign state economies the world over, yet an amount that was neither able to foresee nor forestall 9/11.

There are several important academic institutions that continue to receive major military grants such as the California Institute of Technology (CIT), Columbia University, Dartmouth College, Harvard University, the Johns Hopkins University (JHU), the Massachusetts Institute of Technology (MIT), RAND Graduate School (RGS), Syracuse University (in New York), and the University of California. There are other military institutes that form part of the larger militarist culture that rides like a cultural undercurrent within society. These include the Air Force Institute of Technology (AFIT), Air University (AU), the Defense Acquisition University (DAU), the Defense Language Institute Foreign Language Center (DLIFLC), the Information

Resources Management College (IRMC), the Industrial College of the Armed Forces (ICAF), the Joint Forces Staff College (JFSC), Joint Military Intelligence College (JMIC), the Marine Corps University (MCU), the Naval Postgraduate School (NPS), and the National War College (NWC), among many other units.[6] Each is a recipient of huge multi-million dollar defence budget grants that could run a few Central American republics without cocaine exports.

The importance of the entire military industrial organizational culture is determined by the kind of enemy that is being fought. In the past, the enemy was clearly seen and visible to the naked eye. The enemies of the United States go back a long time in history. It began with the British Red Coats in the eighteenth century; then the German Nazis, the Italians, and the Japanese in World War II; the Koreans, and the Vietnamese from the 1950s to the 1970s; the Soviets from 1955 to 1989; and now the enemies of the post-9/11 era. But if we look at the kinds of funds and the extent of the research done within the MIC, the major work involves conventional warfare and technological application. Unfortunately, the new enemy of the post-9/11 era is very different from the historical enemies of modern American history.

Ever since the Berlin Airlift, America has developed its own view towards assuming the role of a global policeman. This role of global policeman transformed into a global military combat force at the height of the Cold War. However, the post-9/11 era has created another new kind of enemy for the American global combat force. It is no secret that the new enemy is international terrorism where no one is without suspicion, even American citizens themselves who have aided and abetted fundamentalist Islamic reactionary terrorists in their fight for what can only be a cause against human life itself.

The globalized world under the lens of America's military professionals is divided into the following five unified commands that form part of the global geography: Pacific Command (PACOM), Northern Command (NORTHCOM), Southern Command (SOUTHCOM), Central Command (CENTCOM), and European Command (EUCOM). The largest is PACOM, and the smallest is CENTCOM. Therefore, we are talking about a global military force that is highly structured, highly politicized, hierarchical, and contains different sub-cultures and values and emphases that have generated and evolved over the past 200 years.[7] The MIC also has an annual DOD budget of US$371 billion and 2.036 million personnel. Compare this to the largest American MNCs, such as Wal-mart (US$227 billion with 1,383,000 employees), Exxon-Mobil (US$200 billion and 97,900 employees), General Motors (US$181 billion with 365,000 employees), and Ford (US$160 billion with 354,000 employed).[8]

We will now examine the pyramid of military education that has evolved over the years in the politics of American military globalization.

THE PYRAMID OF MILITARY EDUCATION

Military education for children in the United States has a long history dating back to the time of the civil war. Parents send their children to these places for two reasons: firstly, the parents or at least the father was educated there. Secondly, but not exclusively, the parents feel that a military education early in life will instil discipline and patriotism for the country. Many of the schools are themselves stepping stones for ascendance into the higher military academies run by the DOD and serve as a purposeful career path for the future. Ninety-eight percent of these military institutions are coeducational.

If one can imagine a pyramidal structure with an apex made up of five academies and lower level educational colleges, junior colleges, boarding schools, and other preparatory schools with a military dimension, then you would have the impression of a clear set of educational institutions geared specifically towards creating a military culture. This culture represents an important dimension of what Eisenhower, Williams and Moos called the military-industrial complex (MIC).[9]

There are currently five fully-fledged military academies run by the DOD across the contiguous United States. These are the United States Air Force Academy (USAFA) in Colorado Springs, Colorado; the United States Coast Guard Academy (USCGA) in Connecticut; the United States Military Academy (USMA) at West Point; the United States Merchant Marine Academy (USMMA) in New York; and the United States Naval Academy (USNA) in Annapolis. President Eisenhower signed the USAFA into law on 1 April 1954. The USAFA shares the same core values inspired by general Michael E. Ryan, which are "Integrity", "Service before Self", and "Excellence in All We Do". There has been a tradition of executive interest in these military academies that has bolstered the art and science of war since the 1800s. For example, the USMA at West Point was itself established through executive concurrence by President Thomas Jefferson. The mission of this academy is, "To educate, train, and inspire the Corps of Cadets so that each graduate is a commissioned leader of character committed to the values of Duty, Honour, Country; professional growth throughout a career as an officer in the United States Army; and a lifetime of selfless service to the nation" (USMA 2004). In addition to the cadet honour code, cadets at USMA share the army's seven core values: duty, honour, integrity, loyalty, personal courage, respect, and selfless service. It is not easy to get admitted to West Point. To do so, a prospective candidate has to be nominated by a member of the U.S. Congress or a member from the Department of the Army. For over 200 years, USMA's motto of "Duty, Honour, Country" has been imbued in 50,000 graduates that include Stonewall Jackson, Mahan, Polk, Whistler, Ulysses S. Grant, Robert E. Lee (the Confederate general during the American Civil War and a former USMA superintendent), Sherman, Omar N. Bradley, Eisenhower, MacArthur, Patton, Pershing, Buzz Aldrin (astronaut), Schwarzkopf, Westmoreland, Alexander Haig (former president of United Technologies Corporation and U.S. secretary of state), and Brent Scowcroft.

The twice-wounded and decorated military tactician and strategist, Colin Luther Powell, who served no fewer than three U.S. presidents and was the first African-American to assume the position of twelfth chairman of the Joint Chiefs of Staff, was from the ROTC and not a West Pointer. At the end of his military career before he became a Republican politician, Powell was awarded high honours from USMA at West Point. Powell is one of only forty-one Americans over the past 200 years who have been honoured at West Point. They include John Foster Dulles, Cardinal Spellman, Bob Hope, Dean Rusk, Barry Goldwater, Ronald Reagan, Paul H. Nitze, Walter Cronkite, Henry Kissinger, and Daniel K. Inouye. Powell had risen to become the twelfth chairman of the Joint Chiefs, the highest military rank that the military could offer. Powell was a young man during the time the Jim Crow laws were in effect, long before *Brown v. Board of Education of Topeka*, and the enactment of the Civil Rights Act (1965). Powell eventually became the sixty-fifth U.S. secretary of state and the first African-American to hold such high office.

There are seven state military colleges with old historical links to the American civil war in South Carolina, Georgia, Vermont, Texas, and Virginia. Additionally, there are seven maritime colleges across the United States. These include the California Maritime Academy; Great Lakes Maritime Academy; Maine Maritime Academy; Massachusetts Maritime Academy; New York Maritime College; Seattle Maritime Academy; and the Texas Maritime Academy in Galveston. Finally, there are also 47 military high/preparatory schools with various military training options across the contiguous United States with ROTC and JROTC programmes. Not all the military programmes are compulsory: two in Georgia, three in Alabama, one in New Mexico, one in Pennsylvania, three in Missouri, three in Florida, three in California, one in South Carolina, one for Pennsylvania, another for Mississippi, three in Indiana, six in Virginia, four in Texas, one in Kentucky, another in New York, two in North Carolina, one each for Kansas, Wisconsin, Minnesota, Oregon, and Delaware, four in Illinois, and two in Maryland. The roles of these military educational institutions compliment the DOD's Academies for the various military services. The military boarding schools act as feeder institutions that groom and prepare many of its students for life-long careers in the military.

Despite such a grand military tradition and honourable military culture in the United States, there has been a growing series of disjunctions that have begun to unravel. This involves examinations and the problem of gender in a male dominant culture:

> Ultimately, hundreds of cadets had received unauthorized assistance, or cheated, on an electrical engineering assignment and more than 150 cadets were separated for honor violations. The large numbers of cadets involved led to unprecedented congressional and public scrutiny of academy policies and programs. Ultimately, due to the large numbers of the cadets involved and indications that certain institutional practices may have facilitated this behavior, many were permitted to reapply. In the end, nearly 100 returned, and 85 ultimately graduated.[10]

Women now make up about 15 per cent of the population at U.S. military educational institutions. While women personnel have been sailing for at least two decades with the U.S. Navy, they are still not allowed on U.S. submarines.[11] There continues to be an organizational culture within the U.S. military, specific to each of the services. Such cultures and sub-cultures impose specific rituals, traditions, and values on servicemen and service women.

Also consider the USAFA report on sexual improprieties at that academy, or the case of Maj. Gen. David R.E. Hale, a graduate of the USMA. And the following quotation that was carried by the Marine Corps News originating from an article from the Associated Press:

> Statistics on assault cases at the schools are incomplete and difficult to compare. West Point has had 15 reported cases, ranging from unwanted kissing to rape, since August 1999 — or about 4.3 per year. Ten of the 15 accused cadets resigned or were forced out of the academy, three received lesser punishments, one was cleared by DNA evidence and one case is pending. Annapolis had 11 cases reported during the last three academic years, an average of 3.6 per year. Charges were substantiated in four cases, a finding that generally leads to expulsion, three are pending and four

cadets apparently were cleared, based on the fragmentary information the institution provided. The Air Force Academy says it has had 56 cases of sexual misconduct since 1993, an average of 5.6 per year. Six cadets have faced courts-martial during that time, resulting in five convictions. At least eight others were dismissed from the academy, and seven others were reprimanded after disciplinary hearings. Not all the cases involved cadets as victims. Those figures don't reflect a central accusation in the Air Force scandal — that women cadets avoid reporting assaults for fear it will hurt their careers.[12]

American military and its personnel are posted all over the world for all kinds of military and non-military activities. The U.S. Armed Forces are seen as the global force of peace in the fight for freedom and justice. Therefore the United States as a global military force of supreme dominance must seriously accept the role it has chosen for itself and for imposition on the rest of the world.[13] While the United States has not militarily threatened most foreign states, and only invaded a few, the reputation of the U.S. military in all its forms will continue to be tarnished if prevailing realities are not addressed in ways that prevent recurrence.

The U.S. military is a highly efficient and organized global force with a mission to impose peace and stability across the globe for the sake of neoliberal capitalism and "free-trade". Nevertheless, the motto that is accepted by all U.S. military services, "Duty, Honour, Country" is perhaps better understood as an optimistic ideal.

CONCLUSION

There is an urgent and pressing need for the MIC in America which is both alive and well, to take cognizance of what its role actually is within the globalized world. Businesses, academies, and military units within the MIC have to realize that their research and activities have a great impact on the nature of globalization as emanating from the United States.

We saw at the beginning of this chapter the important message that Dwight D. Eisenhower had for Americans in 1960. In his speech, he urged not only Americans but people of all faiths and races and nations towards the importance of freedom and the heavy responsibilities that came with it. He went on to talk about the various ideals that could be removed like poverty, disease, and ignorance so that people can live together in a binding force of "mutual respect and love" (*Public Papers of the Presidents*, Dwight D. Eisenhower 1960, pp. 1035–40). Almost a century after Eisenhower mentioned those words, we can say that we are perhaps more knowledgeable about the planet, about different societies, about racism, about poverty, and about disease. We are perhaps more knowledgeable now than at any other point in human history.

We can see that the gap between the rich and the poor, between rich people and poor people is growing at an increasing rate. Despite the end of the Cold War, the world today is more informed of its class distinctions, as well as the racial divide among people. It is more knowledgeable about disease and disease-control mechanisms. But the globalized world of America, with its allies, enemies, or alone, may not better be off than it was when Eisenhower spoke those words.

Perhaps a more thoughtful comment at this juncture would be the one reiterated by another past president of the United States, Woodrow Wilson, who spoke when America was not a hegemonic power but had some idea of what it would be. Wilson had some sense of the "destiny of America" when he spoke of not wanting "a rivalry of power, but a community of power".[14]

Today that phrase seems equally apt. While Wilson was fearful of other powers such as the Soviets, Chinese, French, and the British, his fears have all but disappeared today. Yet his phrase is equally apt because this is exactly what America needs to do today: to view the world as communities of empowerment if only to realize the later Eisenhower idealism in the politics of American globalization. Perhaps Chomsky's left-leaning politics might be right after all, that America is indeed a one-party state: a business party with two factions — Republicans and Democrats and with party bosses to steer the way forward.

The next chapter deals with a different global reach that the politics of American globalization possesses: American popular culture. The American political culture of neoliberal individualism has created a large middle class. But there remain many questions about success and failure under the American model. The next chapter will examine how popular culture acts as a channel for venting the frustrations of being an American — of all colours and creeds.

The world is in America inasmuch as America is in the world, as the recent economic recession is clearly demonstrating. This is why there continues to be a politics of American globalization. America depends on the world as much as the world, or at least many of its members, are dependent on America. America can export the same levels of terrorism that it receives; America can import the same levels of economic wealth and poverty that it gives; America can provide the same level of cultural commodification overseas that it generates domestically.

Notes

1. Note the U.S. Supreme Court case number 340 U.S. 135 (1950).
2. See for example, the case of *Saeed Rezai v. Immigration and Naturalization Service* (1995); *United States of America v. Oliver L. North* (1990); and *People's Mojahedin Organization of Iran v. United States Department of State and Madeline K. Albright, Secretary of State* (1999).
3. Several political scientists specializing in "American politics" have discussed the reasons why George Bush did not win a second term despite his stellar performance in the first Gulf War in 1991. Most have concluded that it was because even the Republicans did not think too highly of his ability.
4. In 2003, over half a million pro-democracy demonstrators took to the streets of Hong Kong in support of a democratic Hong Kong, doubtlessly supported by the capitalists who are reaping in billions each year from this tiny capitalist nodal point. The British held Hong Kong on a lease from China for 150 years but did nothing for democracy until it was time to hand Hong Kong back to China in 1997, and gave this impossible task to its last British governor Christopher Patten, the former chair of the Conservative Party. The diplomatic fracas and embarrassment that ensued after the return — the United Kingdom reneged on granting British citizenship to thousands of Hong Kong pro-British loyalists — saw Patten elevated to EU commissioner and now Chancellor of Oxford University as a face-saving gesture for the darkened British empire of islands.
5. Noam Chomsky, "History of US Military Involvement: An Interview with Noam Chomsky", *ZMagazine*, 2 January 2004.
6. See also "Office of the Secretary of Defense, Joint Chiefs of Staff, Military Departments, Unified Commands", *US Department of Defense*, 2004. The military departments under the Office of the Secretary of Defense include the US Army, U.S. Air Force, U.S. Navy, U.S. Marine Corps, and the U.S. Coast Guard.
7. See also the pro-government, US-centric report by Walter F. Ulmer Jr., Joseph J. Collins, T.O. Jacobs, eds., *American Military Culture in the Twenty-First Century: A Report of the CSIS International Security Program* (Washington, D.C.: Centre for Strategic and International Studies, 2000).
8. "An Introduction", *US Department of Defense*, 2004.
9. William D. Hartung, "Eisenhower's Warning: The Military-industrial Complex Forty Years Later", *World Policy Journal* 18, no. 1 (2001).
10. "West Point Bicentennial — The Long Gray Line Changes Formation", *USMA*, 2002.

11 Andrea Stone, "Navy Resists Idea of Opening Submarines to Women", *USA Today*, 14 September 1999, 14A.
12 Robert Weller, "West Point, Annapolis Avoid Air Force Academy's Travails", *Associated Press*, 30 March 2003.
13 Kathleen T. Rhem, "Bush Shows 'Deep Disgust' for Apparent Treatment of Iraqi Prisoners", *American Forces Press Service*, 30 April 1004.
14 Henry A. Kissinger, Thayer Award Speech, *USMA West Point*, 13 September 2000.

6

CULTURE

Is culture "political"? An element of the reason why it is not considered political is because it does not seem to be the "stuff" of high politics. The kind of culture that we refer to in this chapter is different from the kind of culture that is referred to in the book as a whole. In this chapter, the focus is on the kind of culture that has emerged in late modernity. The name of that culture is popular culture. The kind of popular culture in globalization that has had the greatest impact in late modernity is American popular culture.

ENTER CULTURE

Unlike Alvin Gouldner's lilting remonstrance titled *Enter Plato*, the cultural considerations of power, authority, and legitimacy in late modernity are not quite as reassuring. Late moderns must learn to accept popular culture whether they like it or not. There is no real choice. It slowly creeps up on you. The influence is subtle and overt, noisy and quiet, hard and fast, soft and slow, entering and exiting as we pass time towards the kind of nihilism that Jean Paul Baudrillard experiments with in the last chapter of *Simulacra et Simulacrum*. We consider and question the sacred cows of modernity's popular fictives and their illusory and captivating devices that project us backwards into the immediacy of existence. Autonomously, these become canons of combat, created to fill spaces of modernity's boredom and languish within late capitalist consumption behavioural patterns that clog up the streets in Greenwich Village. Let us consider some of the more favourite canons of popular culture the world over: (1) Popular culture works because of peer pressure; (2) popular culture is promoted through mass mediated advertising and marketing; and (3) popular culture is about creating instantaneous cultural icons of television, movies, drama, sports, war, philosophy, and science. Examples of cult figures or personality cults in popular culture over the years include Simone De Beauvoir, Hannah Arendt, and Judith Butler (American feminism), Henry Miller (forbidden novels), Toshiro Mifune (Japanese Samurai monochromatic television), John Travolta (American disco), Alec Guinness (British drama), Mika Hakkinen (Formula One sports), Carl Von Clausewitz (war), Michel Foucault and postmodernism (philosophy), Stephen Hawking (physics), Josef Stalin and Mao Tse-tung (communism), Antonio Gramsci (Italian neoMarxism), Eleanor Roosevelt (American icon), Il Duce (Italian Fascism), Martin Luther King, Jr. (American icon), John F. Kennedy (American liberalism), and Fidel Castro (Cuban socialism). This is perhaps the poorest list of names that I can come up with because there are so many more possible areas of popular iconography that could perhaps include Bollywood actors who are watched by hundreds of millions of fans across South Asia and the rest of the Indian diaspora; Chinese cinema, drama, and television stars made and featured almost exclusively in Taiwan and Hong Kong for the Chinese diaspora throughout the world; African-American rappers who influence young Japanese schoolgirls in Tokyo and young Malay schoolboys in Singapore; famous Superbowl quarterbacks; astronauts; cosmonauts; and stand-up comedians like Ellen DeGeneres, Brett Butler, Robin Williams, Sinbad, Jay Leno, Jerry Seinfeld, David Letterman, Bill Maher, Drew Carey, George Wallace, and legendary ones like Sammy Davis Jr., Bob Hope, and Dean Martin. As we proceed we will encounter different discursive elements within American popular culture that have developed and resonated over the years with others fading away in an instant or over several instances. This is why it seems easier, perhaps even better, to consider the notion of American popular culture that is viewed from today as a genealogical trajectory away from the past rather than a single monocotyledonous root tied to the past.

COUNTER-CULTURE

A large part of American popular culture is represented by the counter-culture of the 1960s. Americans have an ability to hark back to that time of their youth and the celebration of that specific zone of leisure and carefree consciousness that evolved out of Woodstock and the anti–Vietnam War sentiment. Perhaps this is another genuine and unique kind of American popular culture.

The counter-culture was itself the popular culture of the era but it had such a politically profound effect on Americans of that generation as embedded and displayed in American music, drama, Broadway musicals, movies, television, radio, sports, and public life of that era.

The American counter-culture of the 1950s and 1960s also saw the rise of American rock music mainly from Southern California. Unlike the cowboy culture that predated it by almost 200 years that had created "country and Western music", the counter-culture of the 1960s was different because it was as brief as it was bloody. The counter-culture was the political uprising of a young generation of Americans who did not want war.

The counter-culture was about battling peaceably against the government. It was not about toppling the government, but it was about being anti-establishment. This meant that the youth were rebelling against their parents, in a way that Mao orchestrated the movement of Chinese youth against theirs in the Great Chinese Cultural Revolution of the 1960s. However, there was no dictatorial hand in the case of the American counter-culture. The American counter-culture was about turning away from American middle-class values. The American middle class believed in monogamy, frugality, filial piety, religious conviction, and a proper education. The counter-culture presented to youthful Americans a channel for asserting their individuality. It was also a form of political resistance against the domestic and foreign policies that had made America into a new nation up till that point in time. In fact, there was a degree of fear among the middle class that the popular culture of rock music would erode the social fabric that had held Americans together. This was not to be the case and that in fact the popular culture of the 1960s was indeed a phase which many Americans if not most at that age had to go through. This was a type of passing phase that would be passed on down to the next generation of young Americans who had not been old enough to have been present at Woodstock or who had been too sheltered by their parents and guardians who did not subscribe to these values. Eventually, the values of the counter-culture of 1960s popular culture would be used as a turning point now called "retro" — a cultural benchmark of what was formerly fashionable. The interesting twist here is that "retro" is also considered current and updated. It is like the fashion industry. Old fashions keep showing up like old wine in new bottles.

In countering the establishment, the ideal composition of the populist counter-cultural ethos was one that was made up of three main ingredients: (1) a radicalization of how America was being viewed; (2) a systematic critique of the establishment policies that had dominated the United States since the end of World War II; and (3) a bourgeoning distrust of made-in-America political institutions. Implicit within these three ingredients was a rejection of the materialism of the American Dream; a proto-nihilistic and alienated view of American life; and a fear that American politics overseas would continue to haunt future generations of Americans by taking their youth for the sake of national interests. While the last two characteristics of the American way of life are consistent with much of the feelings that Americans have today in the first quarter of the twenty-first century, the first characteristic did not come true. In fact, as seen in Chapter 1 of this book, Americans seem to have embraced materialism the god of wealth and material goods.[1] Material goods have therefore taken centre stage in American popular culture and the more luxurious the good, the greater its appeal in terms of the perceived social status that is attributed to the consumption of such expensive labels.

The social mimicry of the consumer behaviour of the minority rich and famous by the majority not so-rich and famous is highly political. The reason why it is highly political is because identity formation is crippled by a need to project images of stability, success, wealth, and power when these are not genuine identities, only means towards an end.

American social scientists and American social science was at the forefront of this revolutionary counter-culture. Almost every American politician, captain of industry, social scientist, researcher, or social worker who grew up in the 1950s and 1960s has been influenced by the counter-culture of the day to some degree. Whether one was a conscientious objector to the Vietnam War draft, a highly decorated veteran, a communal-living protester of "Love Not War", or a draft dodger, the influence of the popular counter-culture was present and had influenced one at some point in that stage of life. The influence of this formative phase of American popular culture would come in three forms: it might have influenced people to go to extremes in experimentation, for example with the effects of psychedelic-inducing drugs. Secondly, it might have resulted in the repression of non-conformist attitudes that would resurrect decades later. And thirdly, it might push some to go to the other extreme of withdrawing totally from the counter-cultural iconoclasms.

Peer pressure continues to be an important factor in making individuals conform to particularistic group behaviour such as smoking marijuana and consuming alcohol to the point of excess; sexual experimentation at a young age, below that which ordinary people and the law would find acceptable; and the difficulties associated with stereotype-casting from one's peers. While the discussion so far has dealt with the psychological impact of the counter-culture, it is important to note that these effects persist over time and may be considered unique for each generational change, but in effect retain certain similarities. Peer pressure and hazing in high schools are common social rituals that people are forced to adjust to. There is only so much avoidance of one's peers that can be achieved in a given school year, for example. Sooner or later one has to maintain a particular stand and become part of some sub-cultural group, listening to its sub-cultural music, dress, values, outlook, accent, and "slang". There is a clear politics of the counter-cultural era and the subsequent periods because people desire to be part of a group but in trying to achieve that goal become beholden to the prevailing expectations of the group's sub-cultural gatekeepers.

PUBLIC SPACE

> The idea of a public contingent on its participants is the analogue of resonance to music because neither would make sense without the other…[and where] the Legal-Autonomous Public Model, and the Multiple Public Model in the work of John Dewey, Walter Lippmann, and Kenneth J. Arrow [exist in the] great contest between Lippmann and Dewey in the 1920s signified a clashing of the two interpretations of the public with one arguing about the need for a return to a constitutionally guaranteed, left-of-centre public philosophy that would entertain the elite while taking care of the poor, and the other a plea for a rationalistic recourse that surmised and envisaged rational public discourse as only one of several possible publics. The article concludes with the notion that the constructions of public space defined by Dewey, Lippmann, and Arrow promote distinct yet related interrogations of public space that is more than an agora of resonating ideas, but includes a kind of automatic reverberation on its own axes.[2]

American popular culture in public space is about a debate over social equations. This is also a political equation because there are some who do not fit in completely because they suddenly discover a consciousness or a mind of their own. There are those who do not fit in because they were coerced in the first place. And then there are those who eventually assume the roles of the new generation of the sub-cultural gatekeepers and their proxies. There is politics because someone gains power and influence over another or over others within the group. Group identity formation and group identity decay are thus central to our complex idea of American popular culture. The wallpaper of popular culture in America is therefore made up of its counter-cultural ballast, "retro", and inter-generational transfers of group identities in public space. Habermas constructed his notion of the theory of communicative action on his reading of the bourgeoisie in nineteenth century Europe. For him, individuals are unable to come together in the revolutionary spirited manner described by Marx because of the structuration of society. In this sense, Habermas must have drawn some inspiration from Gramsci's notion of hegemony. Thus, while Habermas stressed the importance of language dynamics within his theory of communicative action through iterative politics as a way of achieving freedom, Gramsci emphasized the controls designated within society that prevent individuals and imprison them from achieving freedom. The inter-generational transfers from one generation of American pop-cultural consumers to the next therefore cannot employ Habermas's outdated theory of communicative action because it does not allow for revolutionary change.[3]

In fact, it is Gramsci's notion of the soft power of hegemony that presents the challenge for popular culture's consumers. Unlike Joseph Nye's position on soft power, and very much like the U.S. military, the consumers of popular culture as a whole desire an establishment "adversary". This comes in the form of the kind of hegemonic control explained in Gramsci's political thought. But Habermas may be useful because he noticed the importance of language dynamics in his theory of communicative action as a way towards freeing the self from social and political constraints (but not from cultural ones). Any theory of communicative hegemonic action in American popular culture must address the existing mix of ingredients created during the counter-cultural revolution against the establishment which, as previously discussed, involves: (1) the radicalization of the view of America by Americans; (2) a systematic critique of the Establishment policies; and (3) a bourgeoning distrust of made in America political institutions. Elements of the counter-cultural mix of ingredients found in retro can be observed in situation comedies (sitcoms) made in the late 1990s harking back between twenty-five to thirty years through flashback sequences of cast and characters such as *Seinfeld, Third Rock From the Sun, Frasier, Friends, Grounded for Life, The Simpsons, That Seventies Show*, and *The King of Queens*. Examples of these retro-flashbacks help anchor the viewers and the characters with truisms of the past through the reproduction of fictive unions between what actually occurred as fact and what is being presented as a simulacra of that fact.

While these sitcoms are themselves mediated monuments to the modern history of popular cultural norms, they also serve as a way of filling leisure time and occupying space that has been freed up for television broadcasts and receptions. The successful sitcoms of the late 1990s that captured the retro fever in different episodic moments were pre-dated by such prequel sitcoms as *Step by Step, Married... With Children, Home Improvement, Caroline in the City, Ellen*, and *Mad About You*. Thus retrospective iconography through situation comedies, television soaps, drama, and even musicals popularized by Andrew Lloyd Webber instinctively assume the presence of an establishment antagonist. The political structures of control in the public sphere therefore create the poles of disaffection towards which the angst and frustration, satire and Black comedy, love and anger can be directed towards and against as a cultural sounding board. Gramsci's advocacy of the soft power of hegemonic control on one hand, and his ideas involving subordinate behaviour enable a theoretical understanding of how such consumers are able to transmit (iteratively) popular cultural values over time, and across generations within the public sphere through retrospection.[4]

AMERICAN POPULAR CULTURE

"The body and the traces it conceals, the soul and the images it perceives, are here no more than stages in the syntax of delirious language."[5] If one traces the ergonomic lines of an electronic device, one might find its aesthetic lines pleasing and derive pleasure from admiring it *in situ*. Artificial devices have been created to provide stimulation for the human mind, but aesthetics, however pleasing, and ergonomics, however sensual, can only take the senses so far. If it does not work, it is a brick. A brick refers to a useful machine or device that has become incapacitated and no longer works. The capacitor is down and has become dispossessed of having any capacity to deliver a charge. There is no soul if the heart is dead in a way that there can be no facilities if the microchips are down. A bricked microchip has to be replaced entirely because it has virtually no room for error. In the popular culture of American gaming, for example, it is not that rare to have microchips that are liquid, supercooled within large heat sinks and secondary cooling systems. This is because the heart of all PC and high-end electronic devices is the microchip. The charged couple device or CCD is one example of a microchip that can be overheated to the point of meltdown. The more the number of CCDs the more accurate the device, and the more expensive. While there are many who use their computers in all kinds of interesting ways — medical technology is one — globalization has enabled the transfer of real-world actions from motorsports for example, into virtual-world popular culture. High-techies "race" their computers based on clock speed, thermal performance, endurance, cooling capacity, heat absorption and heat dispersal. American popular culture blazes the trail of the global syntax of Japanese, South Korean, Middle Eastern, and other Asian languages while building vocabularies of delirium.

American mass culture or popular culture is defined as that range of activities that are accessible by a majority of people at relatively low cost that can be enjoyed in the private and public domains with or without government regulation or intervention. In order to get onto the list of popular culture, an activity has to satisfy three basic norms: accessibility, use-value, and uniqueness. Accessibility refers to the ease with which the activity and its supporting infrastructure and peripheral devices may be purchased at the lowest possible cost to allow the largest number of participants. Use-value refers to the functional value of an activity to the individual consumer. By and large, satisfaction is derived from participating in popular cultural activities but specifically from the functional value of those activities. Uniqueness is about standing out from other forms, styles, or activities. Uniqueness should involve some degree of originality although this is difficult to achieve in late modernity. *American Idol* is an example of a low cost, high-value entertainment programme that transformed into a popular cultural event of Americans from all walks of life. The impact of this television show — among thousands of other equally successful shows — was so great that it initiated similar shows across Asia, Latin America, the Middle East, and Europe. Most broadcasted programmes do not qualify as being part of popular culture in this strict sense. Another feature of popular cultural programmes is the iconic presence created and the cult of personality that follows. This is clear in Dean Martin, Oprah Winfrey, Howard Stern, and Tupac Shakur. For popular culture to work, there has to be mass participation, and by far the most powerful mass cultural tool at the general level is the Internet.

The competing number of academic books and articles on popular culture is as diverse as the definitions that come with them. Popular culture has similar characteristics all over the world. One is currency. Not the kind of currency that we saw in the previous chapter but a certain fashionableness and trendy set of consumer goods and services. Popular culture is a global industry simply because it is a money spinner. Therefore, popular culture in America and elsewhere in the world constitutes both a currency of fashion and the currency arising out of the sale and purchase of fashionable goods. While this chapter explores some of the different kinds of American popular culture and attempts to show how these cultural tropes inform the politics of American globalization, it cannot possibly encompass all the different kinds of popular culture that has made America what it is today. Some of the more prominent tropes of American popular culture that have been omitted include American cuisine, American pulp fiction, American television, broadcasting and networking, and syndicated networks, and American social sciences as a form of global tertiary popular culture. There are also other aspects of American popular culture that deserve more in-depth treatment such as the metaphorical use of urban legends, the myth of the cowboy, the Big Apple, Manifest Destiny and the Monroe Doctrine, the American Red Indian, the Superbowl and the Sugar Bowl, to name a few. The notion of American popular culture is a deep and important facet of American globalization. The depth and scope of the Internet created by American scientists during the Cold War has broadened significantly in the post 9/11 era. In terms of the conflation of fact and fiction, for example, the Internet is at the forefront of all media technologies. For example, American news, however stilted, biased, or objective has usually been taken for the straight boring stuff. The stuff may be boring but at least most consumers in modernity accepted American news networks like CNBC, ABC News, and NBC News as serious reportage of events considered newsworthy.

Yet the lines between fact and fiction, entertainment, and serious current news reporting changed in the first decade of the twenty-first century. For example, in the run up to the 2008 presidential campaign, the YouTube music video, Obama Girl, featuring a young model singing about her political support for Senator Barack Obama, created a sensation. The sexually implicit lyrics however did not receive a response from either Obama or his wife despite the obvious sexual innuendos in the video about her husband and the young model named Amber Lee Ettinger. Part of the reason is that there is a certain level of tolerance for free expression which would not be accepted in other places. But there is another reason, and that is that Ettinger's video had a tremendous impact when it aired in June 2007 on YouTube, attracting well over two million views and created a positive buzz for the Obama 2008 campaign. However, the lines between fact and fiction become blurred in another example of the popular political culture of the United States. Wolf Blitzer, the respected and popular newscaster and anchor for "The Situation Room" who is a model for many Asian news reporters, received a prank call from a Howard Stern fan during a live interview about the John Mark Karr murder case. This also happened on C-SPAN, Fox News, and twice on CNN. The Internet will continue to serve as a powerful alternative medium for those who resist the establishment's views and traditional information delivery systems. But because the Internet is ungovernable, it allows for great creativity, innovation, and the provision and promotion of truth as well as falsehoods, reality, and lies within the logic of American political culture. The conflation models developed on the Internet have a tremendous impact across the world including Asia which has the fastest growing number of Internet users. Even in Singapore where the government has a low tolerance level for lies, inaccurate reports, and disinformation that undermines state and society, the government of Singapore has never banned the use of the Internet as other governments such as Myanmar, Thailand (a partial and short-lived ban of YouTube videos carrying Thaksin's views), and to a very large extent, the People's Republic of China, have.

HARLEY DAVIDSON AND GLOBAL POPULAR CULTURE

The Harley Davidson Motorcycle Company almost went broke in the 1970s but was eventually revived as an important pillar of American popular culture. This was the beginning of a global popular cultural ethos that commemorated at least two levels. One dimension was the celebration of freedom, individualism, and self-expression; the other aspect was the celebration of an anti-establishment ethos, renegade youthfulness, drug abuse, sexual promiscuity, and a gangster culture that challenged all forms of social propriety and commonsense. Ironically, many state and federal traffic police units all over the world use Harley Davidson motorcycles. The Harley Davidson brand is now a worldwide entity with an MNC that provides the continuity of an old American tradition of the cowboy on his horse with the freedom of the open road to anyone of any colour, age, gender, size, sexual orientation, socio-economic class, or religion with the skill to operate a 1,000 cubic centimetre (twin-cam 88) motorcycle. The negative dimension associated with these powerful machines and the Hell's Angels group has become so diluted over the past half century that they have become an urban legend across the world. Harley Davidson motorcycles at the annual pilgrimage to Sturgis, South Dakota, for example, no longer pose a threat to society. In fact, the popularity of the Harley Davidson culture has become so ingrained over the past sixty-two years that it now seems to be a rite of passage for high-flying CEOs, young executives, and middle managers who still wish to recapture the nostalgic moments of their youth so aptly captured by Marlon Brando in *The Wild One* (1954), Steve McQueen in *The Great Escape* (1963), and the ultimate classic *Easy Rider* (1969) that starred Peter Fonda, Dennis Hopper, and Jack Nicholson. Later versions of the bad-boy image on a Harley include Arnold Schwarzenegger in *Terminator 2* (1991) and Mickey Rourke and Don Johnson in *Harley Davidson and the Marlboro Man* (1991). The popular culture of Harley Davidson motorcycles and the images that they evoke has become a global industry found on every continent and virtually every city and street. It is perhaps one of the most well-known names in global popular culture like Coke and McDonald's or Microsoft's Xbox360.

COUNTRY AND WESTERN POPULAR CULTURE

Many Americans love Country and Western (C&W) music in the songs of Hank Williams, Patsy Cline, Johnny Cash, Randy Travis, the Judds, Garth Brooks, or Charlie Pride. The popular cultural attributes in their songs derive from a history of living out, literally, in the country where self reliance and hardwork were key features of everyday life. Some believe that C&W music only began in the 1930s. This is untrue, and supports too narrow a definition, given the genealogical history of C&W music in America today. C&W music history dates back at least 200 years to the time of the American Civil War.

The epistemological position about C&W music for this book is that it represents C&W popular culture. On the other hand, the study of the meaning of the self is potentially discoverable in C&W music because of its reflection of what is perceived as "natural", "in nature" and "of nature". This is because C&W music is made up of a diverse reflection of different selves, and different approaches to the self turned inside out. This is seen in the variegated genres of C&W music sub-types such as Bluegrass, Dixie, Country Rock, Country Blues, Country Folk, Country Pop, Hawaiian Slack Key, Southern Gospel, Gospel Blues, Hawaiian Gospel, and New Age Country Gospel. C&W music is ostensibly tied, but not exclusively, to a kind of Christian ethos.

Perhaps the most interesting thing about C&W music is that it is easily recognized and enjoyed by people all over the world as being a genuine American invention. Such is the politics of globalization. If the politics of globalization is about influencing people who are not even in America, then this is certainly one example. The global appeal of C&W music — again, as only one example of American popular culture — is in its humility, its simplicity, and its shared "values". The strength of C&W music comes from the use of simple and straightforward themes that are easily recognized almost anywhere there has been access to free radio waves. C&W music also touches the hearts of people with its simple themes about family, losing someone or something, about the "good old days" and nostalgia, emotional wrangles, gambling, alcoholism, success, and joy. Another aspect of C&W music's popular appeal to the consumers of America is that it has a constant set of working metaphors: The "cowboy", "backroads, country roads", the "Lonesome Somebody", "Unrequited Love" and many other metaphors that are presented in a non-threatening, easy-listening, and conventional manner.

Rap music represents a powerful and universal influence in the history of modern music. Ordinary rap music uses more instruments and complex variations in the musical score than C&W music. But its extreme, fundamentalist, right-wing version or Gangster Rap tends to weaken the image and status of rap. Gangster Rap and C&W music are very interesting areas of research because their characteristics are in direct opposition to each other: gangster Rap music often represents the angst, hatred, the suffering, and the power struggles within America's decaying inner-urban cities. It portrays the paraphernalia of alcoholism, drug abuse, sexual abuse, sexism, misogyny, prostitution, misogamy, gang rape, hatred, racism, in-your-face verbal abuse, stealing people's property, treating women as property, and the extended use of expletives in place of adjectives, nouns, and adverbs.

Whether its the booty beat or melodious tunes, both Gangster Rap and C&W music represent popular genres that are equally "real" to their fans. It is just that one emphasizes the violence in human nature and the other does not. Gangster Rap is a reflection of political power and subordination. It is about insubordination. Gangster Rap is the music of political resistance in a way that C&W music is already the music of the empowered and the leisure class. Ordinary rap music is not "laid back" or less politically powerful, but it sends the message without the language of violence.

It is unlikely that many American parents would allow their children to listen to extreme versions of rap. Overseas and away from America, however, rap may be more acceptable by the local establishment because they simply cannot read it. Although both C&W and rap are clearly recognizable as genuine American popular cultural inventions, when sent away, rap tends to be more displaced by time, space, language, and social memory than C&W. Imagine a young Thai teenage consumer of extreme rap music who has never visited America, does not speak Spanish or American English, has no knowledge of "jive" or "street slang", never lived in a "burb" or a "hood", does not know anyone living in the decaying inner cities, nor has ever watched MTV. This is a teenager who will have a highly distorted view of rap. If the teenager's parents were also in the dark about rap, it would serve no less to ameliorate the perception of what rap might mean. Such a feature of globalization makes it political in the sense of a politics of apathy. Another example of political apathy follows.

In the early 1990s, over a period of several months, I noticed some young male teenagers in Singapore and Malaysia wearing T-shirts with a symbol emblazoned boldly on the front. But there was a problem with the symbol. At first I thought that it was the Buddhist swastika, which is common in Southeast Asia where there are relatively large populations of Buddhists. There is even a Red Swastika School in Singapore[6] that belongs to the Tao Yuan sect, also known by its philanthropic arm as the Red Swastika Society (Smith 1970, p. 586; Freedman and Topley 1961, p. 16). However, the symbol in question was the Nazi swastika. But the teens did not know what the symbol of the swastika meant. Had these "non-Aryan" teenagers been alive at the time of the National Socialists they would have been considered one of the lower races and subjected to the usual atrocities of the "non-chosen" people, and very quickly realized that the swastika was the symbol of Aryan supremacy and White-racism under Adolf Hitler.

One day, out of curiosity I asked a young teen loitering along Singapore's Orchard Road whether he knew what the symbol meant. He said that he did not. I politely gave him a brief history lesson about the dangers of (what I later learnt in graduate school to be) primordial and essentialist views of the world. And then I carefully explained what the symbol represented. What made it political? At the end of my explanation, he merely smiled, and shrugged his shoulders. Over a decade has passed since that incident. The fad of wearing such T-shirts has long gone. I only worry when it might come back in time, in a different form. This is the kind of problem that globalization presents when the youth of the world are callous about events and are not willing to bother to discover "the truth" on their own.

Globalization's reach within the popular culture of "trendy fashions" are part of a political problematic that teachers and social scientists need to continually engage.[7] The situation described above may indeed be an isolated episode and is not representative of any one minority. But there was a strong undercurrent of anti-Semitism among the Malaysian political elite under Mahathir Mohamad. The former prime minister blamed George Soros and other currency speculators for the 1997/8 Asian currency crisis. While he could have simply said that Soros was a greedy speculator who preyed on the structural vulnerabilities of developing states, it was Mahathir's suggestion of Soros' Jewish identity that pointed to his anti-Semitism (see also, Groth 1971, p. 89).

Teenagers are particularly vulnerable to the products of pop culture — whether these are made around C&W music, Rap, MTV, California Rock remixes, or the "blue-eyed soul" of Daryl Hall and John Oates. The producers of popular cultural goods and services must themselves be made more socially aware and thoughtful about their products, even though their ultimate desire is to make more money.

On the other hand, C&W music appears much less threatening to many American parents than the extreme versions of rap. But I cannot do justice to the latter genre of music and would urge you to read the work of Pamela Hall, especially her article titled, "The Relationship Between Types of Rap Music and Memory in African American Children" (1988) and Tricia Rose's excellent "Fear of a Black Planet: Rap Music and Black Cultural Politics in the 1990s" (1991).[8]

Yet, the attraction of C&W music to many Americans and to people all over the world is found in its predictability, simplicity of themes and values, and association with a certain "Southern, Confederate culture" that has survived the overwhelming Union victory so many years ago. There apparently is a cowboy in all of us. Even in Elvis Presley, according to the research of David Emblidge in 1976.[9] C&W music may not be able to mesh with American rap music but it certainly has had its share of related criticism. This is seen for example, in the "satire" and jocular diatribes of entertainers such as Jeff Foxworthy. He has indeed made a very good living out of taking the mickey out of American "Southern culture" and what is generally understood as the "Redneck" sub-culture. Foxworthy's success as an entertainer reflects a careful blending of a sub-cultural trait with his own familial history.

The interesting thing about the politics of American globalization is that foreigners often know more about America than Americans know about foreigners. Perhaps because America is more interesting to more people, or perhaps because there are more geographically challenged people in the United States. But this is only a hypothesis because a positivist social scientist in modernity would support the need for the construction of a proper survey instrument, by asking the "right" questions, and by operationalizing the concepts for a representative survey, backed up by ethnographic focus group activities for the absence of a normative bend in qualitative analyses.[10]

THE POPULARITY OF AMERICA

One thing has to be said about the nature of the popular culture of American music: what is considered radical today will no sooner become outdated and old-fashioned, unless the songs and the music remain at the top of the music charts. It is hard to believe that the gilded music of legends like Bing Crosby, Frank Sinatra, Dean Martin, Louis Armstrong, were once a radical set of entertainers. Sinatra, Sammy Davis Jr., and Dean Martin were known collectively as the original "Rat Pack".

American popular culture has continued to invade and occupy the time and space of all social classes, all ethnic communities, and all religious persuasions. This has happened all over the world in an uneven manner. How has the phenomenon of American popular culture come about and why has it continued to stay? More importantly, how is the phenomenon linked to the politics of American globalization? The phenomenon of American popular culture is built on three main ingredients: (1) the American Dream and the Anti-American Dream; (2) the creation of legends, myths, and stories about America's past such as those found in the fictive truths of — *A Horse With No Name*, Abraham Lincoln, American Cowboy, American Pie, Babe Ruth, Big Apple, Big Easy, California Dreamin', *Casey and the Sundance Kid*, Davy Crocket, Easy Rider, From Here to Eternity, *Harley Davidson*, Hotel

California, JFK, John Lennon, Johnny Appleseed, Marilyn Monroe, Marlboro Man, *Miss Saigon*, Paul Bunyan, Route 66, Tom Sawyer, Uncle Sam, Uncle Tom's Cabin, *West Side Story*, Westward Ho! and Woodstock; and (3) the commodification of these legends, myths, and stories into bite-sized bits that can be consumed — through images on television, movie characters on the silver screen, in computer games, in hand-held computer games, in animated films and cartoons, and the export of these to the rest of the world.

It is important at this juncture to note that there cannot be a single comprehensive definition of American popular culture. The best kind would be the broadest, something that sounds like the culture that is readily accepted by the masses, easily commoditized, subject to imminent changes in taste, and has the potential to return as retrospective culture or "retro". However, such a broad definition is not very useful when we consider that American popular culture by nature is about challenging that which is defined and definitive, that which seeks to remain stable and constant, and like the Rat Pack of Sammy Davis Jr., Frank Sinatra, and Dean Martin, designed to ostensibly reject in a politically non-violent way that which is considered to be part of the Establishment culture.

ESCAPE FROM TERROR

It is one thing to have important quotes from the work of Theodore Adorno, Herbert Marcuse, and Max Horkheimer in addition to the specifics of the authoritarian personality but it is quite another to deconstruct the work of Eric Fromm. The dangers of mass consumption were indeed anticipated by Adorno while Heidegger before him had already warned and taught Arendt about the problems that Jaspers had raised about the notion of technology in modernity.

The threat to human life and civilization as we know it comes in the shape of a political paradox. Unlike the paradox that continues to confront Americans that we saw in Chapter 2, this paradox comes from living life itself. Most threats are either biological, environmental, or associated with communications. It is a paradox because the sharing of information in the globalized world means that we have solved some problems of disease and certain aspects of food distribution. We have improved our knowledge in the physical sciences, in pharmaceutical products, and in psychological, clinical and emergency medicine. We have also learnt to develop different lifestyle choices that help us deal with unexpected loss. However, because of globalization's access and speed, modernity has also brought with it the scourge of those who are alienated. Thus it is a paradox because the vehicle that has brought good had also brought bad. It is a political paradox because those who feel that they have been alienated for whatever reason feel the need to use modern technology for destruction. Nuclear maps and explosive devices can be built with the help of the Internet. The ingredients for demolition devices can be purchased discretely and separately over the Internet. Our modes of communication — train travel, sea travel, and air travel — all move us towards efficiently getting there faster in comfort. Yet these modes of communication are themselves targets of alienated persons. The micro-technology used to perform cardiac surgery can also be used to create hidden explosive devices. And soon, nano-technology's advantages will likely be put to bad use. Our greatest achievement has resulted in our worst fears. Globalization is therefore a political paradox of raking in the good and bad without being able to tell the what from the which, quid pro quo within the promise(s) of American life as suggested by Walter Michaels and his discussion of "classes" and "masses".[11]

The world as we know it has increasingly become a tinderbox of terror. The rates of political and social change brought about by globalization's increasing access (to information, resources, talent) and speed have also been taken advantage of by terrorists. The tinderbox of terror might be ignited by people who have the same access to the information and resources with the same speed. In addition to Connolly's analysis of depth in his article "Cosmopolitanism, Speed and Concentric Cultures" we continue to be confronted by people who have spun out of the circle of modernizing cultures. And to have spun out of control is to be made redundant and insignificant.[12] Terrorists desire attention, but want it the easy way. Rather than going through the political process, rather than employing means that will extend bridges of communication, these marginalized groups want to blow them apart.

There appears to be little respite from the threat of someone somewhere plotting to destroy what American families may have been taking for granted for years. It is one thing to consider such a prison mentality as a kind of Gramscian hangover, and a thing of the past. It is quite another thing to consider the prison in a Foucauldian sense that encompasses our modern modes of organizing politics, economics, culture, and society. However, it is because human kind is continually beset and under siege by one form of terror or another that we cannot completely rule out a proto-alarmist position on the possibility that the people we know in a quotidian sense could be the next victim of a terrorist attack. War, it seems, follows the human being like a shadow. And the faster we go, the faster the shadow follows. The communists used the nuclear threat on Americans for the greater part of the lives of most people who are likely to read this book. America, in retaliation, called its own nuclear programme nuclear deterrence. The McCarthyism that followed did not achieve anything but make Americans fear the threat was imminent. There was Korea, Vietnam, Afghanistan, Iran, Iraq, Libya, Lebanon, Kuwait, Haiti, and the indefatigable mess created in the Middle East between the Palestinians and the Israelis. There was also the problem of OPEC's oligopoly and the threat of depleted fossil fuels that were driving the industrialization plans of developing countries, and the post-industrialization of America and Western Europe. The world has become so small and so interrelated that any problem occurring in a distant part of the globe soon becomes an issue of concern for the rest of the world, such as the resurgence in Islamic fundamentalism in the 1970s, AIDS, ozone depletion, global warming, the Savings and Loans scandal, environmental disasters caused by super tankers like the Exxon Valdez, SARS, avian or bird flu virus, Mad Cow Disease, the threat of chemical and biological warfare, Enron, and the horrifying destruction of the World Trade Center's twin towers (9/11), the Bali bombing, the Madrid train bombing, scourge in Southern Thailand, and the continuing problem of latent terrorists trained by the CIA, international waterway piracy, a weakening UN, the rising strength of the euro and the increasing sentiment of European unity and potential protectionism since 1 May 2004.

And American popular culture is part of an important machine within the neoliberal capitalism of America that helps provide that means of escapism. But how does one avoid the real terror exposed to America within its borders, as Michel and Herbeck remind us in their *American Terrorist: Timothy McVeigh and the Oklahoma City Bombing* (Regan 2001) or an earlier harbinger by Raphael S. Ezekiel in *The Racist Mind: Portraits of American Neo-Nazis and Klansmen* (Penguin reprint, 1996). How does one out-think the irrationality of fear(s) that terrorize us from wanting to be over prepared for terror that we inadvertently stultify our own mechanisms for growth and creativity? We need popular culture to escape the horrors of our own images, our own species, and our own world. Popular culture is there at the heart of the social fabric. It could be that popular culture presents itself so instantaneously and on such a vast scale that it helps keep hope alive. Popular culture might be the only thing left for the masses who think they are individuals and are searching to escape the scorching reality of clear and present threats, and vague and future anxieties.

THE POWER OF COMEDY: FANTASY AND ESCAPISM FOR ALL

One of the greatest comedic enterprises and creative talents ever to be generated within American popular culture as a potential school of thought is Black Comedy. Bill Cosby's family-centred comedy routines are an excellent example of centrist Black Comedy. Despite some sarcastic comments about White people in some interviews, the character of Bill Cosby in the vintage *The Cosby Show* adroitly uses his wit and charm to exploit what is known as the "White comfort zone".[13] Black Comedy is usually "funny — Ha! Ha!" encapsulating serious social, political, and economic messages. The difference in function between Black Comedy as a narratival exposition of Black life and death through satire, slapstick, or soliloquy is stridently different from the black comedy that focuses on the dark or evil side as seen in McFadden's view of Nietzsche (McFadden 1981, p. 338). Shakespeare, for example, used black comedy as dark comedy, but his *weltanschauung* addressed a different kind of audience that the Black comedians of American popular culture are addressing in today's globalized world. Black Comedy as a globalizing force of American popular culture is likely to have a greater impact on late modernity than the anachronistic Shakespearean dark comedy or the literary texts of Ben Jonson (1572–1637).[14] More people of the world are likely to empathize with Black comedic routines if only because of the sublimated and subordinated positions of their characters. But the total effect remains to be seen.

As Inniss and Feagin suggest, White people would be more willing to accept knowledge of Black people through a certain level of comfort. The segue into that zone of comfort is comedy. But they also make the important point that such access to Black life, Black problems, and Black happiness are not considered important and hence can be taken lightly. I think that they are wrong about such a hypothesis because they assume too much on behalf of the White audience's level of tolerance and they perhaps misdirect the readers' attention away from a "White" ability to understand the Black problems. The world is not so clearly divided, although many people live life that way because it is easier without complications. It is certainly less tiring and less enervating to think in simplistic terms. Consider the classical Black comedic routine of Sammy Davis Junior and the king of classic Black comedy, Richard Pryor, who even made fun of his own setting himself on fire by accident. In a film with Gene Wilder, titled *See No Evil, Hear No Evil* (1989), Pryor plays a blind African-American man who is self-opinionated and angry at the world for the accident that caused his blindness. In a leap of sudden realization, he stands up in the middle of a crowded commuter train and shouts at the top of his squeaky voice, "you mean, I'm not White?!" Also consider the up and coming comedy sketches of Jamie Foxx in *Breakin' All the Rules* (Screen Gems 2004), Snoop Dogg in *Soul Plane* (MGM 2004), the expletive comedy of Chris Rock and the milder versions displayed by Chris Tucker, and Martin Lawrence in *Martin Lawrence Live: Runteldat* (Paramount 2002).[15]

The power behind Black Comedy lies in the systematic historical and political suppression of Black rights. Black comedy is distinguished from other forms of comedic presentations because of the sustained levels of emotional and cultural abuse that the Black people have received since their ancestors were forced into labour. The transatlantic slave trade between Portuguese Brazil and West Africa, between West Africa and the British isles, and between the Americas and Africa from the fourteenth to the nineteenth centuries would have broken the spirit of any one culture. Furthermore, the internal slavery issues and racism that were systematically implemented in these colonial countries and in the America of the day resulted in the complete denigration and mnemonic erasure of the different "origins" of various Black cultures. Consequently, the lost cultures that were destroyed by mercantilist trade resulted in the re-creation of new American cultures. These new cultures were themselves caught in the political economy of the day, the social and civil strife of the frontier world, and a vicious cycle of impoverishment and political control by the White elites over the Black slave-underclass.[16] There is a clear master-slave dialectic that continues to draw its resources from the Black American experience and I have suggested that Black Comedy as a powerful type of American popular culture provides such an avenue of escapism for the spectatorialism of the sociological *problematique* of leisure within the American public.

PUBLIC SPACE AND LEISURE

The active pursuit of leisure in public space leads to a construction of modes of lifestyle choices in real/reel life that become mimicked over generations through the broadcast media (such as television, radio, the Internet, and film) so that audiences can laugh at themselves while laughing at these characters. The ability to laugh is not limited to the American media but is a reflection of a global and very human phenomenon that requires skill, dedication, focus and hard work to achieve the effect of laughter. This is partially what Neil Postman was darkly trying to convey about the public sphere in *Amusing Ourselves to Death*. Coming close to Lippmann's views on the public, Postman's notion of laughter becomes political when we realize that perhaps in laughing at the characters on TV, those with whom we easily identify, they are indeed a reflection of our own achievements or lack of. Perhaps, this might be why these situational comedies are designed so as to un/cover as wide a range of the social structure as possible.

There is always one sitcom that makes fun of the genteel upper classes and those who desire to be part of that class but fail trying (*Frasier, Dharma and Greg*, and *Just Shoot Me*). There are also sitcoms for those who identify with the working class misery of having to walk the picket line, work on three different shifts, wear a uniform, punch a clock, deal with callous bosses, and fight the problem of being overweight (*The King of Queens*). Also, a third category of sitcom deal with the life of "yuppies" (young upwardly mobile professionals) and "dinks" (double income, no kids) with a limited social circle (*Friends, Herman's Head*) or gender-based ones on television such as *Sex and the City*. A fourth category often deals with teenage and marriage problems that tend to draw audiences from both ends of the spectrum (*That Seventies Show, Grounded For Life, Third Rock From the Sun*). These different presentations of the lighter side of life constitute important images of temporary escape. The audience identifies with one or several characters. The process of identification invites the audience to participate in a fantasy of escapism. There is a politics of escapism in the public space of leisure in these comedic situations because laughter lightens the load of the laden; laughter frees the mind; laughter distracts the audience from the onerous routine of daily work. However, one could make this observation about almost any form of entertainment in the public arena.

So what exactly is unique about these sitcoms? The answer is in the idea of political satire. Most of the sitcoms make sense to the viewer because they take ordinary everyday situations faced by many Americans and place them at the centre of the frame. The focus on one particular event out of many highlights the chosen scene through slapstick routines, exaggeration and hyperbole, or pushing the limits to its logical extremes. This is part of political fantasy but the comedic element prevents the violation of the viewers' choice of the fantasy. Comedy is a means of political escapism because it provides a fantasy of retreat and escape that does not infringe on the rights of the next individual. The moment that comedy goes beyond its bounds it ceases to have its original effect and loses power.

THE AMERICAN DREAM IN PUBLIC SPACE

The American Dream involves "life", "liberty", and the pursuit of "happiness" but it is also made up of a very specific set of historical images that mixes fantasy of fact and fiction to produce a global phenomenon that has changed the way people all over the world perceive themselves, their own cultures, and their own histories. Like its political culture, the novel event that is American popular culture is a deliberate attempt to create a "culture" in a hurry. This is because of America's relatively shorter amount of history as a modern democratic state. People travel to Europe to "see", "feel", and "experience" culture. There is a clear cultural presence in Europe because of its long and bloody history of romance, religion, philosophy, languages, and war. These ingredients have evolved into different sovereign states themselves such as France and the lower countries. In Europe we have cultural production houses that have emerged through violence and conflict over 2,500 years, at least since the time of the classical Greek period. American culture is a breakaway culture, a break from the English colonial traditions that were settled in the first thirteen colonies of the Atlantic seaboard. American culture is a culture in a hurry because the speed of modernization and the need to survive in a rapidly changing world environment has led to less time and space for culture to evolve. This is why many Europeans, perhaps unfairly, criticize Americans for not having a culture. Given the temporal and spatial constraints, there was a clear need for Americans to create their own cultural space within a shorter period of time. The result was a two-pronged effort that began with the founding fathers and the rise of the pioneer culture. The seventeenth and eighteenth centuries were particularly crucial for the development of something out of nothing. As a result, the foundations of American popular culture may be best understood in terms of two strategies of (1) cultural borrowing and (2) the symbiosis of location.

Cultural borrowing meant the copying and mimicry (again we note this important and useful phrase used so effectively by Naipaul and then by Bhabha in different contexts) of so-called original cultures in England. Cultural borrowing also involved the transplantation of migrant cultures from other parts of Africa, Europe, and more recently, Asia and the Pacific, in three stages. The first stage was the transfer of the software through reading material, oral histories, nutrition and dietary habits. The second stage was the amplification of such motherland or "old country" practices and taboos in the new cultural site, with the gateway eventually being called Ellis Island. The third stage involved what is known as the codification of such practices within the first and second generation of migrants who serve as the cultural gatekeepers of these old traditions in the new country through local histories, the oral tradition, entertainment, and leisure activity. The pioneering spirit and the frugality of the early settlers with their year-end celebrations of harvest and Thanksgiving are considered important anchor points for these cultural stake-points.

A cultural stake-point occurs in the public arena. It is the place one might understand to be "ground zero", in the parlance of late modernity. Therefore any values and norms that are created, for example, "pioneer spirit", "frugal", "hard work", or "team effort" as seen in the Anabaptists of yesteryear during a barn-raising or at Thanksgiving, are making use of a cultural stake-point at which to locate the activities that lock in its members. Membership therefore requires participation. Popular cultural traits then begin forming on the fringes of these cultural stake-points not in a subordinate manner but in a way that engages and re-engages those on the public fringe towards the centre, and therefore inwards to the central concerns of the given culture, which in this case is American popular culture. This highly Aristotelian persuasion is nonetheless moot when one considers that cultural anchoring and gatekeeping are concomitant activities that bind members of a community together while promoting their feelings of group solidarity and demoting emotions of insecurity. Consequently, we can see how the cultural stake-points in public space pave the way forward towards a political strategy that I call the symbiosis of location.

The symbiosis of location is the second strategy from where popular culture can be said to truly originate. This symbiosis involves the mixing up and sharing of cultural resources between and among cultural groups and subgroups in the third and subsequent generation of migrants. The sharing of resources includes (linguistic) accents, dietary and nutritional habits, taboos, the function of women, the function of men, and the place of children within the fabric of the new nation. The symbiosis is a result of people of different migrant cultures who have been forced into a new situation where they have no other choice but to live with people of different colours and languages. Over time, a nexus of symbiotic relationships develops among the co-ethics of each community. The resultant product of such cultural mixing is what some call the "melting pot". However, not all co-ethnics within a given community will support the idea of a melting pot and therefore there is a return to the old ways of doing things and of surviving the pressures of urbanization, regionalization, and now, globalization. The symbiosis of location takes place across time and space and involves the marked definition and redefinition of cultural boundaries that change over each generation. Within a given population of Irish-Americans, for example, there will be those who seek to preserve the past for posterity while there are those who completely reject this in favour of the national identity called "America" and "American". In between the cultural preservationists and the cultural rejectionists are those who prefer to keep a little of the old ways while being happy to adapt to changes that take place in the public sphere. The public sphere is where the cultural showcase of ethnic pride is displayed every so often to keep hope alive. In constructing these real displays of culture, one gets an immediate Foucauldian view that involves the construction of discursive formations within society. The public sphere is that container where there are plural cultural activities giving and taking, consuming and producing, demanding and supplying events and activities, action and non-action, upon which the symbiosis of location can settle and take deeper root.

Both cultural strategies that form the basis of American popular culture are understood to have matured by the fourth and fifth generation of migrants, therefore compressing migrant culture into a system of shared diasporic values over a brief period of forty to sixty years. Here, in addition to the counter-culture of the 1960s, C&W music, rap music, and Black Comedy, we discover the other stake-point of American popular cultural celebrations. Consider the commodification of Kwanza, Christmas, and Hanukkah. Other examples are seen in the fictive/fact Christian observance of All Souls' Day and the pagan ritual of Halloween, the neo-animistic Chinese observance of the Hungry Ghost Festival, and the mythical shamanism depicted by some American playwrights.[17] All these festivities represent mixtures of foreign and local, borrowed and invented traditions of filling the chasm devoted to leisure. Celebrations through festivals, parades, song, drama, music, and stories are broadcast across the spectrum of public space. Like Kant's notion of tutelage, the level of creativity rises with the determination to succeed in play as in work. This is all part of the routine that populates the idiom of the American Dream. The dream is volatile and interpretive, enhancing and sublimating texts that rise through history channels of American social, economic and political institutions. The dream is a fantasy world made real in endeavouring to attain and understand liberty. Freedom comes in the form of denial to others. In America, the cultural popularity of the exercise of capitalist choices over goods and services can exist only when these choices are denied to others who do not share the ideological beliefs of neoliberal capitalism. If countries other than the United States and its allies are willing to give up their traditions and differences with American popular culture, they too can share in the hegemonic conquest that is the United States of America; they too can share in the American Dream provided that they use the right currency, stand in line, and get their tickets at the door. And there are a wide variety of films to view at the box office. For example, there are the American classics that celebrate the American Dream of success through perseverance and hard work despite the presence of total calamity that saw the successful launch of such careers as Clark Gable, Olivier De Havilland, Leslie Howard, and Vivien Leigh in *Gone With the Wind* (1939). Classic American movies about Americans wedged in a social class they seemingly cannot escape include Frank Capra's *It's a Wonderful Life* (1946) or a battle of personalities in Elizabeth Taylor's role in a *Cat on a Hot Tin Roof* (1958), and Marlon Brando and Vivien Leigh in Tennessee Williams's *Streetcar Named Desire* (1951). Some American movie classics involved deeper psychological terror skirting a kind of Nietzschean abyss, as with Jimmy Stewart in Alfred Hitchcock's *Vertigo* (1958) and Hitchcock's *Shadow of a Doubt* (1943). In America, there has always been a set of films that depict the saviour-slave metaphor where a marginalized Black Southerner accused of raping a White woman is finally saved by a brilliant White lawyer (Gregory Peck in *To Kill a Mockingbird*, 1962). Could the American civil rights movement have proceeded without the help of real life Atticus Finch personalities or could it have purely depended on the powerful political resistance of real life Rosa Parks' refusal to give up her seat in the White section of a public bus?

We understand now that these "classic" films have become the source for new generations of actors to mimic and hone their own acting skills but there is more to it because many new films often use the American classic movie in a "cameo" piece to add depth or to capture the attention of an older segment of the audience. The entire American movie industry as a popular cultural economy of escapism through war movies centred on John Wayne (who never had any war experience) and a young Elvis Presley (who was posted to Germany and returned an army sergeant with much aplomb) and cowboy movies, called Westerns, that were easy to understand because the bad guys usually wore black, had few clothes, made whooping noises, or threatened White civilization. And then the cavalry returned to decimate the entire native village. The political economy of American film also provided an avenue for rich acting talent that depicted a Sartre's psychological hesitation (Richard Burton and Elizabeth Taylor in the 1966 film *Who's Afraid of Virginia Woolf?*); Bertolt Brecht's tempestuous self-inflicted politics (Orson Welles in *Citizen Kane*, 1941; Robert Redford and Mia Farrow in *The Great Gatsby*, 1976; and Robert Mitchum and Gregory Peck in [the original] *Cape Fear*, 1962); Edward Said's Orientalism (Errol Flynn in *Captain Blood*, 1935); and Henry S. Kariel's widespread desperation (Henry Fonda in John Steinbeck's *Grapes of Wrath*, 1940; and perhaps eventually, Cervantes' *Don Quixote*). While most actors get involved in some kind of social movement or take up some public challenge voluntarily to boost their careers, Gregory Peck was an exception. Peck openly challenged the impoverishment of American values during the civil rights movement when many actors were under intense pressure to stay away from defending "Negroes". He also spoke out against the Vietnam War. He was the most outspoken American liberal actor who believed he could put into practice what he said on film. Peck's movies and the others above are only a few of the movies that constitute the local and global power of the American moving picture industry. The American Dream in the popular cultural political economy of film endeavours to present and represent prevailing versions of truth. Doubtlessly, there will be a war film based on the atrocities of American soldiers in Iraq in the Second Gulf War, but would probably end with American forms of justice and fairness where the good preside over the punishment of evil.

The American Dream is defined as "life, liberty and the pursuit of happiness". The materialistic component is one heavy aspect of the dream and the other heavy aspect is individualism. And all ideological forms of individualism need political heroes and cultural anti-heroes.

> We understand the tragic hero … can never be mad; and that conversely madness cannot bear within itself those values of tragedy, which we have known since Nietzsche and Artaud. In the classical period, the man of tragedy and the man of madness confront each other, without a possible dialogue, without a common language; for the former can only utter the decisive words of being, uniting in a flash the truth of light and the depth of darkness; the latter endlessly drones out the indifferent murmur which cancels out both the day's chatter and the lying dark (Foucault [1965] 1988, p. 111).

If the tragic anti-hero of Gregory Peck were still alive in this racist world, he would have uttered on screen more depths of darkness and more truths in light while looking into the distance at the end of the denouement, and saying, "it would have been a great adventure…but remember it's a sin to kill a mockingbird".

CONCLUSION

We saw at the beginning of this chapter how Americans desire to escape the problems of modernity through the creation of popular cultural activity in public space. And that such leisure activity over generations is transformed into cultural anchor points or stake-points around which acceptable norms of popular culture can grow and spread for the benefit of its members. The examples provided involved publicly overt illustrations of genuine American popular culture such as C&W music, rap music, and the politically charged counter-culture of the 1960s. The chapter showed how such popular cultural programmes are generated through television which has been both a boon and a bane for the promotion of American values overseas and locally. The recreational "sport" of popular cultural activities are part of the politics of American globalization because of the powerful influence over foreigners, strangers who have never set foot on U.S. soil or are ever likely to do so. The political dimension of American popular culture represents a kind of soft power of hegemony where the cultural theory of Gramsci (more so than

Habermas) ignites a certain attraction to America, to its genuine cultural activities, its situation comedies, its war movies, through classic American film, via powerful MNCs that promote Hollywood as an American capitalist idol. Americans have been influencing the world through their popular takes through the broadcast media in ways that are more powerfully residual than gross invasions that lead to undesirable consequences. Once the masses get control of a thing, as they say, it never goes back up and never gets concealed. Look at the end of Louis XIV, and the ultimate political insurrection in the three French Revolutions. Look at what the deterioration and end of the corrupt upper classes had unleashed, despite having lived lives *plaisir à tout prix*. The formal offloading of the elite control of special leisure activities at the end of the Ancien Régime led to a rapid distribution of work otherwise inaccessible without the Guttenberg press and other earlier forms of mass printing. It was, however, the education received by the masses desirous of understanding the written word through the formalization of educational systems across Europe and its colonies as a form of religious expansionism and political control that enabled the rise of crude forms of popular culture. *Rameau's Nephew* was no longer to remain the idle chatter of a circle of *philosophes*. And schools of philosophy that had held intensely to their cherished works from Plato and Aristotle began wavering under the weight of the Enlightenment theorists and their disciples.

Suddenly anyone could listen to Brahms, Beethoven, or Tchaikovsky or read musical scores without having to go through long and arduous training in Switzerland. No one needed to be of Teutonic stock, a German or Russian to create classical music. Consider Lang-Lang, a twenty-two-year-old music prodigy from China. He is one of two great prodigies, the other being a twenty-one-year-old Russian. Now not only can the rich and the swanky afford to listen to Chopin's *Scherzo E Major*, Opus 54, his wonderfully sullen funeral march *Sonata No. 2 in B flat Minor*, Opus 35, or Mendelssohn's *Allegro Brillante in A Major* but anyone who can afford a compact disc (CD) and a Sony CD Walkman can do so.[18] The counter-culture of American rock has indeed created such a demand that it is now more expensive to listen to hard rock bands than classical music ensembles, the tickets of which sometimes cannot be given away even free of charge, not even when one reconsiders the centrality of popular forms of cultural dominance vis-à-vis the practical and functional aspects of the late modern life as suggested by Shusterman,[19] Shapiro, Street, and Docker.

Some examples of the bittersweet ways in which there is systemic failure in American popular culture is the dead hero concept. This is self-explanatory, and tinged with both sadness that someone such as James Dean,

Elvis Presley, Marilyn Monroe, Tupac Shakur had to die at such a young age while simultaneously being a celebration of their universal successes. The systemic failure arises out of the fact of the mysteriousness of their deaths. Death among iconic youth is never simple and always shrouded in mystery. Who really killed Marilyn Monroe? Mystery also surrounds the deaths of Jimi Hendrix, Andy Gibb, John Lennon, Biggie Smalls (Christopher Wallace), Bob Marley, and Kurt Cobain to name a small number. The angst and anger often emerges when people remember their favourite iconoclasts. Chris Rock for example is a well-known celebrity known for resorting to vulgarities and expletives in his punchlines. To an extent, he is a poor imitation of the great and brilliant Richard Pryor who set the cultural standards for many even when his house caught fire. An example of the angst and passion is illustrated from one of hundreds of YouTube clips featuring one of Chris Rock's sell-out, on-the-edge comedies. Millions of people from all over the world have watched his performances that always have a political angle. Oftentimes the disaffection with systemic failure to remedy social ills can only be vented through laughter and repetition.

What will be considered politically correct and acceptable as popular culture then? It points towards a district minority of citizens confined by their own popular political culture of correctness and popular culture of indiscretion. The tension between the two is the reason why teachers exist. Political correctness has led to such a level of hypocrisy and social tolerance that certain words or phrases cannot be used without causing harm to one's career or one's reputation. Perhaps for good reason. On one hand we have a situation where political correctness is the liberal society's effort to be racially sensitive and to serve a higher political ideal of tolerance; on the other hand, political correctness seems to be about hypocrisy and not saying what one truly feels about an issue or subject. Both sides of being politically correct exist within the larger ambit of the freedom of speech. But the freedom to speak or to utter certain words or phrases in the globalized world has its limitations. The rest of the world is increasingly adopting one of America's greatest achievements, to be politically correct. Therein lies the danger.

The popular culture that is circulated by the media also plays to another audience. The public's need-to-know is itself a form of arbitrary justice that has evolved ostentatiously since the time of Lippmann and Pulitzer. The media will always reveal, for whatever reasons of professional ethics, what the world has always known about the fault lines in the conduct of American businesses overseas and the conduct of American foreign policy. And as long as there continues to be an imbalance of power within communities based on tradition, modernization, culture, gender, primordialism, circumstantialism, racism, religion, fossil fuels, and socio-economic class there will be a politics of control, a politics of discord, a politics of resistance, and a politics of subversion that feed into the global reach of American globalization. The extension of life through individualism is very popular in the United States. The entire economy is geared towards the maximization of individualism and the fulfilment of life through materialism. The entire meaning of popular culture may be contained within the spirit of material achievement and the desire for more goods and services that advance instant gratification and promote a wide array of temporary but real options (Rappa 2002). Life is contained within the popular culture of coffee consumption — Starbucks is a spectacular success and has many clones to prove its worldwide undisclosed value of over US$5 billion per annum, clones included — nicotine consumption, alcohol consumption, and the rest of what used to be prohibited in the Progressive Era of 1920s America. It certainly is popular culture now.

An understanding of the politics of American popular culture is important because it continues to have a strong impact on the nature of public culture and public choices across the globe. This in itself makes American culture "political". Consider the acceptability of such displaced persons as Larry Miller whose own sober provocation of Americans (in general) and African-Americans (in particular) seem acceptable because he is an African-American. Or Michael Moore's thrashing of American social problems across the broad backs of White American men as being legitimized and made acceptable to many simply because he is White. But what if the populist roles were reversed?

As this chapter has shown, the American popular culture is indeed a political phenomenon. It is one that is built and designed like General Motors, on the concept of the American Dream. And why should it not? American popular culture has three main legs: (1) the American Dream and the Anti-American Dream; (2) the creation of legends, myths, and stories about America's past such as those found in the fictive stories of Paul Bunyan, Tom Sawyer, Johnny Appleseed, Uncle Sam, the American Cowboy and the Marlboro Man, Harley Davidson, and *Easy Rider*; (3) the commodification of these legends, myths, and stories into bite-sized bits that can be consumed — through images on television, movie characters on the silver screen, in computer games, in hand-held computer games, in animated films and cartoons, and the export of these to the rest of the world. Sometimes known as mass culture, popular culture is perhaps a more accurate term because it conveys the popularity of the instant gratification society while mass suggests a certain lack of discernment and the absence of choice as in the politics of mass mobilization, but you can see why the distinctions between mass and popular continue to be a moot point. The phenomenon of American popular culture(s) continues to maintain a stranglehold over the nameless, faceless, and sometimes masked masses.

Notes

1. Alternatively, consider Daniel H. Levine, "Popular Groups, Popular Culture, and Popular Religion", *Comparative Studies in Society and History* 32, no. 4 (1990): 718–64.
2. Antonio L. Rappa, "Modernity and the Contingency of the Public", in "Modernity and the Politics of Public Space", *Innovation — The European Journal of Social Science Research* 15, no. 1 (2002): abstract.
3. Rappa and Wee, *Language Policy and Modernity in Southeast Asia* (Springer 2006).
4. One cannot expect to draw immediate inspiration from a literal reading of Gramsci's political work because it would seem immediately outdated. This is with regards to the notion of education, unions, and freedom in his political writing of the 1920s. For an understanding we need to turn to the work of Gramsci scholars such as Paul Piccone, "Gramsci's Hegelian Marxism", *Political Theory* 2, no. 1 (1974): 32–45; Paul Piccone, "Gramsci's Marxism: Beyond Lenin and Togliatti", *Theory and Society* 3, no. 4 (1976): 485–512; Walter L. Adamson, "Beyond 'Reform or Revolution': Notes on Political Education in Gramsci, Habermas and Arendt", *Theory and Society* 6, no. 3 (1978): 429–60; James P. Hawley, "Antonio Gramsci's Marxism: Class, State and Work", *Social Problems* 27, no. 5 (1980): 584–600; Joseph V. Femia, "Gramsci's Patrimony", *British Journal of Political Science* 13, no. 3 (1983): 327–64; and the excellent piece by Nadia Urbinati, "From the Periphery of Modernity: Antonio Gramsci's Theory of Subordination and Hegemony", *Political Theory* 26, no. 3 (1998): 370–91.
5. Michel Foucault, *Madness and Civilization* (NY: Vintage, [1965], 1988), p. 97.
6. The Red Swastika Society was the philanthropic arm of the Tao Yuan Sect — formed in 1921 in Tsin-an with the intention of uniting Christianity, Buddhism, Taoism, Confucianism, and Islam. According to Smith, the Tao Yuan Sect spread to Nanyang in the 1930s, and claimed to have a supreme spirit above all the five religious deities called the Tai-i Lao-jen. See R.B. Smith, "An Introduction to Caodaism II. Beliefs and Organization", *Bulletin of the School of Oriental and African Studies* 33, no. 3 (1970): 573–89; See also the earlier work, by Maurice Freedman, and Marjorie Topley, "Religion and Social Realignment among the Chinese in Singapore", *Journal of Asian Studies* 21, no. 1 (1961): 3–23.
7. It is one thing to spread democracy and to support its ideological precepts but it is quite another thing to popularize democracy itself as a culture to be

transplanted to foreign places where there is no tradition of democracy. Western democracies cannot expect newly-democratizing countries to achieve the same level of democratic change that took the West over 200 years to achieve, but must learn to control the urge to interfere. If you were a student in Oxford or New York City, what do you think would happen to American popular culture if China became a superpower and began to export Chinese socialism to Middletown, USA? Or decided unilaterally that it was going to invade America because of all the alleged torture and impoverishment of African-Americans whom it was trying to save? What would be your reaction?

8   Pamela D. Hall, "The Relationship Between Types of Rap Music and Memory in African American Children", *Journal of Black Studies* 28, no. 6 (1998): 802–14; and Tricia Rose, "Fear of a 'Black Planet': Rap Music and Black Cultural Politics in the 1990s", *Journal of Negro Education* 60, no. 3 (1991): 276–90. See also, Errol A. Henderson, "Black Nationalism and Rap Music", *Journal of Black Studies* 26, no. 3 (1996): 308–39; and Houston A. Baker, Jr., "Handling 'Crisis': Great Books, Rap Music, and the End of Western Homogeneity", *Callaloo* 13, no. 2 (1990): 173–94.

9   David Emblidge, "Down Home with the Band: Country-Western Music and Rock", *Ethnomusicology* 20, no. 3 (1976): 541–52.

10 See for example, the work of William S. Fox and James D. Williams, "Political Orientation and Music Preferences among College Students", *The Public Opinion Quarterly* 38, no. 3 (1974): 352–71.

11 Walter Benn Michaels, "An American Tragedy, or the Promise of American Life", *Representations* 25 (1989): 71–98.

12 William E. Connolly, "Speed, Concentric Cultures, and Cosmopolitanism", *Political Theory* 28 (2000): 596–618. See also William E. Connolly, *Neuropolitics: Thinking, Culture, Speed* (MN: University of Minnesota Press, 2002) where he makes a relatively similar argument as Henry S. Kariel did in the early 1990s about the value of the interface between society and images in the screen versions of *Vertigo*, *Five Easy Pieces*, and *Citizen Kane*. Both Kariel and Connolly approach the problem of different ontological paradigms from different angles, meeting at the apex, and then coming away separately. More specifically, Henry S. Kariel rises from the ashes of his *Desperate Politics of Postmodernism* (MA: Massachusetts Press, 1989), and Connolly advances his position based, I think, on the context that he provides in his earlier work. See William E. Connolly, *Ethos of Pluralization* (MN: University of Minnesota Press, 1995).

13 Leslie B. Inniss, and Joe R. Feagin, "The Cosby Show: The View from the Black Middle Class", *Journal of Black Studies* 25, no. 6 (1995): 708.

14 Brian F. Tyson, "Ben Jonson's Black Comedy: A Connection between Othello and Volpone", *Shakespeare Quarterly* 29, no. 1 (1978): 60–66. There is much reference to race in the interpretive and performative aspects of Shakespeare's work and texts but it goes beyond the scope of this book to attempt any deconstruction of his work here. See also James Shapiro, *Shakespeare and the Jews* (NY: Columbia University Press, 1997).

15 See also Leslie B. Inniss, and Joe R. Feagin, "The Cosby Show: The View from the Black Middle Class", *Journal of Black Studies* 25, no. 6 (1995): 692–711. Compare the difference in the use of Black Comedy versus Black Comedy in terms of how McFadden uses Black Comedy as dark comedy. See George McFadden, "Nietzschean Values in Comic Writing", *Boundary* 2 9, no. 3 (1981): 337–58.

16 Despite the so-called advances in politics, law and cultural sensitivity among Americans of all ethnic persuasions, it is impossible for anyone to lift themselves up single-handedly. One cannot deny that the purchasing power of Black America and the leisure time devoted by Black America to leisure activities has increased significantly. But it is another thing to say to a person of colour that another person of a different colour freed you and your family. Perhaps because no human being should be enslaved in the first place?

17 See, for example, V.A. Lucier, " 'Offrenda' on All-Souls' Day in Mexico", *Journal of American Folklore* 10, no. 37 (1897): 106–07; Elsie Clews Parsons, "All-Souls Day at Zuni, Acoma, and Laguna", *Journal of American Folklore* 30, no. 118 (1917): 495–96; Arnold Perris, "Feeding the Hungry Ghosts: Some Observations on Buddhist Music and Buddhism from Both Sides of the Taiwan Strait", *Ethnomusicology* 30, no. 3 (Autumn 1986): 428–48; Ernest Ingersoll, "Decoration of Negro Graves", *Journal of American Folklore* 5, no. 16 (1892): 68–69; and Mae G. Henderson, "Ghosts, Monsters, and Magic: The Ritual Drama of Larry Neal", *Callaloo* 23 (1985): 195–214.

18 Bruce Tucker, "Tell Tchaikovsky the News: Postmodernism, Popular Culture, and the Emergence of Rock 'N' Roll", *Black Music Research Journal* 9, no. 2 (1989): 271–95.

19 Richard Shusterman, "Pragmatist Aesthetics and Popular Culture", *Poetics Today* 14, no. 1 (1993): 99–100.

7

NORMS AND VALUES

WHAT IS A "NORM"?

A norm is a widely accepted social practice. Norms are widely accepted social practices that are contingent on power, authority and legitimacy. Norms serve to guide a community's members along what is considered acceptable behaviour. Because there cannot be specific rules for every single form of human activity, norms provide an important means of social interaction that enables a given society to get on with life in modernity. Norms develop over time and there are always more people in favour of a norm than not. There are also always some people who go against the norm. Sometimes this is considered abnormal behaviour and at other times this is considered anti-social behaviour, both not always meaning the same thing. Acceptable practice usually becomes the norm. And there are several accepted ways of satisfying social norms.

A norm also reflects the average performative actions of a given community. The *American Heritage Dictionary* (4th edition, 2000) states that a norm is "a standard, model, or pattern regarded as typical [such as] the current middle-class norm of two children per family". The word norm is etymologically derived from the Old French word *norme*, and from the Latin root, *norma*, meaning a "carpenter's square". Therefore, the metaphor "to square away" an entity is to get work done, and norms help us organize our lives by getting work arranged into neat compartments to be pursued at a later time or for future reference. Norms are not a priori or universal and tend to be dynamic and moderated by such factors as economics, culture, technology, and philosophy. Norms help regulate and contain the social actions of individuals in the private and public spheres. They are a means of controlling human emotions and keeping people in check vis-à-vis acceptable standards of behaviour. Norms that are accepted in one community are not necessarily acceptable across other communities within societies and across societies. The appealing value of a particular set of norms in one community might be repulsive to another. Traditional societies that subscribe to the killing of old persons and young children would be considered morally reprehensible in modernity and in late modern societies. Nevertheless, the United Nations Declaration of Human Rights is a global document that represents a legal putsch towards basic norms that are considered universally applicable. But as we are aware, the problem of universal human rights is that they are not always universally acceptable. Thus norms require time, space, and cultural space before they can be accepted. This makes the creation of global norms a particularly difficult objective to achieve; as difficult as achieving the moral categorical imperatives of Immanuel Kant.

Norms are an integral part of the world and function at all levels of human interaction. Aristotle believed that human beings are by nature "political". This hypothesis was corroborated some 2,300 years later by the political sociologist, Seymour Martin Lipsett, in *Political Man: The Social Bases of Politics* (Double Day 1963). However, there is no certainty in regulating all instances of human interaction through specific rules and regulations.[1] We need norms to help govern, guide, and process the interstitial aspects of human interaction. Hence computers require programmers to create specific syntax for a computer program to work in terms of generating specific binary instructions for each miniscule step. But human interaction is infinitely more complex and faster than any current computer such that it is not possible to construct a computer that can provide the norms for individual human interaction except through virtual mimicry. One example is IBM's Big Blue and its cloned derivatives that were designed to play chess against Russian and American international chess grandmasters. The computer most often lost to the human challenger/defender though not all the time. At the given level of global technology, there does not appear to be any software that can effectively compute all the different variations and permutations that can mirror the human brain. It therefore becomes virtually impossible to create a human artifice to mimic humanity in terms of the norms that help govern human interaction. Perhaps there is no superior computer software or language currently available that can govern the psychological and emotive norms of the human being. Computer science needs to move away from the binary languages that dominate its mathematical formulae and computing paradigms in order to reconstruct nominal modes that mimic human-to-human interfaces.

Therefore, norms exist as important modes for facilitating the interstitial relationships between a minimum of two human beings. Now that we understand that norms are integral to the human world, we can understand why they are important in globalization. This is because they perform simple tasks that are difficult to mimic or artificially create despite the advances in nano-scale engineering, science, technology,[2] cloning science, and the advances that are claimed by the Human Genome Project and consortiums like the Integrated Molecular Analysis of Gene Expression (I.M.A.G.E.) Consortium.[3] Nevertheless, human civilization can look towards the creative sharing of information across the globe as increasing numbers of think tanks and research institutes approach the nether regions of the frontiers of science. We wait in anticipation of that big break that will cause the next paradigmatic shift.

OPTIMISM AND AUTHORITY

Norms may be governed by optimistic outcomes to situations. So if scientific researchers discover evidence of life on Mars, this might serve to modify and change the norms about alien life in other places and cultures. Man is driven by optimism in modernity to seek and fathom the unknown and the unknowable. Man is the only species on Earth that has developed a highly complex regime of norms and values with the power to change life on Earth. However, man's power to protect other species on earth derives not from some universal belief in the security of other species but from man's ability to destroy and even obliterate other life forms. The prevailing scientific norm on other species is highly optimistic in the sense of creating the belief that all species are part of a larger ecological system. And that the destruction of one part of the authority structure will result in negative repercussions on the system of authority as a whole. This has not been proven to be true, but who is willing to risk going against the norm? Can we justify the presence of global norms that might satisfy alternative imaginations that enable creative worlds where man alone is at the centre and no species exists outside or along the periphery?

PROGRESS AND LEGITIMACY

Globalization is the key to increasing the possibility of global norms because the knowledge that other cultures perform certain activities in certain ways might in reality become acceptable practice in an otherwise non-globally connected environment. Globalization breaks down the political, social, and cultural barriers to the exchange of local norms for global ones. Part of the problem is the fear of losing out on a set of arranged and agreed practices that a given community has come to live comfortably with and a set of norms that a given community has also come to depend and rely upon in past practice.

How do we progress from localized norms towards global ones when there are so many differences that prevent the optimistic creation of universal norms? What impedes the possibility of man's desire for universalizing human norms about the ethics and morality with regard to other species that share planet Earth? Man himself cannot agree because man has consistently been characterized by differences of opinion rather than singularity of thought. Singularity of thought usually breaks down after a while, and cultures that possess frameworks that allow differences to exist in non-violent ways tend to survive much longer. Differences in approaches to global survival techniques also seem to command the most formidable obstacles to the possibility of global norms.

CULTURAL DIFFERENCES

For example, differences in the norms between America and Asia exist. These "normal" cultural differences govern different forms of interaction between and among people from different cultural backgrounds. Being armed with the knowledge of local norms will save the global traveller from potentially embarrassing situations or offending those who might be overly sensitive to the words or phrases used by a person from a different country and ethnic identity.

For example, in Asia, it is the norm to remove one's shoes before entering someone's home. It is not the norm to remove the shoes upon entering an office or public environment. It is also the norm not to talk to strangers on the bus or train. A foreign person who strikes up a conversation with a complete stranger might later discover the extent of his or her embarrassment as time goes by. There are norms for social behaviour at restaurants in Asia that often depend on four main factors: (1) the kind of restaurant — French, Italian, Japanese, Korean, Muslim, or vegetarian; (2) the kind of company — family, friends, colleagues, total strangers; (3) the purpose of the dinner or lunch; and (4) the cost of dining. After a while one will begin to realize that the norms of dining in Asia and the rest of the world are very much the same with the exception of a few subtle differences.

Unlike Paris, pets, especially dogs, are often not allowed in restaurants throughout Singapore, Bandar Seri Begawan, Jakarta, and Kuala Lumpur since this will cause offence to many Muslims who believe that dogs are unclean animals. In Asia it is also considered impolite to offer a Muslim food or drink during the daylight hours of Ramadan, the fasting month.

GLOBAL NORMS

What are the norms that exist in globalization? There are many norms that continue to exist in globalization and that have survived the rapidly changing social, political, and economic world. These global norms are created out of previously existing power structures, authority structures, and methods that legitimize or delegitimize international systems — such as civil society, civil disobedience, and civil-military antagonism. Global norms are needed because you cannot have a rule for everything without the entire system delegitimizing itself. Norms exist for the precise reason of enabling or facilitating everyday human activity. Norms may be established out of political violence, coercion, peace treaties, confidence-building measures, the work of NGOs, the work of the UN, or an agreement between and/or among several states, parties, or communities in order to facilitate the way in which the parties to the norm might proceed over a given matter. The noun "norm" is related to the idea of normalcy, that is, what is considered the normal thing to do in a given context. A norm may also reflect the "traditional" or "conventional" method of doing something. Norms are geographically located and determined so that what is considered a norm in one place would not be the norm in another. In other words, there are different regimes of norms that vary from region to region and are informed by ethnicity, culture, religion, economics, and politics.

One such norm regime exists in the corporate world. There are different norms that make up different corporate structures; they are modified and informed by the demographic makeup and the ethnic, cultural, religious, economic, and political dimensions of place and time. For example, McDonald's failure to adhere to the religious norm against the consumption of beef and related products in India created obstacles and marketing problems despite their public relations endeavours at correcting misconceptions and disinformation created by their competitors who were perhaps more "norm savvy".

Japanese companies used to instil the practice of group exercise before the start of each work-day shift in many of their subsidiary companies overseas until they realized that their group-norm behaviour was perhaps not quite appropriate for all countries. While some Japanese firms continue with these exercises, especially in the manufacturing sector, these norms have become all but diluted versions of their predecessors. Another norm that was discovered about American companies overseas was the fact that they had really fancy-sounding titles. Almost everyone appeared to be a vice-president or senior manager. In the European and Japanese models, the hierarchy and rank-structure remained fairly rigid and high-sounding titles were not part of their norm. However, the successes of many American MNCs and the contacts that were made in the buying and selling of European and Japanese companies, goods, and services resulted in a degree of pressure on non-American firms to change with the times. Very soon there were all kinds of high-sounding titles everywhere in the corporate world. It seemed that customers preferred to have their problems resolved by a senior engineering executive rather than a customer salesperson; or that vice-presidents of marketing and research preferred to deal with people of similar if not greater stature than their own.

There were also new management styles that developed over time because of the intense interaction between MNCs and other businesses the world over through three phases: Phase I — post-World War II (reconstruction); Phase II — Cold War models of developmental corporate behaviour; and Phase III — post–Cold War regenerative corporate management models. These management styles in general saw the flattening of management hierarchies, the broadening of specialist tasks, and the importance of creating better after-sales services for those businesses that were in the corporate competition for the long term. Phase I was distinctive because the old colonial powers continued to possess the management and resources to develop and hone their home-grown industries while being set up as models for "Third World" countries to mimic. Phase II was a result of intense competition between and among corporate styles of management within the "free world" that came under the protection of pro-democratic countries. This phase in particular saw the rise of American norms of management across Europe and the acceptance of the United States as the leader of the free-democratic capitalist world as well as the meteoric but momentary rise of the Asian Tiger or Dragon economies. Phase III saw the rise of Japan as a potential superpower that had the backing of the U.S. Government and other multinational corporate giants. But there was also a decline in domestic confidence within the United States amid rising expectations of the alternate possibility of a European resurrection.

The new world order that supported a multipolar world scenario with large free-trade areas hardly had time to take root before 9/11, and then Bali, Madrid, and Southern Thailand began having trouble with terrorists. Even before the terrorists began making headway into the heart of neoliberal capitalism based on MNCs and the sleepless financial markets, there were already signs of other problems. These problems centred on the outdated norms and the inefficient and illiberal financial structures of the advanced developing nations in Asia such as Thailand, Singapore, Malaysia, Taiwan, and South Korea as well as the lesser developed nations of the Philippines, Indonesia, and Vietnam (to a much lesser extent). The problems in Phase III also demonstrated the weaknesses of the world financial support system modeled after the European Bank for Reconstruction and Development (EBRD) and the International Bank for Reconstruction and Development (IBRD). In addition, there was trouble with the norms that the WTO had tried to implement resulting in worldwide demonstrations at every important summit.

Therefore, the New World Order did not turn out to be a democratically free-trade world but one with several poles that have come under threat from international terrorism. This has led to the creation of new norm regimes such as the need to police air, ship, and rail travel with anti-terrorist security measures. This has resulted in a heightened sense of insecurity as a kind of international norm.

Therefore, 9/11 and the following string of terrorist acts against non-Muslims and Muslims alike from New York City to downtown Jakarta and Jeddah, have created a new kind of international norm: The fear that anyone at anytime could be a terrorist. This has also led to zero tolerance of non-normal behaviour within the travel industry and especially among airlines themselves. New norms are created each time a specific event causes the previous norm regime to blister and break apart. Therefore, the breaking of one set of norms usually requires the ending of that norm regime before a new set of norms can come into play. At the individual level, people must know of such new norms before the norm regime can work efficiently.

Corporate culture often involves business norms that become beholden to the activities of other corporations within globalization. As a result, global norms of dress, etiquette, and behaviour develop and arise over time, despite differences in language, capital size, or the kind of goods and services produced. Also, in order to project the image of success or professionalism, many corporations require their male staffers to wear, at the very least, a long-sleeved shirt and tie, and probably even a two-piece suit when meeting clients, so that one can find busy executives wearing such attire even in the tropical heat of Asia. If not for air-conditioning, the business world would be a very uncomfortable environment to work in in the tropical parts of the world. One would assume that since the tropics are so hot and humid the people would wear clothes that afforded comfort rather than style.

This is clearly not the case in many capital cities in Asia and the Pacific that support the neoliberal corporate culture. Hawaii is one exception to this norm where the accepted office attire for men is a short-sleeve shirt and slacks, while women have greater latitude of choice. Corporate culture therefore determines the type of attire in the tropics as a norm. It is also a norm to dress down on Saturdays where dressing down involves wearing a polo tee-shirt and jeans.

"NORM" AND THE "LAW"

We have examined the nature of the concept of the "norm" in globalization and have ascertained its unique and functional position in daily life. The U.S. political system is built on a system of "checks and balances" and the "sharing of power" between the legislative (law-making), judicial (arbitration and interpretation), and executive (implementation) arms of the U.S. Government. History has shown that all three arms of government are taken very seriously by their defenders and those who occupy the respective seats. The U.S. system of justice is built round a very specific set of legal terms and definitions that guide the officers of the law in their daily work. In other words, the law is very precise and what are considered ordinary definitions of words and phrases often mean something quite the opposite in legal terms. This includes the law of tort, the law of evidence, and power of attorney. Jurisprudence or the theory of justice has evolved over time to adjust to the changing nature of human civilization whether it is under U.S. common law and constitutional law tradition or the British natural law tradition. Natural law underlies both the American and British traditions with American law having evolved from British common law and then adding its constitutional dimension. Despite the gravity of the situation and in spite of hundreds of years of evolution, there is a compelling need to have norms in the search for justice. In other words, there are many situations where the law is unable to specifically dictate what is to be done and hence the judge has to interpret the law according to existing legal norms. The clearest example is in the norm of consensus by the Supreme Court of the United States of America.

The norm of consensus may arguably involve a non-majoritarian decision that is arrived at by the court in its interpretation of the law and the events surrounding the case in question. And therefore, in most cases, it seems that there continues to be a need for the court's majority position and the court's minority report that are themselves based on these legal norms. Some examples of this may be found in *Mutual Life Insurance Company of New York v. Harris*

(1877),[4] *First Security National Bank v. United States* (1965),[5] and the case of *Maryland v. United States* (1965).[6] The norm of consensus is politically charged because it is a reflection of society's values and the impression that the American public projects as discussed by Epstein, Segal, and Spaeth.[7] Apart from the idea of norm of consensus, there are also unanimity norms that arise out of Supreme Court decisions that guide and inform the norms practised by the lower courts, as discussed, for example, by David A. Skeel in "The Unanimity Norm in Delaware Corporate Law" (1997).[8]

There are additional situations when the norm of the law also provides for resolving disputes between the federal government and former elected officials of the federal government and local businesses as illustrated in part by the following cases between the *United States v. Glaxo Group Ltd.* (1973),[9] *Nixon v. Warner Communications* (1978),[10] *Department of the Army v. Blue Fox Inc.* (1999),[11] and the case of the *National Federation of Federal Employees v. United States* (1999).[12]

The U.S. federal system of justice has also become the arena for settling international issues and the differences between MNCs that are headquartered in different countries. It is a political decision on the part of the business corporation because there are compelling reasons for fighting a case on neutral territory or on territory that gives one's position a legal advantage. Some examples of the use of American legal norms in the settlement of business disputes between or among different parties internationally including foreign aliens are: *Alfred Dunhill of London, Inc. v. Cuba* (1976),[13] *Hampton v. Mow Sun Wong* (1976),[14] *Wilson v. Omaha Indian Tribe* (1979),[15] *United States v. Sioux Nation of Indians* (1980),[16] *World-wide Volkswagen Corporation v. Woodson* (1980),[17] and *United States v. Venezuela-Bernal* (1981).[18]

Similarly, the politicization of the law may also arise out of the interaction of legal and public norms that exist in the first instance, to generate new legislation such as the *Voting Rights Act* (1965) and in the second instance the changes that arise within the public arena as a result of normative responses to the initial act that result, for example, in the *Voting Rights (Amendment) Act* (1976).[19] Most of the norms can be traced to the Constitution which is seen by many scholars as a brilliant document. However, a useful example for the sake of brevity and in order to further explain norms in U.S. law can be traced to the Second Amendment within the Bill of Rights (that is, the first fifteen amendments to the U.S. Constitution). The U.S. Supreme Court decision to stay within the latitude of bare bones, literal interpretation of the Second Amendment, despite the advance made by the Brady Act (1993), resulted in more gun-related deaths.

The Second Amendment states that, "A well regulated militia, being necessary to the security of a free state, the right of the people to keep and bear arms, shall not be infringed." This Amendment, dating back to the year 1791, contains the primary subject phrase, "necessary to the security of a free state". Therefore, the adverbial phrase, "the right of the people to keep and bear arms" is in support of the subject phrase. The right to "keep and bear arms" was a reflection of the time when America was still very much an undiscovered frontier, vulnerable to Native Americans who were fighting in defence of their own homeland against the internal colonialism of the American settlers. There were also fears of Spanish and British invasions. The norm-regime created by the Second Amendment and those who support its presence has resulted in the death of more than a million Americans over the past four-and-a-half decades. There are also situations that are potentially norm-blind. This refers to a situation where norms are absent in a given social, economic, or cultural context. In such cases, and in the absence of precedent, U.S. judges may be compelled to arrive at a politicized form of "norm-creation" as illustrated in part by the case of the *National Farmers Union Insurance Companies v. Crow Tribe of Indians* (1984),[20] the *United States v. S.A. Empresa De Viacao Aerea Rio Grandense (Varig Airlines) et al.* (1984),[21] *Air France v. Saks* (1985),[22] and the case of *Chan, et al. v. Korean Air Lines Ltd.* (1989).[23]

The collective norms of the Warsaw Convention and the Montreal Agreement were brought into play to resolve this last international incident. This is, in a sense, a form of norm-creation by an institution that was not designed for norm-creation in specific terms but is not dispossessed of an administrative-cum-legal framework capable of such a function within the set of given statutes. The U.S. system of checks and balances and the sharing of powers among the three arms of government have given rise to a unique context: (1) unanimity of norms, (2) norm consensus-building, and (3) norm creation in situations which are norm-absent or norm-blind. The politics of American globalization in terms of norms and the law serves as a platform for arbitration of not only local and federal issues, but also issues that involve foreign aliens and businesses with or without a legal relationship with a U.S. business or U.S. government agency.

American approaches to the problem of globalization involve the use of legal and rational norms within the public and private spheres. The United States as a sovereign political entity is also becoming a stage for the arbitration of foreign-domestic disputes which result in what may be perceived as increasing neoliberal state confidence in the United States as an arbiter of the last resort in a manner that one day might replace the work done by UN justice tribunals and commissions, the International Court of Justice at the Hague and the smaller European Courts of Justice.

This chapter has shown the various kinds of norms and norm regimes that exist, with illustrations from the United States and Asia. Norms and norm regimes the world over share several basic and common characteristics such as: their adaptation to place; their being modified and informed by ethnicity, religion, culture, society, and politics; their being dynamic; and their being easily replaced when the previous norm regime implodes due to an unforeseen event that interrupts its normal continuance. Those who are part of a given set of norms or a norm regime are also expected to understand the prevailing norms for the efficient running of a norm regime.

WHAT IS A "VALUE"?

The *Merriam-Webster Online Dictionary* (2004) defines a value as deriving from the Latin root *valuta* meaning "to be worth", something or to "be strong". "Value" may also be defined along the following lines: (1) a fair return or equivalent in goods, services, or money for something exchanged; (2) the monetary worth of something or its marketable price; (3) the relative worth, utility, or importance of a good; (4) a numerical quantity that is assigned or is determined by calculation or measurement; (5) the relative duration of a musical note; (6) relative lightness or darkness of a colour; and (7) something (as a principle or quality) intrinsically valuable or desirable. On the other hand, the *American Heritage Dictionary of the English Language* (4th edition, 2000) explains value through its adjectival variants: nominal value, face value, numerical value, expected, surplus, absolute value, truth and market value, et cetera.

To the list of definitions from these two dictionaries, we can add the following modifiers: political value, cultural value, sacred value, residual value, marginal value, and so on. The two patterns that arise from these definitions is that value is a relative term and highly subjective. However, we are concerned with the concept of value in the politics of American globalization.

What do Americans hold dear, that it is also generally considered valuable? This chapter began with a reference to the work of Lipsett on the political nature of human beings. It is this political nature that gives birth to the upholding of the Constitution as a sacred document.

The value of the nation and the sanctity of the Constitution as a sacred document are held in the greatest esteem by many Americans. With the exception of conscientious objectors and those in peaceful and non-violent organizations, there continues to remain a sacred and tragic episode in American life. In order to protect this idiom of American sovereignty, many Americans believe that there is honour in dying for their country. The metaphor of the American Hero and the images created by the consolidation of centuries of giving death for liberty are deeply ingrained in the American public psyche. J. Peter Euben's endeavour at addressing the theoretical implications of the discipline of political theory is a case in point. Euben's work on the democratic roots of America's heritage points towards the tragic narcissism of sacred and traditional "values".

The anti-hero worship common in the popular cultural literature feeds and informs the stereotypical commodification and museumization of the Old Frontier West. Cowboys and Indians was the management idiom and business metaphor used to express the value of these brave warriors defending themselves against the internal colonialism of White America. The old American chieftains have mostly been erased from memory. Those whose memory remains because they were not afraid of being photographed or documented are remembered for enhancing the value of American liberal democratic ex post facto overtures of peaceful coexistence. The men of war must have at least included Chief Cochise, Chief Red Cloud, Chief Little Wolf, and Chief Sitting Bull. The federal state's constrictive amount of time accorded to Native American integration into the urban cultural milieu of America has compressed their cultural space while delimiting their temporality as a resource for ethnic rememberance and political remonstrances. This challenges the naive arguments made by Dobyns, Stoffle, and Jones in their 1975 article.[24] My criticism is supported by David Henige's 1989 reply titled "On the Current Devaluation of the Notion of Evidence: A Rejoinder to Dobyns" in the journal, *Ethnohistory*.[25]

The politics of internal colonialism places a high cultural value on the museumization of ethno-cultural epitaphs to indigenous tribes, because they hope that the preservation of such ethnohistory, ethno-music, and ethno-culture will not only enhance but legitimize the internal colonizing effort over time and space. The speeding up of time by internal colonial post-structural museumization results therefore in the compression of ethnic space in American modernity. According to Wilmer, Melody, and Murdock such inclusiveness extends Almond and Coleman's 1960 work (Wilmer, Melody, and Murdock 1994, p. 269). But the authors are incorrect to suggest that including Native Americans in Political Science courses extends the kind of liberal inclusiveness arguments of the great positivist era supported by Almond and Coleman's own belief in general systems theory.[26] Rather, the value that is derived from such ethno-inclusion leads to the legitimization of the U.S. liberal democratic norm regime. If this is their intention then it makes sense, otherwise it works against the larger multi-universal picture that is postmodernism.

The U.S. Constitution forbids the establishment of an official religion. This means that any religion can be practised in the United States as long as it remains within the ambit of U.S. federal and state law. Religion is a global value and even though the U.S. Constitution expressly forbids the creation of an official religion, it has indirectly sanctioned liberal religious development. At the "Million Man March" in October 1995, the "Reverend" Louis Farrakhan's personal bodyguards were dressed like they were going to a Michael Jackson concert. But the man they were protecting was certainly not like the child-loving Jackson. Farrakhan mentioned Jackson in his speech for being a "drawn out" Black man, but, by 2003, neither Michael Jackson nor the Nation of Islam wanted to have anything to do with one another (Nation of Islam Press Release, 29 December 2003; Fox News, April 2004).

The Nation of Islam is an American Muslim activist group that was "re-established" by Farrakhan in 1977 as a political realignment with the teaching of a former Nation of Islam leader, Elijah Muhammad. Farrakhan (also known as Louis Eugene Walcott), is a kind of religious celebrity who loves the populist limelight. He has great self-confidence in his knowledge of Islam, of his creativity with numerology, and the importance of "19" and "440" in representing the political icons of previous American presidencies. Farrakhan's speeches are usually emotive and provocative. The former virtuoso Calypso singer and dancer (who attained fame in Boston) attack the primordial instincts of African Americans. He provokes them by reminding them of their misery. It does appear that his mannerisms mimic Martin Luther King, Jr., but unlike King, he is afraid to die. That is why Farrakhan has so many bodyguards to protect him from the people he speaks to, from the people he believes in, from the people that he claims to love. These are the people he fears. Unlike Martin Luther King, Jr., who not only had a dream but also stood publicly against racism, Farrakhan is comfortable with rhetoric as some critics believe:

> We cannot be sanguine about the fact that the most ardent and widely listened to voice of un-churched Black Americans is probably Minister Louis Farrakhan. Farrakhan is a separatist who has no commitment to racial reconciliation. He is a persuasive speaker who evokes and manipulates black rage with ambiguous intent and consequences. I believe that tens of thousands of African Americans turn out to hear him, in part, because they are hurting and angry, and they crave the therapy of having those powerful emotions ventilated with style, bombast, and defiance.[27]

The Million Man March was designed for the purpose of Black unity, which was well served. There was no racism or hatred in Farrakhan's speech, despite what former majority leader Senator Bob Dole, Rep. Gary Franks (R-Connecticut), Rep. John Lewis (D-Georgia), and other U.S. political leaders have said about Farrakhan's anti-White, anti-Semitic views. While the march appears to have been planned at some level to elevate Farrakhan into the national spotlight, many Black Americans attended because they wanted to share in the value derived from a sense of unity, a sense of purpose and a sense of being part of America. Farrakhan reminded the audience that if the Jews were held captive by the Egyptians for 400 years, the Black Man had been oppressed for 440 years. The 16 October march was meant to be a turning point for Black men, to turn back on their social ills.[28] The liberal democracy of American politics enables vast differences, racially charged and provocative, to take place within the same agenda. This is why in the aftermath of 9/11, Farrakhan could say in a speech that the attack was "a crime against all humanity". He went on to add:

> When Timothy McVeigh committed the worst act of terrorism on American soil, the first persons accused of this were members of the Nation of Islam and immigrant Muslims. Many followers of Islam were attacked, and then it was found that the perpetrator of this crime was a White American, a soldier who professed to be a Christian. But no Christian of his denomination was attacked ... [later, in response to a question from an American Muslim journalist, he said:] I myself know who and what I am. I know I have never hated Jews. I'm critical of aspects of Jewish behavior in relationship to Black people. I'm critical of the government in aspects of their behavior toward Black people. It doesn't mean I hate America. I'm critical. And because I have the freedom, because of that great constitutional guarantee, to speak even if people do not like what I say, it is the freedom to speak that guarantees America a greater future.[29]

This does not sound like a speaker who is an anti-Semitic, White-hating Muslim preacher that the media and the United Kingdom have painted so vociferously. There are two possibilities. Either there is a "great White conspiracy" against Farrakhan within the politics of American liberalism, or Farrakhan is playing a highly-charged politicized game. Where is the evidence? Where is the public groundswell against Farrakhan's anti-White, anti-Semitic, and sexist comments? So far, the public domain seems content to keep their views on Farrakhan politically "contained" and "non-violent". Perhaps Farrakhan's case is one that seems to illustrate the working value of American democratic liberalism.

The liberal/conservative divide in American domestic politics has itself raised doubts about what is politically achievable apart from empty political rhetoric. Neorealists have never seemed as fashionable as neoliberals since the end of the Cold War. Neoliberals run the world capitalist economy that is intricately tied to (though not dominated) by America. Inside the United States itself, the political ideology of liberalism was supposed to create and support individual rights and protect individual freedoms in the light of hope, optimism, and progress. Yet the tragic mimicry of these end-goals seems to have been outplayed, outlasted, and outwitted by the very people it was designed to protect. Like the so-called reality TV series, *Survivor*, America up-close is armed to the teeth and dangerous. Neil Postman was correct about amusing ourselves to death. So was Michael Moore's book with the essentialist title that catches attention but serves no real purpose in the end.

The servant of liberalism, as we shall continue to re-visit, is already incarcerated by the constitutional rejection of desperate changes to the political institutionalism of the U.S. federal system of government. Liberalism in America was the "answer" and "solution". It is now more of the problem that enhances the gravity of the American political paradox:

> Like the critical theorists, Adorno, Horkheimer, Lefebvre, Berman, Latour, and Kariel, Postman warned of the dehumanizing potential of technologically-based societies. Public and private spaces become increasingly enmeshed as meaningless symbols with worthless teleologies. Postman, however, failed to consider the impact of the internationalization of American media; that the same paradigmatic shift from print to television as the main interface between media producers and media consumers in America of the early 1980s would consume Latin America, Africa, and Asia. These modern cultural masks of death are totems for social normality, and political correctness in society, a correctness that prepares us as we prepare for that last gasp, that last breath, that final rush, '[t]here was no sleeper more elegant than she, with her curved body posed for a dance and her hand across her forehead, but there was also no one more ferocious when anyone disturbed the sensuality of her thinking she was still asleep when she no longer was' (Rappa, *Sincronia*, 1998).

The master of neoliberalism that has engraved the Native American into the iconography of American popular culture remains limited to areas outside of Washington, D.C. Chief Sitting Bull has no place near the Lincoln

Memorial. When U.S. Marines invaded Hawaii on 16 January 1893, they went unceremoniously looking for the Queen Lili'uokalani who was forced to surrender at gunpoint so that the sugar plantation proto-MNC owners could flourish. These White men were hateful of Lili'uokalani's stoppage of the (forced) import of Chinese labour from Shanghai to work on their sugarcane plantations. Because of the unhygienic conditions involved in the long trip, the Chinese labourers were forced to live with malaria, dysentery, and other tropical diseases. This made them vulnerable to sickness and disease. When a smallpox epidemic began in the Chinese population, it came as no one's surprise.

The queen closed the harbour, well before the invasion of the U.S. Marines, in order to prevent further death among the Hawaiian community from the smallpox disease brought in by the forced migrant labour. It is a well-documented fact that the U.S. Government and big business helped destabilize the local economy, naturally with the help of some support from the native elite that they were grooming with promises of entitlement, wealth, and other trinkets. The Bishop Estate today has an endowment fund that is larger than the Harvard Endowment Fund. Americans have taken many sovereign nations by force for hundreds of years and the American values and norm regimes that are recognized today, like other colonial powers transformed into post-colonial democracies, are afraid of remembering the horror that they brought down onto innocent people because of the greed and avarice of Big Business. Panama was nothing compared to Hawaii. The result of political liberalism is the disenfranchisement of people of colour, women, and minorities.

There is little wonder that the primordial backlash from White America continues to find support among a minority of Americans in the racism of David Duke. Is this to be considered a value, when some American citizens consider this to be their constitutional right? I do not think that the families whose relatives were killed or shot in any case of gun-violence — such as the ethnic riots in Los Angeles ("Rodney King Riots") that ostensibly began because of police brutality but erupted into Korean-African American violence, the high-school students shooting one another in Columbine, or the African American New Yorker who hated White people in the Long Island Railway shooting — all have to politically acquiesce to the (deliberate linguistic misinterpretation, as I have demonstrated earlier, of) individual right to keep and bear arms guaranteed under the Second Amendment. All this done in spite of James Madison's clear warning about this form of tyranny in *Federalist Paper Number 51*.

NORM, VALUE, AND THE AMERICAN GLOBE

We have seen that the primary difference between a norm and a value is that one is mainly for functional reasons while the other is for both ideational as well as sacred reasons. Values also take a much longer time to distil while a norm may be created almost instantaneously between two parties that agree on a prescribed mode of carrying out a task. A value requires much debate and consensus before it is informally adopted. There is great difficulty in formally adopting values because one cannot implement values through the legal-rational framework of political, social, and cultural institutions. For example, a society like Japan may value hard work, but if the value called hard work were raised as a bill before the Japanese Diet, chances are that it would not pass into law and, if it did, it would merely be window-dressing or valuable only in a legalistic sense. Another illustration might be to show how the line between the meaning of a value and the meaning of a norm may be vague. Japanese workers are known for their hard work. Hard work is something that is considered a Japanese value. It is not unique to the Japanese but it is something valuable to them anyway. It does not matter who invented hard work at this point. How does one operationalize hard work or measure it? One way that is often widely accepted is through time, that is, the number of hours on the job. The Japanese salaried worker knows that the value of hard work means that he has to work the complete eight-hour day. To do any less is to be considered letting the team down. But most Japanese workers spend more than eight hours a day at work. Let us take a norm of 10.5 hours. We know from social scientific studies that more work after such a norm is merely counterproductive. Yet because of the importance of the position of hard work in the Japanese system and because of the emphasis on common behaviour by the working group, the Japanese salarymen cannot merely leave their desks after 10.5 hours of work a day. This is when a value turns into a norm. The Japanese salarymen pretend to work for more than the 10.5 hours, sharpening pencils, staring at the computer screen, making coffee for the boss, and reading, and generally pretending to do work without working. But once the boss or immediate superior decides that he (and his superiors) have worked "hard enough", he decides to leave the office. This is when there is a sudden and mad scramble for the after-office tête-à-tête. The value is hard work but the norm is to pretend to keep at the place of hard work, that is, the desk, while waiting for the right time to leave the office. Therefore the time spent idling away at the desk re-reading material or surfing the Net or pretending to work is known as a norm. However, to the casual observer it seems like hard work. How can we take our example of the Japanese worker to the American workplace? The Japanese salarymen example is not too different from the American worker who also values hard work but the norms are quite different.

POLITICS AND PHILOSOPHY: QUESTIONING VALUES AND NORMS

Hard work and company loyalty are considered part of the norm regimes implicit in Weber's *The Protestant Ethic and the Spirit of Capitalism*. But the philosophical intrigue goes deeper.

We saw at the start of the chapter that norms are needed to help govern, guide, and process the interstitial aspects of human interaction. The interstitial aspects refer to those "dimensions that exist between spaces" of two points where there are no laws, rules, regulations, or norms to guide human behaviour. The concepts of "norm" and "value" in the politics of globalization is centred on the idiosyncratic work of Western political philosophers. But there is a clear pattern of political empowerment and disempowerment in the history of the specific kind of globalization that we have been examining. The idea of the politics of American globalization has been reiterated politically through its repeated histories of inflicting violence and committing crimes against other sovereign nationalities. Since 1776, after a long and hard-fought war against the British colonial masters, the American form of global dominance has been its strategy of empowerment and control over the security of its future. America has survived because it has learnt that globalization means conquest and control of resources through military conflict and political violence. The politics of American global survival is vested in the extension of its political strategy platform in the Monroe Doctrine and Manifest Destiny.

The philosophical commitment and the incarceration of good and bad ideas, right and wrong norms, are genealogically linked to the Western "tradition". Each generation of divergent philosophies constructed different theoretical positions based on their limited observations of the Western world. Marx made racist comments about India. Mill and his father, both British MPs, similarly made racist remarks despite the differences in their philosophical positions. Naturally, current conceptions of the democratic transition and transformation accorded to the universalism, utilitarianism, and pragmatism of the Enlightenment theorists persists forcefully within the American idiom of conquest, command, and control.

The work of Immanuel Kant and G.W.F. Hegel, the British empiricism of John Locke, as well as George Berkeley and David Hume are also often cited and indicted by postmodern theorists as the philosophical culprits of the past. These culpable constructions of the liberal democratic world have impinged on the direction of the social and political sciences and the humanities over the past 250 to 300 years.

The earlier days of these academic disciplines in the late nineteenth and early twentieth centuries saw the legitimization of liberal democracy while remaining short-sighted, or perhaps blatantly ignoring the violence that was being inflicted outside academis, and across the Great White Plains and prairies of the Western Frontier to the conquest of what is now the modern American colonized state of Hawaii, and New Mexico, to give two examples. The problem was that the Western philosophical view of the world, according to the Enlightenment theorists, co-located the political realism of American conquests with the expansion of the freedom of rights arguments. This led to the belief that a country or people ought to be conquered, if they could not be bought, to force them to accept liberal democratic freedoms. This is exemplified in the "purchase" and "annexation" of the Philippines at the end of the Spanish-American War; the Louisiana Purchase; and the Alaska Purchase. The Western philosophical tradition has come under attack by many American philosophers, theorists and social scientists — modern and post-modern alike — for setting the philosophical pace of survival through violence. After all, they believe that this is in the nature of political man and hence cannot be helped or changed.

A tentative resolution to the problems of democratic liberalism may appear in detailed studies of the politics of philosophical globalization that revolve round the post-Enlightenment, post-Nietzschean narratives of Husserl, Wittgenstein, Hyppolite, Sartre, Arendt, Beauvoir, Foucault, Deleuze, and Guattari.[30] The influence of Fanon, Conrad, Blumenberg, Butler, McClintock, Millet, Cantalini, Narayan, Rushdie, and Gusmao provides a series of overlapping arguments about the individual and the individual's relationship with other individuals. In other words, they have begun paving the way off the *Ship of Fools*. Before the founding fathers founded anything, we discover other nascent problems in the Western tradition that gave birth to American democratic liberalism. Hegel likened women to plants. Nietzsche was a misogynist and a hyper-elitist. Yet these were two of many of the formulators of the Western philosophical tradition whose debates and intellectual criticism, responses, and counter-criticism paved the way for the contortions of the democratic verve that has been inherited today. The point here is to keep interrogating the so-called philosophical foundations that are often taken for granted. Then can we begin to understand the violence and the political paradox of late modernity in terms of these vaunted power structures and self-legitimizing authorities.

Notes

1. Aristotle wrote the eight "books" of *Politics*. In Book VII, Aristotle suggests that, "those who are in a position which places them above toil have stewards who attend to their households while they occupy themselves with philosophy or with politics". Does this not foretell much about the politics of globalization as it is today? See also Books V and VI of Aristotle [350 B.C.], *Politics* (NY: Penguin, 1992).
2. See for example, a brief update by Patricia Dehmer, "The Beauty of Nanoscale Science", *U.S. Department of Energy*, occasional paper on the study of matter at the atomic scale; see also Ivan Amato, "The Apostle of Nanotechnology", *Science* 254, no. 5036 (1991): 1310–11; Michel Hehn et al., "Nanoscale Magnetic Domains in Mesoscopic Magnets", *Science* 272, no. 5269 (1996): 1782–85; P. M. Ajayan, J. C. Charlier, and A. G. Rinzler, "Carbon Nanotubes: From Macromolecules to Nanotechnology", *Proceedings of the National Academy of Sciences of the United States of America* 96, no. 25 (1999): 14199–200; and Karen L. Wooley et al., "Novel Polymers: Molecular to Nanoscale Order in Three Dimensions", *Proceedings of the National Academy of Sciences of the United States of America* 97, no. 21 (2000): 11147–48.
3. See also, "Gene-Rich Human Chromosome 19 Sequence Completed", *Department of Energy, Joint Genome Institute*, 31 March 2004.
4. U.S. Supreme Court case number 97 U.S. 331.
5. Ibid., case number 382 U.S. 34.
6. Ibid., case number 381 U.S. 41.
7. Lee Epstein, Jeffrey A. Segal, and Harold J. Spaeth, "The Norm of Consensus on the U.S. Supreme Court", *American Journal of Political Science* 45, no. 2 (2001): 362–77.
8. David A. Skeel, Jr., "The Unanimity Norm in Delaware Corporate Law", *Virginia Law Review* 83, no. 1 (1997): 127–75.
9. U.S. Supreme Court case number 410 U.S. 52.
10. Ibid., case number 435 U.S. 589.
11. Ibid., case number 121 F. 3d 1357, reversed and remanded.
12. Ibid., case number 132 F. 3d 157, vacated and remanded.
13. Ibid., case number 425 U.S. 682.
14. Ibid., case number 426 U.S. 88.
15. Ibid., case number 442 U.S. 653.
16. Ibid., case number 448 U.S. 371.
17. Ibid., case number 444 U.S. 286.
18. Ibid., case number 458 U.S. 858.

19 Alan Howard, and Bruce Howard, "The Dilemma of the Voting Rights Act — Recognizing the Emerging Political Equality Norm", *Columbia Law Review* 83, no. 7 (1983): 1615–63.
20 U.S. Supreme Court case number 468 U.S. 1315.
21 Ibid., case number 467 U.S. 797.
22 Ibid., case number 470 U.S. 392.
23 Ibid., case number 490 U.S. 122.
24 Henry F. Dobyns, Richard W. Stoffle, and Kristine Jones, "Native American Urbanization and Socio-Economic Integration in the Southwestern United States", *Ethnohistory* 22, no. 2 (1975): 155–79.
25 David Henige, "On the Current Devaluation of the Notion of Evidence: A Rejoinder to Dobyns", *Ethnohistory* 36, no. 3 (1989): 304–07.
26 Franke Wilmer, Michael E. Melody, and Margaret Maier Murdock, "Including Native American Perspectives in the Political Science Curriculum", *PS: Political Science and Politics* 27, no. 2 (1994): 269–76.
27 Robert Michael Franklin, "Response to Leonard Lovett's The Problem of Racism in the Contemporary Pentecostal Movement", *PCCNA National Conferences*, 17–19 October 1994, Memphis, Tennessee, "Pentecostal Partners: A Reconciliation Strategy for 21st Century Ministry".
28 See "Low Turnout for Black Awareness March [in London]", BBC Online, 17 October 1998.
29 "Official transcript", *Nation of Islam*, 16 September 2001.
30 Consider also Wittgenstein's rejection of Husserl; Sartre's resistance against vulgar Marxism; Einstein's response to Newton; Hawkings' bridge to Einstein; and Skinner's defence of conservative liberal thought.

8

TECHNOLOGY AND POPULATION

Chapter One introduced the basic themes of the book: tragedy, hope, optimism, progress, mimicry, and the challenges of culture, money, and terror that were based on the narratives of power, authority, and legitimacy structures. This chapter is concerned with technology and population under such conditions.

The chapter examines developments in technology and population in globalization.[1] Technology and population are critical to any understanding of globalization because these concepts cut across society, economics, culture, and politics. However, the most recently published works on globalization tend to assume that the relationship between these concepts is implicitly ready in theory as it is clearly apparent in life. This chapter hopes to redress this research lacuna and to help begin making these connections finite. The first assumption in this chapter is that the concept of population precedes the concept of technology like the master-slave dialectic in modernity. The second assumption is that technology is capable of existing autonomously without direct human intervention as seen in nanotechnology, space exploration, and robotics.

Emergent technologies develop a life of their own once produced by the international neoliberal economic world order. This leads to the adjustments to suit various social, economic, cultural, and political demands. The power of neoliberal capital flows against the lowering of protectionist barriers to trade has afforded easier access to measurement by academic social theorists, social scientists, and private sector business risk analysts in the Far East, Southeast Asia, and South Asia. The chapter has been organized into five sections: (1) design and manufacturing; (2) technology, society, and population;

(3) technology and addiction; (4) technology and global standards; and (5) technology, the state, and power in the age of globalization.

DEFINITIONS

The official U.S. Census Bureau defines population as all the people living in a geographic area. This is the same for European and Asian definitions of population. In this book, population is specifically defined as a discrete community of persons engaged in a particular activity and possessing cross-cutting ideas, values, skills, and technologies within a given paradigm. Some examples include the intelligence community, the security community, the cultural community, and the InfoTech community. While social demographers are interested in analysing absolute numbers of a given population, social theorists and scientists often assume populations are more abstract and difficult to enumerate than ordinarily recognized. Part of the reason for this is that there is no state (government) that "knows" how many citizens it actually has at any one point in time. This number remains unknown in the Americas, Africa, the Middle East, and Asia. This is because counting the precise number of people has never been accurate except for small populations in the 0–1,000 range. However, the processes of globalization have made it tremendously difficult to measure populations that are now even more mobile than they were a decade ago because of the lower costs of air travel and the liberalization of political borders.

Technology is implicit with "techne", "technique", "technical", "techno", "skill", "guild", "craft", and the "methods" or "ways" of performing, activating, or "doing" something more differently and/or efficiently. The difference or efficacy may involve one or several categories of instruments, media, languages, machines, and other assemblages. Most technologies today will at some point in their life cycle — production and manufacture, innovation, reverse engineering, assembly, packaging, distribution and marketing — involve the Internet. Internet technology is an emergent technology that is underutilized and underexploited. Emergent technology does not have to be thoroughly understood — or understood at all — in order for it to work. One does not need to know the science or craft behind the magic of technology in order to benefit from it. The kind of technology we have today is primarily received technology. When we discuss received technology we are not talking about the potato printing, the invention of the wheel, or Red Bull, a sports energy drink technology,[2] but the kind that William H. Gates created that in the course of his career made him worth US$53 billion. These received technologies catalysed membrane fusion, nanotechnology, biomechanical engineering, and NASA's space technologies.[3] These emergent technologies add to embedded metaphors of hope and optimism when they generate positive economic results but depart towards tragic events when the technologies are abused by homegrown terrorists across Europe, Africa, the Middle East, America, and Asia.

TERRORISM, INTELLIGENCE, AND GLOBALIZATION

Ancient elites in Asia and the West were never interested in having to share their wealth with the masses. They were interested in preserving their wealth for familial posterity. This was similarly the case in Western Europe. Early democratic states in the West themselves did not last long. In the rush of the Enlightenment in the West, the rise of a new kind of modern era promised the greatest good for the greatest number. This utilitarian quest ushered the way for modern mass culture and popular culture. Classical music and opera were no longer the preserve of the rich and famous. But it appears that for every system of governance that attempts to resolve the problem of wealth distribution, there are ideological alternatives that seek to undermine and exploit the status quo.

The ancient Indians and Chinese people documented cosmological sightings, stellar maps, and early modes of measuring time while developing the earliest forms of civilized culture long before Western colonialists began planning their trading posts. However, the failure of the ancient Asians to ensure the longevity of their inventions and emergent technologies — through codification, record-keeping, and dissemination of information — resulted in what might be referred to as a "technological age of death" in Asia during which Western initiative, curiosity, religion, languages, science, economics, and governance caught up and overtook them in one fell swoop. The late modern Asians have examined the nature of the intelligence and security agencies in the West and dropped the U.S. and the U.K. models after 9/11 because they were not effective in their predictive dimension.

To speak of technology is to incorporate its techniques at the linguistic level, while creating the impression that the political leader is aware and knowledgeable about the state of technology. However, decisions made by political masters over intelligence have a deep and serious impact on its overall applications and net outputs. The most important criterion of success in intelligence analysis is not the technology that is used but the predictive accuracy of these technologies. One method to improve the predictive quality of technology is through discrete intelligence security sharing between and among intelligence agencies in the Global War on Terror (GWOT). This war is not a typical war metaphor used in the past such as the war on drugs or a war on crime as Winner suggests in "Technology Studies for Terrorists".[4] It is a war that is being fought against different kinds of enemies with different and mutating signatures:

> A new forecast compiled by U.S. intelligence experts foresees China and India spearheading an expansion of Asian political and economic influence throughout the world. It also sees many Arab countries at a crossroads as globalization spreads.[5]

The religious fanaticism, silence, concealment, belligerance, and/or recalcitrance demonstrated in the Islamic fundamentalism in northeast Malaysia, Mindanao island in the Southern Philippines, Pattani, Narathiwat, and Yala provinces in Thailand, Hindu right wing nationalism in India, border clashes between Pakistan and China, and the Kashmiri region between Pakistan and India, and the stand-off between South Korea and North Korea continue to co-exist uneasily with advances in incremental democracies and comprehensive economic development. The age of globalization has much more potential for peaceful coexistence, some would argue, than not. This potential relies on such value-based preferences as democratic governance and diplomatic and economic pressure (as opposed to hot war syndrome as seen in the Middle East).

The only way that it can spread is via the globalization of emergent technology. It would appear that many Asian countries are now following Western forms of security and intelligence collection and analyses. However, this is not true. Asian intelligence and counter-terrorist cells have been in operation since the time of decolonization. The difference, at some level, is that Asian intelligence services tend not to reveal too much to the public or expose those still under cover. American, European and some former Soviet intelligence service officers tend to celebrate a "tell all" culture that seeks the direct opposite of their previous incarnations. This is not restricted to intelligence but also includes the regular army, navy, air force, marine and police units. When former service personnel write these tell-all books, they compromise the technology platforms and strategies of their former agencies. The intelligence population within any given society in the age of globalization is a porous one. It makes it more difficult for command and control. This situation extends to immigration and customs agencies as well as narcotics and drug enforcement ones. Irma van der Ploeg believes that, "in our era of globalization ... technology in many different varieties is central" to the processes of "fortification, militarization, and informatization" through the installation of "every imaginable sort of detection device, from infrared and seismic scanners to high powered lamps and CO2 scanners to detect exhaled air in containers and trucks".[6] She goes on to argue that:

> The most powerful novelty of recent years in both US and European border control policy and enforcement consists of a range of new deployments of information technology. The practice of building databases and indefinitely keeping growing numbers of records and files on travelling citizens, migrants, cross-border commuting workers, asylum-seekers, and visiting business people, is extending hand over hand. These information systems can be divided into two categories... [those that] facilitate and accelerate border-crossing ... of enrolled persons whose identities and records have been checked as posing no threat to immigration laws and policies; on the other hand there are systems aiming at recognizing and stopping of potential terrorists ... increasingly fitted with biometric systems that unequivocally tie the individual border crosser to the records on file.[7]

Current intelligence security modes and strategies are still based on post Cold War templates which ought to have been revised since 9/11 so that the limits placed on the expandability potential for information gathering and intelligence analysis can be lifted. What intelligence agencies have used with their emergent technologies is to compartmentalize their data according to geospatial references within the intelligence streams rather than at their borders or across these lines. It is a case of not asking probing questions about who is at the dinner table but who is not at the table, and why they were not there for lunch either. A change in intelsec culture is possible because human populations have reached a turning point in modernity which compels reliance on received technologies, those that are immediately intuitive and require little or no in-depth understanding to meet operational efficacy. The other reason why these intelligence agencies — a proxy for the idea of technology and population — are not exploiting technology to their fullest potential is because they are reacting to situations, and reacting badly because it is too late. Every single intelligence agency in the U.S. and in Europe reacted to 9/11 and the WMD scare by reorganizing their structures. They closed some down, shunted others below, and invented new ones with fancy names. They sacked some personnel and redeployed the rest. They put everyone under suspicion and then got out of it because it led nowhere and so returned to the old post Cold War template of profiling. The reason why the international terrorists, as the new global enemy of populations is called, are so successful is because they do not have to report to their handlers and political masters in the same way that Western cells are required to. The reason why the technological population in the public realm is often more aware and technologically sophisticated is because their organizational culture is democratic and there is free entry and exit for all players. Take emergent technologies for example. *Technology Review, CNET, Wired, Scientific American, PC World, Discover, Science, Popular Mechanics, MacWorld* and even the *New England Journal of Medicine* are just a handful of thousands of periodicals that focus on emergent technologies. But why is a focus on emergent technologies so important in globalization?

Part of the reason is that the market demand for something new and different in the capitalist world is always greater than for the old and the ordinary. Old technology often refers to those that have been displaced such as Edison's first light bulb, steam locomotives, the Wright brothers' airplane, the rotary engine, the telephone, the dishwasher, the electric oven, the lawnmower, and Windows NT. Hence technology can refer to old tech, new tech, and emergent tech. Urban, trend-setting populations tend to prefer the latest technology over older ones. Old technology is considered fashionable only when it is repackaged as "retro" or viewed retrospectively. The Internet and its virtually infinite possibilities for emergent technology provide a clear example of the mass appeal and capitalist value of technology in globalization. The tech-savvy population is interested in emergent technologies much more so than older versions of software and hardware.

ASIAN DESIGN AND MANUFACTURING

This age of globalization is the confluence of overlapping extensions — old over new — across the millennia. Specifically, the age is marked by a tendency towards uniformity; the IT and PC revolutions; the commoditization of culture; indirect democracy; capitalist triumphalism; religious discordance; environmental consciousness; terrorism; widespread use of technology. This is why the idea of globalization must be understood as being centred on the development and application of emergent technological development. The age of Western imperialism and colonialism led to a fracturing of memories of the ancient Asian past and a commoditization of Asian histories into a romantic and exotic series of cultural anecdotes. The powerful and influential works of writers like Edward Said, postcolonial theorists and the Subaltern school will eventually change the course of knowledge transmission across Asia, Africa, and the West. One can only imagine the level of change the globe would have witnessed had the Indians and the Chinese been more adamant about their technological posterity and had taken their future into their own hands rather than sequestered it to the chaos theory of fate.

Before the Portuguese and Spanish had divided the world into Catholic halves, these ancient Asians were already considering themselves a highly civilized race intent on changing the world as they knew it. The references in late modernity to ancient technological roots are important only because it gives us a sense of the level of commitment to the development of textual control and ordering of the human brain over the non-human environment. The ancient *Chou I* (The Book of Changes of Chou, *Zhouyi*) or *I-Ch'ing*, is as one of the most important historical Chinese documents written, some believe, by emperor Wen and perhaps even Confucius illustrates this argument. Long before Claude Levi-Strauss's neoMarxist structural anthropology of linguistic symbolism and Noam Chomsky's deep structural analyses at MIT, the *I-Ch'ing* revealed that the written language is symbolic representation of simplicity, man's attempts at early and ancient reductionist cultural cosmology. For example, the character 易 (*yì*) according to Chinese language experts refers to "simplicity" while 經 (*jīng*) symbolizes "continuity" from the past: a simple continuity of changes. This led to the modern connotation of the *I-Ch'ing* as an ancient book of changes. The transmutation across Chinese and Indian history led to the inscrutable and competing interpretations within the Asian and Southeast Asian Chinese diaspora among practitioners of Chinese culture and heritage. The ancient Chinese literati institutionalized the eight trigrams into a sacred and mythical interpretation of the cosmos — heaven, earth, fire, water — as opposed to an autonomous work of Chinese cultural history.[8] This led to its universalistic appeal as an ancient form of anticipating the future based on essential elements within the cosmos.

Asia manufactured technology at a massive scale by using the early inventions of the ancient civilizations across Central Asia and the Far East. Driven by a similar late modern emphasis on war and economic survival, the ancient Chinese and Indian civilizations mobilized entire populations towards survivalist strategies of military and economic consumption. One example reported in the *Harvard Gazette* is a student's thesis that has resulted in the creation of an etching machine for carving ancient jade rings with two types of motion that share common geometric properties used 2,500 years ago in the later Chu period.[9] Ancient Chinese emergent technology created an early version of calculus, simple mathematics, paper-printing, paper and metal currencies, fermented alcohol, agricultural and irrigation techniques, early coastal-going compass, fireworks and gunpowder, and seismic prediction for earthquakes. Indeed, the most accurate technology available for making seismic predictions approximates the ancient Chinese versions in terms of their accuracy. Like the internal combustion engine, the emergent technology of the ancient "Chinese seismograph" is one that has been difficult to better. The Indians made great innovations in systems of governance and law, transportation, engineering, mineral extraction, irrigation and social control, and the attenuation of fate through its variations in ancient cosmologies through the works of Kautilya and Manu. Today, one cannot imagine a globalized world without the value-added services of Indian and Chinese IT specialists who, because of relative labour costs and relative population densities and specialization, are able to outwit, outperform, and outlast their Western contemporaries. The strength of Western forms of emergent technological know-how is the very clever use of Chinese and Indian IT specialists to drive Western capitalist and technological innovation. Scholars of China and India dominate existing academic debates about the origins of ceramics, glass, and pottery and the use of ancient emergent technologies to develop these out of the existing minerals of the day.

Asian states like their global counterparts in the West have at some point wrestled with the problem of population growth. Advances in science and technology have created new realms of knowledge and instruments to predict a range of population issues. While Asian countries tend not to impose their views on population change and development on other Asian or Western countries, such restraint does not generate reciprocity from the West.

Over the millennia when the communists took over China, the sudden boom in population led to the implementation of the one-child policy and the importance of birth-planning laws. In Southeast Asia, since the 1997/8 financial crisis, the question of birth planning and family planning was relegated to religious and community-level actors. Even strong states like Singapore with its long history of family planning and social engineering policies does not enact laws that require contraceptive use. However, China's national law on population and birth planning that was enacted in September 2002 requires couples to practise birth control since there continues to remain a gender imbalance in China. According to the 2000 census, there are 117 male to every 100 female births. And there is an additional problem that has become the trademark of maturing economies like South Korea, Japan, and Singapore. The Chinese case as viewed from a pro-rights U.S. senate committee is intriguing:

> Many Chinese "one-child" couples, lacking siblings, are hard-pressed to support two sets of aging parents ... China's birth planning law and policies retain harshly coercive elements in law and practice. Forced abortion and sterilization are egregious violations of human rights, and should be of concern to the global human rights community, as well as to the Chinese themselves .... Many provincial regulations require women

to wait four years or more after their first birth before making such an application. These regulations also prohibit single women, who become pregnant from giving birth, but enforcement of this prohibition reportedly varies widely throughout China .... Party members and civil servants who parent an "out-of-plan" child are very likely to face administrative sanction, including job loss or demotion. Couples who give birth to an unapproved child are likely to be assessed a social compensation fee, which can range from one-half the local average annual household income to as much as ten times that level .... Women may be allowed to carry the "excess" child to term, but then one member of a couple is strongly pressured to be sterilized. In some cases, they may be asked to go to a hospital under other pretenses, or sterilized without consent.[10]

This example illustrates the use of legislation, technology, and social peer pressure to determine the outcome of populations in globalization. This is a problem when viewed from the United States and other Western countries with different constitutional traditions towards population planning. The Chinese see there is no real alternative, despite the objections from the West. The Singapore case demonstrates the efficacy of a policy implementation regime that had done its work so perfectly it caused a shortage of births. Even today, the unintended consequences of the "stop-at-two" policy continues to take its toll. Unfortunately, alternative measures and policies to counter the negative effects of a lack of children, especially among Chinese Singaporeans, have not met with the same measure of success that resulted in this fertility problem.

TECHNOLOGY, SOCIETY, AND POPULATION

Sulfikar Amir argues that there is a causal link between society and technology. In our discussions, he believes that I have substituted population for society and have deployed it as a proxy for society at large. He consequently argues that the three ps of technology — power, pleasure, and prestige — are applicable through population as a proxy for society.[11] However, I do not necessarily use population as a proxy for society, but do concede that there are clear and distinct links between a given population, which might constitute a segment of society, certainly, but not the whole of it. Nevertheless, Sulfikar explains that the three ps represent discrete, sub-national entities that human beings desire from the utilization of technology. I argue that the technology was initially used by populations to make life efficient and to organize and control human populations' sizes, growth, development, and location in urban centres and rural areas. However, over time it has become almost impossible to separate the nuances between technology and population as observed in the work of post-Heideggerian theorists of technology. This means that human beings are now no mere masters of the technologies that they employ but indeed enslaved to these modes of organization and efficiency.

This means that the concepts of power, pleasure, and prestige are themselves coterminous with the development and enslavement of human populations by the conceit of their own logic and the design of their own ambition. This suggests why Sulfikar is concerned that my work constitutes a kind of technological determinism. While there appears to be some merit to such a claim, it is similarly true that there is room for resisting technological control. Unless one is totally ignorant about the possibilities for resisting coercive technologies, one can avoid coming under undue influence.

TECHNOLOGY AND ADDICTION

Clear illustrations of how human populations have become addicted to technological change exist to support an argument for a limited form of "enslavement". For some this is merely another kind of good and service that have become as indispensible as "butter" and "guns". There are many survey companies which charge a premium for attitudinal and market data. The prohibitive costs of survey research make it difficult for academics to make precise global assessments of Internet use, wireless use, Bluetooth use, handphone preference and choice, and other lifestyle preferences. The latest estimates indicate that close to one billion people now use the Internet and this appears set to increase between 12–16 per cent per capita by 2015. Asian governments are also willing to spend tens of billions of dollars developing emergent technologies including biotechnology, nanotechnology, and 2-D/3-D animation. While the initial growth of computer users was concentrated in the United States, Asia has overtaken the West as the single largest region for computer use and growth especially in South Asia and parts of the developed Far East. Many Southeast Asian governments often include detailed IT strategies in their political platforms during democratic elections. Malaysia, Brunei, and Singapore for example have earmarked billions of U.S. dollars for the use of IT technologies in entrepreneurship development and in public education. When the Chinese government finally removes its state-run firewall, it will similarly unleash a tremendous global market for IT and other lifestyle goods and services, and increase the proportion of human beings exposed to the trappings of IT addiction.

Once a computer user becomes addicted to a given technology, he may lose himself into a seemingly irreversible abyss and must make a concerted effort to break away. One example of addiction is seen in the addictive qualities of electronic mail and the need by some people to constantly check their email, delete spam, and avoid junk mail, even while on holiday. Resistance against checking email is for many workers a strenuous and overt act of reminding oneself not to check one's messages. On the other hand, one could easily argue that email checking is a means of keeping in touch with the business world and with friends, and has become an indispensible tool of modern communications. A second example of addictive behaviour common among the computer literate set is the creation of mindless blogs as an exposé of one's random and innermost thoughts published freely over virtual space. At some level, blogging represents a channel for exhibitionism, a kind of technological fetish that might appear harmless even as it is time-consuming. Perhaps this is simply another form of killing boredom within a larger ambit of studies known as the sociology of leisure. For younger bloggers, it is insufficient to engage with the physical world; modernity has provided a far more interesting virtual world, one that is neither real nor fake. It is a world that mixes fact and fiction; truth and falsehood; desire, fantasy, hope, and fate. A third example of technological addiction has been around longer than the PC and the Mac. This is the addiction to television as the primary source of entertainment.

In all three cases, three characteristics can be discerned: (1) all three addictions have alternatives that could be consumed if only to thwart or control that addiction. For example, there are clear alternative forms of communications instead of email such as letter writing or speaking person-to-person or over the telephone or through Skype (a form of telephony using Internet connectivity). There are alternative forms of self-expression to blogging or vlogging (a vlog is a video log of one's activities), and the alternatives to television as entertainment are of course almost limitless; (2) These are only three forms of technological addiction. There are many other modes where users of technology are unable to break away from its use long after the satisfaction derived at the margin for each unit of good/service consumed has become zero. It reaches a negative state. The examples here would be online gaming, PC gaming, and LAN gaming; (3) It seems clear that these addictions cut across gender, ethnicity, and religion within the globalized world.

TECHNOLOGY AND GLOBAL STANDARDS

Technology depends on commonly accepted standards in order to facilitate manufacturing for international markets. The goods that are produced such as silicon chips, wafers, motherboards, USB devices, infra-red and Bluetooth devices, as well as electronic hardware need to be built according to certain basic guidelines in order to be marketable and to turn a profit. Market goods in modernity are technology-dependent, have a limited shelf-life, and are made according to some global benchmark. There are often competing benchmarks for manufactured goods because of the nature of economic competition across regulated markets.

Ironically, the use of international or global standards itself involves the use of technology to develop such standards, yet the technology used to drive the development of global benchmarks are themselves partially dependent on meeting global standards for technological creation. We can see that the level of standardization is much more easily written about and discussed rather than created. For example, the use of a common platform for electronic mail itself poses different challenges. While an IBM or compatible PC provides a useful benchmark for a common email system, there continue to be different electronic mail types such as Lotus Notes, Eudora Light, MS Outlook, Mozilla and Outlook Express. Most use the Simple Mail Transfer Protocol (SMTP) platform and Post Office Protocol (POP) or Internet Mail Access Protocol (IMAP) protocols with different means of encoding such as MIME and others. Every emergent technology, while dependent on existing technology, endeavours to modify existing standards or prescribe new ones. Rising populations who are computer literate simply increases the levels of technological dependence on derivative software and hardware. The moment that the main operating system changes, however, the entire range of technologies have to be modified or change with it, and hence the literate IT population concerned needs to reconfigure and adapt to the changes. This, as we shall see later, is the case with the shift from Windows NT/2000/XT to Windows Vista.

On the surface, scholars of globalization often view the phenomenon of "standardization", "uniformization", or "universalization" in two dimensions: (1) a process of making globally identical things in the public realm and within private space;[12] and, as a consequence of the first dimension, (2) the need to provide a certain global level of availability of goods and services. However, some political scientists tend to argue that the word "standardization" is one that demands more precise definition because different goods possess different levels of appeal to consumers who represent a highly subjective population.[13] For them, the idea of the global availability of a product to travelling populations needs to be tempered with the preferences of local tastes. This means that apart from the omnipresence of McDonald's, there is a certain level of localization that occurs if only to make that McDonald's separate or distinct from others. They suggested that such differences in "standards" can be seen in terms of the provision of spicy Thai salad (*som tam*) in the Bangkok McDonald's, spicy chicken salad in Chiang Mai KFC, *rendang burger* in Singapore, steamed rice in KFC Manila, and *nasi ayam goreng* in Jakarta McDonald's. This is about the dietary localization of fast food MNCs and the product differentiation of their goods. But this simple example of fast food draws a stark contrast to other kinds of competing standards in the globalized world.

The lack of standardization resulted in different and competing platforms. In the past, the problem was recalling which type of dry cell to get: D size, C size, or penlight; then came AA and AAA, and lithium. The problem today is that there are different kinds of memory cards used in cell phones: Multi-media card (MMC), mini-SD (Secure Digital card) (a mini version of SD), micro-SD, and memory sticks all of which can cause memory loss because of the lack of Random Access Memory (RAM) in our brains due to an information overload. We now live in a world of received technology. We receive technology and no longer need to worry about it because it comes with service and support. But this is only limited, as seen in the case of Windows NT, XP, Windows 2000 to Windows Vista and beyond. Forcing platform change is just another way to make more money while delivering better value goods and services — although the thought that we could live comfortably within the old platform is a gross misnomer. Our world is held up by goods made in China and services provided in India.

Indeed, there continues to remain a set of arguments in social and literary theory that suggests that the globalized world is a kind of postmodern world of homogeneity and uniformity. However, this is too simple a thesis to make for theory and too far distant from political reality to be in practice. There is instead a deeper argument underlying this partial truth. This deeper surface, at another level, involves a political economy of diversification of global standards into competing categories, alternative standards, and divergent classes. This deeper structure of difference results in three main effects: (1) increases in market competition over the efficacy of global methodologies — for example radio versus television; Betamax versus VHS, TV versus HDTV, Mac versus PC, Blu-Ray versus DVD technologies; (2) increase in wealth for global standard service providers through conferencing and networking; and (3) diversification of global markets with different levels of support for these global standards. This is an interesting feature of globalization that did not appear in the past and helps make our understanding of globalization critically unique. It brings us to the importance of global standards.

Why might there be a need for global standards? Can there ever be global standards? Can there be global or international standards if these are set by only one country and foisted upon the rest of the world? The evolution of the global standard is that it begins as originator-dependent and then becomes path-dependent. The problem then is with the multiple origins and the creation of many paths in technology. Increases in the literacy levels of a given population mean that a larger proportion of a given cohort is likely to become devoted to developing particular technological skill sets. These could theoretically mean that larger populations would demand proportionately more medical doctors and computer technicians than smaller populations. Those who prefer making a class-based argument would say that the need for a particular skill set in modernity is dependent on the demand for such services within the global capitalist economy.

One reason for the need for global standards is because of the human need for predictability. We want to know that things will be there when we get there, at least for the sake of convenience. This means more than having Starbucks, Adidas, and McDonald's in every major airport and global city. There appears to be a pressing need for predictability of goods and services so that a predictable level of civilized comfort awaits the global traveller. Hotel chains provide an excellent example of cookie-cutter type rooms and services that create and maintain expectations for travellers. One can expect a certain level of service from say, Holiday Inn, Marriott or the Ritz Carlton. This may mean little to the individual ethnographer or urban anthropologist seeking truth from fact. However, for the family of travellers, or the frequent independent traveller and the more highly prized first class traveller, such levels of predictability make them willing customers for work and vacationing, which translates to important tourist and foreign currency for many Asian and Western cities and states across the globe. Predictability for individuals and families who travel means comfort, portability, and personal safety. But these are too simple to be made into generalized versions of modernity's consequences for technology and vice versa. However, more persuasive arguments have been made in Naipaul's *The Enigma of Arrival*, *An Islamic Journey*, Akira Kurosawa's final film on postmodernity, and that ridiculously brilliant pulp fiction, *Hotel Honolulu*. The idea of global standardization in technology is critical in the age of globalization if its evil twin is the age of terror. Technological standardization and ease of access since the end of the Cold War in 1989 made it easy to learn and apply technology for all kinds of purposes, including ones that the technology was not designed for in the first place.

TECHNOLOGY, THE STATE, AND POWER IN THE AGE OF GLOBALIZATION

Where warrants of economic progress appear and are catalysed through technology, the terrorists of regression themselves emerge as their silent supporters balk at the aegis of Western modernity. This is because progress for Western-styled thinking rides roughshod against the grain of Islamic fundamentalism gone awry. The moral contest, not surprisingly, is a fight for power and control. Western modernity's powerful vacuum and seductive goods and services weaken and undermine the millions who have grown up to see for themselves the values and properties that genuine democracies can attain for the individual as well as the community. Not all who have grown up within the relative luxury of mass consumption are happy with their lot. Many who are well educated similarly take their fight to the streets, silently planning the untimely deaths of innocent members of the public. The fight for power over the masses is one that is immediately political with economic consequences. Traditional political and religious leaders who stand to lose in the global movement towards democracy, secular laws, and economic prosperity are those singularly responsible for agitating the mindless murder of the innocents. The question remains for the reader to decide on which side of the bright line he or she wishes to stand.

Globalization is characterized by uniformity, the IT revolution, and the commoditization of culture. Globalization is similarly marked by indirect democracy; capitalist triumphalism; religious discordance; environmental consciousness; anomie; unrest and terrorism; and emergent technologies. Terrorists depend on technology in the way that the state depends on keeping ahead of terrorists through emergent technology.

There are three bureaus in the United States that saw rapid development towards the end of the Cold War under the larger bureau of Technology Administration within the Department of Commerce. This was set up under the National Institute of Standards and Technology Authorization Act (Public Law 100-519). The highest state office for technology is the Office of Technology Policy (OTP) that reports directly to the undersecretary for technology. The OTP oversees general technology policy, but the detailed work in the field and responsibility for intelligence analysis comes from other lower level agencies.

For example, the U.S. Bureau of Intelligence and Research (INR), which is part of the larger U.S. intelligence community (IC), draws from all intelligence sources and analyses issues for state department policymakers in support of foreign policy and national security. The critical heart of INR is its dependence on emergent technologies to draw together the various aspects of its institutional key performance indicators. Other bureaus that form part of IC include Air Force Intelligence, Army Intelligence, Central Intelligence Agency, Coast Guard Intelligence, Defense Intelligence Agency, Department of Energy, Department of Homeland Security, Department of State, Department of the Treasury, Drug Enforcement Administration, Federal Bureau of Investigation, Marine Corps Intelligence, National Geospatial Intelligence Agency, National Security Agency, National Virtual Translation Center Vacancies, Navy, and the Office of the Director of National Intelligence. In order to sustain the Global War on Terror, the U.S. continues to be dependent on the IC products in order to anticipate enemy activities, courses of action, deployment zones, and their order of battle. The bureaus are agencies of government that up till 9/11 used to work on a competitive basis. This led to an overlapping of intelligence maps, over-mining of the same field, a misallocation and wastage of resources. Ironically it has taken 9/11 and the subsequent terror attacks in Bali, Madrid, London, and Bangkok for states to devolve greater authority and resources to security agencies. The competitive strategy was mainly used by U.S. intelligence services and was different from those employed in the United Kingdom and other Western European states. Looking back after 9/11, when we examine the level of commitment to their competitive-edge strategy and access to global resources, the U.S. intelligence strategy had to change for two compelling reasons. Firstly, as the U.S. government's most important intelligence-gathering and intelsec communities failed to coordinate their information-sharing activities that could have anticipated and prevented the problems that arose during the Iran-Contra affair of 1986; the Cold War in 1989/90; the World Trade Center Tower 1 basement truck bomb on 26 February 1993; the Oklahoma City bombing of the Alfred P. Murrah Federal Building on 19 April 1995; and the second World Trade Center bombing that destroyed both Tower 1 and Tower 2 and the failed attempt to destroy the Pentagon on 11 September 2001. Had there been greater intelsec cooperation across the free world after 9/11, other international disasters could have been avoided. But because the intellgence community of each "free state" in the neoliberal globalized world continues to remain wary of other "free states" because of Cold War experiences, there is a general lethargy towards intelligence sharing. Better intelligence cooperation across the free world could have helped prevent the Tokyo subway sarin gas attack (1995); Khobar Towers, Saudi Arabia (1996); U.S. embassy bombings in Tanzania and Kenya (1998); Kuta Beach Bali, Indonesia (2002); Marriot Hotel, Jakarta, Indonesia (2003); Jakarta and Sulawesi, Indonesia (2004); Madrid, Spain (2004); the hotels (Grand Hyatt; Radisson SAS; and Day's Inn) bombed in

Amman, Jordan (2005); the Babri Mosque and Ram Janmabhoomi in Ayodhya, India and in Bangkok, Thailand (2006), for example. All these examples, and these are only a few, involved terrorists' attempts to kill as many people as possible. The age of terrorism is therefore the age whereby the globalization of emergent technology in which the absence of control over right-wing ethnic and religious communities leads to the massive destruction of human life, rather than devoting their energy and resources towards combating the death and destruction wrought by tsunamis, earthquakes, and other environmental disasters. Time in modernity is being spent on planning to defend or planning to kill populations with emergent and existing technology.

The contradictions in the competing modes of intelligence-gathering and assessment did not mean that some of the agencies were off the mark. Indeed they were more often spot on the mark. For example, on 7 June 1999, the director of the FBI — because he believed that the bureau should confront the challenges of globalization of criminal populations — "placed Usama Bin Laden on the 'Ten Most Wanted' List for his alleged involvement in the 1998 bombings of United States embassies in Africa".[14] Secondly, the competitive-edge intelligence-strategy led to contradictory and often confusing versions over the same intelligence event. It meant that there was information overload and a stilted allocation of resources. This is illustrated in the failure to prevent the first law in intelligence, "keep your nose clean", and the failure of the bright-line principle in the case of Special Agent Robert Hanssen. The misallocation of resources continues today, in large part due to the fact that political considerations carry more weight than non-political ones. Everyone who ever read about the Second Gulf War would have read about WMD, and everyone who knows about WMD will tell you that it appears to have been more of a ruse, a red herring, a deception, or a very bad mistake.

> [Feb. 6, 2004] Today, by executive order, I am creating an independent commission, chaired by ... to look at American intelligence capabilities, especially our intelligence about weapons of mass destruction. Last week, our former chief weapons inspector, David Kay, reported that Saddam Hussein's regime had weapons programs and activities in violation of United Nations Security Council resolutions and was a gathering threat to the world .... America's enemies are secretive, they are ruthless and they are resourceful. And in tracking and disrupting their activities, our nation must bring to bear every tool and advantage at our command .... The commission will compare what the Iraq Survey Group learns with the information we had prior to Operation Iraqi Freedom. It will review our intelligence on weapons programs in countries such as North Korea

and Iran. It will examine our intelligence on the threats posed by Libya and Afghanistan before recent changes in those countries. Members of the commission will issue their report by March 31, 2005. I've ordered all departments and agencies, including our intelligence agencies, to assist the commission's work. The commission will have full access to the findings of the Iraq Survey Group.[15]

Indeed, the international repercussions were greater in the case of the United Kingdom because Tony Blair had to convince his Cabinet, Whitehall and the British people that there were weapons of mass destruction. Nevertheless, the misallocation of resources is clearly illustrated in the fact that,

> The National Security Branch (NSB) was established on 9/12/05, in response to a presidential directive to establish a "National Security Service" that combines the missions, capabilities, and resources of the counterterrorism, counterintelligence, and intelligence elements of the FBI under the leadership of a senior FBI official. In July 2006, the Weapons of Mass Destruction Directorate was created within the NSB to integrate WMD components previously spread throughout the FBI."[16]

The NSB was established four years and a day after 9/11. The mode of intelligence-disclosure to the public is a critical ingredient in legitimizing the tax dollars spent on bureaus like the FBI and sub-bureaus like NSB. In the post-9/11 era there was an initial anthrax mail scare. But up till today, the WMD directorate has not discovered any WMD in the United States or Iraq. The point is that the government took advantage of its position of trust because most of the intelligence community's activities are classified and not appear in the public domain. Returning to the WMD Commission, Bush presents the report but does not really comment on its contents or the fact that the WMD Commission has the following to say:

> We conclude that the Intelligence Community was dead wrong in almost all of its pre-war judgments about Iraq's weapons of mass destruction. This was a major intelligence failure. Its principal causes were the Intelligence Community's inability to collect good information about Iraq's WMD programs, serious errors in analyzing what information it could gather, and a failure to make clear just how much of its analysis was based on assumptions, rather than good evidence. On a matter of this importance, we simply cannot afford failures of this magnitude. After a thorough review, the Commission found no indication that the Intelligence Community distorted the evidence regarding Iraq's weapons of mass destruction. What the intelligence professionals told

you about Saddam Hussein's programs was what they believed. They were simply wrong ... Our review has convinced us that the best hope for preventing future failures is dramatic change. We need an Intelligence Community that is truly integrated, far more imaginative and willing to run risks, open to a new generation of Americans, and receptive to new technologies.[17]

It was a total failure, said the WMD commission members. There was no bias because the Bush administration chose those people. Perhaps that is the beauty of the American system. That for every political problem in acrimony, there are always people of integrity to speak out and say otherwise.

American bureaucracy has demonstrated that each and every successive event/disaster creates a new agency or sub-agency to anticipate such events/disasters. The disasters occur time and again but cannot be anticipated early enough to be circumvented. New intelsec directors and bureau chiefs are excellent at generating new logos, acronyms, words, and phrases. They are not so good at predicting the next disaster from happening which would be an impossible task in any case. Social scientists, economists, policy wonks and spin doctors should realize that there is no beef in fancy phraseology or rhetoric like "core competencies", "key performance indices", "life cycle management", "enterprise architecture", or "information assurance guaranty". But there is great value, good or bad as it might finally be used, such as the FBI's state-of-the-art Integrated Automated Fingerprint Identification System through the Automated Biometric Identification System that is being implemented by signatories of the latest ICAO regulations.[18]

The globalization of technology has empowered states in modernity as well as the agitators against global political and economic empires. Asia is currently playing catch-up with the rest of the developed world and it appears more likely than not that the rise of Asia will contrast the demise of Pax Americana. This is likely to occur because of the massive international debt the United States is shouldering because it is still paying for World War II, the Korean War, the Vietnam War, the Cold War, the Gulf Wars, and the Global War on Terror. The United States is able to maintain its global superpower status because it has relied on the shared political ideology of export democracy and economic dependence. It undermines states that do not share its democratic values and invades those who openly challenge its moral authority to lead. Its adversaries from the Cold War era such as China, India, the former Warsaw Pact countries, and Russia have adjusted their politics, systems of governance, and economic strategies into greater alignment with the neoliberal economic system of globalization. That is power.

The world wants to follow America's lead but the recessionary pressures may be too much to bear. Note that every time America spends more than five years in any one place as an invader, a global recession usually ensues. One recalls that the system of barter trade in the pre-medieval ages broke down because of its inherent inefficiencies. Mercantilism and neofeudalism worked for decades during the colonial period but also gave way to early capitalism. By the end of World War II, in the European colonies the shift towards a new economic paradigm was already well under way. Then there was the OPEC crisis in 1973 that served to caution Westerners about their incredible civilizational dependence on fossil fuels. Then Reaganomics and the American "Star Wars" Programme — in addition to *Glasnost* and *Perestroika* — helped cripple and destroy the Soviet economy. The First and Second Gulf Wars were meant to destroy terrorists and boost a flagging American economy. The Gulf War is not over and most of the critical terrorist leaders have still not been captured. The sub-prime crisis was ignored until it mushroomed into a bigger problem than Congress could fix. By 2008, the largest banks that were over-exposed had fallen not only in the United States but across the world. That is how interconnected and interdependent globalization technology has made our populations, economies, social networks, and financial institutions.

Notes

[1] The chapter title was named "Technology and Population" because technology appears to be driving population. Although some would prefer the argument that "population precedes technology" in terms of origins and authenticity; or that "technology appears *before* population" because human beings are invariably and inevitably trapped by technology. Technology has become an/Other. Human beings appear to be chaining themselves to an/artificial/Other. Such self-incarceration brings about addiction to a particular technology or several technologies, or addicted to processes such as annual/biannual upgrades; purchasing immediate obsolescence (that is by the time one begins deriving satisfaction from a good or service, the implicit technology it uses is obsolete); and buying insurance as a guaranty against risk that the technology might break down and become in need of after sales service support. The purchase of immediate obsolescence is tied to the argument about the many contradictions of survival in late modernity (Rappa 2002, *Modernity and Consumption*). This idea of technology as an/Other is a common thesis among researchers interested in science and technology. If science is knowledge that is designed to make humanity more civilized, more efficient, more livable, and more wholesome then technology should be an extension of science. But it is not that kind of extension. It is after all rather

close to what Martin Heidegger had warned Hannah Arendt about in the early 20th century. See for example, Andrew Feenberg, *Heidegger and Marcuse: The Catastrophe and Redemption of History* (Routledge 2005).
2. Red Bull technology is based on a simple formula that has been protected by international licences and patents. See Forbes.com and *Forbes* "Thailand's 40 Richest" (2005, 2007).
3. See "Conspiracy Theory: Did We Land on the Moon?" television programme aired on 15 February and 21 March 2001. See also, *Apollo 11: The NASA Mission Reports: Vol. 1 (NASA Mission Reports)* (Apogee Books); Charles D. Benson and William B. Faherty, *Moon Launch! A History of the Saturn-Apollo Launch Operations* (University Press of Florida, 2001) <http://liftoff.msfc.nasa.gov/news/2001/news-moonlanding.asp>.
4. Langdon Winner, "Technology Studies for Terrorists", in *Surveillance and Security: Technological Politics and Power in Everyday Life*, edited by Torin Monahan (London and New York: Routledge, 2006), p. 276.
5. Gary Thomas, "US Intelligence Report Sees Sharp Rise in Asian Influence", *Voice of America*, 14 January 2005.
6. Irma van der Ploeg, "Borderline Identities: The Enrollment of Bodies in the Technological Reconstruction of Borders", in Monahan, op. cit., pp. 178–79.
7. Ibid.
8. See C.F. Baynes and R. Wilhelm, *The I Ching or Book of Changes*, trans. by Richard Wilhelm and Cary F. Baynes (Bollingen 1950). It would appear that Carl Jung and other scholars were more interested in the earlier Chinese to German translations; and S.J. Marshall, *Mandate of Heaven: Hidden History of the I-Ching* (Columbia University Press, 2002).
9. Peter J. Lu's work published in Science and announced in Steve Bradt (2004) "Ancient Chinese Technical Tango", *Harvard Gazette* 17 June 2004. See also, Rod Campbell, "The Chinese Neolithic: Trajectories to Early States by Li Liu", "Governance in Asia", *Harvard Asia Pacific Review* 9, no. 1 (Winter 2007).
10. Arthur E. Dewey, "One-Child Policy in China", Assistant Secretary for Population, Refugees and Migration, Testimony before the House International Relations Committee, Washington, D.C., 14 December 2004.
11. Discussion with Sulfikar Amir, ISEAS, B103, 2007. See also Sulfikar Amir, "Power, Culture and the Airplane: Technological Nationalism in New Order Indonesia", Ph.D. dissertation, Department of Science and Technology Studies, Renssleaer Polytechnic Institute, Troy, New York, USA, 2005.
12. The importance for such "identical things" arises from a psychological need and economic demand that provides comfort in a foreign and alien environment. This seems part of modernity's attempt at injecting a certain level of humanity into a rapidly dehumanizing world. However, one might argue that it is also true that one need not necessarily feel comfortable with things that one can identify with. I would like to thank Napisa Waitoolkiat for this criticism.
13. Ardeth Maung Thawnghmung (Ph.D., political science, University of

Wisconsin, Madison) and Napisa Waitoolkiat (Ph.D., political science, Northern Illinois University).

14 "Usama" is the way that it is spelt on the website. "In June 2001, FBI Director Freeh retired from federal government service. On 4 September 2001, Robert S. Mueller III became the Director of the FBI. On 11 September 2001, terrorists attacked the World Trade Center in New York City and the Pentagon in Washington D.C. In October, the FBI confronted another challenge: Anthrax-laden letters." "The History of the FBI" at <FBI.gov>. An official site of the U.S. Federal Government, U.S. Department of Justice. See <http://www.fbi.gov/libref/historic/history/prepare.html>.

15 CNN, "Transcript: Bush Announces WMD Panel Members", Friday, 6 February 2004.

16 <http://www.fbi.gov/hq/nsb/nsb.htm>.

17 *The Commission on the Intelligence Capabilities of the United States Regarding Weapons of Mass Destruction*. Report to the President of the United States, 31 March 2005.

18 <http://www.fbi.gov/hq/ocio/cc_progress.htm>.

9

WAR

This chapter examines the complex connections between globalization and war. There are many reasons for war today. It appears that there are wars on virtually every front. There are cultural wars and social wars at different levels in each economy. But perhaps the most consequential in a neoliberal capitalist world order are financial wars. When the Americans "won" the Cold War, everyone thought that capitalism was the economic answer to the less attractive and more inefficient alternative provided by the Soviets. No one could have imagined that the sub-prime crisis that actually began in the late 1990s — not ten years after the Cold War ended — would eventually balloon and burst all over Wall Street in 2008. People are making comparisons in the streets of New York City. They are comparing the consequences of 9/11's terrorist attack on the WTC and the financial terrorism of 2008 that has so far cost an estimated US$16 trillion and counting.

While the discussion of globalization involves competitive world markets and local entrepreneurialism, all these seem like empty words in the face of the financial wars of the economic world. In 2007 experts warned of a new economic recession because contemporary financial (but expert) speculation — based on sophisticated predictive tools — indicated that the global economy had run into a ten-year economic boom-and-bust cycle. There were others that argued that the global economy was experiencing increasing levels of intense economic competition with the amount of time between peaks and troughs being reduced through the compression of time into space by new technologies. Hence the operational hypothesis here is that new technologies compress time into space. The collapse of time into space means that an increasing set of events can be carried out in a shorter frame of time, but there are problems with such a compression. One of the most significant consequences of such compression is that the entities that occupy each discrete event are not prepared for extraneous adversity. Therefore, the rapid compression of financial time into political space often creates internal pressures which expose systemic weaknesses. The weaknesses become magnified when structures built for specific events are stressed beyond their limits. The sub-prime crisis is a case in point. And all this was fuelled by greed. Greed on the part of the banks and institutions and other underwriters as well as individuals. The belief that relationships between domestic markets are relatively shielded from the larger global ones is a false belief. This is because greed cuts across national space, cultural boundaries, and economic markets. The sub-prime crisis was a guerilla war that began in several different parts of the globe and few thought of linking them up with the larger neoliberal capitalist ideology till its worst effects were realized. This is the punishment of modern society that James C. Scott, Jean Elshtain, David Garland, and many other scholars have long since identified in social theory.[1]

The longer we wait for cultural and monetized baggage to be cleared from the refuse bins of society, the longer it will take for the economy to drive itself out of a global recession. At the end of 2008, anyone could have told you that we had not yet reached the bottom of the depressed globe. When George W. Bush began his war in Iraq, his staffers crunched out numbers that put the total cost at about US$50 billion based on the premise that all troops would return within five to eight years or between 2008 and 2012. Bush's chief economic aide, Lawrence Lindsey, thought he had immunity when he predicted that the war would cost two to four times more than Bush had indicated. Not long after, Linsey was sacked. Added to the toll are those who were sacked in the line of duty. According to Stiglitz and Bilmes, the war as of 2006 would have cost US$2 trillion. This is not even to add the amount of money spent on arms and bases reduction since 1992. It makes the billion dollars worth of defence contracts won by pro-Republican neoconservatives such as Eric Prince and his associates at Blackwater seem like chump change. Should President Obama's new administration make the mistake of engaging another enemy in another prolonged war — such as North Korea or Iran — then the United States would have seen the end of its ability to hold onto its superpower status. The Middle East is the poison chalice of the United States. Gleaming and beautiful in the purest gold, those who drink from it eventually die.

There is a war-like range of relationships between global markets and local firms. Yet both global and local markets in their war garb are similarly dependent on talents, technology, and capacity. Their successes are dependent on sentiments of culture, money, and terror. Whether a firm is located in Asia or the North American continent is less important than whether one's firms are able to produce more for less, maximize profits while minimizing losses, and re-invent itself every other quarterly war during the financial year. The location of the firm in a designated zone is contiguous with larger political boundaries of the nation state. While many political scientists have argued for the disappearance of the nation state and the dissolution of boundaries with globalization for the past twenty years, nothing much has changed. For example, every agreement that weakens political divisions or boundaries is often challenged by new statal functions that demand a re-institutionalization of the boundaries in question. One new function that has clearly reinvigorated the importance of the state is terrorism. In the United States, this has resulted in the creation of an entirely new department called Homeland Security. In the United Kingdom, the Ministry of Home Affairs has traditionally held this portfolio in conjunction and in cooperation with the Ministry of Defence. Many former British colonies also follow the U.K. model. In such a case, Asia views the West in a way that is a reflection of the old ways in which the former colonial masters used to control insurgent activities, irredentism, religious and ethnic separatism when Stalinism and Maoism were at the height of power in Asia and the West. Indeed, if anything, the importance of the nation state and national boundaries during decolonization of the 1960s became more pronounced by the end of the Cold War in 1989 with the fall of the Berlin Wall. The place of the nation state would then reach a critical stage when the terrorists bombed the Twin Towers of the New York World Trade Center.

The waxing and waning of the nation state's political fortunes paled in the successes of Asian, African, Latin American, Pacific, Middle Eastern, and Western forms of globalization in late modernity. Their economies have been ironically tied to various wars since the end of World War II. Asian firms continued to learn, adapt, and innovate from their "advanced" Western counterparts throughout the 1970s and 1980s which came to be known as the PC (hardware) and the IT (software) revolutions. The position of the capitalist firm was safe as long as economic and business planning models became more concrete, discrete, and realistic than when compared to economic theory a decade earlier. However the local qualities of the firms within different industries became increasingly mistaken as direct representatives of local abilities and talents when indeed they were mere economic units belonging to global MNCs such as Exxon-Mobil, Wal-Mart, Royal Dutch Shell, BP, General Motors, Chevron, DaimlerChrysler, and Toyota, to name a few. The cars and gasoline might be marketed locally, but the most successful companies were market leaders because they were global. By 2010 these corporations would have had sufficient intra-industrial wars to have weeded out the weakest players and promote the viability of the strongest performers.

Therefore the so-called "localization thesis" of the firm in the global twenty-first century is not about the adaptability of indigenous firms but about the adaptation to internationally-recognized practices to suit local tastes, talents, and technologies. Localization is deceptively presented by many politicians as the new way forward because their own political fortunes are tied directly to the local economic activities of their political constituents and the security of the nation state as they know it. Localization is no more than a subset of globalization and not an alternative to globalization. So when politicians and policymakers talk about localization taking precedence over globalization, they are of course re-telling one side of the story, and a very skewed one at best. The entire process of globalization involves re-invention at the local level and a simultaneous global borrowing of ideas and innovations that emerge from other firms and communities. The transmission and revaluation of these ideas and innovations are rapidly mediated by the global advertising and marketing networks that define their life cycle.

Youths look towards the West for manifold reasons, some produced out of war, others for reasons associated with war. Often it is because there is a human need to fill spaces before boredom sets in. In the past it was only the middle class and those who had sufficient disposable income who could venture into divergent forms of entertainment not found within their own homeland or region. The PC and IT revolutions — two pistons of globalization — dramatically changed the situation. While those who wanted to "get out" in the past had to rely on some form of inherited, earned, or disposable wealth to prevent boredom from seeping into their lives, globalization radicalized the norms that govern the avoidance of boredom and undermined the sociological paradigm that explained it as a phenomenon. Indeed, any individual who wishes to "break out" of her or his own system has only to stop caring, and move elsewhere. The phenomenon of entertainment as the avoidance of boredom shifted from a monetized dependence to one where it became possible to enjoy the fruits of modernity without any currency, and with only a willingness to try something new or different that would change one's entire life. The world of Asian traditions and exotica once ended at the doorstep when Asians removed their footwear, but in modernity, Asia now views the West in an entirely different, post-Occidental idiom. Younger generations of Asians growing up in Asia are now more willing and more able to travel with the myriad of possibilities provided by globalization and in this sense, these youthful Asians are now more willing than ever to rid themselves of past traditions and customary practices. Perhaps V.S. Naipaul's "Mimic Men" is the best metaphor to explain the adoption of different Western tongues in communications and Western tastes in consumption. But it does not remain as simple as Naipaul's allegory suggests. The complexity of Asia's mimicry of the West is now ironic as it is critical. This invites us to realize through Said that Asians are much closer to influencing Western perspectives and images than they think. Unfortunately, there are some cities in the Asian world that are less circumspect. They tend to identify, mimic, and uphold Western norms to the point of denigrating their own sexuality, gender, ethnic composition, and cultural heritage. In rejecting the self these Asians exist on the same plane of certitude as the old European conquerors who went native, knowing full well that they could always return to their former self with opportunity costs.

Youths brought up under the girdle of post-nationalist pride are more likely to meld more confidently with the challenges of globalization and the importation of new ideas and values. This explains why as Asia views the West, certain distinct economic structures emerge that deepen the divide between the stereotypical perception of Asian traditions and Western modernity. The claim that the West brought modernity into Asia, Africa, and the Pacific while Asia managed and moderated the meaning of this Occidental overture is one part of the argument that the West created modern Asia, Africa, and the Pacific (for example), which for its own part has done economically well. Asian economies have roughly generated a relatively shorter learning curve than other non-Western places. Since the end of the Cold War (figuratively and ostentatiously since 1989), Asia seems adamant in playing catch-up with the advanced, post-industrial societies of Japan and the West. With the exception of the two belligerent, autarkic, economic non-players of North Korea and Myanmar, the Asian view of the West has fast become the most important variable in the future template of the world. There is hardly any place in reality and virtual reality that Asian products and services have not penetrated. The ironic penetration of Western civilization and militarization into Asia has resulted in rapid and successful materialistic gains by many Asian nations whose populations lived in abject poverty under the British, French, Dutch, Spanish, and Portuguese before them. This is not to say that before first contact with the West that all Asian people enjoyed some kind of heavenly existence. Rather, if we understand the rise of modernity as the concordant development of Western Enlightenment and the breakdown of both Asian and European empires across the past 500 years, we will begin to understand why it took such a short time for Asia to play catch-up with the West. It was not just technology, but another very real variable. But this variable is the subject of another book to be written. As Asia views the West, it reifies a kind of hope, optimism, and progress associated with the American Dream. Recently, former American President George W. Bush, said that the reason why America had to do what it did in Iraq (and possibly Iran) is that there was a dire need to protect the American Dream, the dreams of the youthful glorification of culture, while side-stepping the violence and terrors of its tangents.

Asian economic planners and financial analysts reading the West in general and America in particular, are quick to add that the American Dream is now mired in the problematic quagmire known nowadays as the sub-prime loan disaster. Greedy banks were willing to extend loans to unworthy customers without proper or proprietary credit checks which resulted in the ballooning of throwing good money after bad loans. The global impact of the sub-prime debacle in the United States has not yet been fully understood, though what is clear is that the nature of unrecoverable loans continues to generate a multi-billion dollar undercurrent for which everyone pays eventually. Nevertheless, the combined effects of the steady rises in oil prices and banks that are wary about further consequences of the sub-prime problems on the world economy will be no less than startling if properly aligned. If these two singular and discrete events do not in themselves illustrate the meaning of interdependence in globalization, then there is little else that can be used to convince the supporters of the localization debates. In the search for peace and stability, the preparedness for hot wars has caused policymakers and post-industrialists to jockey for power regardless of the costs to the environment, because after all, that is the other person's problem and non-jurisdictional.

In historical terms, globalization involves the outgrowth of the capitalist machine from the colonial period. Globalization is the offspring of the tension between war and peace. It is the economic vehicle that drives the world. The breakdown of the old European colonial empires in World War II presented their former colonies with a nationalist opportunity to break away. The nationalist awakenings of the proto-globalized world were also read against the grain of the ideological movements of the mid-twentieth century. Empires in decline shed blood. The Seven Years War, the French Revolution, the Crimean War, the Boer War, The Russo-Japanese War, the Balkan Wars, and World War II all signalled the end of empires.

The break-up and breakdown of the European empires through war and internal old world terrorism would signal hardship and disaster. These wartime failures were harbingers of the fate of their former colonies. The new post-9/11 allies of the United States and Western Europe now stand ready to collapse with a rapidly declining American economy. America's final test as an economic superpower is on the line. In every previous test, America has come out stronger. In every previous test, America has had to start a war in order to prime the economy. For the first time, America started a war without realizing that there already was a war within.

The Korean War, Cuban Missile Crisis, Vietnam War, the War in Afghanistan, the Cold War, the Persian Gulf War, the Second Gulf War, and the Global War on Terror are a pattern of events signalling the fight to remain alive despite the losses and untold suffering of America as a "benign hegemony". While America does not seem ready to give up, it may already be too late. Former adversaries like China, Vietnam, and Russia have deep investments in America. Once the Middle East, North Korea, Myanmar, and Africa jump on the bandwagon of American-style democracy, the real problems can begin. Indeed, most economies in modernity have no choice but to remain tied to the American economy. The fall of the United States will mean the end of a critical set of arrangements that have been put in place since 1945.

Part of the reason is that America has made itself so useful and valuable that it cannot be ignored. Another reason is that America tends to bully countries that do not share its ideals. The globalization of financial services — where America is again a world leader — has become the largest profit-making industry since the end of the Cold War. While financial services covers a broad area of credit and banking, it also includes the globalization of investment instruments such as Exchange Traded Funds (ETF), mutual funds, bonds, annuities, tech stocks, and hedge funds. These are the unseen but real instruments of consumption in modernity. New products and services created by banks and other financial institutions create experiences of hope, optimism, and progress for their customers. They help keep in place the neoliberal structures of modernity. Most money is made through some form of financial service either directly or indirectly. But most people do not even have access to a brokerage or understand the difference between mortgage, debt, and equity. They have never heard of JPMorgan Chase, Goldman Sachs, BCG, or Lehman Brothers. They never went to any school, let alone business school. And they will probably die not knowing. So it is not difficult to understand the fact that most people in modernity live below the poverty line, and only a disproportionate minority are wealthy. The middle class that makes up the rest of the population are potential workers, current workers, or retirees. It is the middle class that suffers from the desultory effects of hope, optimism, and progress in a world desensitized by culture, money, and terror. Globalization is the dominant paradigm of the twentieth and twenty-first centuries. It has two main dimensions: (1) a neoliberal MNC-driven economic ideology and (2) democracy, also known as the political ideology of capitalism.

Think of globalization as having many levels and creating an impact at each of these levels across time and space. Resistance to globalization is more than just a few days of protests against WTO meetings. Resistance arises out of states and societies that have fallen behind politically, economically, and culturally. The perception of being left behind leaves these states with two main alternatives. To play catch-up, or to resist. Examples of states that are playing catch-up include Indonesia, Vietnam, Laos, Cambodia, and the Philippines. Russia too. India has had a long democratic gestation period while the Philippines has been in the economic doldrums for decades. Examples of states that resist include Myanmar, North Korea, Cuba, Libya, Iran, and communities across the globe that rejects globalization. In each state of resistance are various social classes that demonstrate the tension between the "haves" and the "have nots". They are caught in a tension between (political and economic) elites — the beneficiaries of globalization and the masses (wage workers, the unemployed, and the retired).

But the complex runs deeper than this simple explanation. Within each class are different communities often with competing demands and limited resources. Traditional religious leaders who have lost power to the seductive effects of Westernization live in fear of further cultural erosion. Their only recourse, according to them, is to fight globalization with those followers who continue to support their just cause. Justice for some is injustice for others. While America and its allies viewed the First Gulf War as a just war, there are many who are diametrically opposed to that form of justice. For many Muslim communities, Judaism and Christianity are gaining ground through globalization. For them, globalization = Westernization = Americanization = the erosion of Islamic values. Marginalized communities will resist this (simplistic) equation. Those who believe in the West will similarly fight as hard, if not harder to maintain the status quo and the balance of power. There are other Muslim communities who are discovering a middle path which allows for their economic progress without sacrificing their religious beliefs. Indeed the majority of Muslims do not support terrorism. The greatest fear in late modernity is not the fight over Islamic or Jewish civilizations but an all-out religious war reminiscent of the Crusades. The overall assessment in late modernity is that human beings are incapable of civilization or of being civilized. The reason why Muslim communities are fighting desperately for their own political space across the world is because their religious leaders believe that their own traditional power bases have been encroached and subsumed under Western modernity. Western modernity is so attractive to many young Muslims because of the freedom that materialism provides; because of the attraction of not being restricted by dietary practices or cultural norms. Western education, laws, entertainment, culture, and food are all attractive to many Muslims all over the world. Late modernity is also about a different kind of terror that Muslims cannot explain. If one is born Catholic or Jew, how can one reject one's religion? Similarly, to reject Islam for those who are born into that faith is to reject oneself and one's own identity, the identity of one's parents and perhaps one's ancestors. In Islam as practised in some countries, there is no freedom for the Muslim to reject his or her own faith without dire social and familial consequences. In Singapore for example, a non-Muslim who marries a Muslim is expected to convert to Islam, not vice-versa. The pressure may be gentle and persuasive. But if there is no religious conversion, then the couple simply breaks up and does not marry. There is no data on the number of people who elope because of religion in Singapore.

In Malaysia, the pro-Islamic courts frown upon Muslims who marry outside the Islamic religion. This is part of the reason why many Muslims who wish to marry non-Muslims marry in a neighbouring country. In this manner they can avoid what V.S. Naipaul has described in *Among the Believers: An Islamic Journey*, "a kind of prying religious police" in Malaysia that checks on Muslims with regard to their religious duties and religious taboos. Two taboos are *khalwat* or physical proximity to a person of the opposite sex who is not related to you, and consumption of alcohol, which is *diharamkan* or prohibited. There are good reasons for both. And there are fines and prison sentences for those who are caught in *khalwat* or consuming liquor. The religious laws and punishment applies to all as long as one party is Muslim. Ask any scholar to make a public comment about the number of converts away from Islam to another faith and you will get no reply. Perhaps the reason is because there are no official statistics. Islam is a defining characteristic — in the Malaysian Constitution — of a Malay. So to reject one's religion is a serious matter. It is to reject oneself. But Islam practised in America for example, is quite different. The social and familial pressures are not as intense and indeed, can be rather inviting, given the growing number of Muslims in America today. This is just one side of a multifaceted coin. Each side of the coin is politicized.

TECHNOLOGICAL GLOBALIZATION

Technological globalization facilitates the exploitation of trust, disinformation, and misleading strategies between allies and enemies, if the allegations in the media are true. But perhaps they are more than true. No one seems to be talking because of the cellular structure of these international intelligence agencies. Globalization affords even greater means of cover and stealth. While Hollywood creates interesting and entertaining versions of this spooky world, many consumers believe that some of these allegations are true, such as the U.S. spy planes flying out of Pakistan and into Soviet airspace, or the Russian Foreign Security Service that caught four British spies in Moscow, although this was denied by the British Foreign Office (ITAR-Tass News Agency, 2006). In 1983, Yang Ping-Wang was charged with espionage and imprisoned in the Beijing Remand Centre. Strangely, he managed to escape to Hong Kong and resume his activities (The Australian Broadcasting Corporation, 2005). However, on 8 April 1995, Yang was again arrested in Hong Kong. In 2003, Xinhua News Agency and *China Daily* reported that twenty-four Taiwanese spies and nineteen citizens of mainland China were arrested regarding the location of 496 Chinese missile sites currently pointed at Taiwanese cities. All this was denied by the Military Intelligence Bureau (Taiwan).[2] There is a deeply embedded underworld of espionage that exists in the post 9/11 era while consumers living on the surface world continue to be distracted by the fears and horrors of 9/11 and the global reaction to terrorists. The resistance to the dominant neoliberal democratic paradigm since 9/11 has resulted in a continuation of war against the infidels and other non-believers. As a result, we have reached a stage in modernity, called late modernity, where there are significant technological advances in all epistemologies (except philosophy and history) and also a clearer distinction between the rich and the poor, the right and the wrong, non-terrorists and terrorists, freedom fighters and insurgents, and other naturalized, bright-line, Hegelian dichotomies. This is where neoMarxist scholars are predicting the ultimate revolution because the rich are getting richer and the poor are getting angrier. The problem, for neoMarxist scholars, is that the angry poor are disorganized, but when the disenfranchised come to the realization that there is more to life than revolution, they open the door to possibilities. When they make it to the bourgeois class, they become role models for hope, progress, and optimism. Rejecting the Jamesonian cultural theory of late capitalism, postmodernism represents the movements and struggles of alternative identities, marginalized communities, insignificant persons, and discarded ideals. Postmodern theorists were blamed for their liberalism. They were the ones, it was said, who suggested that the marginalized be given a chance and embraced with open arms.

The political ideal of non-state interference in the private sphere has weakened from the measures designed to combat terrorism. It is now clear that the targets of terror are no longer aimed at the symbols and bastions of successful economies. Innocent children and ordinary hardworking people in both Muslim and non-Muslim dominant states are the targets of terror. It appears on the surface that Marx was correct since these terrorists are clearly revolting against the widening gap between the world's richest people and the world's poorest ones; where the wage and income differentials between the rich and poor across the world are increasingly caused by the exploitative nature of neoliberal capitalism. Indeed, the owners of the factors of production today are a mixture of hyper-wealthy individual billionaires plus 2,500 MNCs and their global corporate boards.

These late modern megaliths of production and consumption are driven by a highly complex mesh of financial, banking, and services industries searching for global market domination and power over consumption and modernity, or in nano-science that only began taking root in China in the late 1980s with the advent of deMaoization, and Deng Xiaoping's liberal socialism. Some Chinese researchers believe that China is on the cusp of joining the international scientific community of countries that have a worldwide impact on science.[3] Taiwan is still ahead but will weaken and diminish as China exerts its economic and political muscle as it competes internationally with India and begins reclaiming old territory lost after 1949. Nevertheless, both Taiwanese and Indian manufacturers are already claiming to have manufactured the compound that is Tamiflu, a wonder drug created by the powerful pharmaceutical MNC, Roche, which uses neuraminidase inhibitors to attack the influenza virus.

The prescription medicine sells for US$91 for a strip of ten capsules/tablets. That was in mid-November 2005. Despite its side effects, Tamiflu is believed to offer hope and treatment for those struck down with avian influenza or in an avian flu pandemic. The drug is only one example in millions that offer an epistemological view of scientific advancement over the millennia and offers a stark contrast from just a few hundred years ago when diseases were blamed on women, witches, black magic, heretics, and the wrath of god. But what about those who cannot afford Tamiflu? Well they need not worry too much.

By January 2008, critics began wondering what had actually happened to all those predictions by pharmaceutical companies and states that had begun stock-piling Tamiflu as a precaution against a pandemic. Yet there were no visible signs of an avian influenza pandemic in any part of the globe, just some sporadic deaths, terrible as that might be, such as the three reported deaths in China. Indeed, more people have died in Iraq from the war on all sides than from the avian flu since the beginning of 2005.

Is the future of modernity designed on the prospect of survival for only those who are sufficiently wealthy to extend life? Therefore, the problem is not as simple as one envisioned by Marx in the nineteenth century. They say that one man's freedom fighter is another man's terrorist. But some deaths and executions are simply too large to ignore. In the reign of terror of 1793, the perpetrators were known, and their intentions were clear. In the late modernity of the twenty-first century, neither the perpetrators of global terrorism nor their intentions are immediately obvious. There is no set pattern to global terror, and no single vision that unites global terrorists. Were people like Saddam Hussein, Chemical Ali, Kadyrov and Azahari terrorists? There is no doubt. As long as innocent people are killed, it is an act of terrorism and these men killed innocent people. What about the U.S. soldier who misdirects artillery fire and bombards a village of innocent men, women, and children like in Vietnam? Is that an act of terror? This is where the intention to commit the crime comes into question. And the *mens rea*. But what if the accused is of unsound mind, does that make the crime any less criminal? Does it make the act of terror any less terrible? It seems clear to me that Hitler was of unsound mind. And so was Saloth Sar, better known as Pol Pot. His intention was to get rid of one-third of his countrymen of the bourgeois decadence of the French. Born in French Cambodia in 1925, Pol Pot was fluent in French, studied overseas in Paris, and eventually rose to become Prime Minister of the Kingdom of Cambodia. His Khmer Rouge party mass-murdered over one million Cambodians (between 1976 and 1979). Pol Pot died in 1998 without receiving a "proper" trial like Saddam and without any international power seeking him out of the jungle foxhole where he lived ignominiously into his seventies.

Terrorism has become a nefarious, multi-headed hydra that has many lives of its own with a new head of terror arising out of a recently decapitated one. The old political structures of the nineteenth and twentieth centuries have worn thin in their ability to cope with the dynamics of global terror. These political institutions have to be changed dramatically in order to cope with rising prospects of terror. Terrorism in Southeast Asia, the Middle East, Australia, New Zealand, and in Europe has ironically created new forms of citizens. These are citizens who now refuse to move from danger zones, as seen in the two London bombings and those in Jakarta and Bali in 2005. Foreigners and expatriates in Southeast Asia, South Asia, the Middle East, and Europe have refused to be put off by acts of terror in Jakarta, Bali, Pattani, Madrid, Tel Aviv, Amman, and Chechnya. The problem of global terrorism is as unpredictable as it is uncontrollable. One thing is clear, terrorism is one of the themes in human civilization that refuses to disappear. States in late modernity are unable to cope with terrorist activities as these reinvent themselves over time, and overnight. Idealists seeking a more open world without political controls and fewer restrictions have lost the battle to the new conservatism that has taken place all over the world. Everyone is now a potential terrorist, and the most innocent prospects are indeed ironically viewed with the highest suspicion. Ordinary travellers will continue to be bothered by an array of bureaucratic controls if only to protect them from themselves. The police who have always been vulnerable to corruption have now been given greater powers to investigate, detain, and interrogate suspects.

On 22 July 2005, London policemen shot and killed an innocent, unarmed Brazilian man, Jean Charles de Menezes. While the incident may not have caused British Prime Minister Blair to transfer power to Gordon Brown, death of the innocent Menezes was certainly bad karma for Blair's political fortunes. After Menezes was killed (no one has been charged with this crime), Blair lamented losing political ground in Parliament over giving police greater powers of detention. That did not solve the real problem and explains little about the actual failure of existing institutions to curb terror. Two days after the killing, the BBC reported that:

> Met[ropolitan] police chief Sir Ian Blair has apologised to the family of the Brazilian man shot dead by police in south London on Friday. He said the death of Jean Charles de Menezes was a "tragedy", but admitted more people could be shot as police hunt suspected suicide bombers.

Did the police chief mean that more innocent people could be shot or that the police have no control over whom they arrest or shoot in London? On 24 July 2007, the Independent Police Complaints Commission concluded an investigation into the activities of six police officers from the West Midlands for the use of excessive force:

> The Independent Police Complaints Commission (IPCC) has concluded its investigation into the conduct of six West Midlands Police officers involved in the arrest and detention of a man in January 2006. The investigation was triggered by a member of police staff who reported the use of excessive force on a detainee. The man concerned was subsequently traced and recorded a complaint against police. As a result of the IPCC managed investigation, one officer received a written warning, with a second receiving a written warning and words of advice — both due to failings identified in respect of their conduct towards the complainant. A third police officer received words of advice for failing to take appropriate action when the initial complaint was brought to

his attention. There was no evidence to support the allegations of use of excessive force. John Crawley, IPCC Commissioner said, "Our findings clearly demonstrate that the incident was not treated appropriately or initially investigated as it should have been by officers. It sometimes takes courage to challenge the behaviour of others when you believe a colleague has misbehaved, but the willingness of officers and staff to do so is crucial to the maintenance of the professional standards that are rightly highly valued in our police service".[4]

Foucault warned us of the police. If innocent people are killed by terrorists and police forces, why have police forces in the first place? If the police continue to be open to corrupt activity the world over and abuse their powers of arrest by brutalizing innocent citizens in New York, South Africa, Malaysia, and elsewhere, what is the point of having such forces? Globalization would be much easier to understand if the problems were merely bickering over aid-for-poverty or European farm subsidies and the more horrifying acts of terror that weaken economic markets and global trade. Unfortunately, there are more other problems. Since 2004, the world has been wrecked by the earthquakes in South Asia, in India and Pakistan, Hurricane Katrina in the U.S. southwest, and increasing dangers of AIDS, avian influenza, Californian forest fires, and new computer viruses.

OUR GLOBE

Since October 2004 when the first edition of this book was first published, new changes have occurred in terms of neoliberal capitalism. OECD reports that the U.S. economy is likely to grow by 3.25 per cent annually by 2007 in spite of rising energy costs. The weak short-term sentiment for OECD countries is supplemented by a strong and globally competitive Euro, with Japan, the United States, and the European Community taking the lead in an upward movement towards 1996 trade levels. Japan appears to be coming out of its economic doldrums with new domestic confidence under the political leadership of former Prime Minister Junichiro Koizumi. The BBC reported that Japan's GDP increased by 0.4 per cent in the third quarter of 2005, which has lifted the Nikkei to a "closing four year high".[5] China's retail market volumes expanded by almost 13 per cent[6] while its national and regional economic assets gained 28 per cent. This was in addition to the US$12 billion surplus in trade and an inflation rate of 1.2 per cent. The importance of Western European economies to China was reinforced by Chinese President Hu Jintao's visit to Spain, Britain, and Germany to boost trade in an event that would have been unthinkable in the Cold War era less than two decades ago. The bombings in New Delhi's city of 14 million people may have shaken many citizens and political observers, but it has not prevented the U.S. treasury secretary from endeavouring to open up India's archaic financial sector and highlighting the problematic economic infrastructure of the world's largest democracy.[7] But CNN Money reports of problems between the proposed barriers to trade between Brazil, the United States, and the European Union as the latter remains the world's largest trader accounting for over 20 per cent of global trade volumes. While neoliberal capitalists continue to dominate the world stage in pushing new and different forms of pharmaceutical goods, hybrid automobiles, and influenza vaccines, the poorest poor continue to live in squalor across Africa, Latin America, India, and China. Hurricane Katrina provided another kind of terror. It devastated the world's largest economy and rolled back resources originally intended for the Second Gulf War where the untimely, but preventable deaths of innocent Iraqis and innocent Americans have become daily news of horror.

Globalization contains the answers to the problems created by natural and artificial events in modernity. The problems of terrorism, human viruses, and biological viruses have widened the scope for new goods and services for neoliberal MNCs. We continue to live in a world that has witnessed the transformation of former colonial centres of economic and political power into transnational economic, political, cultural, and social power bases. Where recent memories of regime abuse are not quickly forgotten as seen in the July 2007 demands by the Democratic Alliance Against Dictatorship of Thailand, made up of political scientists and academics loyal to former Prime Minister Thaksin and others who are not Thaksin's men but demand the resignation of retired General Prem Tinsulanonda, a former Prime Minister and president of the Privy Council by special appointment by the King. The use of the Internet and cellular phones are examples of simple emergent technologies used for organizing anti-coup protests and demonstrations in Bangkok. This was made worse by then Prime Minister General Surayud Chulanont's calls, to Muslim and Buddhist communities in Pattani, Narathiwat and Yala, which contrasts significantly with Thaksin's strategy for the south when he was Prime Minister.[8] By December 2007, new protests emerged after the NLA decided to pass new legislation before the democratic elections could be held. The election commissioner also made a police report against a member of the PPP, a pro-Thaksin political party, about the forging of documents. The EC was approved by the Council for National Security junta of former and current Thai generals. Observers argue that the intention is to make sure that the "right people" get into the NLA.[9]

Technology in 1960 used to be something that could be touched, seen, and felt. We were amazed when they introduced the radio, the monochromatic television, air-conditioning, hydroelectric power, manned space flight. The state of technology forty-eight years later in 2008 is a world apart from before. Technology today seems omnipresent. It is marked by the convergence of global standards, the shortening lifespan of electronic goods, low cost production, and high rates of return. IT conferences which were unheard of in the past are large meetings where capitalists agree on how to attain win-win outcomes for the corporate bodies they represent. Three-year-old children understand and play online games dexterously long before advancing their linguistic skills. There is a melding of technology into humanity and vice-versa. The result is not always fortuitous. Technological change is the vestibule into the vagaries of globalization. Technology is about change and English is the language of technology. English has survived because it has been able to adapt and change in the face of globalization's challenges. English no longer belongs to the English people and perhaps it never did. Eighty years ago, English gave many people in Africa and Asia something to think about and eventually something to rebel against. Eighty years ago the world witnessed the decline of a formerly great empire, reduced to a motley group of islands living off the wealth that was extracted out of the colonies and "the broad brown backs of Asian people" (Rappa 1997). The British and French colonialists have gone the way of the Spanish Conquistadors and Portuguese and Italians before them. Part of the reason why London continues to remain a great financial hub is because of the concentration of these services there for the past 200 years, an epitaph to a shell of its former self.

Globalization tends to set a dizzying pace for those who participate in its widening gyre, and, as Michael Perelman reminds us, creates and forces contradictions on us. The modern world has become so complex that we are coerced into leading increasingly dependent lives that ironically make us more detached and self-absorbed. The arguments involving truth-fact distinction appear real in the reel life of *The Queen* (2006), *The 300* (2007), and *Apocalypto* (2007) which reveal the traditional inconveniences of primitive, self-contained societies that were built on superstition as religion and myth as scientific fact. The word that was introduced into the primitive jungles failed to resolve the problematic of the jungle economy in Conrad's *Heart of Darkness* which has seen little real economic and political development since the time of Belgian colonialism.

We have doubtlessly been let down by the senses, by our cognition, and then misled into thinking that technology will save us. Nothing can save us from death, and technology can only prolong its end. For every wealthy and influential environmentalist who says that the world is warming us to death, there will be another who says that this has been one of the coolest periods in the millennia of civilization. The dizzying pace of globalization thwarts resistance, it demands us to go with the flow or risk it all. As they say, we are preparing our children for a world that no longer exists. We are indeed cognizant of the fact that something is wrong out there and virtually helpless to apprehend it. Yet this claim is different from the one that says that the world we grew up in no longer exists. To say that we are preparing our children for a world that no longer exists means that the world in which these children themselves are growing and experiencing youth itself disappears with the present moment; that the world of ideas and changes dissipates into nothingness like Nietzsche believed. But contrary to what Nietzsche claimed in eternal recurrence, the world perhaps is not going to reinvent itself. It has not happened before in the precise same manner. That even the spider on its web in the moonlight is one that looks like the first spider but it is on a different web. And we are indeed forced to become virtual web-crawlers, distracted by the images, videos, and blogs across the World Wide Web. As an academic virus with a long ideological past, history seems to have been forced to reinvent itself across American campuses into some kind of multidisciplinary humanities subject that has stretched historiography into the chasm of popular culture. History has become non-history, moving into areas it had not ventured into previously because of the fear of becoming another dinosaur like the departments of philosophy that used to rule university campuses.

The problem of method in globalization is, of course, not limited to history. The social scientific paradigm, the scientific method, and the research of knowledge has for the past 100 years remained a faulty reinvention of itself in order to remain relevant. But in remaining relevant it has lost the romantic value of its past. Marx had deluded himself into thinking that he was some kind of social scientist and his economic theories were skewed and twisted into causing untold misery and death. But Marx had stumbled upon something important. Something that great cultural scholars and political scientists have known all along: the value of any academic discipline is dependent on the base. The superstructure is basically dependent. That survival in the globalized world means going with the flow rather than resisting it. That was the revolution that Marx should have confessed to rather than impatiently calling for the global revolution of workers. While communism was revolting, democracy was reinventing itself as the political ideology of neoliberal economic theory — at least since decolonization in the 1940s to

1960s — and has eventually proven to be the least worst alternative in late modernity. Capitalism is politically dependent on regulated global markets.

Apart from offering some insights into ancient political life, the work of Socrates appears to present a value-added but a romantic and archaic anti-solipsism of "ideal government". Yet Socrates' real monetary beneficiaries are mass market publishers who derive profits from periodically publishing his *The Republic* (collated by his student Plato and re-edited over the centuries by political philosophers and theorists) and other philosophical classics. Publication in the age of globalization has become an important profit centre. The publishing industry dates back to the time of the ancient Chinese, and much later to the time of Johann Gutenberg (1468) who might be considered the Steve Jobs (Apple, 1976; Pixar, 1986) and the William H. Gates (Microsoft, 1975, and Corbis) of fifteenth century Europe for his technical innovation in printing techniques. No one really remembers Gutenberg today or pays much attention to the value of the Gutenberg press. A hundred years ahead of our time, no one may even know who Steve Jobs, Bill Gates, or Walter Cronkite are. Even today, no one easily recalls who invented the Internet or the World Wide Web. But many have benefited from these inventions. Indeed, the power of information transcends the individual inventor in the globalized world of late modernity. One can think of a million teenagers in thousands of cities across the world with more knowledge of science and technology, and with greater urban survival skills than Socrates himself. Plato, Aristotle, Aquinas, Hobbes, Locke, Berkeley, Hume, Vico, Rousseau, de Pizan, Wollstonecraft, Marx, and Weber would have to reconstruct while revising their entire theories if they were alive today. Diachronic change has become the trademark of globalization.

Which philosopher should we read to avoid the calamities that globalization has inflicted upon us? Marx got his theory right but his method wrong. This made his social theory particularly vulnerable to misinterpretation by politicians greedy for self-aggrandizement. So should we believe politicians who are themselves as much the cause of problems as the solution to the problems that they and their predecessors have caused? It is clear to me that people move into politics because they believe that they can make a change, and that they would like to contribute to society. Politicians join politics because they desire the trappings of political power. Or the prestige of receiving special treatment. They may not say that they do, but they certainly want to remain in politics — and to retain political power — for as long as they can. It is very difficult for a politician to voluntarily step down from office because once her or his political voice is no longer captured in the global and/or local media, they will then find another way to get the public's attention, as demonstrated by Mahathir Mohamad, Prem Tinsulanonda, B.J. Habibie, and Megawati Sukarnoputri, for example.

STABILITY AND SUCCESS

A large part of Singapore's success can be attributed to the Economic Development Board (EDB) and its role in the early 1960s to launch Singapore into what former Deputy Prime Minister S. Rajaratnam called, "the global village". He said this almost thirty years before the word globalization had taken academic root, although its economic underpinning had already been established. S. Dhanabalan, a former Singapore cabinet minister and chairman of one of the world's largest investment houses, Temasek Holdings, which is reported to be worth over US$130 billion, said in an interview in late 2007 that, "in many political systems, the politician doesn't rank very far above a second-hand car dealer". A staunch Christian, S. Dhanabalan was the elite Singapore administrative officer in 1961 who was asked to prepare and collate Singapore's policy plans for the EDB built out of the Industrial Promotion Board (IPB). Goh Keng Swee decided to break up the EDB into several different organizations in 1968. When Milton Friedman asked about Singapore's "Plan B" for its economy after separation from Malaysia in 1965, in the absence of a common market, what they all believed back then was that their plan had to work. It was only admitted in 2007 that there was no Plan B. Singapore's success as an Asian economic tiger was in no small part due to the work of politico-economic leaders who eschewed political ideology and cut deeply into the importance of what was formerly known by Asian economic insiders as Singapore's "pragmatic economics". This economic school, which exists in a different form today, was a result of Asia viewing the West very seriously.

Singapore's pragmatic economics involves a post-socialist social welfarism balanced by nationalistic economic tripartism and collective arrangements between the state, businesses, and workers (in that particular order). As Lee Kuan Yew once said, "there is no free lunch". But what he meant also was that no Singaporean should starve or go without his or her basic physiological necessities. At that point in time, "The sole objective was survival. How this was to be achieved, by socialism or free enterprise, was a secondary matter. The answer turned out to be free enterprise, tempered with the socialist philosophy of equal opportunities for education, jobs, health, and housing".[10] Since Goh Chok Tong became Prime Minister and now that Lee's eldest son is Prime Minister, the idea of a socialist philosophy as described by Lee has all but disappeared. New public policies in Singapore continue to adhere to a kind of neo-socialist ideal often mistaken for benign authoritarianism, but suffering no fools either.

Marx's contribution to globalization was the concept of human unity through class disenfranchisement. However, he underestimated the ability of the owners of the factors of production to outwit the masses just as he underestimated the masses' desire for unity and organization. The end of the Cold War was ostensibly marked by the fall of the Berlin Wall in 1989 and signalled the advent of the failure of Western socialism. To make matters worse, Marx did not specify the time period it would take for the shift from one set of political contradictions to the next stage, from capitalism and socialism to the ultimate communist utopia. Marx's faithful followers, Western neoMarxists such as Rosa Luxembourg, Karl Kautsky, Antonio Gramsci, Louis Althusser, and Nicos Poulantzas have been unable to sustain their intellectual influence over politics let alone challenge the widening gyre of Western neoliberal democratic capitalism. Marx cannot be said to be useful as a philosopher in globalization except for being a sounding board for liberal capitalism, a variation on a theme. This is clearly demonstrated in Cuba, China, Vietnam, and North Korea where pragmatic reinterpretations of Marxism, Leninism, and Maoism continue to keep the forces of globalization somewhat at bay.[11]

In the search for a philosopher of globalization, this book has tried but mainly failed to resist recognizing the increasing importance that the adherents of realism, liberalism, and nominalism (the old name for what is ostensibly known as constructivism in political science parlance) have come to play in late modernity. Therefore, it seems insufficient for us to believe, like Nietzsche, that our entire life's goals and achievements begin and end in an eternally recurring soup of nothingness. Nietzsche was too depressed, too insane, even though his intellect reflected nothing less than complete genius. His philosophy cautioned of the dangers of modernity long before the Frankfurt school's Adorno and Horkheimer warned of the dangers of mass consumption. Nietzsche's philosophy of complex layers of intricacy continue to challenge and provoke students in late modernity till each one singularly reaches a point of greatest resistance. In the continuing search for theorists of globalization, we find that Jean Paul Sartre vacillated too much in his early dalliances with communism and the left, and eventually rejuvenated a philosophy of life that was as limited as it was a compelling narrative, a lineage traceable through Heidegger and Wittgenstein, Marx, Hegel, and Kant. Sartre's own contribution to globalization theories of personal politics is his concept of the being-in-itself and being-for-itself appropriated deeply within the vicissitudes of globalization where the importance of the existence of an individual citizen precedes the essence of his or her own being. Perhaps above all is the common accessibility of Foucault's obsession with crime and punishment as discursive platforms for understanding authoritarianism and its agents of discipline as power in late modernity. This is why Foucault features significantly more than other philosophers in this book. Yet all philosophy and philosophers have their value and have something to share with us about the world in which we inhabit.

We live in a world of competing ideals, competing choices, and seemingly competing lifestyles on an increasingly uneven playing field. Advertisements in the globalized marketplace are formulated on trickery and misplaced optimism. Their messages of self actualization and goal achievement conflate hope, freedom, and success of materialism and conspicuous consumption. Indeed, the public sphere has taken on insidiously powerful political languages that capture and determine private lives and personal moments (Rappa, "Modernity and the Politics of the Public", 2002; Rappa, *Modernity and Consumption*, 2002; Rappa and Wee, *Language Policy and Modernity*, 2006). The impact of globalization is not a mistake or fluke of evolution. Modern man created technology for its usefulness. Indeed, globalization seems increasingly tied to an irreverent politics of useful postmodern interventions (Rappa 1998). These are the modern death dances that produce good, bad, positive, negative, neutral, moral, immoral, and amoral circumstances; situations in which one wrong turn can lead into a right one; where riding off into the epistemological sunset is pure ontological kitsch. The postmodern world, living parasitically within modernity, is for the wealthy elites. This is the theoretical confluence where Habermas' sphere of communication seems insufficient; Rorty's bourgeois postmodernity (1983) is indifferent; Stephen White's weak ontology spirits premium; and where Foucault is dramatically ensconced. But the postmodern world is to be enjoyed by the few, if we are to believe Rorty's original position, and the theories of postmodernists continue to appear as laments before the oracle of unknown optimism, hope, and progress. It is wealth that most people are after. Not the theories that explain how it might be derived.

Wealth in this globalized world is concentrated in the hand of the power elite, said C. Wright Mills. Ironically, currencies that were invented to ensure that such wealth circulates upwards to those in power can also bring them down. Wealth and power in globalization creates winners and losers. Momentary winners are celebrated as the true victors in the commoditized globe. But it is momentary success because as our fame and fortune dissipates, so do the condiments of success that surround us. It is a moral dilemma. We need to avoid getting morally entrenched in late modernity. And one way out, apart from death, is to follow the words of the Buddha who urged his followers to seek their own destiny (Rappa, "The Buddha's Last Meal and Nietzsche's Last Supper", 2005). Hence when Sartre said "everything in life has been figured out except how to live it", he was really referring to those who could afford the time and the luxury to think about thinking. But because most people are caught up in the world of consumption's marketing ploys, they become committed too soon and too quickly. Before they know it they are spending the rest of their lives enslaved to vituperous capitalist bankers. That is one kind of loser. The kind that believes that everyone has to be like her or him because the majority is like that anyway and there is no turning back, no escape from the kind of freedom that goes beyond the chain of Eric Fromm's personal demons. There are many other losers in the global picture. Such as the 17-year old Singaporean Chinese teenage blogger who was sentenced to a two-year probation and 180 hours of community service within the Malay ethnic groups he had made racists remarks about. Or Ahmed Abu, a 24-year-old Muslim fanatic from Falls Church, Virginia, who signed a confession after being charged with conspiracy to assassinate U.S. President George Bush with the support of Al-Qaeda. There are more examples of moral losses and losers in globalization: The U.S. marines accused of rape in various parts of the world; the increasing anti-Semitism labelled as the "protocols of Zion"; the murder of Carlo Giuliani by the *carabiniere* who ran over Giuliani's dead body while ironically fleeing from the scene of their own crime during an anti-globalization protest on 20 July 2001; or the story of the 28-year-old Singaporean Malay lecturer and law graduate, Abdul Basheer Abdul Kader, reported in the local news as "a self-radicalized terrorist" in June 2007. Terrorists in the globalized world are well-educated and resourceful. They are skilful at using technology to leverage on the limitations of their resources.

One advantage of technology in the globalized world is that it eventually allows for cheap and market-wide dispersal of its products such as digital camcorders, 3G camera phones, miniature hi-fi and wi-fi systems, and Blu-ray discs. Relatively affordable technology has captured what social, political, and cultural theorists have been warning about for decades: police brutality. Neo-anarchists and social constructivists argue for the necessary evil of the police. Large global populations have led to the need to control the criminal element that prey on innocent, law-abiding citizens. However, there appears to be a strong tendency among police forces to "cover-up" abuse by their own personnel until situations of intimidation and abuse are leaked to the media. Police intimidation is the use of public-legitimized power to cause fear in innocent people. Intimidation involves psychological and emotional abuse, and may lead to physical abuse of persons under detention and away from the public eye. Police brutality involves the physical, emotional, and psychological abuse of citizens by the police. Both intimidation and abuse by police are illustrated in the 1979 Arthur McDuffie case; the 1991 case of Rodney King who was beaten up by three policemen while their supervisor watched. There are other cases of police brutality in South Africa during the worst excess of apartheid politics. In 1995, a U.S. Department of State report stated that a suspect in a burglary case died from injuries during police detention by Royal Malaysian Police; in 1998, a former Malaysian inspector general of police (IGP) allegedly punched former Deputy Prime Minister Anwar Ibrahim on the left side of his forehead while he was in police custody as a crime suspect; and so on. The presence of intimidation and abuse by police forces across the world is indicative of societies that have some form of counter-abusive system in place. These often include constitutionally-guaranteed citizens' rights, the role of investigative journalism, human rights' watchers, and academic scholarship investigating police intimidation and brutality. One thing is clear, any organization empowered with the use of force such as the police and the military will result in intimidation and abuse regardless of institutionalized checks and balances within the political system. Citizens are themselves wary of both illegal acts of terror and illegal acts of police intimidation and brutality. In the age of globalization, the fear of global terrorism has given police, paramilitary, and military units greater powers of arrest and detention and has resulted in creating more avenues for abuse inasmuch as there appear to be more safeguards against abuses by legitimate state organizations. This returns us to the anarchists' warning of statal abuse because of its concentration of political power that Foucault warned us about as seen in the civilized protests versus uncivil-like treatment by the authorities from London to Bangkok.

Late modernity involves the processes of globalizing terror, money, and culture. Globalization links up different aspects of life, in war or in peace. Globalization bonds different events into our globe: ETFs and other indexed stocks, the engineering of biological and chemical weapons in hidden laboratories all over the world, child-labour on Indian farms, African American support for the Clintons, the forgive-and-forget attitude of the American people, and the pardon to 50,000 convicts by King Bumiphon on the sixtieth anniversary of his reign and on his eightieth birthday in December 2007 — all these activities, nice and not so nice, come together in a rough blend of modernity and consumption in peaceful times. We can only limit ourselves to momentarily reminiscing about fallen heroes, forgotten relatives, and public servants because to stop is to admit boredom and death into our lives. The politics of forgetting means that those POWs from the United Kingdom who used to visit Changi Prison Museum and Chapel in Singapore are slowly dwindling. The number of years away from 1945 increases stealthily as these former prisoners return to say their last goodbyes to comrades long forgotten, whose memories will end with the lives of those who could remember. Then only the scars and experiences of the war years will be able to present the memories in museums to visitors who will no longer have any attachment to that past; where visitors will no longer know what it was like to be at the receiving end of Japanese water torture except from the old photographs at the Eurasian Association Community House or the Changi Prison Memorial Chapel and Museum in Singapore, for example.[12] And once these museums stop receiving guests and visitors, once the novelty of place and memory have evaporated, and once they stop making money, the place will disappear, like graves that are exhumed and their beautiful marble features destroyed forever.

Notes

[1] See James C. Scott, *Seeing Like A State: How Certain Schemes to Improve the Human Condition Have Failed* (Yale University Press, 1998) and Jean Elshtain, *Just War Theory: Readings in Social and Political Theory* (NYU Press, 1991).
[2] Willy Lam, "China Cracks Taiwan 'Spy Ring'", CNN, 24 December 2003.
[3] See Chunli Bai, "Ascent of Nanoscience in China", *Science* 309, 5731 (July 2005): 61–63.
[4] According to its website, "The Independent Police Complaints Commission (IPCC) became operational on 1 April 2004. It is a Non-Departmental Public Body (NDPB), funded by the Home Office, but by law entirely independent of the police, interest groups and political parties and whose decisions on cases are free from government involvement. We have a legal duty to oversee the whole of the police complaints system, created by the Police Reform Act 2002, our aim is to transform the way in which complaints against the police are handled." See <http://www.ipcc.gov.uk/index/about_ipcc.htm>.
[5] "Domestic Sales Aid Japan's Growth", BBC News World Edition, 11 November 2005. There was significant improvement by the end of March 2006, where the BBC reported that "Japan's economy grew by 3.2%, its fastest rate of expansion in 15 years".
[6] Bloomberg News, 11 November 2005. This amount is expected to hit US$200 billion by the first quarter of 2008, according to Chinese sources. Western media and financial experts predict much lower volumes.
[7] BBC News, 8 November 2005.
[8] Between 2003 and till the time of the September 2006 coup, the Thaksin government wavered between negotiations and harsh suppression of Islamic

radicals in the southern Thai provinces. This, however, had little to do with his ouster by Surayud Chulanont in late 2006, and everything to do with the age-old contest between the centuries old differences between Muslims and Buddhists in Southeast Asia.

9   Social scientists from Thammasat University, Chulalongkorn University, Phitsanulok, and Bangkok (2007 to 2008).
10 Lee Kuan Yew, speech at the 26th World Congress of the International Chamber of Commerce, 5 October 1978.
11 I have consistently been less interested in fledgling communist movements in the Philippines, Thailand, Malaysia, and South Asia than in the theories that govern their existence. But I am confident that I live in ignorance of many great Chinese, Indian, Korean, Vietnamese, and Cuban Marxist theorists whose work have influenced many lives since the People's Revolutions of the 1940s and 1950s, but only because I have not read them yet. This is offered as an explanation of a widening gap in my own reading of Marxist epistemology as a global phenomenon.
12 Antonio L. Rappa, *Saudade: The Portuguese Roots of Eurasian Communities in Singapore and Malaysia* (Singapore: Institute of Southeast Asian Studies, 2008).

10

END THOUGHTS

In the first edition of this book, the themes of hope, optimism, and progress were examined in Asia and America based on a distinction between Americanization and globalization within a neoliberal capitalist world order. The second edition, *Globalization: Power, Authority and Legitimacy* analyses how a new pessimism has descended on the globalized world. The America that was once the bastion of hope, optimism, and progress is now showing clear signs of a superpower in decline. The first sign of the American decline since 1941 in Pearl Harbor was the destruction of the World Trade Center in New York City on 11 September 2001. The other signs are the "Vietnamization" of Iraq, a nuclear stand-off with North Korea, increasing trade imbalances with China and India, a stalemate with terrorists in Afghanistan, the challenge of European protectionism, a belligerent politics in the Middle East, overt American dependence on oil and fossil fuels, and the mushrooming of various sub-prime crises into an escalating global recession. This second edition incorporates the latest developments in terms of culture, wealth, and terrorism around the world and provides possible solutions to salvage the American Dream. *Globalization* began with several assumptions. Firstly, the American public has become beholden to the U.S. government and that the latter made unilateral policy decisions that did not reflect the views of the public. In late modernity, that dependence has expanded to include many non-Americans. Secondly, the mismeasurement of cultural tropes existing in late modernity has entrenched neoliberal capitalist structures and embedded financial problems that emerge when the cracks occur at the surface. The most recent spate of cracks that led to Black October was the U.S. sub-prime crisis. It was a crisis ignored because Bush and his administrators were bogged down with discovering or inventing weapons of mass destruction as well as fighting hidden terrorists in Iraq and Afghanistan.

On the home front, the powerful superpower in decline sometimes reveals its economic underbelly. America would not be able to function without illegal Mexican workers. Nevertheless, the U.S. Senate has approved the building of a state-of-the-art, triple-layered fence worth US$8 billion that is about 800 miles long for the 1,900 mile long U.S.-Mexico border. This plan seems ill-conceived and does not take into account the complex history of Hispanic Americans, non-Hispanic Americans, and Native Americans in late modernity. The rush to lower labour costs in the United States has led to American entrepreneurs devising new and creative ways of legally avoiding overheads, or at least lowering them. The earlier chapters have shown how money is made in the United States and how profits are derived overseas in tax-free shelters. We also saw how the problem of back-room operations and other service related work are outsourced overseas, and how foreign illegal workers are willing and able to work for less than minimum wages. This tells us several things. Firstly, the structure of the U.S. economy is weakened by the number of wars that it has conducted and the fact that individual American citizens are the world's largest debtors. Hence the accumulation deficit crunch overshadows the economy. Apart from debt, U.S. companies have to survive within a highly regulated system of bureaucratic structures that are restricted by high wages, union regulations, and environmental controls. This makes U.S. companies less viable and flexible under the pressure of globalization. The automotive industry and the airline industry are two examples of companies that have to compete with state, federal, and international laws governing emissions standards and foreign market requirements in addition to the high sunk technological costs. Secondly, the U.S. public is divisive and fractured along a range of divergent ideological lines. These differences cannot be easily captured by demographic surveys and tend to change at a high rate, thereby making survey data obsolete within the short to medium terms. Additionally, the reliance on exit polls, Gallup polls, Harris polls, and other impressionistic assessments that try to capture data at the cusp of change provides a vague and often skewed image of the political situation. Thirdly, the U.S. media is posited on the profit motive and while media idealists argue for the objective of accurate and unbiased reporting, the media tends to focus on events and situations that sell their stories and raise their ratings rather than documentaries and debates over the Public Broadcasting Service and CSPAN.

While the U.S. media MNCs play a critical role as political watchdogs over errant politicians, the media themselves are not free from internal politicking within their own organizational structures. On the other hand,

PBS documentaries tend to educate their viewers for the long term but most viewers appear to prefer to spend an average of eight hours a day on entertainment channels, sports, soaps, game shows, sitcoms, reality television, talk shows, and limited blips of foreign and local news reports. Hence the shaping of public opinion and identity is constructed over time by hundreds of different channels over broadcast television, network TV, radio, talk radio, and by changing patterns of consumer choices. This worsens the divisive nature of the public so that no single public can possibly exist, it would seem. Let us assume that (1) most Americans watch television; (2) most Americans rely on television for their information about the world and to be entertained; (3) only a minority of American viewers watches PBS, CSPAN; (4) only a minority of Americans read the serious articles in established newspapers such as the *New York Times* or the *Wall Street Journal*. This means that the limited content of serious news garnered by the average American viewer is restricted to the talking-heads of newscasters, information blips, and one-line ticker-tape and crawler messages. How much can the public, with all its ideological divisions, economic constraints, and entertainment distractions, really care about the rest of the world? Why should they care as a whole? So therefore it comes to no one's surprise that the Republicans were swept into power on a restricted information diet of images of terror and xenophobia. It would be churlish and ungracious for anyone to conclude that all Americans were so easily swayed by the state. Indeed the problem seems to be similar in any modern civilization.

The thinkers and intellectuals constitute a fragment of society and are hardly able to influence the masses. This also means that any single person who tries to establish rapport with the masses must become a politician. But being a politician means playing to the audience and those who constitute the majority of the audience. Hence Jesse Helms, Pat Robertson, and Pat Buchanan continue to have many supporters and fans not because their politics are superior but because the majority of American conservatives align themselves with their ideas in order to safeguard what has become their idea of the American way of life. And it is politically clear that at this point in time, America remains entrenched within the conservative stronghold. This has little to do with the fact that America is an ageing society and that people tend to become more conservative with age. Rather, the role of the media and the preferences of the viewers have shaped the current identities that dominate the public domain and have indeed become symbolic of the public itself. In order to reach out to the people, a politician must be able to reduce his or her own ideas and thoughts into small bite-sized pieces for easy consumption, and that is something that will convey less than half of what the truth might approximate. The American public is fractured with different fissures and cracks that make it seem complicit with American motives overseas.

Fifty years ago the amount of information available to individual citizens was limited by old fashioned and sluggish means to discover it. Today, information is virtually served to us in various guises and exists at the tips of our fingers — from the Internet to our palm pilots and cellular phones. The problem of information overload is precisely what it is described as — too much information within a brief period of time, therefore making it virtually impossible to make sense of anything before the next event occurs.

THE PARADOX OF POWER POLITICS

Some of our greatest achievements this century accompany our worst fears: poverty, terrorism, viruses, diseases, psychoses, clinical dependency, future uncertainty, cultural insecurity, unemployment, failure, debt, pessimism, and loss. This was represented in this book by Foucault's *Ship of Fools*. Seen from the perspective of Asia, a view that is as far away from the United States as is geographically possible, the picture of globalization meets the metaphorical symbolism of the *Ship*. If we gaze at the ship long enough, the layers that make up its construction begin to unravel, and we start to understand Foucault's much maligned subject.[1]

Jean Baudrillard extended the *Ship* metaphor in his *Simulacra et Simulacrum* when he wrote about the "end of the panopticon". By this he meant that technology in the globalized world had attained such dramatic proportions as to provide unlimited access to several original starting points; that human life and activity is not only viewed and controlled from a single panoptic perspective, but from multiple ones. Foucault himself treated the idea of the panopticon as a structural device, a functional method of keeping up a permanent gaze over the prisoner in *Discipline and Punish: The Birth of the Prison*. Further back in history, John Stuart Mill's reinvention of the panopticon enabled a single gatekeeper with the all-seeing eye of a demi-god that controlled and watches over us all. Baudrillard, Foucault, and Mill all have one theme in common — they come together in making a distinction between two types of people in modernity. One type desires exhibitionism, and the other desires voyeurism. Globalization is political because it is the net effect of gazes that enhance the meaning of exhibitionism and the voyeurism across the world. We see this in marketing, advertising, public calls to attention for beheading, talking heads, weddings, funerals, baptisms, and birthday parties. We are knowingly and, often, unknowingly held victim to the public gaze of authorities and the coercive structures that we invent to protect us from our own kind.

In attempting to promote peace, life, liberty, happiness, hope, optimism, and progress across the world, America's role since the Louisiana Land Purchase and the acquisition of Alaska from Czarist Russia in 1867 has seen the unintended consequence of promoting war, death, incarceration, sadness, hopelessness, pessimism, and regression across the globe. American men and women have paid the ultimate price for American involvement in defending the free world but in that defence, in Korea, Vietnam, the Middle East, and in Latin America, the world has not always accepted the kind of democratic practices that the United States has imposed upon these places. Czarist Russia offered to sell off Alaska to the Americans in 1859 and with the defeat after the Crimean War it became even more imperative that the Czar stave off burning a candle at both ends. The balance of power in those days was highly tilted towards the British as a world naval power. British power was so extensive in those days that I would eventually be educated at a Christian missionary school as a result of British power far away from the British Isles. The school was set up by the Christian Brothers in 1852 and named St. Joseph's Institution, on the tiny, backwater island called Temasek (Singapore) that most people had not heard about since its "discovery" by Stamford Raffles in 1819. The year 1819 marked the end of the Xhosa War with Britain, the end of the Seminole War with America, and the American decision on the Florida Purchase. There are many Americans who prefer to forget the horror and death that was brought about by America in its neo-imperial quest. The ideals of life, liberty, and happiness that brought the early Americans together against the Red Coats of King George would ironically be pursued under America's quest for global supremacy. This is not to say that the world has not benefited from Pax Americana. And there are many reasons for remembering that neoliberalism in the post-9/11 era is a much lesser evil than the kind of political ideology that the Soviets were espousing had they won the Cold War.

LEGITIMACY AND THE GLOBAL GAZE

The power of the Foucauldian gaze is itself a reminder of the other kinds of political derivations that we have experienced in modernity and continue to experience as experience itself, the being of being as an anthology of the arrested self. The deference to expert counsel, the importance of the scientific event, the mercy killing of medical science, the need for pharmaceutical drugs that dominate through the false camouflage of highly paid public relations executives who guarantee turning water into wine. The old modernity's dependence on science and technology that Martin Heidegger anticipated and Henry S. Kariel warned about, reveals much about the extent and depth of the new modernity's tentacular forms of control over our daily lives. There are uppers and lowers — drugs to make you high, stoned, forget, or remember. There are so many kinds and variations within the global political economy of drugs that after two decades of exposure to the international pharmaceutical giants, we have become as much dependent on them as they are on us. The gaze of the giant pharmacies have been returned with the blank and empty stares of people in late modernity who have been over-medicated, self-medicated, and over-dosed their boredom-filled lives with the reckless cacophony of competing streams of information.

How many of us now alive and well in the late urban, post-advanced industrial suburbs of a luxurious life really care about the wondering and suffering masses whose own lives hang on a thin thread of our decisions; whose worthless lives disappear vapidly into the swirling pool of Nietzschean cultural abysses sometimes mistaken for a balanced life of work and play? If you managed to watch television last night, it would be remarkable if you could recall the main stories that were headlined on the screen. It would be remarkable if you could recall the pain or the anguish that you might have felt at seeing innocent lives being wasted, or the joy of witnessing youthful playfulness with hope and promise in the local kindergartens and classrooms. It would be even more remarkable if you even remembered telling yourself that tomorrow was going to be another and a better day. But it would have been most remarkable if you said that you did not recall anything at all, and did not bother to remember because you believe that there is really nothing good on television. And that Neil Postman was really amusing himself as he thought of our cultural ends dipping their feelers into the quagmire of a Nixonian death dance — perfectionism till the end. Kant and Hegel may have anticipated the great cosmological motifs that they believed dominated the universal and moral landscapes of philosophy. And they must have gone happily to death because they thought that they were on to something really powerful, and really unique, something that had never had an original starting point, or an image of a simulated past.

But is there hope in late modernity and can all the convictions of past practice convince us that we ought to return to ourselves and know where we stand, know what grounds us and are sufficiently knowledgeable about our own weaknesses and strengths to want to embark on that journey of optimism, hope, and progress? It is one thing to think that the post-Enlightenment world is a large and duplicitous deceit; a matrix of confusion that has been cunningly concealed and contrived to convince us of the plausibility of reality and the certitude of truth. But it is quite another to take the urban and legendary bull by the horns and admit to ourselves that we are indeed the inheritors of a great destiny, a great people, a positive and a real future that admits no boundary or structure can bend us from living life to the fullest. We do not really need to build bridges to the eighteenth century as Postman argues, but bridges that can withstand the weight of late modernity as we know it today. We do not need the textbook histories and confidence tricksters who would have us believe in solid ground but in the kind of controversial and interrogative methods used by Foucault and less ordinarily and more conventionally by writers such as Marshall Sahlins, Henri Lefebvre, David Harvey, and Zygmunt Bauman.

Similarly, one would want to consider carefully before being convinced by the latter-day prophets in the work of Aldous Huxley, Michael Mann, D.H. Lawrence, Zhang Yimou, George Santayana, George Orwell, Louis Hartz, Gabriel Garcia Marquez, Akira Kurosawa, Paul McCartney, Carl Sagan, and especially Salman Rushdie. We ought to be forewarned about these prophets of modernity because their moral epistemologies — through fiction, film, or fact — are genuine, too authentic, too clever, and too believable. Their work has come to be too readily accessible to the mass marketplace of modernity and consumption. And each of these writers has savagely vindicated the possibility of man's propensity for failure at his own hands, all by himself. In other words, their books are too optimistic to really be read in broad daylight, and are therefore too blinding for globalization viewed from any other part of the world. Yet they continue to exist at the top of the trade and in fact revealed interesting values about globalization through their stories and methodical disjuncture. The Asian view would warrant a longer list of non-English sounding names whose ethnic ancestry would gravitate towards syntax and symbols that trace the global picture for East Asia, the Pacific Rim, New Zealand, and Australia. There are simply too many books that try to explain the view of America from the outside in qualitative terms or through quantitative analyses. These books share the clear and purposive direction of all modern texts, aims, objectives, definitions, frameworks for analyses, charts, diagrams, illustrations, and conclusions.

Globalization appears to be shifting us periodically, knowingly, incrementally towards some predestined place and time. We are not necessarily in agreement with the direction of the globe because we really have not many choices for all that is said and done in modernity. There are problems in the *Ship of Fools* because everyone thinks that someone is steering the ship, some people have noticed people steering the ship, and still others think that someone ought to be steering the ship. But there may not be anyone at all in the wheel-house, and the ship is really moving fast and purposefully with all the verve and deliberateness of a new-found faith. These accounts were demonstrated through the various quotes on Sahlin's argument on the multiple searches for the origins in the apotheosis of a colonial sea-master to the death, and Harvey's Weberian-influenced linear delineation of the condition of postmodernity contrast heavily with Lefebvre's contentious predictions about terrorism in his *Everyday Life in the Modern World* (Transaction 1984) and Zygmunt Bauman's reinvention of modernity from gas, to solid to its liquid states are all remarkably detailed and well thought out conceptualizations of globalization from within the "United" something or other. These works bear the imprint of powerful diatribes against the urban legends that have returned from the rapid turning of pages over the past sixty years into a political reality that confronts us in life-like images in the newspapers on a daily basis.

Globalization appears to centre on a political paradox of taking in the good and bad without being able to tell them apart. Like the philosophical moralism of Aldous Huxley or the first and last postmodern film of Akira Kurosawa. It is like voting for the Republican or Democratic parties and hoping that some of our grassroots ideals will be attained and some of our fears vindicated. Globalization involves the sexual innuendoes of Lawrence's wicked novels that have been recast incorrectly and by mistake in the films of a Michael Mann intoxicated with the beauty and power of love in the time of cholera in a soliloquy about the directionless textual motifs of late modernity. The central paradox of the politics of American globalization is that American citizens are left responsible and vulnerable as targets because they have been continuously betrayed by their own governments that they never really elected except through some neutralizing platform and dehumanizing mechanism. Some people call this the Electoral College. Others blame the Senate or the House of Representatives.

Let us recapitulate the paradox of American politics that has impacted modernity. Most Americans since 1945 have not voted for the kinds of politicians and the kind of policies that have come out of American government, but still pay the price for being American anyway. This is why Americans seem to believe in one thing but their government appears to be doing something else.

THE AUTHORITY OF AYN RAND

Ayn Rand was influential in New York among the socialites and Republican crème de la crème. Her "analytical philosophy", camouflaged under the guise of "objectivism", belied her libertarian economic beliefs. The Republican Party supporters loved it. Rand lived through the people that she influenced most, and most of them seemed to have attained high positions in American life. If there was anyone who has tried to achieve greatness as her ideal man in *Atlas Shrugged* (1957), it was Alan Greenspan. Greenspan was to work under many American presidents and became one of her most ardent fans and a cherished and favoured supporter. The problem is that Rand by all accounts is an economic idealist. Like the idealist hero in *Atlas Shrugged*, Rand's vision of the ideal could only be attained through rationality. For her, objectivity is best promoted through economic libertarianism. Rand was great at understanding some parts of the big picture of business but poor on its mathematical aspects and even worse about predicting the performance of economic markets. Perhaps this was why she was such a convincing novelist, as seen in *The Fountainhead* (1943) and the bestseller, *Atlas Shrugged*. This means that a significant aspect of her philosophy lacked making sense of the kind of data available to her when she was alive. But this was not even a big problem in her philosophy.

The biggest problem was her trust in the kinds of assumptions that she made about economic markets, more specifically, the free market. Her philosophy has been twisted out of its weakness to support what is ostensibly touted as the free market but what is in effect a democratically controlled, regulated, and contrived market. The "free" aspect of the market has nothing to do with that dubious phrase, "the invisible hand". The "free" dimension of the free market refers to neoliberalism and neoliberal capital across the globe. But how do we get to go across the globe? This is where the democratically controlled aspect rides into the arena. In other words, as long as a country is willing and able to accept the fable of the democratic free market, it can join the club or remain in fear of being intimidated and bullied into opening up its markets. To wit, Atlas merely shrugged. He could not get rid of the weight. But what kind of democracy does neoliberalism offer? We can see that the absence of a proper training in philosophy has misled Rand and her disciples who have tried vigorously to promote her as a philosopher in ways that Arendt never needed help. Rand is not on the compulsory reading lists of the major centres of philosophy, not even economic philosophy. But her name was raised in this concluding chapter to revise the value of her street worthiness as a philosopher of sorts. Since Greenspan and others seemed so taken in by her, she has indirectly influenced the nature of the American political economy and hence the politics of its causeway to globalization.

POWER, AUTHORITY, LEGITIMACY: ONE MAN, ONE VOTE

The politics of American globalization is not about the "one-man, one-vote" system. Instead, the democratic dimension of American globalization revolves round the "one-dollar, one-vote" manifesto popularized by the former pro-Republican satirist Arianna Huffington.[2] Money buys votes and as long as players within the public politics of American globalization are willing to remain within the idiom of the American Dream[3] — dramatically supported by its variegated global popular cultures, a willingness to wage war, defended and propped up by the U.S. military in the pursuit of life, liberty, and the pursuit of happiness — and to go to the fullest extent of which the law does not expressly forbid. But Huffington is being too harsh. People need hope, optimism, and progress in this post-Enlightenment world, but not the kind of so-called objectivism that Rand provided. Yet, ironically, Rand gave to the world a kind of street-level philosophy of elitism that enabled the layman to think that he actually had a hand in changing the economy through free-market libertarianism when in fact all they were doing was buying her popular novel(s). If Rand had not influenced Greenspan's conservatism, America would have taken bigger risks and would have achieved much more materially than it has today. Part of the problem of the politics of American globalization is that no one knows who is going to become the next power holder and no one can predict the next set of elites that will take hold of political power or economic power in America.

> How do we know when irrational exuberance has unduly escalated asset values which then become the subject of unexpected and prolonged contractions as they have in Japan over the past decade? (Greenspan, 1996)

The former chairman of the U.S. Federal Reserve Board admits that he was very concerned about speculation in the stock market in 1996. A few months later in the summer of 1997, the Asian financial crisis struck. He does have some sense of the impending gloom of the immediate future. In testifying before a congressional committee in mid-April 2004, Greenspan said that no one knows the number of illegal immigrants in the country. What they have at best is an estimate. However, they do know that the payroll data and the family income data surveys have matching results. He deduced that the value of the illegal work must be captured by either survey since both surveys have the same result. He also said that it would be a major step ahead in their statistical methods if they manage to figure out the illegal migrant issue. This is clearly a situation where there are problems with the statistical methods used, and perhaps the wrong instruments are being used to compute something that these instruments are not designed to capture. Greenspan also said that there are no indications of wide-scale inflationary pressures. And he did support permanent tax cuts in 2002. He also suggested that Social Security be cut in order to solve the problems that the Republicans and the Democrats have created since the end of World War II. What does it mean when influential economic proctors like Greenspan represents both the problems and the solutions of American neoliberal capitalism?

THE POWER OF THE VAINGLORIOUS

Certainly, there are political and economic institutions for controlling the Foucauldian gaze. But an intimate knowledge of these formal institutions flowing from the checks and balances system and the structure of shared powers that were created by the founding fathers only leads to higher levels of bureaucratic knowledge. Bureaucratic knowledge is limiting because someone who is intimately knowledgeable about the red tape in a system can only quote more red tape. This was what Foucault meant when he referred to the decentring and then the recentring of the author. Foucault did not mean that we should do away with authors because they were clearly part of the entire set of discursive formations that revelled in society. Rather, that the author — whether s/he was armed with the power of bureaucratic knowledge or not — should take a sidestep and not be made the focal point of power relations. Yet if we look at any of the Washington crowd of high powered attorneys and MNC CEOs with Wall Street accomplishments, to the senatorial class of regenerative political families, we immediately know that the author is surviving well in spite of public necessities and public problems. Each vainglorious politician and political hopeful, to borrow a phrase from Thomas Hobbes' *Leviathan* (1651), hopes to achieve more than the fifteen minutes of fame prophesized by the twisted brilliance of Andy Warhol. This makes alignment with popular but nonsensical and elitist authors like Rand a clear strategy in itself? However, the politics of American globalization and its norms, values, and rules have been influenced more directly by other writers than Rand. Rand's effect on the politics of American globalization was indirect. However, there are those within the academe who have directly affected America's process of globalization. One of them never even saw America. Adam Smith's highly influential book, *An Inquiry into the Nature and Causes of the Wealth of Nations* (Oxford University Press 1975) also available as the *Wealth of Nations* (Penguin 1982; Modern Library 1994) presupposes the continuing existence of an inordinate mechanism known as the "invisible hand". The "invisible hand" seemed politically resolute. Its role was to resolve all the problems and questions of the economy and hence of civilizational survival. If you needed food, the market mechanism and the "invisible hand" would provide it for a fee. If you needed clothing or exotic wares, same thing, you would go to the market. The idea of the "invisible hand" and the "free market mechanism" became so popular among the elite that it actually seemed to work. The culminating point of these successes, inventions, and economic activities in the West was called the Industrial Revolution. The "invisible hand" of Smith is felt throughout the neoliberal capitalist world. Smith's ideas have in fact outlasted many of the criticisms of his peers and those who came later. Apart from his economic idealism as the *economic advent* of over two hundred years (and counting), the most important reason why Smith has become so influential is that his work is so old and crusty that it has been whittled down to its very bare assumptions and continues to be twisted this way and that by economic libertarians, Republicans, Democrats, and greedy neoliberal capitalists on the ascent.

Therefore Smith's work has an impact on the process of politics in American globalization because of its idealism and its distance from today's global macroeconomy. He achieves this effect in a way that Rand could not. Rather than the value of his microeconomic theories and concepts, Smith's farsighted vision provides the politics of American globalization with "hope", "optimism", and "progress". These are the three central values of the politics of American globalization. These are the three values that will propel America to selfish individualism and vulgar material achievement regardless of how many times the Al-Qaeda, the CIA-trained Osama bin Laden, the Abu Sayyaf, and the Jemaah Islamiah rear their ugly heads. But like Frankenstein of Mary Shelley's novel of the same name, America has to come to terms with the monster that it has been mainly responsible for creating. The sooner that Americans realize that these terrorists are Cold War relics who now have personal grievances to resolve, the faster will the paranoia that is clouding the United States subside and fade away. The terrorists are not as organized as Americans think they are. It is the media that gives some semblance of organization and cohesion in their up-to-the-minute updates to ensure that they too survive the politics of American globalization.

The terrorists have to be made redundant so that the focal point of debate and discussion can continue to centre — not on the authors and talking heads — but on the three values that are propelling America towards greater selfish individualism and vulgar materialism. Greed is very important, according to the neoliberal capitalists, for without which there would be no American global economy and political scientists would have much less work to do. It would appear that there are significant reasons for giving moral support to these neoliberal capitalists, since there does not seem to be any viable alternative in modernity thus far. Neoliberalism is like the war in the Middle East. It will never end as long as the oil is there. And since the only viable alternative — socialism — exploded in ethnic violence across Eastern Europe at the end of the Cold War and only manifested unaccountable greed and corruption among the top communist leaders. Over the past fifteen years since the end of the Cold War, ostensibly with the fall of the Berlin Wall, the former communist cadres have slowly been reinventing themselves as neocapitalists of a new American age. Human beings have achieved so much failure up till now, and it is sad to think that no one has truly come up with a viable and practical alternative to it. But life must go on despite the drawbacks of the system. Perhaps by understanding its core values, its norms and rules, and its main weaknesses we can create a newer and better system.

AUTHORITY ACTING AGAINST TERRORISM

Terrorists are wrong because they do not know what they want except to destroy what most sane people desire. They hate the ideals of hope, optimism, and progress and are entirely against big business in America because they can never be part of that American Dream. They are callous and unfeeling not because they possess some superior political philosophy but because they have marginalized themselves.

Nevertheless, what seems more interesting despite all that pessimism is that the three values of "hope, optimism, and progress" are also central to motivating the rest of the neoliberal capitalist world as we know it today. This represents the politics of global economic mimicry writ large. The world today is about innovation, reverse engineering, blatant imitation of ideas, concepts and products that seem original. The global village concept has been one that continues to grow and give birth to new ways of getting round government restrictions, loopholes in regional and international agreements, copyright laws, and new ways of making great imitations of overpriced and overvalued merchandise. Modernity no longer needs the management advice of Peter Drucker and his failed attempt at explaining anything when he wrote *The End of Economic Man* (Transaction 1939) and the *Age of Discontinuities* (1968). Modernity needs to listen more carefully and attentively to the politics of Noam Chomsky. Look for example, without prejudice, at his work titled, *Hegemony or Survival: America's Quest for Global Dominance (The American*

Empire Project) (Metropolitan 2003) and you will understand better the meaning of America's sorrow.

Despite his age and celebrity status, Drucker has managed to reinvent himself repeatedly to the signs of the changing times. The politics of re-inventing government and economic productivity by Ted Gaebler and David Osborne in their aptly misnamed, *Reinventing Government: How the Entrepreneurial Spirit is Transforming the Public Sector* (Addison-Wesley 1992), or Thomas Friedman's *Lexus and the Olive Tree: Understanding Globalization* (Anchor 2000) and his *Longitudes and Attitudes: The World in the Age of Terrorism* (Anchor 2003) were no less U.S.-centric, capitalistically self-serving, and onerously preachy, and not the much vaunted guides to globalization and everything else they are supposed to be.

Enter Samuel Huntington's remarkable best-selling *Clash of Civilizations and the Remaking of World Order* (Touchstone 1996) that paved the way for more Fukuyama-type work. Huntington proved finally to the American public that he was capable of glossing over minority cultures and zoom in on what he thought were the pre-eminent cultures that would dominate the world. However, many of the problems of the simplistic arguments in his *Clash of Civilizations and the Remaking of World Order* were glossed over and perhaps even corrected by a more intellectually convincing version that he co-edited with Peter L. Berger called *Many Globalizations: Cultural Diversity in the Contemporary World* (Oxford University Press 2003). Based on the work of less-than-prominent authors, Huntington illustrates once again his prowess as an editor and of work done for his functional array of books, as seen in the Kovacs chapter on Hungary and the Kellner one on Germany. The most provocative aspect was the final part of the book by Hunter and Yates. Perhaps if we could recommend a book that contains some interesting views, this might be the book, although readers are warned that it repeats its own caution about globalization's steadfast promise of remaining with us from here to eternity.

Globalization is indeed not here to stay forever. But the politics of globalization and the politics of American globalization will continue to manifest itself across the globe for much longer than Smith, Rand, Friedman, Huntington and others think it will. The secret is that neoliberal capitalism has finally found its new enemy, now that the Soviet bear is gone, while China and India look too promising as neoliberal markets to destroy militarily through an arms race. The new enemy of neoliberal capitalism is in fact a bugbear from the Cold War. "International" terrorism is the new enemy. Despite its Islamic front, it is not an Islamic-only organization. There are many marginalized Americans who have converted to Islam despite being raised on a diet of American popular culture and who have now come under the shadow of suspicion of the American public. This is not surprising. The politics of American globalization and its influence on the world stage can only make it legitimate if the American leadership takes cognizance of the extent of the real problems that plague the world today: poverty, the widening divide between the rich and the poor, terrorism, AIDS, and environmental degradation through the burning of fossil fuels.

THE ILLEGITIMATE ROOT OF WAR: OIL

The beauty of the American system is that the crooks eventually get found out. Perhaps one could say that such a system is missing in draconian, authoritarian states where the entire system must break down and fail before the crooks are exposed completely as seen in Marcos' Philippines, the Soviet Union, the Shah's Iran, and Saddam Hussein's Iraq.

The chapter on war in this book examined the problems associated with American global commitment to its neoliberal ideological design that ostensibly facilitates the democratic transformation across the world. How far true can this be from an America that is struggling to keep its international debt down, its currency afloat, and its citizens safe? To what degree can Americans themselves trust their own governments when it takes years if not decades for the legitimate system of checks and balances to run its course? What do we really know about the war in Iraq today and how might it be related to oil and the Cold War? The following story tells us about the CIA involvement in propping up and bringing down foreign governments. But it also reveals much about what has been taken for granted about the American way of life.

Honest, hardworking, taxpaying Americans who dutifully vote for their governments have little control over the kinds of decisions that their democratically elected representatives take on their behalf. The primaries are often considered standard benchmarks for the outcome of presidential nominees, but the extent to which these nominated leaders are capable of effectively marshalling the resources of political office is an entirely different ball game from the process of getting elected. This is why the distance between idealistic promises and actual political delivery in policy terms appears to be both wide and at times misleading. The American voter ought to expect clarity and purposefulness during the hustings. The most idealized versions of any political mandate ought to be articulated in the run-up to the polls. However, as we have seen, this is much more complex a problem than it appears on the surface. The political candidate in American modernity has to satisfy the basic funding issues to gain sufficient exposure in the public space. But such exposure also means that long forgotten events and incidents in the candidate's life are subject to scrutiny.

At the level of presidential candidates, there are considerably greater pressures on the person in question to take a stand about, for example, the foreign policy direction towards the Middle East, or the real military and economic threat posed by the People's Republic of China. The presidential candidate also has to be aware about past and present political benefactors and those politicians already in the milieu who might support one aspect of a programme but not others. There are many aspects to any one bill before the Houses of Congress, and many more miniscule aspects to the way in which it passes into law. Even in the construction of bills to be passed, the meaning of a law might be debatable. There are variances in interpretation by the candidate, the senior senators, congresspersons, chairs of congressional committees, ordinary members of the candidate's political party, and the mass media.

Then there is the American public and the perceived demands of the American people — different people with different views, changing across time and space. Since 2002, Kerry showed himself to be a democratic hawk. However, when word got out that the Democratic caucuses wanted an anti-war candidate, he began back-paddling. This resulted in his flip-flopping on whether he was for or against the war in Iraq. He was at first against the US$87 billion supplementary budget for the war and then voted for it. On the other hand, the administration of the Republican incumbent George W. Bush misled Americans with regard to the weapons of mass destruction. No wonder Americans prefer to uphold the old adage, "In God We Trust, Everyone Else Pays Cash".

In 1979, the Shah of Iran was forced to go into exile by a revolutionary Islamic groundswell against his fifty-seven-year-old regime. The Shah, or emperor, had virtually ruined the Iranian economy through a systematic squandering of national resources on cronyism and nepotism; torturing of dissidents by the Savak or Iranian secret police; acrimonious business deals with British, French, and U.S. oil companies; and widespread corruption among Islamic leaders, local and foreign businessmen, family members of the Shah, the military, and the government. Two years after the Shah's fall, U.S. Executive Order 12284 raised "Restrictions on the Transfer of Property of the Former Shah of Iran", as noted in the *American Journal of International Law* 75, no. 2 (1981): 431–32. This indicated the extent and depth of the wealth owned by the former monarch in America.

During his reign, the Shah was caught in a complex political triangle involving the United States, the United Kingdom, France, and several Arab nations. He was also torn by growing disaffection within his autocratic regime and haunted by his own indecision and political compromises that dogged him till the very end. At one point in the mid-1970s it appeared that he was courting the French with a US$4 billion deal that would resolve some of France's economic problems and in return France promised delivery of five nuclear reactors. Ironically, France was also home to the Islamic ideologue and widely respected Islamic cleric Ayatollah Khomeini, who would eventually be swept into power by the pressures from the Islamic groundswell against the Shah's regime. Mohammed Reza Pahlavi the Shah thought he had the Americans in the palm of his hand, but the Americans thought that it was the other way round. So did the French. And the Soviets had their own agenda. In many ways, so did the CIA. American intelligence agents were already deeply embedded in Iranian society after World War II. The Americans also feared that without the Shah, the American economy that was virtually built on oil would be irrevocably disrupted. This was also the Cold War era. The Soviets hated the fact that American interests could be protected by the Shah so close to their long geographical border with Iran. The Shah ultimately was a Cold War pawn, but his fall saw the rise of more problems for America and confirmed the death knell for many future American soldiers who would fight in the two Gulf Wars in 1990 and in 2003. The Shah himself had other plans. He toured India, Pakistan, and Singapore to establish warm ties with countries that needed oil. He lived in great splendour in the tradition of his ancestors. He was adored and loved by many within Iran and across the world.

The British Government continued to control much of the Iranian economy after 1945. The popular Islamic lawyer, Mohammed Mossadeq, was perceived as a threat to U.S. and Allied oil interests and this resulted in their plot against him. The plotters involved anglophile Iranians, clerics and businessmen as well as members of the British intelligence agencies. Both Conservative Party leaders Anthony Eden and Winston Churchill suggested an Anglo-American strategy against Mossadeq. By the mid-1950s, American economic interests were higher than any previous point in history. Iran was also increasingly being courted by Soviet intelligence agencies, given its proximity to the Soviet Union. CIA operations already in place since the end of World War II were in position to conduct black operations on behalf of U.S. national interests. British MI6 was also involved in kidnapping and coup plotting. Despite these invidious conditions, the Shah continued to rule through the 1970s with the aid of U.S. special advisers and the formation of the notorious secret police called the Savak in 1954. Naturally, in the months that led to the fall of the Shah, attacks against American citizens domiciled in Iran increased. The details of the 1953 coup are documented in Mark J. Gasiorowski's 1987 article, "The 1953 Coup D'etat in Iran", published in the *International Journal of Middle East Studies* in 1987.

Henry Kissinger met with the Shah to negotiate oil prices. The Shah antagonized the other Arab countries by saying that Iran would sell oil to Israel in 1976. Rockefeller's meeting with the Shah involved future business deals that both were planning on implementing. The *New York Times* on 8 July 1977 headlined a shouting woman who had disrupted traffic on Fifth Avenue at a luncheon in honour of Empress Farah, the Shah's wife. The writing was on the wall. On 13 September 1977, a car carrying the Shah of Iran's twin sister in Paris, Princess Ashraf Pahlevi, was attacked by gunmen on the French Riviera. Her lady-in-waiting was killed. In November 1977 Jimmy Carter, a wealthy peanut planter from Georgia who became the Democratic President to succeed Republican President Gerald Ford, assured the Shah of the strong relationship between the United States and Iran. He praised the Shah for the "strong, stable and progressive Iran". By 12 January 1978, the *New York Times* reported an incident where several hundred police officers had to protect the Waldorf-Astoria Hotel where Empress Farah Pavlevi was at a party. There were 200 demonstrators outside, across Park Avenue that shouted "Shah is a fascist butcher, down with the Shah!" Apart from Jimmy Carter, support for the Shah also came from Richard M. Nixon. In 1978, *Time* magazine carried an article where the Shah accused the CIA of using dirty tricks since the 1960s to destabilize his regime. On 16 January 1979, the Shah landed at Reese AFB in Texas and by 12 February 1979, the Soviet Union recognized the government of Ayatollah Ruhollah Khomeini. By 16 February 1979, Iran's Islamic Revolutionary Council executed four of the Shah's generals, including the head of Savak, by firing squad.

CONCLUSION

Herodotus' view of the ancient world was a romantic beginning for those who subscribe to the utopian ideals of Western civilization. The romance of these ancient ideals provides a sense of security because it creates the possibilities for concretized and "original" starting points. The globe then and the globe now are geographically very similar. But the political globe then compared to the globe in late modernity is vastly different. Globalization in late modernity today has made us virtually unrecognizable by Herodotus and the ancients. Yet the tragedy and the sadness of the past seems to permeate our late modern world. We seem to have come closer to Nietzsche's willingness to break with the past despite the pressures by cultural gatekeepers to retain historical validity, as if that could preserve the future. The role that America will now play will become increasingly pessimistic as if a pall of economic doom had descended to choke the living. We saw how America is both real and unreal. How it remains one of the most peaceful countries in the world yet is not dispossessed of a history of political and economic violence. America suffers poverty on its own shores, while the richest of the rich bask listless on the widening shores of the almighty greenback. In a sense, this was a book that has shown how the world celebrates American successes while simultaneously condemning America's failures. But Americans are the ones who must learn to accept the consequences of the decisions made by their political leaders. The choice is sometimes as simple as voting for the Democratic Party that will complicate domestic policies and vacillate on foreign policy. On the other hand, those who vote for the Republican Party are likely to realize better returns for MNCs and wealthy Americans, while living under the fear of hawkish foreign policies. America, like the world, needs a non-partisan leader who can rise above ideological and party differences and tackle the real problems without having to consider political loyalties or make policy decisions that are driven by term limits and voting patterns of the past.

Despite the challenges of culture, money, and terror, globalization continues to be driven by sentiments of hope, optimism, and progress. The new rhetoric involves a kind of politics of forgetting; it involves phrases like "letting go", "moving forward", and "moving on". This book has been about the politics of globalization and how it has manifested itself through its use of cultural norms, neoliberal wealth, and military power. Culture gives rise to idealism and meaning; money makes for a common currency of communication, while terrorism continues to violate the free world.

The book is about the need to readjust the formal and informal institutions of power, authority, and legitimacy that constitute globalization in late modernity.

EPILOGUE: THE SHIP OF FOOLS

A familiar stranger turned and insisted that he listen to the rest of my story about that Black Prison Ship aptly named the *Courageous and Highly Valiant*.

End Thoughts

The *Ship of Fools* called Courageous where prisoners are wardens; and sheep look like goats. Insanity rules norm while value steers forward. The Ship is moving tremendously as if it were on "speed". There is a cacophony of voices from various wooden crosses recessed on board that are saying this or arguing about that, and trying to convince each other of the differences and the similarities about "being" and "time". In the time being, the wooden sailing ship speeds on famously. It has twelve main decks made of wrought iron from a little known foundry. There are seven minor decks, seventy-seven cabins, twelve masts, a little known Masonic Lodge, and cotton white wide sails that stretch across thousands of nautical miles. The entrance to the ship is guarded by Joseph Conrad's two women knitting wool with a funereal air and smoking really expensive Cubans. Yes, sometimes, there is a fire on board the ship. Or someone cuts down the mizzen mast and replaces it with 3M duct-tape. But because its imaginary pine furniture is sponsored by Ikea, no one can hope to realize that they are being incarcerated by their own vanity, and ego.

Sometimes it takes a few years, sometimes centuries. Eventually the memory is erased and the *SMS Courageous and the Valiant* speeds along. It goes on anyway because the *Ship* is much bigger than one can stretch one's eyeballs. One needs at least six days to complete the tour while resting on the seventh day. Millions die on its revolutionary year-round voyages especially in Tourist Class. But at least they serve good Portuguese port. People are committing suicide from the Crow's Nest, hurtling themselves into the Pacific, making nuclear bombs, killing and maiming one another, surfing the Internet, making small holes in the plywood sideboards, setting fire to the sails, and running amok naked through the narrow passageways with scissors. But there is also loud singing and rejoicing. And old people shaking their heads. Some people look bright-faced and illuminated, smiling while pointing skywards. They hug and embrace each other. There are happy campfire songs, as a stuttering Johnny Mathis wannabe sings *A Ray of Hope*. Old salts shove people overboard after torturing them for hours. Many watch in horror. And then go back to their shopping at Borders. Karen does not allow rubbernecking for more than two seconds. Others return to the football game played across a colossal plasma screen on a high definition television. Those who believe that they are steersmen and oarsmen work strenuously. An original, but friendly slave-driver who looks like a cross between Lawrence Olivier and Joseph Stalin beats a battle drum while Robin Williams tells really good jokes to the rhythm of Gloria Estefan's The Miami Sound Machine. In a dark and wet corner of the lower deck is a sacred shrine where pilgrims pay homage to an old picture of Dean Martin and Sammy Davis Jr. while drinking cheap tequila and vodka shooters. On the quarter deck, Woody Allen hums the *Battle Hymn of the Republic of the Galapagos* because *Manhattan* was all right, *Annie Hall* was too real, and *Mighty Aphrodite* was a canvass mop. No one leaves their post even when the fast food galley begins flooding from tropical torrential rains that are a common feature in these parts. The Grand Council of Economic Advisers is made up of the original cast of Monthy Python and a fiercely armoured rabbit wearing a wire with sharp, pointy teeth. Meanwhile, anadromous sturgeons work quietly in the ship's general infirmary, cutting away flesh that causes pain while extending life *For a Few Dollars More*. Do not worry. It is only a flesh wound.

Sometimes a miracle happens. But there is only room for one more waiter behind Mel Brooks' reprise of the Last Supper. The National Dance is called the "Fish Slapping Dance". The State Crest is missing, and the State Bird was mugged by a taxi driver in a New York borough. Every Halloween, millions wear Montezuma's death masks and gather under the moonlight to watch Major League Cow Acrobats. The dead are heaped overboard after a quick ceremony involving flowers, wire mesh, chanting, and some police brutality. The prophet tells them that it is all right, because they have put a man-in-the-moon, the cat-in-the-cradle, a dog-in-a-manger, and a pig-in-a-poke. Parts of the floorboards are made of marble chips from fallen boulders along the Pacific Coast Highway. Ancient temples in late modernity are inhabited by carpet-weaving, peace-loving, Persian-tourists while taking a break from acting as suspects for the terrorism police. Other parts of the main deck feel like sinking cabbages and sealing wax that the Hunchback of Notre Dame got for Christmas from the walrus and the carpenter's shopping trip to Jiffy Lube and Home Depot. The staple drink is Lewis Carroll's Diet Soda but some concoct their own brews while hiding from anal retentive bureaucrats wearing horn-rimmed glasses and cheap leather shoes.

The upper deck is carefully regulated and lined with pictures of David Hasslehoff, Sidney Poitier, and *The Third Rock from the Sun*. This deck is outfitted with security cameras, false mirrors, disappearing stairs, inappropriate midriffs, foreign accents, and glass ceilings. People everywhere are dying for television, while more promises made by used car salesmen are broken by small-time teamster politicos. Unfortunately, the *Ship*'s only library near the only 7-Eleven was burnt down by the First Emperor in a tantrum because the Turtle Dove Soup caught cold. Ancient Greeks throw decaying philosophical monuments at wondering *Bands of Brothers*. All of a sudden, six characters from Pirandello's shallow sea chest decide to rest uneasily against the creaking mizzen mast while spying another author walking hurriedly. Women and animals, as usual, are "known" in common at the upper deck, while men stand in line for years waiting to contract gonorrhea and syphilis. There is blood in the urine and pus on the beer-nuts at all seventy-seven "all-day, all-night" taverns. There is an abundance of food and pornography. Shoes that are made for less than ten cents on the Upper East Side are sold for 300 times that amount in Greenwich Village. The port side dwellers do not know why the starboard-siders get all the sun. The starboard-side complains that the port-siders stole an ancient effigy of their god who claimed to have killed as many people in the name of religion as Attila the Hun. Once in a while, some approved communities see God and commit mass suicide. Other communities are charged with writing letters, sewing, and feeding stray cats for their dinner. There is one major disease on board the *Ship*.

There is also an annual Pride Parade (PP). The PP seems long but in fact is very brief. The route always taken is from the port-side to the starboard-side. They navigate by the hot air balloons sponsored by MetLife filled with Sports Commentators and energy watch dogs eating Ruffles Potato Chips (even though McDonald's fries taste better) and chugging huge vats of pink champagne while the Eagles are forced to replay *Hotel California* on air guitars, or need to travel to faraway places like Bangkok's Impact Center (15 October 2004), Singapore's Indoor Stadium (15 October 2004), Hong Kong's Coliseum (19 October 2004), Sapporo at the Sapporo Dome (24 October 2004), and Tokyo at the Tokyo Dome (30–31 October) in order to drum up support for their final years. The PP takes place at the same time each year except for heavy flow days when tropical torrents flood Main Street. Reviewing the PP is a must for the ecotourist. For as far as the eye can see, there are rich people, poor people, child molesters, murderers, saints, agnostics, democratic aristocrats, the Queen, her deceased mother, and Howard Stern standing behind them. There are Republicans, winos, straight talkers, backstreet walkers, David Soul, the Pope, Liv Tyler, communists, Grand Central Station, and the CEOs of all the major food groups. There are comedians, a milk powder factory, a war-time *consigliere*, Billy Bob Thornton's acting debut, the Young and the Restless, ACDC, Lavern and Shirley, Satan, one million marchers from Cambodia's holocaust from 1975–79, an image of the Pharaoh Akhenaton in drag, all the second runners-up of the Miss World Pageant, 1929, and *My Favourite Martian*.

The PP is watched by hundreds of millions all over the ship, some from the portholes, some from the decks, some from the mastheads, from under the rotting wood, under milkwood, and under cover. Some watchers watch through tiny holes in their log cabins, while others become scurrilous when they think that they have been caught on poorly-made rip-offs of *Candid Camera*. Sometimes during the PP, prophets dressed in sequins appear. They often sound like the character played by that John Travolta–look alike in *Pulp Fiction*, speaking truthfully but duplicitously while looking at Demi Moore's acting double in *Striptease*. So they drag one across the Arc De Triumph and sell pictures of him taken on digital cameras to the locals, as the *Courageous and the Valiant* with the decaying remains of terrorists displayed in public for entertainment, and as a warning to future entrepreneurs and struggling capitalists that whatever they have built can be destroyed in a matter of seconds.

Notes

1. Mark Bevir, "Foucault and Critique: Deploying Agency against Autonomy", *Political Theory* 27, no. 1 (1999): 65–84. See also, Mark Philp, "Foucault on Power: A Problem in Radical Translation?", *Political Theory* 11, no. 1 (1983): 29–52. At a higher level of theoretical generality, Connolly might agree with my assertions here. William E. Connolly "Taylor, Foucault, and Otherness", *Political Theory* 13, no. 3 (1985): 365–76; and Laforest's similar claims that were published in the same year as Connolly's critique of otherness in Guy Laforest "Regards genealogiques sur la modernite: Michel Foucault et la philosophie politique", *Canadian Journal of Political Science* 18, no. 1 (1985): 77–97.

2. See also Arianna Huffington, *How to Overthrow the Government* (New York: HarperCollins, 2001) and her *Pigs at the Trough: How Corporate Greed and Political Corruption are Undermining America* (New York: Random House, 2003). It has become clear to me that there are really very few differences, if at all, between the Republican Party and the Democratic Party. In their scramble to win over the traditional voters and swing voters on either side over the past fifty years, nominees from both parties have conceded so much ground that traditionally fell under the purview of the other side that there are no real differences that can be discerned nor measured. I would like to thank Deane E. Neubauer for reminding me that the two parties are like Tweedle-Dee and Tweedle-Dum. The predominance of the Democratic party in the south, for example, has been eclipsed by the presence of strong Republican support. The national voting public is really not voting along party lines but along personalities as subsequent presidential electioneering contests continue to demonstrate. This means that if Alice in Wonderland were part of the voting public, and she met the Tweedles in the forest, they would be of no help to her at all.

3. As the reader would have anticipated by the end of this book, my first constructions of the idea of the American Dream concept rely heavily on the romantic detachments outlined by Fitzgerald's interpretation. There are many relevant interpolations and here are some that might be useful for garnering depth

from the surface structure of this book: John F. Callahan "F. Scott Fitzgerald's Evolving American Dream: The "Pursuit of Happiness" in Gatsby, Tender Is the Night, and The Last Tycoon", *Twentieth Century Literature* 42, no. 3 (1996): 374–95; Michael Rogin, "Nature as Politics and Nature as Romance in America", *Political Theory* 5, no. 1 (1977): 5–30; and Wilson's unsuccessful lament in the wonderful article on pessimism, see Francis G. Wilson "Pessimism in American Politics", *Journal of Politics* 7, no. 2 (1945): 125–44.

REFERENCES

Adamson, Walter L. "Beyond 'Reform or Revolution': Notes on Political Education in Gramsci, Habermas and Arendt". *Theory and Society* 6, no. 3 (1978): 429–60.
Aghion, Philippe and Jeffrey G. Williamson. *Growth, Inequality, and Globalization: Theory, History, and Policy*. Cambridge University Press, 1999.
Ajayan, P., M.J.C. Charlier, and A.G. Rinzler. "Carbon Nanotubes: From Macromolecules to Nanotechnology". *Proceedings of the National Academy of Sciences of the United States of America* 96, no. 25 (1999): 14199–200.
Akaka, Daniel Kahikina. "US Senator's Speech before the Kukahi Coalition", 21 November 1998. University of Hawaii-Center for Hawaiian Studies.
Alesina, Alberto and Edward Glaeser. *Fighting Poverty in the US and Europe: A World of Difference*. Oxford: Oxford University Press, 2004.
Althusser, Louis. ([1968]). *For Marx*. Verso, 1996.
Amato, Ivan. "The Apostle of Nanotechnology". *Science* 254, 5036 (1991): 1310–11.
American Heritage Dictionary of the English Language. Fourth edition. Houghton Mifflin, 2000.
Aristotle. ([350 B.C.]). *Politics*. New York: Penguin, 1992.
Axelrod, Paul and Michelle A. Fuerch. "Flight of the Deities: Hindu Resistance in Portuguese Goa". *Modern Asian Studies* 30, no. 2 (1996): 387–421.
Baker, Jr., Houston A. "Handling 'Crisis': Great Books, Rap Music, and the End of Western Homogeneity". *Callaloo* 13, no. 2 (1990): 173–94.
Bacchetta, Paola. "When the (Hindu) Nation Exiles Its Queers". *Social Text* 61 (1999): 141–66.
Berger, Peter L. and Samuel P. Huntington. *Many Globalizations: Cultural Diversity in the Contemporary World*. New York: Oxford University Press, 2003.
Bolce, Louis and Gerald de Maio. "The Anti-Christian Fundamentalist Factor

in Contemporary Politics". *The Public Opinion Quarterly* 63, no. 4 (1999): 508–42.
Borofsky, Robert. "CA Forum on Theory in Anthropology: Cook, Lono, Obeyesekere, and Sahlins". *Current Anthropology* 38, no. 2 (1997): 255–82.
Bowen, Roger W. "Japan's Foreign Policy". *PS: Political Science and Politics* 25, no. 1 (1992): 57–73.
Bragg, Steven M. *Outsourcing: A Guide to Selecting the Correct Business Unit, Negotiating the Contract, Maintaining Control of the Process.* John Wiley, 1998.
Burks, Arthur W. "Icon, Index, and Symbol". *Philosophy and Phenomenological Research* 9, no. 4 (1949): 673–89.
Calvo, Guillermo A. and Enrique G. Mendoza. "Capital-Markets Crises and Economic Collapse in Emerging Markets: An Informational-Frictions Approach". *The American Economic Review* 90, no. 2 (2000): 59.
Camroux, David. "State Responses to Islamic Resurgence in Malaysia: Accommodation, Co-Option, and Confrontation". *Asian Survey* 36, no. 9 (1996): 852–68.
Case, William. "The UMNO Party Election in Malaysia: One for the Money". *Asian Survey* 34, no. 10 (1994): 916–30.
———. "Comparative Malaysian Leadership: Tunku Abdul Rahman and Mahathir Mohamad". *Asian Survey* 31, no. 5 (1991): 456–73.
Chambers, Paul and Napisa Waitoolkiat. "Thaksin or 'White September'? The Year 2006 has been a Year of Living Dangerously in Thailand". *The Nation*, 11 October 2006.
Chi, Leeisha. "Anwar Ibrahim's Arrest Not Good for Business". *Bloomberg News*, 17 July 2008.
Chin, James. "Malaysia in 1997: Mahathir's Annus Horribilis". *Asian Survey* 38, no. 2 (1998): 183–89.
Clarke, Susan E. and Gary L. Gaile. "Local Politics in a Global Era: Thinking Locally, Acting Globally". *Annals of the American Academy of Political and Social Science* 551 (1997): 28–43.
Clinton, William Jefferson. "Apology Resolution to Native Hawaiians". *Public Law 103–150*, 23 November 1993.
Cnudde, Charles F. and Deane E. (eds.). Neubauer. *Empirical Democratic Theory.* Chicago: Markham Publishing, 1969.
Collins, Susan M., Barry P. Bosworth, and Dani Rodrik. "Economic Growth in East Asia: Accumulation versus Assimilation". *Brookings Papers on Economic Activity* 2 (1996): 135–203.
Connolly, William E. *Ethos of Pluralization.* University of Minnesota Press, 1995.
———. "Speed, Concentric Cultures, and Cosmopolitanism". *Political Theory* 28 (2000): 596–618.
———. *Neuropolitics: Thinking, Culture, Speed* University of Minnesota Press, 2002.
Crafts, N.F.R. "Some Dimensions of the 'Quality of Life' during the British Industrial Revolution". *The Economic History Review* 50, no. 4 (1997): 617–39.

Deeb, Mary-Jane. "Militant Islam and the Politics of Redemption". *Annals of the American Academy of Political and Social Science* 524 (1992): 52–65.
Desker, Barry and and Kumar Ramakrishna. "Forging an Indirect Strategy in Southeast Asia". *Washington Quarterly*, 25, no. 2 (2002): 161–76.
Dobyns, Henry F., Richard W. Stoffle, and Kristine Jones. "Native American Urbanization and Socio-Economic Integration in the Southwestern United States". *Ethnohistory* 22, no. 2 (1975): 155–79.
Doner, Richard F. "Approaches to the Politics of Economic Growth in Southeast Asia". *Journal of Asian Studies* 50, no. 4 (1991): 818–49.
Drucker, Peter F. *The End of Economic Man*. Transaction, 1939.
———. *Age of Discontinuities*. Transaction, 1968.
Dubin, Steven C. "Symbolic Slavery: Black Representations in Popular Culture". *Social Problems* 34, no. 2 (1987): 122–40.
Earman, John "Causation: A Matter of Life and Death". *The Journal of Philosophy* 73, no. 1 (1976): 5–25.
Emblidge, David. "Down Home with the Band: Country-Western Music and Rock". *Ethnomusicology* 20, no. 3 (1976): 541–52.
Epstein, Lee, Jeffrey A. Segal, and Harold J. Spaeth. "The Norm of Consensus on the U.S. Supreme Court". *American Journal of Political Science* 45, no. 2 (2001): 362–77.
Eribon, Didier. *Michel Foucault*. Cambridge, MA: Harvard University Press, 1991.
Espino, Ovidio Diaz. *How Wall Street Created a Nation: J.P. Morgan, Teddy Roosevelt, and the Panama Canal*. New York: Four Walls Eight Windows, 2001.
Euben, J. Peter. *The Tragedy of Political Theory*. Princeton, NJ: Princeton University Press, 1990.
Evans, Martin. "A Note on the Measurement of Sahlins' Social Profile of Domestic Production". *American Ethnologist* 1, no. 2 (1974): 269–79.
Fanon, Franz. *Black Skin, White Masks*. MacGibbon and Kee, [1952] 1968.
———. *The Wretched of the Earth*. MacGibbon and Kee, [1961] 1965.
Farazmand, Ali. "Globalization and Public Administration". *Public Administration Review* 59, no. 6 (1999): 509–22.
Femia, Joseph V. "Gramsci's Patrimony". *British Journal of Political Science* 13, no. 3 (1983): 327–64.
Fernea, Elizabeth Warnock and Basima Qattan Bezirgan (eds.). *Middle Eastern Muslim Women Speak*. Austin, TX: University of Texas Press, 1978.
Fish, Stanley. *Is There A Text In This Class? The Authority of Interpretive Communities*. Cambridge, MA: Harvard University Press, 1980.
Foucault, Michel. *Madness and Civilization*. New York: Vintage, [1965] 1988.
Fox, William S. and James D. Williams. "Political Orientation and Music Preferences Among College Students". *The Public Opinion Quarterly* 38, no. 3 (1974): 352–71.
Franchot, Jenny. "Unseemly Commemoration: Religion, Fragments, and the Icon". *American Literary History* 9, no. 3 (1997): 502–21.

Franklin, Robert Michael. "Response to Leonard Lovett's The Problem of Racism in the Contemporary Pentecostal Movement". PCCNA National Conferences, 17–19 October 1994. Memphis, Tennessee: "Pentecostal Partners: A Reconciliation Strategy for 21st Century Ministry".

Freedman, Maurice and Marjorie Topley. "Religion and Social Realignment among the Chinese in Singapore". *Journal of Asian Studies* 21, no. 1 (1961): 3–23.

Friedman, Thomas. *Lexus and the Olive Tree: Understanding Globalization*. Anchor, 2000.

——. *Longitudes and Attitudes: The World in the Age of Terrorism*. Anchor, 2003.

Gaebler, Ted and David Osborne. *How the Entrepreneurial Spirit is Transforming the Public Sector*. Addison-Wesley, 1992.

Gaston, John C. "The Destruction of the Young Black Male: The Impact of Popular Culture and Organized Sports". *Journal of Black Studies* 16, no. 4 (1986): 369–84.

Geertz, Clifford. "Culture War — Book Review of Gananath Obeyesekere's *The Apotheosis of Captain Cook: European Mythmaking in the Pacific* and Marshall Sahlins's *How Native Think, About Captain Cook, for Example*". *The New York Review*, 30 November 1995, pp. 4–6.

Gellner, Ernest. *Anthropology and Politics: Revolutions in the Sacred Grove*. Blackwell, 1995.

Gillespie, Jr., J. Lodge. "Rhetoric and Reality: Corporate America's Perceptions of Southeast Asia, 1950–1961". *Business History Review* 68, no. 3 (1994): 325–63.

Griffin, James M. and Weiwen Xiong. "The Incentive to Cheat: An Empirical Analysis of OPEC". *The Journal of Law and Economics* 40, no. 2 (1997): 289–316.

Groth, Alexander J. "The Politics of Xenophobia and the Salience of Anti-Semitism". *Comparative Politics* 4, no. 1 (1971): 89–108.

Gunnell, John G. "Political Theory and the Theory of Action". *Western Political Quarterly* 34, no. 3 (1981): 341–58.

Gutmann, Amy. "The Challenge of Multiculturalism in Political Ethics". *Philosophy and Public Affairs* 22, no. 3 (1993): 171–206.

——. "Moral Philosophy and Political Problems". *Political Theory* 10, no. 1 (1982): 33–47.

—— and Dennis Thompson. "Moral Conflict and Political Consensus". *Ethics* 101, no. 1 (1990): 64–88.

Hall, Pamela D. "The Relationship Between Types of Rap Music and Memory in African American Children". *Journal of Black Studies* 28, no. 6 (1998): 802–14.

Harrison, Bernard. "Judaism". *Annals of the American Academy of Political and Social Science* 256 (1948: 25–35.

Hart-Landsberg, Martin and Paul Burkett. "Contradictions of Capitalist Industrialization in East Asia: A Critique of 'Flying Geese' Theories of Development". *Economic Geography* 74, no. 2 (1998): 87–110.

Hartung, William D. "Eisenhower's Warning: The Military-Industrial Complex Forty Years Later". *World Policy Journal* 18, no. 1 (2001).

Hawley, James P. "Antonio Gramsci's Marxism: Class, State and Work". *Social Problems* 27, no. 5 (1980): 584–600.

Hehn, Michel, Kamel Ounadjela, Jean-Pierre Bucher, Francoise Rousseaux, Dominique Decanini, Bernard Bartenlian, and Claude Chappert. "Nanoscale Magnetic Domains in Mesoscopic Magnets". *Science* 272, no. 5269 (1996): 1782–85.

Henderson, Errol A. "Neoidealism and the Democratic Peace". *The Journal of Peace Research* 36, no. 2 (1999): 203–31.

———. "Black Nationalism and Rap Music". *Journal of Black Studies* 26, no. 3 (1996): 308–39.

Henderson, Mae G. "Ghosts, Monsters, and Magic: The Ritual Drama of Larry Neal". *Callaloo* 23 (1985): 195–214.

Howard, Alan and Bruce Howard. "The Dilemma of the Voting Rights Act — Recognizing the Emerging Political Equality Norm". *Columbia Law Review* 83, no. 7 (1983): 1615–63.

Huffington, Arianna. *Fanatics and Fools: The Game Plan for Winning America Back*. Hyperion, 2004.

———. *Pigs at the Trough: How Corporate Greed and Political Corruption are Undermining America*. Random House, 2003.

———. *How to Overthrow the Government*. HarperCollins, 2001.

Huntington, Samuel P. *Clash of Civilizations and the Remaking of World Order*. Touchstone, [1996] 1997.

Hussaina J. Abdullah and Ibrahim Hamza. "Women Need Independent Ownership Rights". Paper presented at an International Workshop on Women and Land in Africa, Emory University Law School, Atlanta, Georgia in collaboration with Associates for Change, Kampala, Uganda at the Entebbe Beach Hotel, 24–25 April 1998.

Ilinitch, Anne Y., Richard A. D'Aveni, and Arie Y. Lewin. "New Organizational Forms and Strategies for Managing in Hypercompetitive Environments". *Organization Science* 7, no. 3 (1996): 211–20.

Ingersoll, Ernest. "Decoration of Negro Graves". *The Journal of American Folklore* 5, no. 16 (1892): 68–69.

Ingold, Tim (ed.). *Key Debates in Anthropology*. London and New York: Routledge, 1996.

Inniss, Leslie B. and Joe R. Feagin. "The Cosby Show: The View from the Black Middle Class". *Journal of Black Studies* 25, no. 6 (1995): 692–711.

Inoguchi, Takashi. "Japan's Response to the Gulf Crisis: An Analytic Overview". *Journal of Japanese Studies* 17, no. 2 (1991): 257–73.

Jackson, Bernard S. "The Prophet and the Law in Early Judaism and the New Testament". *Cardozo Studies in Law and Literature* 4, no. 2 (1992): 123–66.

Johnson, D. Gale. "Population, Food, and Knowledge". *The American Economic Review* 90, no. 1 (2000): 1–14.

Jorion Philippe, and William N. Goetzmann. "Global Stock Markets in the Twentieth Century". *The Journal of Finance* 54, no. 3 (1999): 953–80.

Juergensmeyer, Mark. "Christian Violence in America". *Annals of the American Academy of Political and Social Science* 558 (1998): 88–100.

Kahin, Audrey R. "Crisis on the Periphery: The Rift Between Kuala Lumpur and Sabah". *Pacific Affairs* 65, no. 1 (1992): 30–49.

Kariel, Henry S. *Desperate Politics of Postmodernism* University of Massachusetts Press, 1989.

———. "The Feminist Subject Spinning In The Postmodern Project". *Political Theory* 18, no. 2 (1990): 255–72.

Karliner, Joshua. *The Corporate Planet: Ecology and Politics in the Age of Globalization.* Sierra Club Books, 1997.

Katzenstein, Peter J. "Regionalism in Comparative Perspective". *Arena Working Papers*, 96/1, 1996.

———, Robert O. Keohane, and Stephen D. Krasner. "International Organizations and the Study of World Politics". *International Organization* 52, no. 4 (1998): 645–85.

Kissinger, Henry A. Thayer Award Speech. USMA West Point, 13 September 2000.

Kwa, Chong Guan (ed.). *S. Rajaratnam on Singapore: From Ideas to Reality.* S. Rajaratnam School of International Studies, 2006.

Laclau, Ernesto. "Politics and the Limits of Modernity" in Thomas Docherty (ed.). *Postmodernism: A Reader.* New York: Columbia University Press, 1993, pp. 329–43.

LaFleur, William. "Points of Departure: Comments on Religious Pilgrimage in Sri Lanka and Japan". *Journal of Asian Studies* 38, no. 2 (1979): 271–81.

Larmore, Charles. "Political Liberalism". *Political Theory* 18, no. 3 (1990): 339–60.

Landsberg, Marge E. "The Icon in Semiotic Theory". *Current Anthropology* 21, no. 1 (1980): 93–95.

LaPalombara, Joseph. "International Firms and National Governments: Some Dilemmas" in Brad Roberts (ed.). *New Forces in the World Economy.* Cambridge, MA: MIT Press, 1996.

———. *Politics Within Nations.* Englewood Cliffs, NJ: Prentice-Hall, 1974.

——— and Stephen Blank. *Multinational Corporations and Developing Countries.* NY: Conference Board, 1979.

Laurence, Henry. "Financial System Reform and the Currency Crisis in East Asia". *Asian Survey* 39, no. 2 (1999): 348–73.

Levine, Daniel H. "Popular Groups, Popular Culture, and Popular Religion". *Comparative Studies in Society and History* 32, no. 4 (1990): 718–64.

Levy, Gidon and Udi Adiv. "The Jew the State Thinks is an Arab". *Journal of Palestine Studies* 13, no. 2 (1984): 176–78.

Lewis, Bernard. "Islam and Liberal Democracy: A Historical Overview". *The Journal of Democracy* 7 (1996).

Liebman Charles and Bernard Susser. "Judaism and Jewishness in the Jewish State". *Annals of the American Academy of Political and Social Science* 555 (1998): 15–25.

Long, William J. "Nonproliferation as a Goal of Japanese Foreign Assistance". *Asian Survey* 39, no. 2 (1999): 328–47.

Lucier, V. A. "Offrenda on All-Souls' Day in Mexico". *The Journal of American Folklore* 10, no. 37 (1897): 106–7.

Mahbubani, Kishore. *Beyond the Age of Innocence: Rebuilding Trust Between American And the World*. PublicAffairs/Perseus Book Group, 2005.

———. *Can Asians Think?* (Third edition) Times Editions by Marshall Cavendish, 2004.

Makin, Tony. "Preventing Financial Crises in East Asia". *Asian Survey* 39, no. 4 (1999): 668–78.

Martinez, Delores (ed.). *The Worlds of Japanese Popular Culture: Gender, Shifting Boundaries and Global Culture*. Cambridge: Cambridge University Press, 1998.

Mauzy, Diane K. and R. S. Milne. "The Mahathir Administration in Malaysia: Discipline through Islam". *Pacific Affairs* 56, no. 4 (1983–1984): 617–48.

May, Brian. "Memorials to Modernity: Postcolonialism and Pilgrimage in Naipaul and Rushdie". *ELH* 68, no. 1 (2001): 241–65.

Maynard, Patrick. "The Secular Icon: Photography and the Functions of Images". *The Journal of Aesthetics and Art Criticism* 42, no. 2 (1983): 155–69.

McClure, Kirstie M. "The Strange Silence of Political Theory: Response". *Political Theory*, 23, no. 4 (1995): 657–63.

McFadden, George. "Nietzschean Values in Comic Writing". *Boundary 2*, no. 9 (1981): 3, 337–58.

Michaels, Walter Benn. "An American Tragedy, or the Promise of American Life". *Representations* 25 (1989): 71–98.

Miller, David B. "Legends of the Icon of Our Lady of Vladimir: A Study of the Development of Muscovite National Consciousness". *Speculum* 43, no. 4 (1968): 657–70.

Mittelman, James H. *The Globalization Syndrome: Transformation and Resistance*. Princeton: Princeton University Press, 2000.

Moen, Matthew C. "The Evolving Politics of the Christian Right". *PS: Political Science and Politics* 29, no. 3 (1996): 461–64.

Monroe, Kristen Renwick (ed.). *Contemporary Empirical Political Theory*. Berkeley: University of California Press, 1997.

Norton, R.D. "Industrial Policy and American Renewal". *Journal of Economic Literature* 24, no. 1 (1986): 1–40.

Nye, Jr., Joseph S., Philip D. Zelikow and David C. King. *Why People Don't Trust Government*. Harvard University Press, 1997.

O'Loughlin, John and Luc Anselin. "Geo-Economic Competition and Trade Bloc Formation: United States, German, and Japanese Exports, 1968–1992". *The Journal of Economic Geography* 72, no. 2 (1996): 131–60.

Olafson, Frederick. "Nietzsche's Philosophy of Culture: A Paradox in *The Will to Power*". *Philosophy and Phenomenological Research* 51, no. 3 (1991): 557–72.
Parsons, Elsie. "All-Souls Day at Zuni, Acoma, and Laguna". *The Journal of American Folklore* 30, no. 118 (1917): 495–96.
People's Mojahedin Organization of Iran v. United States Department of State and Madeleine K. Albright, Secretary of State (1999).
Perris, Arnold. "Feeding the Hungry Ghosts: Some Observations on Buddhist Music and Buddhism from Both Sides of the Taiwan Strait". *Ethnomusicology* 30, no. 3 (1986): 428–48.
Peterson Indira V. "Singing of a Place: Pilgrimage as Metaphor and Motif in the Tevaram Songs of the Tamil Saivite Saints". *Journal of the American Oriental Society* 102, no. 1 (1982): 69–90.
Pfaltzgraff, Jr., Robert L. "The Emerging Global Security Environment". *Annals of the American Academy of Political and Social Science* 517 (1991): 10–24.
Piccone, Paul. "Gramsci's Hegelian Marxism". *Political Theory* 2, no. 1 (1974): 32–45.
———. "Gramsci's Marxism: Beyond Lenin and Togliatti". *Theory and Society* 3, no. 4 (1976): 485–512.
Powell, Colin L. Thayer Award Acceptance Remarks. *USMA West Point*, 15 September 1998.
Pryor, Frederic L. "The Impact of Foreign Trade on the Employment of Unskilled U.S. Workers: Some New Evidence". *Southern Economic Journal* 65, no. 3 (1999): 472–92.
Putnam, Hilary. "To Think with Integrity". *Harvard Review of Philosophy* VIII (2000): 4–13.
Ra'Anan, Uri. "Soviet Strategic Doctrine and the Soviet-American Global Contest". *Annals of the American Academy of Political and Social Science* 457 (1981): 8–17.
Ramasamy, P. *Plantation, Labour, Unions, Capital and the State in Peninsular Malaysia*. New York: Oxford University Press, 1994.
Rappa, Antonio L. "Saudade: The Portuguese Roots of Eurasians in Singapore and Malaysia".
———. "Singapore-Thailand Bilateral Exercises as part of Regional Security Architecture". Paper presented at the Konrad Adenauer Stiftung international conference on Regional Security Architecture, Bangkok, Thailand, 9–10 April 2009.
———. Review of Bilveer Singh's *The Talibanization of Southeast Asia*, Praegar Security International, 2007 in *Contemporary Southeast Asia*, 2009.
———. "Thai Military Culture". (Unpublished manuscript).
———. "Insight: Thailand's Politics". Channel NewsAsia, 18 December 2008.
———. "Protest Culture: The Case of Thailand". *RSIS Commentaries* 124 (2008).
———. "Wither Civil Society in Thailand?". *RSIS Commentaries* 92 (2008).
———. "A Critique of Modernity". *Alternatives: The Turkish Journal of International Relations* 2, nos. 3/4 (2003): 1–25.

―――. *Modernity and Consumption: Theory, Politics and the Public in Singapore and Malaysia.* Singapore and New Jersey: World Scientific, 2002.

―――. "Modernity and the Contingency of the Public" in "Modernity and the Politics of Public Space". *Innovation — The European Journal of Social Science Research* 15, no. 1 (2002).

―――. "The Classical Origins of Altruism in Plato's Dialogues" in Basant Kapur and K.C. Chong (eds.). *Altruism's Reveries: Perspectives from the Humanities and Social Sciences.* Netherlands: Kluwer Academic Press, 2002.

―――. "Urban Political Theory and the Symmetrical Model of Community Power," *Innovation: European Journal of Social Science Research* 14, no. 1 (2001): 5–16.

―――. "On A Common Currency for East Asia: Some Political Considerations" in *A Common Currency for East Asia: Dream or Reality?* Kuala Lumpur: AIDCOM-Konrad Adenauer Stiftung, 2000, pp. 42–58.

―――. "Werlin on Wolin: A Misrepresentation of Political Theory". *International Review of Administrative Sciences* 66, no. 1 (2000).

―――. "Surviving the Politics of Late Modernity: The Eurasian Fringe Community". *Southeast Asian Journal of Social Science* 28, no. 2 (2000).

―――. "Political Pluralism and Governance in Singapore". In Frank Delmartino, Amara Pongsapich, and Rudolf Hrbek (eds.), *Regional Pluralism and Good Governance.* Baden-Baden: Nomos Verlagsgesellschaft (1999): 81–97.

―――. "Political Pluralism and Governance in the Federation of Malaysia". In Frank Delmartino, Amara Pongsapich, and Rudolf Hrbek (eds.), *Regional Pluralism and Good Governance.* Baden-Baden: Nomos Verlagsgesellschaft (1999): 99–120.

―――. "Imprisoning the Other". *Peace Review* 11 (1999).

―――. "The Politics of Ageing in Singapore: Perspectives from State and Society". *Southeast Asian Journal of Social Science* 27, no. 2 (1999): 123–38.

―――. "Modern Death Dances: The Irreverent Politics of Postmodernism". *Sincronia* (Spring/Primavera 1998).

Rappa, Antonio L. and Lionel Wee. *Language Policy and Modernity in Southeast Asia: Malaysia, Philippines, Singapore and Thailand.* Netherlands: Springer, 2006.

Rappa, Antonio L. and Sor-Hoon Tan. "Political Implications of Confucian Familism". *Asian Philosophy* 13, nos. 2/3 (2003): 46–60.

Rejali, Darius. *Torture and Democracy.* Princeton University Press, 2007.

Reischauer, Edwin O. and Marius B. Jansen (eds.). *The Japanese Today: Change and Continuity.* Cambridge, MA: Harvard University Press, 1995.

Rocco, Christopher. "Between Modernity and Postmodernity: Reading Dialectic of Enlightenment Against the Grain" *Political Theory* 22, no. 1 (1994): 71–97.

Romm, James S. *Herodotus.* New Haven, CT: Yale University Press, 1998.

Rorty, Richard. "Postmodern Bourgeois Liberalism". *The Journal of Philosophy* 80, no. 10, Part 1 (1983): 583–89.

Rose, Tricia. "Fear of a Black Planet: Rap Music and Black Cultural Politics in the 1990s". *The Journal of Negro Education* 60, no. 3 (1991): 276–90.

Rosenfield, Sarah. "Factors Contributing to the Subjective Quality of Life of the

Chronic Mentally Ill". *Journal of Health and Social Behavior* 33, no. 4 (1992): 299–315.

Roy, Denny. "Singapore, China, and the 'Soft Authoritarian' Challenge". *Asian Survey* 34, no. 3 (1994): 231–42.

Roy, Parama. "Oriental Exhibits: Englishmen and Natives in Burton's Personal Narrative of a Pilgrimage to Al-Madinah & Meccah". *Boundary* 2, 22, no. 1 (1995): 185–210.

Rushdie, Salman. *The Satanic Verses*. Viking, 1989.

———. *The Moor's Last Sigh*. Vintage, 1997.

Sahlins, Marshall. "The Sadness of Sweetness: The Native Anthropology of Western Cosmology". *Current Anthropology* 37 (1996): 395–418.

———. *How "Natives" Think — About Captain Cook for Example*. Chicago: The University of Chicago Press, 1995.

———. *Islands of History*. Chicago: University of Chicago Press, 1985.

———. *Historical Metaphors and Mythical Realities: Structure in the Early History of the Sandwich Islands Kingdom*. Ann Arbor: University of Michigan Press, 1981.

———. "Poor Man, Rich Man, Big-Man, Chief: Political Types in Melanesia and Polynesia". *Comparative Studies in Society and History* 5, no. 3 (1963): 285–303.

Said, Edward W. *Orientalism*. New York: Vintage, 1979.

Sawyer, Darwin O. "Public Attitudes Toward Life and Death". *The Public Opinion Quarterly* 46, no. 4 (1982): 521–33.

Scalapino, Robert A. "The United States and Asia in 1998". *Asian Survey* 39, no. 1 (1999): 1–11.

Schilling, Mark. *The Encyclopedia of Japanese Pop Culture*. Weatherhill Publications, 1997.

Schlosser, Eric. *Reefer Madness and Other Tales from the American Underground*. London: Penguin Books, 2003.

Scholte, Jan Aarte. "Global Capitalism and the State". *International Affairs* 73, no. 3 (1997).

Shamsul, A.B. *From British to Bumiputra Rule*. Singapore: Institute of Southeast Asian Studies, 1986.

Shapiro, James. *Shakespeare and the Jews*. Columbia University Press, 1997.

Shusterman, Richard. "Pragmatist Aesthetics and Popular Culture". *Poetics Today* 14, no. 1 (1993): 99–100.

Sikorski, Douglas. "Effective Government in Singapore: Perspective of a Concerned American". *Asian Survey* 36, no. 8 (1996): 818–32.

Sisci, Francesco. "La démaoization de la Chine". *Le Grand Soir: Asiatimes* (10 November 2002).

Skeel, Jr., David A. "The Unanimity Norm in Delaware Corporate Law". *Virginia Law Review* 83, no. 1 (1997): 127–75.

Smil, Vaclav. "China's Energy and Resource Uses: Continuity and Change". *The China Quarterly* 156 (1998): 935–51.

Smith, Adam. *An Inquiry into the Nature and Causes of the Wealth of Nations*. Oxford University Press, 1975.
———. *The Wealth of Nations*. Penguin, 1982.
———. *The Wealth of Nations*. Modern Library, 1994.
Smith, R. B. "An Introduction to Caodaism II. Beliefs and Organization". *Bulletin of the School of Oriental and African Studies* 33, no. 3 (1970): 573–89.
Song, Xue. "American Poverty and Welfare Reform". *Perspectives* 2, no. 6 (30 June 2001).
Spieser, J. M. "The Representation of Christ in the Apses of Early Christian Churches". *Gesta* 37, no. 1 (1998): 63–73.
Stark Oded. "Altruism and the Quality of Life". *The American Economic Review* 79, no. 2 (1989): 86–90.
Sugimoto, Yoshio. *An Introduction to Japanese Society*. Cambridge: Cambridge University Press, 2002.
Taylor, Charles. "Connolly, Foucault, and Truth". *Political Theory* 13, no. 3 (1985): 377–85.
Thiele, Leslie Paul "Twilight of Modernity: Nietzsche, Heidegger, and Politics". *Political Theory* 22, no. 3 (1994): 468–90.
———. "Reading Nietzsche and Foucault: A Hermeneutics of Suspicion?" *American Political Science Review* 85, no. 2 (1991): 581–92.
Tilly, Charles. "Violence, Terror, and Politics as Usual America's 'New War' Reflects an Epochal Change in the Nature of Collective Violence". *Boston Review* 27, nos. 3–4 (Summer 2002).
———. "Processes and Mechanisms of Democratization". *Sociological Theory* 18, no. 1 (2000): 1–16.
———. "Charting Futures for Sociology: Inequality Mechanisms, Intersections, and Global Change". *Contemporary Sociology* 29, no. 6 (2000): 782–85.
———. "Social Movements and (All Sorts of) Other Political Interactions — Local, National, and International — Including Identities". *Theory and Society* 27, no. 4 (Special Issue on Interpreting Historical Change at the End of the Twentieth Century) (1998): 453–80.
———. "A Primer on Citizenship". *Theory and Society* 26, no. 4 (1997): 599–602.
Tucker, Bruce. "Tell Tchaikovsky the News: Postmodernism, Popular Culture, and the Emergence of Rock 'N' Roll". *Black Music Research Journal* 9, no. 2 (1989): 271–95.
Tully, James. "Wittgenstein and Political Philosophy: Understanding Practices of Critical Reflection". *Political Theory*, 17, no. 2 (1989): 172–204.
Tyson, Brian F. "Ben Jonson's Black Comedy: A Connection between Othello and Volpone". *Shakespeare Quarterly* 29, no. 1 (1978): 60–66.
Ulmer Jr., Walter F., Joseph J. Collins, and T.O. Jacobs (eds.). *American Military Culture in the Twenty-First Century: A Report of the CSIS International Security Program*. Washington, D.C.: Center for Strategic and International Studies, 2000.

United States of America v. Oliver L. North (1990).

Urbinati, Nadia. "From the Periphery of Modernity: Antonio Gramsci's Theory of Subordination and Hegemony". *Political Theory* 26, no. 3 (1998): 370–91.

Wacker, R. Fred. "Assimilation and Cultural Pluralism in American Social Thought". *Phylon* 40, no. 4 (1979): 325–33.

Weiss, Anita M. "Women's Position in Pakistan: Sociocultural Effects of Islamization". *Asian Survey* 25, no. 8 (1985): 863–80.

Werbner, Richard. "The Suffering Body: Passion and Ritual Allegory in Christian Encounters". *Journal of Southern African Studies* 23, no. 2 (1997): 311–24.

West, Cornel. "A Matter of Life and Death." *October* 61 (1992): 20–23.

———. *Keeping Faith: Philosophy and Race in America*. New York: Routledge, 1993.

White, Richard. "The Return of the Master: An Interpretation of Nietzsche's 'Genealogy of Morals' ". *Philosophy and Phenomenological Research* 48, no. 4 (1988): 683–96.

Wilmer, Franke, Michael E. Melody, and Margaret Maier Murdock. "Including Native American Perspectives in the Political Science Curriculum". *PS: Political Science and Politics* 27, no. 2 (1994): 269–76.

Witkin, Robert W. "Constructing a Sociology for an Icon of Aesthetic Modernity: Olympia Revisited". *Sociological Theory* 15, no. 2 (1997): 101–25.

Wooley, Karen L., Jeffrey S. Moore, Chi Wu, and Yulian Yang. "Novel Polymers: Molecular to Nanoscale Order in Three Dimensions". *Proceedings of the National Academy of Sciences of the United States of America* 97, no. 21 (2000): 11147–48.

Woodall, Brian "The Logic of Collusive Action: The Political Roots of Japan's Dango System". *Comparative Politics* 25, no. 3 (1993): 297–312.

Yasutomo, Dennis T. "Why Aid? Japan as an Aid Great Power". *Pacific Affairs* 62, no. 4 (1989–90): 490–503.

Young, Kenneth T. "Asia and America at the Crossroads". *Annals of the American Academy of Political and Social Science* 384 (1969): 53–65.

Zahralddin-Aravena, Rafael X. "Chile and Singapore: The Individual and the Collective, A Comparison". *Emory International Law Review* 12, no. 2 (1998): fn. 153.

INDEX

A
ABC News, 195
Abdul Basheer Abdul Kader, 282
Abdullah bin Haji Ahmad Badawi, 67, 91, 93, 94, 120, 130n20
Abdul Rahman, Tunku, 75
Abe, Shinzo, 117
Abhisit Vejjajiva, 124–25
ABRI (Angkatan Bersenjata Republik Indonesia). *See* Tentara Nasional Indonesia (TNI)
Abu, Ahmed, 282
Abu Ghraib prison, 36
Abu Sayyaf, 297
Aceh, 69
Achebe, Chinua, 92
Adidas, 252
Adorno, Theodore, 201, 232, 280
Afghanistan
   Chinese Muslims in, 103
   Soviet occupation, xiv
   stalemate in, xi, 286
   U.S. casualties in, xviii
   U.S. decline and, 267, 286, 287
   U.S. intelligence on, 256
   U.S. motives in, 103
   U.S. special forces in, 65
Africa
   British colonial times, xiii, 276
   democracy in, 267
   labour market, 128
   media globalization and, 232
   nationalist movements, 2
   ongoing wars, 3
   poverty, 49, 275
   slave trade, 205
   U.S. embassy bombings, 254, 255
Age of Discontinuities, 298
Aghion, Philippe, 18–19
AIDS, 203
AIG (American International Group), x, 156
Airbus Industries, 63, 78
Air Force Institute of Technology (AFIT), 178
Air France v. *Saks,* 227
airline industry, 62–64, 77–80, 224, 287
Air University (AU), 178
Alabama, 181
Alaska, 147, 236, 290
Aldrin, Buzz, 181
Alesina, Alberto, 53
Alfred Dunhill of London, Inc. v. *Cuba,* 226
Algeria, 85
Al Jazeera English, xix
Almond, Gabriel A., 229
ALPA-S (Airline Pilots Association–Singapore), 78–79

Al-Qaeda, 53, 90, 102, 103, 121, 282, 297
Althusser, Louis, 280
Amazon.com, 153
American Dream
　counter-cultural rejection of, 189
　expatriate Americans and, 13
　inflation and, 42
　Iraq invasion and, 266
　military-industrial complex and, 177, 295
　multinational business and, 162
　oil and, 99
　popular culture and, 25–26, 47, 200, 206–11, 214, 295
　salvaging the, 286
　terrorists and the, 298
American Idol, 194
American Soldiers, 87
American Terrorist, 203
Amman, 255, 272
Amnesty International, 103
Among the Believers, 269
Amusing Ourselves to Death, 205
Analytic Services Incorporated (ANSER), 52
Annan, Kofi A., 173
Annapolis, 180, 182
Anwar Ibrahim, 91, 92, 130(nn17, 20), 283
ANZUS treaty, 73
Apollo-Education Group, 154, 161
Apple, 140, 159
Arendt, Hannah, 15, 142, 188, 201, 236, 259n1, 294
Argentina, 45
Aristotle, xvi, 28, 134, 212, 219, 237n1, 278
Armed Forces Preparatory Academy, 125
Arrow, Kenneth J., 191
Artaud, Antonin, 211
ASEAN (Association of Southeast Asian Nations), 86, 90, 110, 124

Ashland University, 158
Asian financial crisis, 75–76, 77, 93, 104–10, 118, 199, 295
Asian Free Trade Agreement (AFTA), 88
Associated Press, 182
Astana, 126
Atlas Shrugged, 294
Auckland, 126
Australia, x, xiii, 61, 73, 81, 84, 292
Avineri, Schlomo, 9
Azahari Husin, 272
Azizan Abu Bakar, 130n20

B
Babri Mosque, 255
Badawi. *See* Abdullah bin Haji Ahmad Badawi
Bahamas, 13
baht (THB), 76, 104–5, 126
Baku, 126
Bali terror attacks, 67, 121, 203, 223, 254
Balkan Wars, 266
Bandar Seri Begawan, 126, 222
Bangkok, 61, 66, 123, 124, 126, 127, 254, 255
Bangladesh, 84
Bank of America, x
Barbados, 13
Barbieri, Pierpaolo, 134
Barings Bank, 109
Barisan Nasional (BN), 91–92
Bashir, Abu Bakar, 121
Batey Ads, 80
Baudrillard, Jean Paul, 187, 289
Bauman, Zygmunt, 9, 292, 293
Bay Area Rapid Transit (BART), 76
BBC, 57, 172, 273, 274
Bear and the Lion: Soviet Imperialism and Iran, 37
Bear Stearns, 154, 160
Beauvoir, Simone de, 188, 236

Index   325

Beck, Ulrich, 9
Bell, Charlie, 155
Benelux economic confederation, 37
Berger, Peter L., 299
Berkeley, George, 235, 278
Berlin Airlift, 179
Bhabha, Homi K., 127, 163, 207
Bharathiya Janata Party (BJP), 114
Bhumibol Adulyadej (King of Thailand), 125, 126, 275, 283
Biggie Smalls, 213
Bilmes, Linda J., 262
Bin Laden, Osama, 2, 41, 102, 103, 255, 297
Birkinshaw, Julian, 29
Bishkek, 102
Bishop Estate, 233
Black Swan: The Impact of the Highly Improbable, 31
Blackwater Worldwide, 262
Blair, Sir Ian, 273
Blair, Tony, 256, 273
Blitzer, Wolf, 195
Blumenberg, Hans, 9, 236
Boeing, 63, 78
Boer War, 266
Bollenbach, Stephen F., 154
Botwinick, Aryeh, 9
Bouts, Thierry, 55
Bowling for Columbine, 51
Bowling Green University, 86
Bradley, Omar N., 181
Brady Handgun Violence Prevention Act (1993), 51, 226
Brando, Marlon, 196, 209
Brazil, 45, 205, 275
Breakin' All the Rules, 204
Brecht, Bertolt, 210
Bretton Woods system, 18
Brigham Young University, 161
Britain
  anti-terrorism efforts, 263
  ban on Louis Farrakhan, 231

  colonial empire, 29–30, 32n11, 56–58, 66, 81, 120, 265, 276
  global financial crisis and, x
  as a great power, 145, 290
  Hong Kong and, 57, 175, 185n4
  Hu Jintao's visit to, 274
  immigration, 101
  natural law tradition, 225
  North American possessions, 137
  race relations, 57–58
  Shah of Iran and, 302
  slave trade, 205
  soccer hooliganism, 36
  spies in Moscow, 270
  system of government, 97
  U.S. war of independence and, 14, 179, 207, 235
  during World War II, 176, 284
British Overseas Airline Corporation (BOAC), 64
British Petroleum (BP), 77, 263
Brooks, Garth, 196
Brown, Gordon, 273
Brown v. Board of Education, 36, 181
Brunei, 69, 84, 248
Buchanan, Pat, 288
Buddhism, 198, 215n6, 282
Building of the Panama Canal in Historic Photographs, 144
Bunau-Varilla, Philippe, 144
Burke, Edmund, 97
Burton, Richard, 210
Bush, George Herbert Walker, 88, 173, 185n3
Bush, George W.
  conspiracy to assassinate, 282
  election, 11, 95, 178
  Iraq invasion and, 2, 256–57, 262, 266, 301
  Malaysian prime ministers and, 93, 120
  political allies, 158, 160
  sale of Harken stocks, 42

September 11 and, 98
Singapore prime minister and, 173
sub-prime crisis and, 287–88
troop withdrawals and, 170
Business @ the Speed of Thought, 159
Business Times, 77
Butler, Brett, 188
Butler, Judith, 188, 236

C
Cairo, 173
California, 137, 181
California Institute of Technology, 178
California Maritime Academy, 181
Caltex, 77
Cambodia, 2, 65, 126, 268, 272
Canada, 13, 83
Canberra, 126
Cantalini, 236
Cantalupo, Jim, 155
Cape Fear, 210
Capra, Frank, 209
Captain Blood, 210
Carey, Drew, 188
Carter, Jimmy, 93, 303
Cash, Johnny, 196
Cassidy, John, 99
Castro, Fidel, 188
Catell, Robert B., 163
Catholic Church, 72
Cat on a Hot Tin Roof, 209
Cayman Islands, 13
Cayne, James E., 154, 160
Cendant, 154, 157, 158, 165n17
CEO and the Monk, 163
Certificates of Entitlement (COEs), 76
Cervantes Saavedra, Miguel de, 210
Challenging the Mandate of Heaven, 87
Chan, et al. v. Korean Air Lines Ltd, 227
Chang, Iris, 2
Changi International Airport, 78
Changi Prison Museum and Chapel, 284

Chavalit Yongchaiyudh (General), 105
Chechnya, 272
Chemical Ali, 272
Chen Shui Bian, 164n5, 175
Chevron, 263
Chiang Mai, 122
Chile, 45
China. *See also* Hong Kong
 ancient technologies, 245, 278
 Asian financial crisis and, 110
 ban on the Internet, 195, 248
 corruption, 112–13, 128
 Cultural Revolution, 189
 educational system, 81
 emigrants to Singapore, 82–84
 financial reform, 108
 Hawaiian labour from, 233
 invasion by Japan, 119, 168
 as investment destination, 84, 99, 127
 investments in the U.S., 267
 Japanese pop culture and, 119
 language, 127, 128
 Lee Hsien Loong's Taiwan visit and, 66
 Marxism in, xiii, 280
 military, 73
 Muslim population, 96, 100–104
 as neoliberal market, 299
 per capita GDP, 113
 population control, 246–47
 poverty in, 58, 275
 relations with ASEAN, 110
 relations with India, 115, 175
 relations with Pakistan, 242
 relations with Russia, 175
 relations with Soviet Union, 87, 100
 relations with Taiwan, 82, 89, 173–75
 relations with U.S., 87–88, 89, 100–104, 110–13, 174, 257
 trade imbalances with U.S., xi, 286

U.S. Treasury bond holdings, 61, 104, 111, 113
war against Vietnam, 2, 3
China Aviation Oil (Singapore), 113
China Daily, 270
China Life, 153
Chinese Communist Party (CCP), 88, 89, 111, 175
Chomsky, Noam, 9, 95, 184, 245, 298
Christianity, 21, 197, 215n6, 268
Christine de Pizan, 278
Chua, Amy L., 124
Chuan Leekpai, 125
Chulachomklao Royal Military Academy, 124
Chulalongkorn University, 124
Churchill, Winston, 302
CIA (Central Intelligence Agency), 12, 65, 85, 97, 203, 297, 300, 302
CitiGroup, 154
Citizen Kane, 210, 216n12
Civil Rights Act (1965), 181
Clarke, Susan E., 20
Clarke Air Force Base, 71, 173
Clash of Civilizations, 299
Clausewitz, Carl von, 17, 188
Cline, Patsy, 196
Clinton administration, 108, 283
CNA (Channel News Asia), 126
CNBC, 126, 195
CNN, 172, 195
CNNMoney, 157, 275
Cobain, Kurt, 213
Coca-cola, 115–16, 196
Cochise, Chief, 229
Cold War
 airline industry and, 62
 American propaganda during, 26
 Asian countries and, 71, 81, 100, 114, 120, 122
 cost of, 14, 257
 end of, 88, 100, 280, 298
 Germany and, 118
 globalization and, 37–38
 intelligence gathering, 243, 254
 military industrial complex and, 171, 177, 179
 oil crisis and, 84–85
 place in modern history, xiii–xiv, 267
 technology and, 195, 253
 terrorism and, 176, 297
 triumph of capitalism, 141, 261
Cold War and Soviet Insecurity, 37
Coleman, James S., 229
Colgate-Palmolive, 154, 156
Colombia, 45, 144
Colombo, 126
Colorado, 180
Columbia University, 178
Communist Party of America, 115
Communist Party of Thailand, 122
Computer Associates, 153
Condillac, Etienne Bonnot de, 138
Condorcet, Jean-Antoine-Nicolas de Caritat, Marquis de, 138
Confucianism, 215n6, 245
Congo, Republic of, 98
Congress Party (India), 113, 115, 116
Connecticut, 180
Connolly, William E., 9, 19, 202, 216n12
Conrad, Joseph, 236, 276
Conservative Party (UK), 185n4, 302
consumer price index (CPI), 43–44
Corruption Perceptions Index (CPI), 70
Cosby, Bill, 203–4
Cost of Living Index, 43
Council for National Security (Thailand), 125
country and western (C&W) music, 196–200
Crimean War, 266, 290
Cronkite, Walter, 181, 278

328 Index

Crystal, Graef S., 165n15
C-SPAN, 15, 195, 287, 288
Cuba, 2, 56, 268, 280
Cuban Missile Crisis, 267
CUNY (City University of New York), 160

D
DaimlerChrysler, 48, 263
Darden Graduate School of Business Administration, 157
Dartmouth College, 178
D'Aveni, Richard A., 20
David, George, 154, 157
Davis, Sammy, Jr., 188, 200, 204
Dean, James, 212
Death the Leveller, 151
Defense Acquisition University (DAU), 178
Defense Language Institute Foreign Language Center (DLIFLC), 178
DeGeneres, Ellen, 188
De Havilland, Olivia, 209
Delaware, 182
Deleuze, Gilles, 236
Dell, Michael, 160
Dell Computers, 160
Democratic Party (U.S.)
  Asian financial crisis and, 107
  foreign policy and, 52, 96
  liberal values and, 11–12, 145, 297
  "one-party state" and, 94, 177, 184, 308n2
  as voting choice, 293, 304
Deng Xiaoping, 88, 271
Department of Homeland Security (DHS), 52, 98, 263
Department of the Army v. *Blue Fox Inc.,* 226
Depression, Great, xiii
Detroit Project, 46, 48
Dewey, John, 142, 191
Dhaka, 126

Dhanabalan, S., 279
Diaz Espino, Ovidio, 144
Dicey, A.V., 36
Dili, 126
Discipline and Punish, 289
Dittmer, Lowell, 104
Dobyns, Henry F., 229
Docker, 212
Dole, Bob, 231
Don Quixote, 210
Dow Jones Industrial Average, 107
Drucker, Peter, 298, 299
Drug Enforcement Administration (DEA), 11
Duke, David, 233
Dulles, John Foster, 181
DuPont, 85

E
Eagleburger, Lawrence S., 27
Earman, John, 20
East Timor. *See* Timor Leste
East Turkestan Islamic Movement (ETIM), 102, 103
Easy Rider, 196, 214
Economic Development Board (EDB), 279
economic theory, 138–41
Ecuador, 45
Eden, Anthony, 302
EDSA People Power revolution, 71
Egypt, 173–74, 176
Einstein, Albert, 36, 238n30
Eisenhower, Dwight D., 169, 173, 176, 180, 181, 183–84
Eisner, Michael D., 154
Electronic Road Pricing (ERP), 76
Elijah Muhammad, 230
Ellison, Lawrence J., 154, 159, 160
Elshtain, Jean, 262
Emblidge, David, 200
End of Economic Man, 298
End of History and the Last Man, ix

English language, 26, 81, 82, 101, 127–28, 198, 276
Enigma of Arrival, 252
Enlightenment, 138, 151, 212, 235, 236, 241, 265
Enron, 109, 154, 165n15, 203
Enter Plato, 187
environmental disasters, 203
Epstein, Lee, 226
Esso-Mobil, 77
Ettinger, Amber Lee, 195
Euben, J. Peter, 1, 9, 229
Eurasian Association Community House, 284
euro (EUR), 203, 274
Europe
  American Idol clones in, 194
  cultural production, 206–7
  dependence on oil, 84, 203, 258
  dependence on U.S., 37
  immigration, 113
  neoliberal capitalism and, x
  neo-Marxist movements, 2, 169
  potential protectionism, 203, 286
  special force units, 65
  welfare state in, 54
European Bank for Reconstruction and Development (EBRD), 224
European Community, 118, 274
European Courts of Justice, 228
European Union, 175, 275
Everyday Life in the Modern World, 293
Exxon-Mobil, 77, 180, 263
Ezekiel, Raphael S., 203

F
Fannie Mae, x
Fanon, Frantz, 236
Farah, Empress, consort of Shah of Iran, 303
Farrakhan, Louis, 230, 231
Farrow, Mia, 210
Fast Food Nation, 44

FBI (Federal Bureau of Investigation), 255, 256, 257
Feagin, Joe R., 204
Federal Energy Regulatory Commission (FERC), 85
Federalist Paper Number 51, 178, 233
Federal Power Act (1920), 85
Ferguson, Kathy, 27
Financial Development of Japan, Korea, and Taiwan, 38
Financial Times, 153
First Security National Bank v. *United States,* 226
Five Power Defense Arrangements (FPDA), 73
Florida, 11, 85, 181, 290
Flynn, Errol, 210
Flynt, Larry, 50
Focke, Heinrich, 36
Fonda, Henry, 210
Fonda, Peter, 196
Forbes, 124, 154, 156, 157, 158, 160, 166n27
Ford, Gerald R., 36, 93, 303
Ford Motors, 46, 47, 116, 180
Forest Labs, 154, 160
Fortis, x
Foucault, Michel. *See also* "ship of fools" metaphor
  on crime and punishment, 281
  interrogative methods, 292, 296
  liberalism and globalization, 236
  Madness and Civilization, 123
  on modernity and humanity, xvii, 55
  personal imperfection, 35, 36
  on the police, 274
  as pop culture icon, 188
Fountainhead, 294
Fox News, 195
Foxworthy, Jeff, 200
Foxx, Jamie, 204
France
  arms sales, 173

as colonial power, 29, 66, 145, 265, 276
as immigration destination, 101
Shah of Iran and, 302
U.S. territorial expansion and, 37, 137, 143
Franks, Gary, 231
Freddie Mac, x
Freedom of Information Act (1967), 5
free trade, 11, 17, 57, 88, 99, 224
French language, 26, 82, 272
French Revolution, 168, 212, 266
Friedman, Milton, 279
Friedman, Thomas, 299
Friquegnon, Marie-Louise, 6
Fromm, Eric, 201, 282
Fukuyama, Francis, ix, 15
Fuld, Richard S., Jr., 154, 157
Fuyushiba, Tetsuzo, 117

G
Gable, Clark, 209
Gabon, 85
Gaebler, Ted, 299
Gaile, Gary L., 20
Gandhi, Sonya, 113, 115, 116
Gang of Four, 88
Garland, David, 262
Gasiorowski, Mark J., 303
Gates, Bill, 140, 159–60, 240, 278
Gates, Melinda, 159
Geiger, Theodor, 19
General Motors (GM), 48, 180, 214, 263
Georgia, 181
Gerakan Aceh Merdeka (GAM), 32n4
Gerakan Mujahideen Islam Pattani (GMIP), 32n4
Germany, x, 30, 118, 168, 274
Gibb, Andy, 213
Gibraltar, 13
Gillespie, J. Lodge, Jr., 61
Gilpin, Robert, 16, 17

Giuliani, Carlo, 282
Giuliani, Rudy, 161
Glaeser, Edward, 53
global financial crisis (2008)
  Asia and, 129
  causes, xvii, 258, 262, 266, 286–87
  effects and solutions, x–xi, 104, 164
  as financial terrorism, xiv, xviii, 261
  social behaviour and, 134
globalization
  defining traits, xiv–xvi, 5, 15, 253, 283
  democracy and, 215n7, 268, 277, 290
  demographic matters and, 82, 148–49
  financial services and, 267–68
  intelligence gathering and, 241–44
  localization and, 250–51, 264
  modernity and, 28–29
  the nation-state and, 263
  norms and, 218–28, 234–37
  origins in colonialism, 29–30
  permanent residency status and, 130n12
  police powers and, 282–83
  politics of, 5, 289–90, 293
  popular culture and, 198–99, 201–3
  quality of life and, 22–25, 33n17
  religion and, 21–22
  values and, 228–37
  vs. Americanization, 25–27
  war and, 261–84
  youths and, 198–99, 264–65
Globalization and Its Discontents, 123
Globalization Syndrome, 19
Goetzmann, William N., 16
Goh, Ryan, 79
Goh Chok Tong, 67, 109, 279
Goh Keng Swee, 74, 85, 279
Goldman Sachs, 151
Goldwater, Barry, 181

Golkar, 107
Gone With the Wind, 209
Gorbachev, Mikhail, 88
Gore, Al, 90–91
Gouldner, Alvin, 9, 187
Gowa, Joanne, 17
Gramsci, Antonio, 188, 192, 193, 211, 215n4, 280
Granger, Clive, 139
Grant, Ulysses S., 143, 181
Grapes of Wrath, 210
Great Escape, 196
Great Gatsby, 210
Great Lakes Maritime Academy, 181
Greenspan, Alan, 104, 107, 111, 294, 295
Growth, Inequality, and Globalization, 18–19
Guangzhou, 100
Guanxi and Business, 112
Guattari, Pierre-Félix, 236
Guinness, Alec, 188
Gulf of Mexico, 85
Gulf War, First
   Asia and, 81
   background, 2–3
   economic effects, 117–18, 258
   George H.W. Bush and, 185n3
   motives behind, 99, 258
   U.S. and, 4, 176, 257, 267
Gulf War, Second. *See also* Iraq
   American Dream and, 210–11
   Asia and, 81
   cost of, 14, 257, 275
   George W. Bush and, 2, 256–57, 262, 266, 301
   motives and justifications for, 56, 99, 255, 258
   Singapore's support for, 75
   UN opposition to, 173
   U.S. and, 4, 176, 203, 267
Gusmao, 236
Gutenberg, Johannes, 278

H
H1N1 bird flu pandemic, 124
Habermas, Jürgen, 9, 191–92, 212, 281
Habibie, B.J., 106, 130n24, 279
Hague, 228
Haig, Alexander, 181
Haiti, 203
Hakkinen, Mika, 188
Hale, David R.E., 182
Hall, Pamela, 199
Hampton v. Mow Sun Wong, 226
Hang Seng index, 61, 107
Hanssen, Robert, 255
Harken Energy Corporation, 42
Harley Davidson and the Marlboro Man, 196
Harley Davidson motorcycles, 196, 214
Hartz, Louis, 292
Harvard Gazette, 134, 245
Harvard University, 156, 157, 178, 233
Harvey, David, 9, 292, 293
Hat Yai, 123
Hawaii, 27, 119, 147, 225, 233, 236
Hawking, Stephen, 188, 238n30
Heart of Darkness, 276
Hefner, Hugh, 50
Hegel, Georg Wilhelm Friedrich, 235, 236, 280, 291
Hegemony or Survival, 298
Heidegger, Martin
   among other thinkers, 9, 280
   Hannah Arendt and, 15, 142, 201, 259n1
   ideas on technology, xvii–xviii, 15, 24, 62, 140, 291
Hell, 55
Hell's Angels, 196
Helms, Jesse, 288
Hendrickson, Mason, 68, 90
Hendrix, Jimi, 213

Henige, David, 229
Herbeck, Dan, 203
Hermocrates, 170
Herodotus, 1, 303
Herzog, Chaim, 68
Hewlett-Packard, 85
Hilton Hotels, 154
Hinduism, 21, 113–14
Hindustan Coca-Cola Berverages (HCCB), 115
Hiroshima, 1
Hispanic Americans, 287
History of the Peloponnesian War, 38, 150
Hitchcock, Alfred, 210
Hitler, Adolf, 199, 272
HKTV-B, 126
Hobbes, Thomas, 17, 133, 171, 278, 296
Ho Chi Minh, 87
Homeland Security Institute (HSI), 52
Honasan, Gregorio "Gringo" (Colonel), 71
Hong Kong
 British handover, 57, 185n4
 China Life IPO, 153
 emigrants, 82
 mini-Constitution, 112, 175
 as part of Chinese economy, 111, 112
 pop culture, 188
 stock exchange, 62
 subway system, 77
 Yang Ping-Wang and, 270
Hong Kong dollar (HKD), 105
Hon Sui Sen, 85
Hope, Bob, 181, 188
Hopper, Dennis, 196
Horkheimer, Max, 201, 232, 280
Hotel Honolulu, 252
Howard, Leslie, 209
How Wall Street Created a Nation, 144
Huffington, Arianna, 50, 295

Hu Jintao, 274
Hukbong Mapagpalaya ng Bayan, 2
Huk Rebellion, 2, 3, 31n3
Hulland, John, 29
Human Genome Project, 220
human rights, 98, 219
Hume, David, 235, 278
Hundred Years of Solitude, 92
Huntington, Samuel P., 30, 299
Hussein, Saddam, 2, 27, 56, 255, 272, 300
Husserl, Edmund, 236, 238n30
Hustler, 50
Huxley, Aldous, 292, 293
Hyppolite, Jean, 236

I
IBM, 219
IBRC, 17
I-Ch'ing, 245, 259n1
Ilinitch, Anne Y., 20
Illinois, 147, 182
I.M.A.G.E. Consortium, 220
IMF (International Monetary Fund)
 American globalization and, 10, 57, 104, 123
 Asian financial crisis and, 93–94, 104, 107, 109, 110
 as organ of neoliberal capitalism, 17, 162
 projections for future, 149
Immigration and Naturalization Service (INS), 11, 146
India
 British colonial times, xiii
 corruption, 113, 114, 128
 democracy, 268
 emigration to Singapore, 84
 Hindu nationalism, 113–14, 242
 as investment destination, 84, 127–28
 Karl Marx on, 235
 as neoliberal market, 299

Index   333

New Delhi stock exchange, 62
petrochemical industry, 77
poverty, 275
relations with ASEAN, 110
relations with China, 115, 175, 271
relations with Pakistan, 242
relations with U.S., 58, 113–17,
   222, 257
Shah of Iran's visit, 302
terrorism, 255
trade imbalances with U.S., xi, 286
U.S. Treasury bond holdings, 61,
   104
Indiana, 182
Indian Oil Corporation, 116
Indonesia
   airline industry, 63
   Asian financial crisis and, 76, 105
   corruption, 70, 71
   educational system, 81
   financial structures, 224
   McDonald's in, 251
   military, 65, 67, 68, 70, 73
   Muslim population, 96
   as oil producer, 85
   as potential Al-Qaeda hub, 176
   relations with Malaysia, 67, 69, 121
   relations with Singapore, 86, 173
   response to globalization, 268
   standards of living, 46
   terrorism, 67, 121, 203, 223, 254,
      272
   U.S. investment in, 84
   U.S. sale of weapons to, 29
Indonesian Democratic Party–Struggle
   (PDI–P), 107
Industrial College of the Armed Forces
   (ICAF), 179
Industrial Promotion Board (IPB), 279
Industrial Revolution, xii, 9, 138, 140,
   297
Information Resources Management
   College (IRMC), 179

Inniss, Leslie B., 204
Inouye, Daniel K., 181
Institute for Research on Poverty, 39,
   41
Internal Revenue Service (IRS), 11, 13
International Bank for Reconstruction
   and Development (IBRD), 224
International Court of Justice, 228
Internet
   addiction, 248–49, 277
   Bill Gates and, 140, 159
   invention, 36, 278
   structures of power and, 28, 194,
      195
   U.S. and, 38
In the Past Lane, 42
Iran
   fall of the Shah, 26
   globalization and, 268
   Islamic revolution, 3, 172–73
   relations with Soviet Union, 302,
      303
   U.S. and, 65, 85, 203, 256, 262
Iran-Contra affair, 254
Iran-Iraq war, 2–3, 26–27, 173, 176
Iraq
   causes of terrorism and, 1
   deaths in, xviii, 11, 146, 271
   invasion of Kuwait, 2–3
   John Kerry and, 301
   oil reserves, 99
   signs of U.S. decline in, xi, 286,
      287
   U.S. invasion of, 56, 75, 173, 203,
      255–56, 262, 266
   U.S. military malfeasance in, 27,
      211
   U.S. special forces in, 65
Irian Jaya, 69
"iron cage" syndrome, 52
Isaac, Jeffrey C., 29
Islam
   cultural norms and, 222, 269

fundamentalist movements, 169, 203, 242, 253, 299
   globalization and, 21, 268–69
   Tao Yuan Sect and, 215n6
   in the U.S., 230, 231, 300
Islamabad, 126
Islamic Association of China, 100
Islamic Journey, 252
Israel, 66, 86, 92, 99, 173, 176, 203
Italy, 101, 176, 276
It's A Wonderful Life, 209

J
Jackson, Michael, 42, 230
Jackson, Stonewall, 181
Jakarta, 61, 126, 222, 251, 254, 272
Jameson, Fredric, 9, 30
Japan
   business and work culture, 222–23, 234–35
   demographic problems, 246
   as economic model, 75, 90, 93, 265
   economic outlook, 274, 295
   educational system, 81, 118
   financial reform, 108
   as investment destination, 127
   relations with U.S., 117–20, 173, 223
   Tokyo stock exchange, 62, 107
   U.S. investment in, 84
   U.S. military and, 27, 36, 175
   U.S. Treasury bond holdings, 111, 117
   war with Russia, xiii, 3, 266
   World War II, xiii, 119, 168, 179
Japanese Red Army, 68
Jaspers, Karl, 201
Java, 105, 121
Jefferson, Thomas, 180
Jemaah Islamiah, 53, 297
Jessop, Bob, 146
Jesus CEO, 163
Jews, 2, 52, 67, 92–93, 100, 120–21, 231

Jinan, 100
Jobs, Steve, 159, 160, 278
Jogjakarta, 121
Johns Hopkins University, 178
Johnson, Don, 196
Johnson, Lyndon B., 39, 93
Johor, 66
Joint Forces Staff College (JFSC), 179
Joint Military Intelligence College (JMIC), 179
Jones, Kristine, 229
Jones, Laurie Beth, 163
Jonson, Ben, 204
Jordan, 255
Jorion, Philippe, 16
Journal of Politics, 136
Judaism, 21, 268
Judds (country singers), 196
Jung, Carl, 259n8

K
Kabul, 126
Kadyrov, Akhmad, 272
Kahneman, Daniel, 139
Kammen, Michael, 42
Kant, Immanuel, 141–42, 209, 219, 235, 280, 291
Kaplan, Robert D., 163
Kariel, Henry S., 136–37, 210, 216n12, 232, 291
Karr, John Mark, 195
Kashmir, 98, 242
Kathmandu, 126
Katrina, Hurricane, 4, 12, 275
Katzenstein, Peter J., 9, 16, 24–25, 28, 31, 104
Kautilya, 246
Kautsky, Karl, 280
Kay, David, 255
Kedah, 3
Kelantan, 3, 121
Keller, Ulrich, 144
Kellner, Douglas, 29

Kennan, George F., 17
Kennedy, John F., 188
Kentucky, 182
Kerry, John, 301
Keynes, John Maynard, 18, 139
Khmer Rouge, 2, 272
Khomeini, Ruhollah (Ayatollah), 2, 3, 172, 302, 303
Khunying Potjaman Shinawatra, 72, 124
Kim Il-Sung, 89
Kindsvatter, Peter S., 87
King, Martin Luther, Jr., 188, 230
King, Rodney, 36, 233, 283
Kissinger, Henry, 181
Koizumi, Junichiro, 117, 274
Konfrontasi, 69
KOPASUS (Komando Pasukan Khusus), 69–70
Korean War, xiv, 81, 87, 176, 179, 203, 257, 267
Kota Tinggi, 67
Kovacevich, Richard M., 154, 160
Krueger, Anne, 94
Kuala Lumpur, 62, 90, 94, 120, 126, 127, 222
Kumar, Sanjay, 153
Kumpulan Mujahiden Malaysia (KMM), 32n4
Kuomintang (KMT), 174
Kupperman, Robert H., 4
Kurosawa, Akira, 118, 252, 292, 293
Kuwait, 2–3, 203
Kyrgyzstan, 102

L

Lang-Lang, 212
Language Policy and Modernity in Southeast Asia, 81
Laos, 268
Larmore, Charles, 9
Lash, Scott, 9, 19
Late Capitalism, 148

Latin America, 45, 128, 194, 232, 275
Lauper, Cyndi, 163
Laurence, Henry, 108
Law of the Constitution, 36
Lawrence, D.H., 292, 293
Lawrence, Martin, 204
Lay, Kenneth (Ken), 165n15
Leadership Secrets of the World's Most Successful CEOs, 163
Lebanon, 203
Lee, Robert E., 181
Lee Hsien Loong, 66, 68, 75, 90, 279
Lee Kuan Yew, 64, 67, 78–79, 90, 279
Leeson, Nicholas, 109
Lefebvre, Henri, 30–31, 232, 292
Lehman Brothers, x, 154, 156, 165n16
Leigh, Vivien, 209
Leninism, 280
Lennon, John, 213
Leno, Jay, 188
Letterman, David, 188
Leviathan, 296
Levi-Strauss, Claude, 245
Lewin, Arie Y., 20
Lewis, John, 231
Lexus and the Olive Tree, 299
Liberal Democratic Party (Japan), 117
Libya, 203, 256, 268
Lili'uokalani, Queen, 233
Lilly Ledbetter Fair Pay Act (2009), x
Lincoln Memorial, 232–33
Lindsey, Lawrence, 262
Lippman, Walter, 191, 205, 213
Lipsett, Seymour Martin, 219, 228
Little Wolf, Chief, 229
Lloyd Webber, Andrew, 192
Location of Culture, 127
Locke, John, 35, 56, 235, 278
Lockheed Corporation, 63
London terror attacks, 254
Longitudes and Attitudes, 299
Los Angeles, 36, 233

Louisiana Purchase, 37, 236, 290
Lucas, Robert, Jr., 139
Luhmann, Niklas, 148
Luo, Yadong, 112
Luxembourg, Rosa, 280
Luzon, 3
Lyotard, Jean François, 9

M
MacArthur, Douglas (General), 120, 181
Machiavelli, Niccolò, 17
Maclear, Michael, 87
Madison, James, 178
Madness and Civilization, 123
Madrid terror attacks, 67, 203, 223, 254, 272
Mahan, Alfred Thayer, 181
Mahathir bin Mohamad, 67, 74, 75, 90–92, 94, 120, 130n20, 279
Maher, Bill, 188
Mahsum, Hasan, 103
Maine Maritime Academy, 181
Makati incident, 71
Makin, Tony, 108
Malacca Straits, 66, 99
Malayan Communist Party, 2, 122, 177
Malaysia
  airline industry, 63
  anti-Semitism in, 92–93, 199
  Asian financial crisis and, 75–76, 105, 108
  constitutional definition of Malay, 269
  economic policies, 74, 90, 93–94
  educational system, 81
  financial structures, 224
  Islamic movements, 3, 96, 242, 269
  IT technologies, 248
  Kuala Lumpur stock exchange, 62, 107
  military, 66–67, 68, 70, 73

  petrochemical industry, 77
  police, 274, 283
  population, 100
  as potential Al-Qaeda hub, 176
  race relations, 74, 92
  relations with Indonesia, 67, 69, 121
  relations with Singapore, 66–67, 74–75, 77, 85–86, 173
  relations with U.S., 90–91, 120
Malaysian Airlines (MAS), 64
Malaysia-Singapore Airways (MSA), 64
Male, 126
Malindo Darsasa, 67, 73
Malott, John, 91
Malthus, Thomas, 138
Manchester City Football Club, 72, 124
Mandel, Ernest, 148
Manifest Destiny, 137, 194, 235
Manila, 126
Mann, Michael, 148, 292, 293
Man of the People, 92
Manoogian, Richard A., 154
Manu, 246
Many Globalizations, 299
Maoism, 2, 280
Mao Zedong, 87–88, 174, 188, 189
Marcos, Ferdinand E., 71, 300
Marcuse, Herbert, 9, 201
Marine Corps News, 182
Marine Corps University (MCU), 179
Mark, Reuben, 154, 156
Marley, Bob, 213
Marquez, Gabriel Garcia, 292
Martin, Dean, 188, 194, 200
Marx, Karl, xiii, 150, 191, 235, 272, 277, 278, 280
Maryland, 182
Maryland v. *United States,* 226
Masco, 154
Massachusetts Maritime Academy, 181

Mass Rapid Transit (MRT), 76
Mass Transit Railway (MTR), 77
Mastny, Vojtech, 37
McCartney, Paul, 292
McClintic-Marshall Company, 144
McClintock, Anne, 236
McClure, Kirstie M., 29
McCullough, David, 144
McDonald's Corporation, 115–16, 155–56, 196, 222, 250–51, 252
McDonnell Douglas, 63
McDuffie, Arthur, 283
McFadden, George, 204
McKinley, William, 143
McQueen, Steve, 196
McVeigh, Timothy, 231
Mearsheimer, John, 17
Melody, Michael E., 229
Menezes, Jean Charles de, 273
Merrill Lynch, x
Merton, Robert C., 139
Mexico, 13, 45, 287
Michaels, Walter, 202
Michel, Lou, 203
Microsoft, 159, 160, 196
Middlebury College, 156
Middle East
 American Idol and, 194
 democracy and, 267
 hot war syndrome, 242
 Islamic fundamentalism, 169
 oil and, 98, 99, 298
 special forces, 65
 U.S. politics and, 52, 98, 99, 203, 262
 U.S. ports and, xviii
Mifune, Toshiro, 188
Military Intelligence Bureau (Taiwan), 270
Mill, John Stuart, 235, 289
Miller, Henry, 188
Miller, Larry, 214
Miller, Nathan, 145

Millet, 236
Million Man March, 230–31
Mills, C. Wright, 281
Mimic Men, 127, 265
Mindanao, 72, 242
Minnesota, 182
Mississippi, 182
Missouri, 181
MIT (Massachusetts Institute of Technology), 95, 178, 245
Mitchum, Robert, 210
Mittelman, James H., 19
Mobil, 85
Modelski, George, 29
Mohammad Reza Pahlavi, Shah of Iran, 3, 26, 85, 103, 301–3
Mohammed Dato Abdul Aziz, 93
Mok Hin Choon, 79
Mongolia, 119
Monroe, Marilyn, 213
Monroe Doctrine, 137, 194, 235
Montreal Agreement, 227
Moody, Peter R., Jr., 88
Moore, Kenny, 163
Moore, Michael, 50, 51, 214, 232
Moos, Malcolm, 180
Morgan, J.P., 144
Morgenthau, Hans Joachim, 17
Moro Islamic Liberation Front (MILF), 3
Moro National Liberation Front (MNLF), 3
Morris, Edmund, 145
Morrison, Allen, 29
Mossadeq, Mohammed, 302
MSNBC, 159
multinational corporations (MNCs)
 American globalization and, 10–11, 163, 196, 212, 223
 Asian, 64
 fast food, 44–45, 115–16, 250–51
 impermanent monuments of, 177
 Japanese bond holdings and, 117

new opportunities for, 275
oil and, 85, 99
outsourcing and, 145–49, 162
Panama Canal as, 137, 143
rise of, xiv
SEC scrutiny of, 153, 165n13
U.S. system of justice and, 226
Western European, 37, 85
Murdock, Margaret Maier, 229
Mussolini, Benito, 188
Mutual Life Insurance Company v. *Harris,* 225
Myanmar, 81, 195, 265, 267, 268

N
Nagasaki, 1
Naipaul, V.S., 127, 163, 207, 252, 265, 269
Najib Tun Razak, Datuk, 4
Nandy, 126
Nanjing, 100, 168
Narathiwat, 3, 242, 275
Narayan, Uma, 236
NASA, 241
Nasution, Abdul Haris (General), 69
National Farmers Union Insurance Companies v. *Crow Tribe of Indians,* 226
National Federation of Federal Employees v. *United States,* 226
National Front (NF), 91
National Incident Management System (NIMS), 52
National Justice Party, 90, 130n17
National Rifle Association, 51
National Security Branch (NSB), 256
National War College (NWC), 179
Nation of Islam, 230–31
Native Americans, 137, 194, 229, 232–33, 287
NATO (North Atlantic Treaty Organization), 27, 37, 175

Naval Postgraduate School (NPS), 179
Nazis, 2, 168, 176, 198–99
NBC News, 195
Nelson, Todd S., 154, 161
neoliberalism
  beneficiaries of, 152
  China and, 90
  globalization and, x, 6, 268, 275
  positions and preferences, 17–18, 57, 107–8, 277, 296
  poverty and, 149–51
  sub-prime crisis and, 262
  supporting structures, 85, 232, 297–98
  terrorism and, 270, 299
Nepal, 84
Netherlands, x, 29, 66, 81, 82, 265
Neubauer, Deane E., 9
New Delhi, 126, 275
New Jersey, 160
New Komeito Party, 117
New Mexico, 181, 236
Newton, Isaac, 238n30
New York, 153, 177, 274
New York Maritime College, 181
New York Post, 153
New York State, 147, 160
New York Times, 49, 288, 303
New York University, 157
New Zealand, xiii, 73, 81, 84, 292
Nicholson, Jack, 196
Niebuhr, Reinhold, 17
Nietzsche, Friedrich
  American politics and, 55
  the anti-hero and, 211
  Aristotle and, xvii
  ideas, xvi, 136, 142, 277, 304
  McFadden's view of, 204
  personal traits, 236, 280
Nigeria, 85
Nikkei index, 62, 107, 274
Nine Network, 126

Nitze, Paul H., 181
Nixon, Richard M., 36, 87, 93, 303
Nixon v. Warner Communications, 226
North Carolina, 147
Northern Virginia Roundtable, 158
North Korea
  intelligence on, 255
  rejection of globalization, 265, 268, 280
  threats from, 89, 242
  U.S. decline and, xi, 262, 267, 286
Norton, R.D., 37
Nuclear Regulatory Commission (NRC), 85
NVR, 154, 158
Nye, Joseph S., 17, 192
Nye, Robert, 29

O
Obama, Barack Hussein, x, 2, 195, 262
Obama Girl, 195
OECD (Organization for Economic Cooperation and Development), x, 61, 274
Office of Technology Policy, 253
Okinawa, 175
Oklahoma, 85
Oklahoma City bombing, 169, 254
OPEC (Organization of Petroleum Exporting Countries), 39, 84, 85, 203, 258
Opposition and Dissent in Contemporary China, 88
Oracle, 154, 159
Oregon, 182
Organization of the Islamic Conference (OIC), 67–68, 92
Orientalism, 85
Orwell, George, 292
Osborne, David, 299
outsourcing, 128, 145–49
Oxford University, 124, 185n4

P
Pahlavi, Ashraf, Princess, 303
Paine, Thomas, 142
Pakistan, 4, 84, 242, 270, 302
Palestine, 120, 203
Panama Canal, 136–37, 143–44, 161, 233
Pan-American World Airways, 64
Papua, 69
Pareto, Vilfredo, 139, 140
Pareto's law, 139, 148
Parks, Rosa, 210
Partai Demokrasi Indonesia Perjuangan (PDI–P), 107
Parti Keadilan Rakyat, 90, 130n17
Path Between the Seas, 144
Patrick, Hugh, 37
Pattani, 3, 242, 272, 275
Pattani United Liberation Organization (PULO), 32n4
Pattaya, 123
Patten, Chris, 57, 185n4
Patton, George S., 181
Paul Samuelson, 139
Paulson, Henry (Hank), 151
PBS (Public Broadcasting Service), 287
Pearl Harbor attack, xi, xiii, xviii, 171, 286
Peck, Gregory, 210–11
Pedra Branca, 67
Pennsylvania, 181, 182
Pentagon, 254
Penthouse, 50
People's Liberation Army (China), 88, 175
People's Liberation Army (Philippines), 2
Perak, 3
Perelman, Michael, 276
Perlis, 3
permanent residency status, 130n12

Perry, Elizabeth J., 87
Pershing, John J., 181
Peru, 45
Peshawar, 4
peso (PHP), 105
Pettis, Michael, 29
Philippines
  Asian financial crisis and, 105
  corruption, 71
  educational system, 81
  financial structures, 224
  insurgencies, 2, 3, 66, 71, 72, 242
  KFC outlets in, 251
  military, 65, 68, 71–72, 73
  as potential Al-Qaeda hub, 176
  response to globalization, 268
  U.S. annexation of, 236
  U.S. investment in, 84
  U.S. military bases in, 71, 173, 175
  World War II, 119
Philippine Special Warfare Group, 72
Phillips, 85
Pillay, J.Y.M., 79
piracy, 203
Piven, Frances Fox, 40–41
Plato, 212, 278
Playboy, 50
Ploeg, Irma van der, 242
Political Man: The Social Bases of Politics, 219
Polk, James K., 181
Pol Pot, 272
popular culture
  American culture and, 196–201
  American Dream and, 200, 206–11, 214
  comedy, 203–6
  Japanese, 119
  theories of, 187–88, 191–95, 201–3, 277
  vs. counter-culture, 188–91
Port Authority of New York and New Jersey, 158

Port Moresby, 126
Portugal, 81, 105–6, 265, 276
Postman, Neil, 136, 205, 232, 291, 292
Poulantzas, Nicos, 280
poverty, 38–42, 43–44, 45–46, 122, 149–51, 162, 275
Powell, Colin L., 181
PowerGas, 77
PowerSenoko, 77
PowerSeraya, 77
Prem Tinsulanonda, 124, 125, 275, 279
Presley, Elvis, 200, 210, 213
Pride, Charlie, 196
Prince, Eric, 262
producer price index (PPI), 43
Protestant Ethic and the Spirit of Capitalism, 235
Pryor, Richard, 204, 213
Pulau Batu Putih, 67
Pulau Bukom, 68
Pulitzer, Joseph, 145, 213
Puzo, Mario, 9

Q
Qatar, 85
Quayle, Dan, 120

R
Racist Mind, 203
Radio Free Asia, 103
Raffles, Thomas Stamford, 290
Rafidah Aziz, 91
Rajaratnam, S., 279
Rameau's Nephew, 212
Ram Janmabhoomi, 255
RAND, 38, 89, 97
Rand, Ayn, 293–94, 295, 296
RAND Graduate School, 178
Rape of Nanking, 2
rap music, 197–98
Rappa, Antonio L., 81

Rappaport, Roy A., 9
Rat Pack, 200, 201
Reagan, Ronald, xiv, 181
Reaganomics, 41, 88, 258
realism, 17
Red Cloud, Chief, 229
Redford, Robert, 210
Red Swastika Society, 198, 215n6
Reefer Madness, 44
Reich, Robert, 139
Reid, Roddey, 35
Reinventing Government, 299
Rejali, Darius M., 12
Reliance Industries, 116
renminbi (RMB), 111, 175
Republic, 278
Republican Party (U.S.)
  Asian financial crisis and, 107
  Colin Powell and, 181
  conservative values and, 11–12, 297
  defence contracts and, 262
  foreign policy and, 52, 96
  George H.W. Bush and, 185n3
  Northern Virginia Roundtable and, 158
  "one-party state" and, 94, 177, 184, 308n2
  terror and xenophobia and, 1, 288
  Theodore Roosevelt's presidency, 145
  as voting choice, 293, 304
Reuters, 153
Ricardo, David, 138
Rice, Condoleezza, 98
Rich, Frank, 49
Rifkin, Glenn, 163
ringgit (MYR), 76, 93, 105, 109
Rise of Theodore Roosevelt, 145
Robertson, Pat, 288
Robinson, Douglas, 145
Robinson, William I., 87
Roche, 271
Rochester, J. Martin, 29

Rock, Chris, 204, 213
Rollei, 85
Roosevelt, Eleanor, 188
Roosevelt, Franklin D., 144
Roosevelt, Theodore, 143, 144–45, 152
Rorty, Richard, 9, 281
Rose, Tricia, 199
Rosetta Stone, 176
ROTC (Reserve Officers' Training Corps), 181
Rothman, Robert, 158
Rourke, Mickey, 196
Rousseau, Jean-Jacques, 278
Royal Bank of Scotland, x
Royal Dutch Shell, 263
Royal Society for the Prevention of Cruelty to Animals, 36
rupiah (IDR), 105, 109
Rushdie, Salman, 236, 292
Rusk, Dean, 181
Russia, 175, 257, 267, 268, 290
Russian Foreign Security Service, 270
Russo-Japanese War, xiii, 3, 266
Ryan, Michael E., 180
Ryanair, 64

S
Sabah, 69
Sagan, Carl, 292
Sahlins, Marshall D., 9, 292, 293
Said, Edward, 30, 85, 210, 244, 265
Samak Sundravej, 124
Santayana, George, 292
Sarawak, 69
Sartre, Jean-Paul, 20, 146, 236, 238n30, 280, 282
Saudi Arabia, 85, 99
Savings and Loans scandal, 203
Sawyer, Darwin O., 21
Schar, Dwight C., 154, 158
Schlosser, Eric, 44, 49, 50
Schram, Sanford, 40

Schultz, George, 27
Schwarzenegger, Arnold, 47, 59n12, 196
Schwarzkopf, H. Norman (General), 181
Science and Technology Directorate, 52
Scotland Yard, 57
Scott, James C., 262
Scowcroft, Brent, 181
Sea of Japan, 117
Seattle Maritime Academy, 181
Securities and Exchange Commission (SEC), 153, 165n13
See No Evil, Hear No Evil, 204
Segal, Jeffrey A., 226
Seinfeld, Jerry, 188
Seminole War, 290
Seoul, 62, 126
September 11 terrorist attacks. *See also* terrorism
 American globalization and, xiv, 41, 203, 223
 Asia and, 81
 compared to sub-prime crisis, 261
 effects on foreign policy, xviii, 65, 98, 176
 intelligence gathering and, 241, 243–44, 254, 270
 Malaysia and, 67, 90, 92, 121
 the nation-state and, 263
 sign of U.S. decline, xi, 286
 swing to conservatism, 30, 146
Seven Years War, 266
Shadow of a Doubt, 210
Shah of Iran. *See* Mohammad Reza Pahlavi, Shah of Iran
Shakespeare, William, 171, 204, 216n14
Shakur, Tupac, 194, 213
Shanghai, 100, 101, 112, 233
Shapiro, James, 212
Shell, 77
Shelley, Mary, 297

Shenzhen, 111
Sherman, William Tecumseh, 181
Shin Corp, 73
"ship of fools" metaphor
 epilogue, 304–8
 Europe and, 54
 globalization and, 289
 India and, 115
 iron cages and, 52–53
 meaning, xi
 neoliberal capitalism and, 30
 Panama and, 143
 theories of liberalism and, 236
 U.S. and, 31, 99
Shirley, James, 151
Shusterman, Richard, 212
Sicker, Martin, 37
Sikorsky, Igor, 36
Silkair flight MI185, 129n3
Silverman, Henry R., 154, 157
Simpson, O.J., 42
Simulacra et Simulacrum, 187, 289
Sinbad, 188
Singapore
 airline industry, 63–64, 77–80
 Asian financial crisis and, 105, 109
 colonial era, 284, 290
 economic strategies, 279–80
 educational system, 81–82
 fall of Barings, 109
 fertility rate, 82, 246–47
 global financial crisis and, x
 globalization and, 74–77, 127, 224, 251
 immigrants, 82–84
 investments in China, 111, 113
 IT technologies, 248
 lack of corruption, 70
 Malayan Communist Party and, 177
 Muslims in, 222, 269
 oil crisis and, 85
 per capita GDP, 113

pop culture and, 119, 188, 198–99
race relations, 282
relations with Malaysia, 66–67, 74–75, 77, 85
relations with Thailand, 73
relations with U.S., 68, 75, 173
Shah of Iran's visit, 302
stock exchange, 61, 107
as tax haven, 13
terror incidents, 68, 69, 80
traffic management, 76–77
use of the Internet, 195
U.S. investment in, 84, 126
U.S. military training and, 65, 73
Singapore Airlines (SIA), 64, 68, 75, 77–80
Singapore Airlines Pilots' Association (SIAPA), 78
Singapore Armed Forces (SAF), 68, 80, 129n3
Singapore dollar, 76, 105, 109–10
Singapore Petroleum Company (SPC), 77
Singapore Power, 77
Sitting Bull, Chief, 229, 232–33
Six-Day War, 176
Skeel, David A., 226
Skilling, Jeffrey, 165n15
Skinner, B.F., 238n30
Skinner, Jim, 156
Smil, Vaclav, 110
Smith, Adam, 18, 137, 138, 139, 296, 297
Smith, Ellen, 151
Smith, Fred, 158
Smith, R.B., 215n6
Snoop Dogg, 204
Socrates, 278
Solomon, Howard, 154, 160
Somchai Wongsawat, 124
Song, Xue, 41
Sonthi Boonyaratkalin (General), 72, 73, 125

Soros, George, 36, 76, 108, 110, 199
Soul Plane, 204
South Africa, 274, 283
South Carolina, 181, 182
South China Sea, 67, 173
South Korea
  demographic problems, 246
  dependence on oil, 84
  economic disparities, 105
  financial structures, 224
  Japanese pop culture and, 119
  relations with North Korea, 89, 242
  relations with U.S., 27, 81, 82, 120, 173
  stock exchange, 62
Soviet Union
  airline industry, 62
  arms sales, 173
  Cold War adversary, 26, 84, 120, 179, 270
  end of Cold War and, 88, 100
  ideological defeat, 57, 261
  occupation of Afghanistan, xiv
  relations with China, 87, 100
  relations with India, 114
  relations with Iran, 302, 303
Spaeth, Harold J., 226
Spain, 81, 137, 265, 274, 276
Spanish-American War, 236
Spellman, Francis Joseph (Cardinal), 181
Spratly Islands, 67
Sri Jayewardenapura Kotte, 126
Sri Lanka, 84
Stalin, Josef, 188
Stanford University, 160
Starbucks, 214, 252
Star News Network, 126
Star Wars programme, xiv, 41, 88, 258
State Theory, 146
Steinbeck, John, 210
Stern, Howard, 194, 195
Stern Business School, 157

Stewart, Jimmy, 210
Stewart, Martha, 42
Stewart B. McKinney Homeless
  Assistance Act (1987), 45
Stiglitz, Joseph, 108, 123, 139, 262
St. Joseph's Institution, 290
Stoffle, Richard W., 229
Straits Times, 68, 79, 106
Street, 212
Streetcar Named Desire, 209
Subic Bay Naval Base, 71, 173
Sudan, 98
Suharto, 46, 69, 71, 76, 105, 125,
  130n24
Sukarno, 69
Sukarnoputri, Megawati, 107, 279
Sulfikar Amir, 247–48
Sullivan and Cromwell, 144
Sumatra, 69
Sun TV, 126
Surayud Chulanont (General), 72,
  125, 275, 285n8
Survivor, 232
SUVs (sport utility vehicles), 46–49,
  60n12
Suzhou, 111, 113
Sweden, 70
Switzerland, 13
Sydney, 61
Syracuse University, 178

T
Taft, Charles P., 144
Taft, William H., 143
Taiwan
  Chen Shui Bian's presidency, 164n5
  espionage, 270
  financial structures, 127, 224
  Japanese popular culture and, 119
  Lee Hsien Loong's visit to, 66
  pop culture, 188
  relations with China, 87, 89–90,
    99, 174–75, 270, 271
  relations with U.S., 84, 98–99, 173,
    174–75
Taiwan Relations Act (1979), 173
Taiwan Straits, 82, 174
Tajikistan, 102
Taleb, Nassim Nicholas, 31
Taliban, 103
Tamiflu, 271
Taoism, 215n6
Tao Yuan Sect, 198, 215n6
Taylor, Elizabeth, 209, 210
technology
  addiction, 248–49
  Asian design and manufacturing,
    244–47
  defined, xvii–xviii
  globalization and, 24, 239–58,
    269–74
  global standards and, 249–52
  human nature and, 52
  omnipresence, 276, 282
Tel Aviv, 272
Temasek Holdings, 73, 279
Tentara Nasional Indonesia (TNI), 69
Tentera Laut DiRaja Malaysia
  (TLDM), 66–67
Ten Thousand Day War, 87
Terminator 2, 196
terrorism. *See also* September 11
    terrorist attacks
  causes of, 1, 253
  combatting, 65–66, 263, 272–74
  globalization and, 203, 241–44
  incidents, 2, 68, 223
  intelligence-gathering and, 254,
    270
  Malaysia and, 67
  vs. freedom-fighting, 3
Texas, 85, 147, 181, 182
Texas Instruments, 85
Texas Maritime Academy, 181
Thailand
  airline industry, 63

Asian financial crisis, 104–5, 109
Bangkok stock exchange, 61
ban on the Internet, 195
Constitution, 125
corruption, 70–71, 72–73, 105, 123
educational system, 81
globalization and, 122–23, 224, 251
insurgencies, 3, 66, 121, 203, 223, 242
military, 65, 68, 70–73, 121–22, 125
political unrest, 275
relations with Singapore, 73
social structure, 121–22
U.S. investment in, 84
Thai Rak Thai, 124
Thaksin Shinawatra, 71, 72–73, 124, 125, 195, 275, 284n8
Thammasat University, 125
Theodore Roosevelt, 145
Thimpu, 127
Thomas Aquinas, Saint, 278
Thucydides, 17, 38, 150
Tiananmen Square incident, 89
Tiger Air, 64, 79
Tilly, Charles, 9
Timor Leste, 69, 98, 105–6, 107
To Kill a Mockingbird, 210
Tokyo, 62, 127, 169, 175, 188, 254
Torres, Carlos A., 30
Toyota, 263
Transparency International, 70
Travis, Randy, 196
Travolta, John, 188
Tsang, Donald, 175
Tuas Power, 77
Tucker, Chris, 204
Tung Chee Hwa, 175
Turnbull, Phyllis, 27
TWA (Trans World Airlines), 64
Two Treatises on Government, 35

U
Uighurs, 101–4
UMNO (United Malays National Organization), 91
United Kingdom. *See* Britain
United Nations (UN)
  Abdullah Badawi's letter to, 120
  Declaration of Human Rights, 219
  neoliberalism and, 17
  Timor Leste and, 106, 107
  U.S. invasion of Iraq and, 75, 100, 173, 255
  weakening of, 203
United States. *See also* U.S. military
  African Americans, 181, 203–5, 214, 217n16, 230–31, 283
  airline industry, 62–64
  arms sales, 29, 173
  Articles of Confederation, 14
  bureaucracy, 11, 52
  Cold War and, xiv
  decline, xi, 4, 266–67, 286
  defence agreements, 73
  demise of socialism in, 115
  domestic politics, 10–13, 61, 94–97
  dropping of atomic bomb, 1–2
  economic outlook, 274
  educational system, 81, 101, 135, 180–83
  foreign policy, 95–104
  freedom of speech, 50
  Global War on Terror, 65, 241, 254, 257, 267
  gun rights, 50–51, 226–27, 233
  illegal immigrants, 287, 295
  immigration, 83, 84, 101, 113, 148–49, 207–9
  intelligence-gathering, 241, 243–44, 253–54
  international debt, 257
  invasion of Iraq, 56, 75
  investments in Asia, 84–86, 126–27, 129

military-industrial complex, 177–85
nature of power, 55–57
neo-imperialism, 4–5
oil consumption and policy, 61,
    84–85, 98–99, 103, 203, 258,
    286
pet food industry, 45–46
popular culture, 187–215
pornographic industry, 49–50
poverty in, 38–42, 43–44, 45–46
race relations in, 36, 40–42, 45,
    53–54, 233
relations with China, 87–88, 89,
    100–104, 110–13, 174
relations with India, 113–17
relations with Japan, 117–20
relations with Malaysia, 90–93
relations with Taiwan, 173
rise to superpower status, 37–38,
    42
Shah of Iran and, 302
system of government, 14, 97, 225,
    227, 232
territorial expansion, 137, 143, 236
War of Independence, 3, 31n3,
    207, 235
xenophobia, 113, 146
United States Air Force Academy
    (USAFA), 180, 183
United States Coast Guard Academy
    (USCGA), 180
United States Merchant Marine
    Academy (USMMA), 180
United States Military Academy
    (USMA), 180, 182
United States Naval Academy
    (USNA), 180, 182
United States v. *Glaxo Group Ltd*, 226
United States v. *Sioux Nation of
    Indians*, 226
United States v. *Varig Airlines et al.*,
    227
United States v. *Venezuela-Bernal*, 226

United Technologies (UTX), 154,
    157, 181
University of California, 86, 178
University of Colorado, 157
University of Hawaii at Manoa, 86
University of Nevada at Las Vegas
    (UNLV), 161
University of Pennsylvania, 157
University of Utah, 161
University of Virginia, 157
University of Wisconsin-Madison, 39,
    41
Urban Institute, 40
Urry, John, 19
Uruguay, 45
U.S. Bureau of Citizenship and
    Immigration Services (USCIS),
    11
U.S. Bureau of Intelligence and
    Research (INR), 253
U.S. Bureau of Labor, 43
U.S. Bureau of Public Debt, 14
U.S. Census Bureau, 41, 240
U.S. Constitution, 13, 35–36, 225,
    226, 228–30
U.S. Corps of Engineers, 144
U.S. Department of Commerce, 253
U.S. Department of Defense (DOD),
    11, 87, 178, 179
U.S. Department of Energy, 85
U.S. Department of State (DOS), 13,
    87, 100, 103, 176, 283
U.S. dollar (USD), 5, 42, 101, 104–5,
    111
U.S. Federal Reserve, 10, 61, 104, 295
U.S. Hispanic Chamber of Commerce
    (USHCC), 157
U.S. House of Representatives, 12, 14
U.S. military
    anti-American sentiment and, 27,
        36
    in Asia, 27, 36, 71, 82, 84, 95–96
    desire for adversary, 192

global presence, 170
military-industrial complex, 177–85
training for foreign forces, 65, 73
U.S. expatriates and, 13
U.S. Navy Seals, 72
U.S. Pacific Command, 173, 175, 179
U.S. President, 14. *See also individual presidents*
U.S. Senate, 14
U.S. Supreme Court, 14, 36, 95, 225–27

V
Vajpayee, Atal Bihari, 113, 114
Van Opstal, Debra, 4
Vattimo, Gianni, xi, 9
Venezuela, 45
Vermont, 181
Vertigo, 210
Vico, Giambattista, 278
Vietnam
  communist theory in, 280
  educational system, 81
  financial structures, 224
  foreign investments in, 84, 126
  investments in the U.S., 267
  response to globalization, 268
  U.S. special forces in, 65
  war against China, 2–3
Vietnam War
  oil crisis and, 85
  place in modern history, xiv, 81, 176, 179
  social and cultural reaction to, 86–87, 188, 190, 203, 210
  terrorism and, 169
  U.S. casualties in, 2, 87
  U.S. decline and, 267
  U.S. economy and, 38, 257
Vindication of the Rights of Women, 36
Virginia, 158, 181, 182, 282
Voting Rights Act (1965), 226

W
Wahid, Abdurrahman, 106, 107
Wallace, George, 188
Wallerstein, Immanuel M., 30
Wall Street Journal, 288
Wal-Mart, 160, 179, 263
Walsh, Colleen, 134
Walt Disney, 154
Walton, Sam, 160
Waltz, Kenneth, 17
Wan Aziza, 130n17
Warhol, Andy, 296
Warrior Politics, 163
Warsaw Convention, 227
Warsaw Pact countries, 257
Washington Mutual, x
Washington Post, 107
waterboarding, 12
Wayne, John, 210
Wealth of Nations, 138, 296
Weber, Max, 52, 163, 235, 278
Wee, Lionel, 81
Welles, Orson, 210
Wells Fargo, 154, 160
West, Cornel, 21
Westmoreland, William Childs (General), 181
Westphalia, Treaty of, xii
West Point, 180, 182
Whistler, James McNeill, 181
White, Stephen, 281
Who's Afraid of Virginia Woolf?, 210
Wilberforce, William, 36
Wilder, Gene, 204
Wild One, 196
Williams, Hank, 196
Williams, Ralph E., 180
Williams, Robin, 188
Williams, Tennessee, 209
Williams College, 157
Williamson, David, Jr., 4
Williamson, Jeffrey G., 18–19
Wilmer, Franke, 229

Wilson, Woodrow, 143, 184
Wilson v. *Omaha Indian Tribe,* 226
Winfrey, Oprah, 194
Winner, Langdon, 242
Wiranto (General), 106–7
Wisconsin, 182
Wittgenstein, Ludwig, 236, 238n30, 280
Wollstonecraft, Mary, 36, 278
won (KRW), 105, 109
Wong Kan Seng, 79
Woodlands Naval Base, 66
Woodstock, 188, 189
Words of Welfare, 40
World Bank, 10, 57, 94, 149
World on Fire, 124
World Trade Center, 169, 177, 203, 254. *See also* September 11 terrorist attacks
World Values Survey, 53–54, 55, 162
World War I, xiii, 144
World War II
   Egyptian pyramids and, 176
   end of colonial empires, xiii, 258, 266
   Germany and, 168
   Japan and, 119–20
   U.S. and, 86–87, 171, 179, 257
World-wide Volkswagen Corporation v. *Woodson,* 226
Wright brothers, 36
WTO (World Trade Organization), 17, 57, 224, 268

X

Xhosa War, 290
Xinhua News Agency, 270
Xinjiang, 101, 103

Y

Yala, 3, 121, 242, 275
Yale University, 160
Yang Ping-Wang, 270
Yaverbaum, Eric, 163
yen (JPY), 119
Yom Kippur War, 176
YouTube, 195, 213

Z

Zee TV, 126
Zhang Yimou, 9, 292

www.ingramcontent.com/pod-product-compliance
Lightning Source LLC
Chambersburg PA
CBHW020121020526
44111CB00048B/154